# CHINESE GOLD

## THE CHINESE IN THE
## MONTEREY BAY REGION

### SANDY LYDON

# CHINESE GOLD

I shall therefore, with patience and resignation continue to dig with an abiding hope for something better . . .

Chung Sun
digging ditches,
Watsonville, 1871

SANDY LYDON

# CHINESE GOLD

## THE CHINESE IN THE
## MONTEREY BAY REGION

CAPITOLA BOOK COMPANY

Capitola Book Company
1601 41st Avenue, Capitola, CA 95010

© 1985 by Sandy Lydon. All Rights Reserved.
Printed in the United States of America

86  85  87        5  4  3  2  1

*Library of Congress Catalog Card Number: 84-72699*

ISBN 0-932319-00-9
ISBN 0-932319-01-7 (pbk.)

TO MY WIFE, ANNIE,
*for understanding the importance of this
and not letting me forget.*

# Contents

# List of Maps

# Acknowledgments

THIS BOOK was inspired fifteen years ago at a San Francisco conference on Chinese-American history organized by the Chinese Historical Society of America. The remarkable syllabus (Chinn, Lai, and Choy, *A History of the Chinese in California: A Syllabus*) and the extremely active Chinese Historical Society have guided and encouraged me throughout the research and writing of the book. A number of institutions assisted the project along the way; the Chinese Historical Society of America was always willing to let me test some of my findings before the membership, whether in San Francisco or on field trips in the Monterey Bay Region. A National Endowment for the Humanities Summer Fellowship in 1974 and a grant from the Sourriseau Academy of San Jose State University supported early research. A Fellowship for College Teachers from the National Endowment for the Humanities in 1982–83 and a sabbatical leave from Cabrillo College provided the time to write the first draft. A decade's-worth of students patiently permitted me to digress and test new ideas, and many of their research projects illuminated new materials and interpretations. Chinese Historical Society founders Philip Choy and Him Mark Lai read the manuscript, and Thomas W. Chinn, the patriarch of all Chinese-American historians, encouraged my research, read the manuscript, and helped me trace important information.

The staffs of the California Historical Society, California State Library, California State Archives, Bancroft Library, Huntington Library, Special Collections of Stanford University Library, Pajaro Valley Historical Association, and Monterey County Historical Society were all extremely helpful. In the early 1970s Robin Gottfried of the Federal Archives and Records Center in San Bruno told me about the thousands of habeas corpus cases in the center's basement, and she and the Archives staff gave invaluable assistance as I sought out cases relating to the Monterey Bay Region. Rita Bottoms, Carol Champion and Paul Stubbs of Special Collections at the University of California, Santa Cruz, patiently put up with my repeated requests for materials and always let me know when new information came to their attention. Stan Stevens, the Map Librarian for the University of California, Santa Cruz, found a number of treasures in his map collection which he shared with me. Don Clark, Librarian emeritus at the University of California, Santa Cruz, sent me place-name derivations as he found them. Marnell Hillman, Interlibrary Loan librarian at Cabrillo College, helped unravel the mysteries of MOBAC and got the precious microfilm newspapers. Sudy MacDonald of the Pebble Beach Company provided several invaluable pieces of the puzzle from the company's collection in Pacific Grove. Charles Prentiss and John Lane of the Santa Cruz City Museum and Al Schadle of the Santa Cruz County Museum found a number of visuals which appear here. Rob Edwards, colleague, friend, and archaeologist, always shared new reports and findings in regional archaeology and a number of those reports are cited in the references. Robert J. Schwendinger, Director of the Maritime Humanities Center in San Francisco, provided several opportunities to present new material as well as reading the manuscript. Patty Dunn, curator of the Monterey County Historical Society, took time out on the day before her wedding to find several important photographs of Salinas. Sucheng Chan, Provost of Oakes College, University of California, Santa Cruz, read and commented on the manuscript.

The interviews were aided by the Kitchen Sisters (Nikki Silva and Davia Nelson) who recorded many of them on radio-quality tape. Kate Ashcraft acted as a go-between in the Watsonville Chinese community in the early stages of the interviews, as well as bringing to my attention a number of important photographs. Mrs. Bernice Porter allowed me free access to the Porter family's priceless collection of artifacts from Watsonville's Chinatown. Lillian McPherson Rouse, Duncan McPherson's granddaughter, shared all of Duncan McPherson's papers and together we tried to better understand his feelings toward the Chinese. Lillian's mother, Matye Patton McPherson, dutifully clipped all of Ernest Otto's columns over the years, and those clippings formed the basis for the sections on Santa Cruz's Chinatown.

The Chinese communities throughout the Monterey Bay Region gave unfailing assistance and hospitality. Florabelle Wong introduced me to a number of Watsonville's Chinese families and invited me to that wondrous reunion in May 1982. Annie de la Pena, Elmer Shew, Ida Wong, Ernie Wong, Mae Wong, Earl and Evelyn Goon, and Wally Lew shared their stories and ideas with me. Hoy Lew, the patriarch of the Watsonville Chinese, and his wife, Margaret, spent many hours going over their recollections and their photographs. Henry and Alice Leong of San Jose spent a rainy afternoon with me as we put together the life story of Henry's mother, Leong Low Shee.

In Monterey, Ben Hoang, Jack and Frances Yee, Al and Rose May Jung allowed me to interview them. Margaret Lam helped explain the secrets of fish drying while Suellen and Munson Kwok provided invaluable information about Monterey and Watsonville. The Salinas Chinese, including Emma Dong, Wellington Lee, Henry Chin, Bill Young, and Walter Wong all patiently endured my questions, while Sam Chinn gave me several tours of his farm to help me understand the process of reclamation. Long-time Spreckels Sugar Division employee, Tom Ryan, shared his knowledge of the history of Spreckels and contemporary beet sugar production in the Salinas Valley.

Jimmy Lam showed me the inner workings of a China Dryer, and one wonderful afternoon he and Charlie Leong took me on a tour of the drying process, explaining the differences between the old-fashioned dryers and today's modern ones. The Chinese community of Santa Cruz may be one of the smaller ones in the region, but it made giant contributions to this book. Priscilla Lee translated all the written Chinese in the photographs while George Lee took a number of the historic photographs of Santa Cruz Chinatown as well as the contemporary portraits. George's brother, Jun Lee, loaned me his personal papers and took the time to elaborate his political career in Scotts Valley. George Ow, Sr. gave two lengthy interviews which provided some of my basic understandings of Chinese-American businessmen, while his wife, Emily, filled in her version of the long hours working in a small market.

Thanks go to Bruce Bratton and Carolyn Swift for reading and commenting on the first draft. A special thanks to Bruce MacGregor for his careful reading of the railroad sections as well as his continuous encouragement and support over these many years. Ruthanne Lum McCunn read the first draft and then spent precious days going over the draft and sharing her unique sensitivities and expertise; Don McCunn helped me understand what the publishing business involved. Photo archivist Pat Hathaway, one of Pacific Grove's greatest natural resources, gave me unlimited access to his photographs and maps. Margot Berg-quist generously shared her family's (J. K. and Myron Oliver) photograph collection, loaning me the rare post-fire scenes at Point Alones. Henrietta Latour Vieille helped me track down the owners of an important early painting of Point Alones. Betty

McGlynn introduced me to several important drawings and paintings of the Chinese fishing villages and shared her wealth of knowledge about Monterey Peninsula artists.

Cate Brady put up with a lot as she edited the three drafts it took to get the book in order and to shake out all the "glitches" that had crept into the manuscript. Betty Gee guided the book through all the bewildering stages of production. Mark Ong is responsible for the distinctive beauty of the book and its cover.

George Ow, Jr. provided much of the energy and inspiration to complete the book. From telephone calls of encouragement and critical comments on the manuscript to the vision to see how it might be published, George has been the book's midwife.

My family deserves a special vote of thanks for sharing me for so long with library, archive, typewriter, and word processor: my son, Christopher, my daughter, Sasha, and Mac who took me for walks when I needed to go. My wife, Annie, encouraged me every step of the way even though it meant foregoing a regular home life with movies, eating out, vacations, or weekends.

Two special people did not live to see the finished product. Sharon Lew, Hoy Lew's granddaughter, became involved in Asian-American studies at Cabrillo College, going on to San Francisco State, and had just begun interviewing her grandfather when she was killed in a traffic accident. Charlie Leong spent hours with me discussing his boyhood days in Watsonville, and he was instrumental in helping me track down the descendants of many of the region's families. His reporter's eye was keen, and he helped me hone some of the ideas put forth in this book; he also helped me understand the inner workings of an apple dryer. I am sorry that Sharon Lew and Charlie Leong were not able to see this book.

All the help notwithstanding, errors of fact or interpretation are mine alone.

# Introduction

No MONUMENTS, no prominent place names, no gilt "Chinese-style" buildings, and no large concentrations of Chinese people attest to the Chinese presence in the Monterey Bay Region. In 1982 a local newspaper gave the following assessment of Asian immigration when reconstructing the arrival of immigrant groups into the Pajaro Valley:

> Original Spanish subjects [were] replaced by early American settlers of European background, followed by the arrival of the Croatians, who became a dominant economic factor, and the Portuguese, and now the Mexicans, with a sprinkling of Orientals down through the years.

The Chinese, like the Japanese, Koreans, Filipinos, and Southeast Asians, have consistently been thought of as "sprinkled" throughout history, marginal participants who made no major contributions.

Yet Chinese contributions were fundamental to the region's economic development. In Watsonville, known for its diverse agriculture, Chinese farm laborers provided the muscle and ingenuity which led to agricultural diversification in the Pajaro Valley. Until their arrival in the 1860s, wheat was the dominant crop. The sugar beet industry which led an agricultural revolution in both the Salinas and Pajaro Valleys was built on the backs of dependable Chinese workers. At the turn of the century the

Chinese helped pioneer the fruit-drying industry which made the difference between profit and loss on the apple crop. In Salinas the Chinese reclaimed thousands of acres of Salinas Valley tule swamps and brought them into production as well as providing the labor for a diversification similar to that which transformed the Pajaro Valley. In Monterey, where Cannery Row is now a tourist attraction, the Chinese founded the commercial fishing industry and for a half-century inspired other fishermen in the area to expand the definition of marketable products to include squid, mussels, abalone, and seaweed. Santa Cruz became a resort town because Chinese made the cuts, drilled the tunnels, and laid the rails which brought trainloads of tourists into Santa Cruz and Monterey counties. In fact, most of the large development projects undertaken in the region in the nineteenth century, whether they were railroads, irrigation projects, or major water systems, relied on Chinese laborers.

Should you try to find these Chinese contributions listed in local and regional histories you will be disappointed. Regional histories written in the nineteenth and early twentieth centuries often fail to mention the Chinese at all. The first histories devoted exclusively to the Monterey Bay Region were subscription histories prepared by the Charles Elliott Company of San Francisco, called "mug books" by historians today. Local residents subscribed to the book before it was written; each subscriber's place in the history was in direct proportion to the number of books ordered. The books give a fair measure of the social and economic leaders of the region in the late 1870s and early 1880s, but they do not mention the contributions of the Hispanics and Chinese, nor do they mention the anti-Chinese hysteria which blazed at the time they were written. A decade later E. S. Harrison, an insurance salesman, took up a subscription to write a history of Santa Cruz County, and though there are several tantalizing, oblique references to Chinese working in Pajaro Valley strawberry and hop fields, this history, too, was prepared primarily to stroke the egos of the socially prominent. These early writers had no motive to consult the history of California by Hubert Howe Bancroft, where they would have found numerous references to the Chinese in the Monterey Bay Region. The Elliott and Harrison mug books primarily recorded the history and traditions of newly-transplanted Yankees in a region settled by Spaniards, Mexicans, and Californios (Hispanic people born in California).

In their two-volume *History of Monterey, Santa Cruz and San Benito Counties, California*, Major Rolin C. Watkins and Millard F. Hoyle included the heretical notion that the Chinese made contact along the California coast long before the Spanish, but failed to mention the Chinese in their analysis of the region's economy. The 1950s and 1960s produced a new generation of local and regional histories, and for the first time the Chinese were included. Augusta Fink, Anne B. Fisher, and Margaret Koch all make brief references to the Chinese, but for the most part the emphasis is on the "exotic" or "picturesque" nature of the Chinese, not their importance to the region's development. During the late 1960s and 1970s, academic papers and limited-edition books dealt with various aspects of the region's Chinese, but these are rarely available outside academic libraries.

The reasons the Chinese received so little recognition in regional histories are embedded in the story of their experience in the United States. In the late 1960s it was fashionable to say that white historians conspired to leave the Chinese out of the general histories, but as with many theories advanced during those tumultuous times, this one is too simplistic. The silence resulted, at least in part, from the ferocious struggle between the Chinese immigrants and all levels of government in the United States. Both the Chinese and white participants wished to obscure this struggle; the Chinese to avoid further harassment by immigration officials, and the whites to cover the often embarrassing facts of the conflict.

The Chinese Exclusion Act, signed into law in May 1882, set the official guidelines for the struggle, and though dozens of restrictions were directed at the Chinese both before and after 1882, the Exclusion Law looms over the entire experience of the Chinese in America from 1850 to the present day. The Exclusion Law prohibited the further entry of Chinese laborers into the United States (merchants, scholars, and students could still enter); also included by Congress in the law was the reminder that Chinese immigrants were ineligible to become naturalized citizens of the United States. Harassment at the hands of government officials was nothing new for the Chinese; they arrived in the United States with a healthy suspicion of government honed over centuries of dealing with Chinese bureaucrats. The technique the Chinese used to thwart the government here on the Golden Mountain was not new either—avoiding contact with the government was the best defense on either side of the Pacific. In China anonymity could never be complete, as the individual was a member of a family, lived in a family village, and had roots stretching back for hundreds of years. In the United States, where Chinese faces and names blurred under government scrutiny, Chinese immigrants quickly developed systems of artifice in order to avoid the threat of deportation.

Early in my research I was delighted by the subterfuge practiced by nineteenth-century Chinese immigrants in California. I cheered for the Chinese, their crib books (used during interrogations by immigration officials), and their use of aliases to confound government authorities. But when I began to try to follow those Chinese pioneers through the historical records, the sand which they threw in the eyes of their pursuers also obscured my vision.

Many Chinese immigrants bobbed and weaved through their public life using one name in the white community, another in the Chinese community, and another (their true identity) within

the immediate family. Many times when I inquired about ancestors who came into the United States after 1882, the interviewee would reach over to cover the microphone and explain
that the surname was changed to avoid detection by immigration
officials. Often the immigrant took the name of a person already
legally residing in the United States, becoming for the record a
close "relative," and in fact a paper person. These paper names
are not just some academic curiosity. Many Chinese-Americans
still harbor a deep-seated fear of immigration officials which
manifests itself in a distrust of interviewers and a reluctance to
apply for a passport for fear that the required birth certificate
might set off a chain reaction which could result in uncovering a
parent or grandparent who entered the United States illegally.

The historian or genealogist attempting to find specific Chinese individuals in the nineteenth-century records is confronted
with a nightmare of aliases and nicknames. In *China Men* Maxine
Hong Kingston describes how her father gave a different name
to the Stockton police department each time he was arrested for
gambling. Stockton police records list dozens of Chinese men
arrested for gambling who may have been one person. Often
record keepers, census takers, and tax collectors were culturally
hard of hearing, not able to transliterate the polytonal Chinese
name into anything resembling the actual pronunciation. In two
door-to-door lists of Salinas' Chinatown made less than a year
apart, only three of the fifty-four names on the two lists even
resemble each other, a result of poor transliteration and the cus-
tomary use of several names on the part of the Chinese.

One of the saddest legacies of the Exclusion Law is the inability of many Chinese-Americans to trace their genealogies
back more than two or three generations. During its existence
(1882–1943) the Exclusion Law destroyed most of the Chinese
families it touched, permanently separating members in America
from those in China. Even though the law was repealed forty

years ago, it continues to work, scrambling the record and keeping Chinese families from learning about their forebears. Third- and fourth-generation Chinese families frequently know as little about their ancestors as do historians and census-takers. Often during interviews the subject responded to the question, "When did your parents/grandparents come to California?" with a sad shake of the head. In *China Men* Maxine Hong Kingston offered several versions of her grandfather's arrival in the United States —first in a box, then as a regular ship's passenger—demonstrating the state of many Chinese-Americans who have no firm idea how their grandparents came to the United States. For the family-conscious Chinese, this inability to trace their genealogies back beyond 1900 is tragic.

While the nineteenth-century Chinese immigrants diligently obscured their individual identities, white observers of the time often went a step farther and obscured the existence of the entire Chinese community. Individual Chinese may have changed their names, pulled down their hat brims, and moved quietly along the edges of roads, cities, and towns, but groups of them still dotted the region's field, railroad projects, and beaches. After an initial flurry of curiosity when the Chinese first came into the region in the 1860s, white writers at best took them for granted and treated them like part of the landscape. The Chinese presence was recorded by the federal census and county records, but for weeks and months at a time local newspapers failed to mention them. Newspapers often failed to report important events involving Chinese; when Watsonville's Chinatown moved across the Pajaro River and into Monterey County during the summer of 1888, the *Salinas Weekly Index*, the leading Monterey County newspaper, made no mention of the move for a year, even though the move meant that Monterey County's Chinese population doubled instantaneously.

Even with huge projects like the building of the region's railroads, the fact that hundreds of Chinese railroad workers filled the right-of-way gained desultory mention, if any, while the name of the railroad president became a household world. This silence about the laborers in the region's history goes beyond the Chinese; consider how often laborers have received credit for their accomplishments, whether they were Italians, Japanese, Greeks, Slavs, or Filipinos.

Added to the humble nature of the Chinese laborers' work was the wide difference between the culture of English-speaking observers and Chinese immigrants. For most journalists in the Monterey area in the nineteenth century, the Spanish-speaking Mexicans and Californios were foreign enough, and it is no surprise that they found the Chinese to be beyond understanding. After the initial curiosity wore off, journalistic stereotypes for the Chinese became set; most reporters and editors could not get beyond the "heathen Chinee" level of reporting. Because there were few bilingual persons to act as go-betweens, Chinese culture was perceived as remote and alien.

Finally, any possibility for cultural exchange and understanding was dashed by the anti-Chinese movement. The derisive and often savage treatment that the Chinese received in the California press beginning in the 1850s was universal. Even when the Chinese did something commendable, it was impossible for any writer to credit them for fear of being branded a "Chinaman lover." The cliches became so commonplace, and the Chinese so disliked by whites in the region, that all but 7 of the 5,000 voters in the region voted against continued Chinese immigration in the 1879 referendum. That kind of mandate precluded any meaningful cultural or personal understanding between the Chinese and the press. But to inflame local feelings against the Chinese, the anti-Chinese proponents had to describe them, and ironically, these accounts, often filled with racial slurs and exaggerations, provide rare documentation of the Chinese presence. Sometimes cities tried to use health ordinances to rid themselves of a China-town (Santa Cruz took this approach); a newspaper reporter on a fact-finding tour of the Chinese quarters would then produce a prejudicial but detailed description of the Chinatown.

The silence which cloaked the Chinese experience in America was first broken during the late 1960s when third-generation Chinese-American university students began to demand that research and course work be instituted to document the contributions made by Chinese pioneers. But most of the studies focused on the urban Chinese and the larger Chinatowns where many Chinese still live. Research on rural Chinatowns has only begun to gain rightful recognition for the Chinese—for railroad work, for placer mining, for developments in agriculture.

The Chinese have been viewed outside the mainstream of the Monterey Bay Region's historical, economic, and social development. By placing them in a more central position, we can gain both a more accurate picture of the region and a new perspective on the experience of "outside" groups in the region. (I am intentionally avoiding the word "minority," as a group may have a numerical majority and still be considered "outside," as were Hispanics in the 1850s and 1980s.) The relationship between each Chinatown and the white community in which it grew reveals much about both; each community's response to its Chinese inhabitants dramatically defines the widely varying character of each community. Prejudice toward immigrants from Asia, which began with the Chinese, continues throughout the region's history (as it does elsewhere in the United States), a blueprint repeated with the arrival of later immigrants from Japan, the Philippines, Korea, and Southeast Asia.

The fortitude and courage of the Chinese pioneers, exemplified by individuals such as Tim Wong of Monterey, the apple drier Lam Pon, Charlie Chin Goon, Shorty Lee, Jim Jack, Len Puk, Emma Dong, and Charlie Leong, deserves to be included in the region's history. Although many other Chinese remain unnamed, their presence has also left its mark on the region. Though the Chinese are not explicitly mentioned in the local and regional histories, if you hold each page to the light you can make out a faint pattern. The longer you look, the stronger the pattern becomes. The Chinese are in the very paper, they are the watermark. The rhythm of the car's tires crossing the railroad tracks will beat out, "Chi-na-man," calling up the image of a crew of Chinese railroad workers with picks, shovels, and dynamite sweating, swearing, and singing as they cut the grade for those tracks a century ago. Driving Highway 17 north of Santa Cruz, you will cross the dark and deserted Laurel-Glenwood tunnel and the sounds of the Chinese tunnel crews, the ring of the sledge, the explosions, will haunt you for miles. Or looking out over Monterey Bay, you will see the lateen-sailed sampans tacking toward the beach in the afternoon wind, and the boat will land and the Chinese fishermen will sort and carry the day's catch to the drying racks behind their cabins. The fields alongside the road will be dotted with hundreds of laborers wearing conical hats and quilted coats. In the sloughs around Watsonville and Salinas you will see Chinese in the waist-deep mud digging out the willows and tules, turning swamps into prime agricultural land. Obscure street corners, vacant lots, and parking lots will become filled with the sounds and smells of Chinatowns long since burned down and redeveloped in Watsonville, Castroville, Pacific Grove, Monterey, and Santa Cruz. The entire Monterey Bay Region is a monument to the Chinese. This book is intended to help you see it.

PART ONE

# CHINESE PIONEERS

Leaving behind my writing brush and removing my sword, I came to America.

Poem written on the wall at Angel Island by a Chinese immigrant.

# 1

# The First Immigrants

THE WORD *pioneer* calls to mind images of buckskin, gingham, dusty covered wagons swaying across the plains and through the mountains. The image is only partially correct; many California pioneers arrived by sea from Hawaii and Hong Kong, and wore neither buckskin nor gingham. The image of the California pioneer must be broadened to include the Chinese standing on a beach near Monterey looking east and wearing cotton and queue.

California is most often described as being the outer edge of the continent, the last frontier, and land's end. All these labels are based on the notion of Europe as the world's center. The stereotypical California pioneer left Europe or New England, came across the Great Plains and through the Rockies and Sierra Nevada, and arrived out of breath on the California coast. Our historical lexicon is filled with phrases that describe this east-to-west flow—Go West, beyond the 100th meridian, Manifest Destiny. None of this applies to immigration from China. To better understand Chinese immigration to California (and California history in general) we need to move our perspective from Greenwich, England, to a point high above the Hawaiian Islands.

From this viewpoint the west coast of North America takes on an entirely different aspect—California becomes an integral part of the Pacific Basin and China and Japan neighbors sharing the same sea. The presence of Asians in California history has always been treated as exotic, requiring special explanation, and yet when California is seen as but one shore of the Pacific, it becomes as logical for Asians to cross the Pacific to California as it was for Europeans to cross the Atlantic to the east coast of North America. For Asian immigrants California was not the end of the continent but the nearest shore of a land stretching eastward. Seen from our perch above Hawaii it is the *European* presence in California which becomes extraordinary (and even tenuous).

California is even closer to China than it appears. Flowing clockwise around the northern Pacific is the relentless current known by its Japanese name, the *Kuroshiro*, or Black Tide. The current was given the name *Wei-Lu* (ultimate drain) in early Chinese literature. Both the Chinese and Japanese names hint at the one-way nature of the current, and Chinese histories cite a number of expeditions which set out on the current and never returned.

The strongest hint of early Chinese contacts along the California coast is found in the legendary history of the land of Fu-Sang. In 499 a Buddhist monk named Hui-Shen returned to China and recounted his visit to a land called Fu-Sang which lay east of China. Hui-Shen's description of the land was vague and fanciful, and ever since, a controversy has raged among Sinologists about where Fu-Sang might have been. Though the mystery of the exact location of Fu-Sang may never be solved, even the cautious Sinologist Joseph Needham admits that:

> A mountain of evidence is accumulating that between the −7th century and the +16th, i.e., throughout the pre-Columbian ages, occasional visits of Asian people to the Americas took place, bringing with them a multitude of culture traits, art motifs and material objects (especially plants), as well as ideas and knowledge of different kinds.

One of the few histories of California to dwell on the subject of early Asian contacts by sea is Charles Chapman's *History of*

*California: the Spanish Period,* published in 1921. Chapman indicates that for some Chinese and Japanese sailors the problem was not how to make the journey, but how to *avoid* making it, as the Black Tide could easily drag the incautious sailor and his craft over the horizon. A scholar who specialized in the Spanish colonial period in California, Chapman states that many sightings of strange sailing craft along the California coast were recorded during that time: "There is said to be an authentic record of some sixty oriental craft which were driven across the Pacific in the eighteenth and nineteenth centuries."

Some of those craft were sighted around the Monterey Peninsula. In 1774, when the Spanish explorer Juan Bautista de Anza visited Carmel Bay, "he saw a strange wreck, of a type of construction which none of the Spaniards there had ever seen—no doubt, an oriental boat." Eventually, the sketchy physical evidence of early contacts by Asian sailors became intertwined with the story of Fu-Sang.

Soon after the Del Monte Hotel was constructed in 1880, a wagon driver named Alex Early began giving guided tours to visitors, and he told them that the Monterey Cypress was actually the tree of Fu-Sang and had been originally planted on the Monterey Peninsula by Chinese Buddhist monks. The tree was unique to the Monterey Peninsula, and into the early twentieth century, amateur naturalists continued to credit the Chinese with bringing the tree to the Monterey Peninsula in the fifth century. In 1915 a Monterey naturalist took the story and a branch of the tree to the Panama Pacific Exposition in San Francisco, where she showed a visiting Buddhist monk a branch of what she believed to be the tree of Fu-Sang. The monk consulted his texts and connected the tree with the account of Hui-Shen and began to spread the story among his Buddhist colleagues. In 1927, while traveling on the train from San Francisco to Monterey, a Monterey newspaper columnist met and interviewed a Buddhist monk from India who was on a pilgrimage to the Monterey

Peninsula to visit the place that the fifth-century Buddhist monks called Fu-Sang. The wheel had turned full circle.

Further research may prove that the legend of Fu-Sang records actual voyages to the California coast. Already research has demonstrated that Chinese and Japanese sailors sailed across the Pacific to the coast of North America long before the arrival of the Spanish. It was easier to make the voyage than it has been to get California historians to give serious consideration to these early Asian contacts. The theory of early Chinese contacts was originally put forward over a century ago, yet few histories of California devote much attention to it, as the idea of Chinese explorers on the coast centuries before Cabrillo, Portolá, and Serra borders on heresy. Perhaps now that the idea has been argued so eloquently by Stan Steiner in his book *Fusang*, California historians will not only include the Chinese and Japanese mariners in their works, but also will see the California coast as an integral part of the Pacific Basin and not just the farthest reach of European expansion.

## SPANISH RULE IN THE PACIFIC

The Spanish were the first Europeans to envision the Pacific Basin as a single administrative unit. When they combined the territories discovered by Columbus and Magellan, they established a colonial system which spanned the Pacific. The clockwise currents and winds connected the colony of New Spain; beginning in 1565 Spain dispatched a single annual ship to make the Pacific loop and deliver a year's worth of directives, letters, and payroll. From 1565 to 1815 the ship's annual voyage tied the Philippines to Mexico City, the capital of New Spain.

The galleon usually left Acapulco in June, dropped south until it caught the prevailing easterly trade winds, and sailed quickly to the Philippines, usually completing the trip in sixty days or less. On the Acapulco–Manila leg, the galleon was loaded with Peruvian and Mexican silver which was traded in Manila for goods from all over Asia, particularly Chinese silks, porcelains, and jewelry. The Spanish galleon, patterned after the huge ocean-going Chinese junks, often weighed more than 1,500 tons (compared to the 200-ton ships used by Columbus and Magellan). Designed and built by Chinese craftsmen in Manila, crewed in part by Chinese sailors, the Manila galleons were known as the *naos de China*—China Ships.

To return to Acapulco from Manila, the galleon sailed due north until it caught that marine conveyor belt, the Kuroshiro current, which carried it across the northern Pacific to the coast of North America. Upon sighting the California coast, the galleon turned south and ran before the prevailing northwesterly to Acapulco. The ship was often out of sight of land for six months on the eastward journey, and the crew usually caught beri beri or scurvy long before reaching Acapulco. It was not unusual for half of the crew to be incapacitated with scurvy by the end of the voyage, and in one particularly ill-fated instance, the entire crew died on the return trip—the galleon was found drifting off Acapulco filled with "silk and cadavers."

The return voyage of the galleon so tested human endurance that in 1602 the government of New Spain sent Sebastian Vizcaino north from Acapulco to find a harbor which the galleons might use as a place to refit and take on fresh water and food before making the last leg of the trip down the coast. Sailing against the prevailing currents and northwesterly winds, Vizcaino selected the oval-shaped depression between Punta de Año Nuevo (New Year's Point) and Punta de Pinos (Point of Pines) as the best available harbor, naming it after the Viceroy of New Spain, the Conde de Monterey:

. . . we found ourselves to be in the best port that could be desired, for besides being sheltered from the winds, it has many pines for masts and yards, and live oaks and white oaks, and water in great quantity, all near the shore.

Soon after Vizcaino returned with the news of his discovery of a perfect haven for the China ships at Monterey, the Spanish bureaucracy was distracted by other international concerns, and for 160 years more, the China Ships sailed down the California coast, past New Year's Point, the Point of Pines, and Monterey Bay, the crew usually suffering from the advanced stages of scurvy. Concerns about Russian and English encroachment on the shores of the Pacific in the Pacific Northwest eventually revived Vizcaino's Monterey plan. In the 1760s the Spanish decided to set up a buffer colony along the upper California coast which would also provide a harbor of refuge for the China ships at Monterey.

Monterey had grown to be such an ideal harbor in the imagination of the Spanish that when Portolá's expedition finally came north to the site in 1769, the "best port that could be desired" did not fit the reality of Monterey's open roadstead. The plan to make Monterey the harbor of refuge for the China ships had gained such bureaucratic momentum that even when one of the greatest natural harbors in the world was discovered nearby at San Francisco, the Spanish tenaciously stuck to their original plan of making Monterey the capital of the province and a harbor for the galleons from Manila. By the late 1770s the Franciscan priests, under Junipero Serra's leadership, had established a string of missions along the coast.

Monterey never became a regular harbor of refuge for the galleons, however, as but a half-dozen of the China ships stopped there between 1769 and 1815. Most galleon captains preferred to stay out to sea and make the final run to Acapulco rather than risk either the shallow harbor or the rocky coasts nearby. But the province of Alta California (upper California), which was administered from the provincial capital at Monterey, did succeed as a deterrent to Russian and English expansion, for the energetic Franciscans transformed the California coast from San Diego to San Francisco into a shabby but healthy Spanish region.

Though often faulted for their heavy-handed treatment of the Indians, the Spanish had a very liberal attitude toward other races and cultures. In the Spanish view, anyone could become a *gente de razon* (person of reason) by converting to Catholicism, learning Spanish, and taking a Spanish name. Thus a small group of Spaniards could enter an area like Alta California and through persuasion (and sometimes force) convert the existing population into loyal Spanish subjects rather than import large numbers of Spanish citizens to occupy the region; intermarriage was also encouraged between Spanish subjects and the local population. As a result, the word *Spaniard* applied to all manner of racial peoples—Indians, Spanish, blacks, and Chinese.

A large number of Chinese merchants had found their way to Mexico via the galleons, and over the years they had taken the necessary steps to become citizens of New Spain, taking Spanish names and marrying local women. When the colonial system spread north to Alta California after 1769, some of the "Spanish" who came north were, in fact, ethnic Chinese or Spanish Chinos. Stan Steiner notes in *Fusang* that Antonio Rodriguez, one of the original twenty-three settlers who came to the pueblo at Los Angeles, was Chinese. We will probably never know just how many Chinese were living in Alta California during the Spanish period, but along with African blacks, Mexican Indians, mulattoes, and Spanish, Chinese "Spaniards" took part in the original colonization of California.

The first documented Chinese resident in the Monterey Bay Region was Annam (Ah Nam?), a native of a village six miles from Macao in Kwangtung Province, in *gran China*. Annam, who was employed as cook for Pablo Vicente Sola, the Governor of Alta California, was baptized with the Spanish name Antonio Maria de Jesus. It is possible that Sola brought Annam to Monterey when he took over as governor in 1815. Annam died two years later and was buried April 20, 1817.

One other tantalizing Chinese remnant of the Spanish-Mexican period is the name *Arroyo del Chino* (ravine of the Chinese), which is found in old deeds. Given to the ravine near present-day Aptos cut by Aptos Creek on its way to the sea, the name dates from the Mexican period when Rafael Castro was granted the Aptos Rancho by the Mexican government. The only Chinese listed in either Monterey or Santa Cruz County in the 1850 federal census lived in the house of Rafael Castro, next to the Arroyo. The handwriting on the manuscript census is difficult to read, but the name appears to be Sanquie (San Kee?); the man was twenty-one years of age and a native of China. Possibly there is a connection between the Arroyo del Chino and Sanquie, but at this stage of the research, it is only conjecture.

The scattered references to Chinese in the Monterey Bay Area before Alta California became part of the United States in 1848 are probably a fair representation of the extent of the Chinese presence. The local Indians provided the raw labor for the agriculture which was the primary industry in the region, and there was little commerce to attract Chinese merchants to Monterey, because the Spanish and Mexican governments had severely restricted commerce along the Alta California coast. But circumstances were permanently altered by unrelated events on opposite sides of the world in the late 1840s—unrest in Kwangtung Province and the California Gold Rush.

## REASONS FOR CHINESE EMIGRATION IN THE 1850s

People emigrate for a complex tangle of economic, political, and social reasons. Most Chinese immigrants to California came from Kwangtung Province primarily because of revolt, civil war, and economic difficulty in their native province and because the California Gold Rush offered a great opportunity to make a fortune. Emigration was something of a tradition in the province and acted like a safety valve; when times were difficult (flood, famine, or war) some of the men would seek their fortunes elsewhere. Prior to the mid-nineteenth century, Kwangtung men had found their way into Southeast Asia, Borneo, South America, and, as we have seen, the Philippines and Mexico. Economic and political dislocation brought in part by British military activity around Canton in the 1840s increased the pressure on the people of Kwangtung. Revolt and civil war raged through Kwangtung in the late 1840s and 1850s, and many families looked again to the sea and sent sons and husbands away to supplement the family's income and reduce the number of mouths to feed. Large numbers of Kwangtung men had already gone to Southeast Asia and South and Central America when word of the California Gold Rush reached Hong Kong in 1849. The men of Kwangtung at home and overseas wheeled and headed for California, *Gum Shan*, the Golden Mountain.

The physical similarities between areas of California and Kwangtung Province also help to explain the arrival of Chinese in the region. Examples abound of European immigrants who settled in places in North America which had climates and geography similar to that of their homeland—the Swedes in Minnesota are perhaps the best example. Descendants of Genovese immigrants to the Monterey Bay Region show photographs of Italian fishing villages near Genoa which bear a remarkable resemblance to the coastline near Santa Cruz. Konavle Valley and the area around Dubrovnik on the coast of Yugoslavia have a climate and configuration identical to that of the Monterey Bay. The Chinese who settled in the Monterey Bay Region could easily adapt the fishing and farming skills of their region to the new setting.

Kwangtung Province has a large delta where several major rivers converge and then languidly find their way to the sea. The alluvial soil and sub-tropical climate permit double and triple cropping of the land as the winters are usually mild. Most of the region's rainfall comes with the dreaded summer typhoons which swing up out of the South China Sea and sometimes slam into the province. Climate, soil, and abundant water combine to make Kwangtung Province one of the richest rice-producing areas in China. Visitors from California to Kwangtung Province are often struck by the similarities between the Sacramento Valley and the Chinese delta country with its flat land crisscrossed by rivers and levees.

The Monterey Bay Region has a more temperate climate, with most of the rainfall during the winter, colder winters, and a shorter growing season than Kwangtung. But the low, flat, swampy lands in the Salinas and Pajaro Valleys are remarkably similar to Kwangtung. The men of Kwangtung had centuries of experience creating farmland out of swamps, and not surprisingly, they quickly saw the agricultural potential in the marginal lands in the region. Both Kwangtung and the Monterey Bay Region have long, irregular coastlines. Many of the immigrants from Kwangtung traded their coastal villages in China for similar sites along the Monterey coast.

These factors coincided with the Gold Rush, which brought immigrants from all over the globe. Yet the Chinese have been singled out as "sojourners" who wanted to make their fortune and return to Kwangtung. The debate over the intentions of the Chinese immigrants still rages today. When many Chinese immigrants returned to their homeland later in the century, anti-Chinese proponents condemned the Chinese for opportunism. The intentions of the Chinese attracted to the gold fields were no different than those of any other Forty-Niner: most of the people who came to California at that time came to make their fortune and take it back whence they came. Only after circumstances made it difficult to return did most Gold Rushers settle down and become permanent residents. Chinese immigrants, however, had greater difficulty in settling permanently, because they were barred by immigration restrictions and discriminatory laws. Despite these additional handicaps, many Chinese families who came before immigration laws were tightened settled in the new country, undermining the notion that the Chinese were "mere sojourners."

Many immigrants who came seeking gold did not find it, but they remained in California to mine her other riches. European and Yankee pioneers saw the potential of the natural resources (redwood trees into lumber, limestone deposits into lime), but Chinese immigrants saw resources they could not, thanks to cultural differences and a resourcefulness bred of centuries of overcrowding.

The Chinese came from a land which had been populated and exploited for hundreds and thousands of years. Flood, drought, and famine always threatened their existence and livelihood. Food, such a scarce resource, became central (Chinese greet each other with the question "Have you eaten?"), a legacy of life in an over-populated country. With eyes sharpened by necessity and imaginations spurred by famine, the Chinese arriving in California saw opportunity everywhere they looked. The value and potential in a lump of gold was obvious and universal, and both the Yankee and Chinese immigrant recognized it. When circumstances (including discrimination and prejudice) forced the Chinese out of the best claims, they moved out to the fringes of the diggings, working areas that had been overlooked or mined hastily by other miners. The Chinese did well because they had an abundance of the primary ingredients in the alchemist's equation—inspiration and muscle. California was the Golden Mountain not because there was gold, but because there was the opportunity to transform so many different things into wealth.

The Chinese knew the potential of every plant and creature

they saw. The Chinese knew how to harvest, prepare, dry, and cook the abalone clinging to rocks in the bay, which the Yankees passed by. When a Yankee farmer looked at the mustard growing wild on his land, he saw a nuisance, something to be eradicated; the Chinese saw an opportunity, as mustard was highly valued in Chinese cuisine, and the Chinese knew how to harvest the plants and separate the seeds with their flails. Clumps of willow meant a swamp to the Yankee, and each farmer had a "worthless" section of "willow land" which he grumbled about and ignored. But to the Chinese the willow was a symbol of life and regeneration. Willow branches were part of many of the spring celebrations in China, and a clump of willows indicated fresh water and fertile land. The Chinese cleared and drained the willow land, turning it into the richest and most productive in the Monterey Bay Region. The ability to see the potential in the most mundane things may be the greatest contribution of the Chinese immigrants to the history and development of the Monterey Bay Region—they showed the Yankees and Europeans the infinite *possibilities* that the region offered. Yankees who snorted derisively when the Chinese began harvesting some worthless creature or crop later had to change their minds.

## THE MONTEREY BAY REGION IN THE 1850s

The Gold Rush in the Sierra Nevada instantly realigned California geography, erasing the legacy of Vizcaino and his harbor of refuge for the China Ships. Monterey had been the capital of Alta California from the 1770s to 1848, and though there were better harbors in the province (San Diego, San Francisco), Monterey remained the point of entry for foreign visitors to California during that entire period because of bureaucratic inertia on the part of the Spanish and Mexican regimes.

Monterey could not withstand the force of the Gold Rush,

however. The thousands of gold seekers found that the shortest route to the gold took them into the grand natural harbor of San Francisco, up the Sacramento River, and into the Sierra. When the provisional military governor of California moved his headquarters from Monterey to San Francisco to be closer to the action, the Monterey Bay Region was left behind. The route from San Francisco to the Mother Lode became the most important area in California, and places like Stockton and Sacramento flourished. California soon became a state and the state capital was moved to Sacramento.

Monterey lost the capital not only because it was on a second-rate (some said non-existent) harbor and off the beaten track, but also because it was a Mexican town. After seventy years as the provincial capital under the Spanish and Mexican governments, Monterey in the late 1840s and early 1850s was strongly Mexican in its style and way of life. Rather than try to wrench the land and lifestyle of the town away from its Mexican inhabitants, the impatient Yankees moved the capital to a new site where there were few Mexicans and where opportunities were not stifled by complicated Mexican land grants. In a few short years, Monterey went from a capital and port city to a small, quiet, out-of-the-way Mexican town. The simple adobe buildings, meandering streets, and relaxed style of living gave Monterey the appearance of having been there much longer than it had. Monterey became the Old Capital, and more often than not, the emphasis was on the word old.

Not all of the Monterey Bay Region reflected the Mexican heritage as strongly as did Monterey. On the north side of Monterey Bay, a knot of Yankees was turning Santa Cruz into the image of New England. Neither the Santa Cruz Mission nor the pueblo founded across the San Lorenzo river in 1797 (the Villa de Branciforte) had been successful in converting Indians or attracting Mexican settlers, so in the 1840s the vacuum around Santa Cruz filled up with Yankee settlers. By 1845 more Yankees and foreigners lived near Santa Cruz than anywhere else in Mexican Alta California. The abundant and easily accessible tracts of redwood timber and limestone also attracted many Yankees to the area. When California became a state in 1850, the Monterey Bay was braced by two communities—a small replica of New England at Santa Cruz on the north and a small replica of Mexico at Monterey on the south.

When the census taker took his hurried census in the Monterey Bay Region during the autumn of 1850, he found Monterey to be predominantly Californio and Spanish-speaking. The primary diet of the region was beef and beans, and most of the ranches were unfenced, the precise number of cattle on each unknown. The only Yankee enclave was at Santa Cruz, and even in Santa Cruz County, with many of the men "away at the mines," the Californios outnumbered the Yankees. Most of the men from Kwangtung were also at the mines or had set up shop along the San Francisco–Sierra axis to provide services and merchandise for the flood of humanity that moved in and out of the Sierra.

In the early 1850s the Monterey Bay's earlier importance as a potential stopping place for the China Ships had been forgotten. For the moment the residents of the region were distracted by the Gold Rush, and the Monterey Bay slipped into a state of suspended animation. The galleons no longer rode the Kuroshiro Current, but the ocean continued to whirl slowly, connecting the continents of Asia and North America. While most of the Chinese immigrants boarded British sailing ships for the journey to the Golden Mountain, a half-dozen families set sail in their junks, and just as their predecessors had done when exploring the land of Fu-Sang, and the galleon captains when leaving Manila, the small junks headed north to follow the Black Current to the Golden Mountain. The first Chinese colonists to the Monterey Bay Area came not from the Sierra gold fields or San Francisco, they came directly from China by sea.

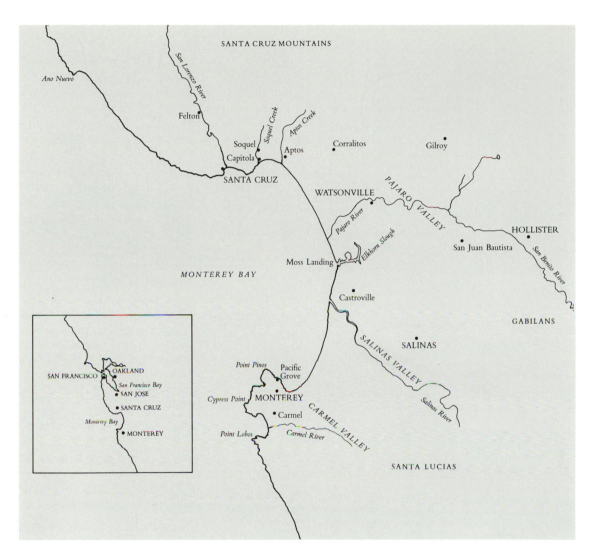

SANTA CRUZ MOUNTAINS

*Ano Nuevo*

*San Lorenzo River*

Felton

*Soquel Creek*

Soquel

Capitola

*Aptos Creek*

Aptos

Corralitos

Gilroy

SANTA CRUZ

WATSONVILLE

*Pajaro River*

PAJARO VALLEY

HOLLISTER

*Elkhorn Slough*

San Juan Bautista

*San Benito River*

Moss Landing

MONTEREY BAY

Castroville

GABILANS

SALINAS VALLEY

SALINAS

*Point Pinos*

Pacific Grove

*Cypress Point*

MONTEREY

*Salinas River*

Carmel

CARMEL VALLEY

*Point Lobos*

*Carmel River*

SANTA LUCIAS

SAN FRANCISCO

OAKLAND

*San Francisco Bay*

SAN JOSE

SANTA CRUZ

*Monterey Bay*

MONTEREY

Map 1-1

THE MONTEREY BAY REGION

"With an untiring industry their quaint looking sea craft urged o'er the waters from early dawn to dusk, and everything from a shark to a shiner is dried, pickled or salted, preparatory to shipment abroad."

*Monterey Gazette*, 1864

# 2

# Fishing

COMMERCIAL FISHING brought the first groups of Chinese into the Monterey Bay Region. The skilled and imaginative Chinese fishermen who set up fishing camps along California's central coast challenge the stereotype of the Chinese as mindless, machine-like workers who provided nothing but the labor for railroad or levee building.

The first Chinese colonists to the Monterey Bay Area came not from the Sierra gold fields, the Transcontinental Railroad, or San Francisco, but directly from China by sea. A number of Chinese in California have passed down the story of their ancestors coming to California from Kwangtung Province in thirty-foot junks in the early 1850s. In a 1967 interview in Mendocino County, Joe Yee, grandson of Chinese fishing pioneers, related the story that seven thirty-foot boats left Kwangtung in 1854, with two landing in California—one in Mendocino County and the other at Monterey. When I asked Ben Hoang, descendant of the founders of the Chinese fishing colony at Monterey, if he knew when his grandmother, Jone Yow Yee, had come to California, he replied, "She was born at Point Lobos." When? "In 1851." When did her parents come to California? "I'm not certain, but they came by boat from China." To corroborate the story of these early pioneers, the 1900 manuscript census for Monterey County lists a forty-nine-year-old Chinese woman living in the fishing village who gave her birthplace as California, and though her name is unintelligible, it may have been Ben Hoang's grandmother. Munson Kwok, another Monterey descendant, also told of his ancestors coming directly to the Monterey Peninsula by boat in the 1850s.

Though the evidence is circumstantial, it is quite possible that families who came directly to the Monterey Peninsula from China were "boat people." The boat people (or *Tanka* as they are called in Kwangtung Province) were a distinct minority group living along the Southeastern coast. Their origins are obscure, but they have fished and lived aboard their boats in South China for all recorded history. Because of their distinctive dialect, form of dress, and occupation, the boat people were treated as outcasts by the land-based Cantonese, and during the early eighteenth century the Cantonese prohibited the boat people from living on shore. Even an imperial edict issued in 1730 which forbade discrimination against the Tanka could not enforce social equality for them. To this day in Hong Kong, the Tanka are born, live, and die aboard their boats. Though they lived on boats, the Tanka were not immune to the social and economic dislocation which gripped Southeastern China in the mid-nineteenth century, and without the traditional family ties to land, ancestral hall, and village, the Tanka had much more latitude to move. When the Tanka heard the news of the Golden Mountain, they set sail—wives, children, and all.

Though most observers of Chinese in California did not make distinctions between different Chinese dialects and districts of origin, a newspaper reporter living in Santa Cruz became familiar enough with the Santa Cruz Chinese community to be sensitive to linguistic and cultural differences. Ernest Otto had grown up when the Chinese fishermen were still on the beach near Capitola and in several of his reminiscences, he referred to the early Chinese fishermen on Monterey Bay as "boat people": ". . . in the early [1850s], a group of fishermen settled in this county [Santa Cruz] as in Monterey. It was always said that these were Chinese who lived on houseboats and fished in their own country around Canton." Ben Hoang noted that the fishing families spoke a different dialect of Chinese from that of the single men who lived in Monterey; their fishing techniques, village composition, and attitude toward the fishing resources all add weight to the idea that the Monterey Chinese fishermen were distinct from their counterparts in other occupations in the region.

## THE ABALONE RUSH

Marine biologists rave about the wealth of sea life around the Monterey Peninsula. The upwelling of colder ocean currents from undersea canyons results in one of the richest tapestries of sea life anywhere in the Northern Pacific, from migrating whales to mussels on the rocks. The Chinese had the knowledge, skills, and energy to turn those resources into gold.

Perhaps better than any other people who came to live on the Central California coast, the Chinese immigrants knew the value and potential of the sea. In an interview one of their descendants, Margaret Lam, explained why the Chinese were so attracted to the Monterey coast, quoting an old Chinese saying: "It is safer to live on the seashore than on a hillside." She explained, "The sea has so many things to offer, mussels, seaweed, sea cucumbers; to a Chinese, the seashore is the best insurance against starvation."

Prior to the arrival of the Chinese, Indians had fished extensively for shellfish, salmon, and steelhead, but the Indian impact on the region diminished during the 1830s and 1840s as their population dwindled under the pressures of colonization. Commercial use of the marine resources before 1850 was extremely limited. Yankee whalers taking on supplies at Monterey sometimes killed migrating whales that wandered into the bay, and Yankee otter hunters (with Mexican partners) worked up the coast killing otters for their pelts. Though neither the Spaniards nor Mexicans had developed a taste for abalone meat, they periodically harvested abalone for their shells, which were shipped to the United States to be manufactured into buttons and jewelry. The Spanish left us with the mollusks' unusual name, which is either a variation on their Indian name, *Aulon,* or a "corruption of the Spanish 'orejones,' sea ears."

The otter hunters inadvertently set the stage for the abalone rush; once the otters, natural predators of abalones, were removed from the Monterey Peninsula's waters, the abalone population exploded. In the early 1850s abalone shells covered the rocks all around the peninsula.

To the Chinese fishermen from the heavily fished shores of Southeastern China, where dried abalone was a delicacy, the Monterey coastline probably looked like heaven. In April 1853, while thousands of Chinese miners combed the Sierra looking for their Golden Mountain, a half-dozen Chinese set up a camp on the beach near Monterey and began harvesting abalone. Word of the abundant abalone near Monterey swept through the Chinese community in San Francisco, and a month later each vessel leaving San Francisco for Monterey carried dozens of Chinese eager to join in the Monterey abalone rush. Six weeks after the first group arrived, "five or six hundred [Chinese were] engaged in gathering the [abalone] and drying and packing the meat." Some of the Chinese built small cabins along the shore, spreading the abalone on railings and roofs to dry.

As the more accessible abalone were harvested around Monterey, the Chinese abalone hunters spread down the coast, landing

Pescadero Fishing Village, c. 1900. Abalone shells in foreground, with older sampans. Seventeen-Mile Drive bridge on extreme left of photograph.
MONTEREY PUBLIC LIBRARY

their sampans in deserted coves along the steep coastline south of Point Lobos. In the summer of 1856 a crew of Chinese abalone fishermen was observed working on the rocks near Point Sur.

The Chinese abalone hunters worked with such energy that, as early as 1856, observers declared that the Chinese had "cleaned nearly all the [abalone] from the waters around Point Pinos." This theme of "decimation of the resources" was a background chorus for the entire half-century that the Chinese fished in the Monterey Bay Region, and whether they harvested abalone, rockfish, squid, or salmon, the Chinese fishermen were accused of lacking concern for the future of the fishing industry. In 1866 the Monterey County Assessor declared that the abalone supply was exhausted between Monterey and San Diego. A quarter-century later, the abalone were still abundant, but predictions that the Chinese would soon wipe them out were still made. Charles H. Shinn, editor of the *Overland Monthly*, lamented that ". . . in a decade or two more this curious and delicious mollusk will probably be extinct."

Pescadero Shell Stand, c. 1900. Jung San Choy on left. Shows myriad varieties of shells sold as souvenirs to tourists on the Seventeen-Mile Drive.
MONTEREY PUBLIC LIBRARY

These predictions of extinction took into account neither the resilience of the abalone nor the restraint of the Monterey Chinese. Although only a few Chinese in the region occasionally behaved without restraint, all Chinese fishermen were painted with the same brush whenever the issue of conservation was raised. Generally, the complaints about the Chinese decimating the marine resources were exaggerated.

Harvesting abalone involved some risks for the Chinese fishermen, particularly when it was necessary to wade into the rocky tidal areas at low tide to find the abalone. According to an oft-told Monterey story, one afternoon a Chinese went abalone hunting alone in the rocks near Point Joe. While reaching over to pry the creature off the rock with his pry-bar, he dropped the bar. Rather than retrieve his bar, the fisherman reached under the edge of the abalone's shell, and the powerful muscle clamped down on his fingers, pinning him to the rock. No one heard his cries for help, and unable to free himself, the Chinese fisherman was drowned by the incoming tide. According to the story, other Chinese abalone fishermen avoided the area for many years following the tragedy.

During the 1850s and 1860s, the Chinese concentrated on drying and selling the meat of the abalone: "With singular improvidence, however, for such an economical people, they [the Chinese] have hitherto thrown away the shells. . . ." Just as shell middens marked the sites of previous Indian habitation, mounds of abalone shells marked the sites of Chinese abalone camps along the Monterey coastline. When a market for the shells developed in China in the mid-1860s, the Chinese backtracked along the coast to collect the shells they had tossed aside. The shells were used for mother-of-pearl cabinet inlays and Chinese jewelry. In the summer of 1874 two large orders came in from New York for a total of 30,000 abalone shells to be used in button and jewelry manufacture; by October 1874 the price of abalone shells rose to fifty dollars per ton. The price rose and fell during the 1870s, and even when it dropped to twenty dollars per ton in the summer of 1875, the Chinese continued to ship shells to France, Germany, and China, as well as New York. By the 1880s the shell mounds were exhausted, and shells could only be obtained from continued harvesting. As the supply of shells dwindled, the price rose steadily, reaching one hundred dollars per ton in 1888. A local market for abalone shells as souvenirs also developed in Monterey, and well into the twentieth century, Chinese vendors sold shells to sightseers along Monterey's scenic drives. After the Monterey abalone fishing industry passed into the hands of Japanese immigrants around the turn of the century, the value of abalone shells soared to $1,000 per ton, and in 1912 the Japanese shipped one and a half tons of shells out of Monterey.

## DIVERSIFICATION

During the late 1850s and 1860s, the Chinese fishermen at Monterey, facing few restrictions and little competition, were free to expand the variety of their catch. The isolation which gave them the freedom to explore and experiment with different types of fishing was also a drawback, as Monterey was too far from San Francisco to ship unrefrigerated fish to the fresh fish markets there. Chinese peddlers sold a few fresh fish each day in Monterey and Santa Cruz, but the local fresh fish markets absorbed but a small part of the Chinese catch. Of necessity, the primary method used by the Chinese to preserve their catch was drying fish in the open air. Fish drying required skill, labor, and a market, and the Chinese met all three requirements. With their vast experience drying fish in China, the fishermen knew which fish could be dried without cleaning, which could be dried by hanging rather than spreading on racks, and how long to leave them in the open air before bundling them for shipment. Finally, since other Chinese made up the largest market for dried fish and controlled access to that market, the Chinese fishermen virtually monopolized the commercial fishing industry in the region.

By the early 1860s the Chinese expanded their catch beyond abalone to include "everything from a shark to a shiner." The smaller fish were dried on the ground or spread flat on racks while larger fish were split, salted, and hung by the tail from poles. Each year the size of the catch grew, until in 1867 the Chinese shipped three hundred tons of dried fish by steamer from Monterey, the bundles and sacks filled with a wide variety of fish. When flounder were particularly valuable, the "platforms [were] covered with the fish," while at other times lists of fish caught and dried by the Chinese read like an inventory of the Bay: ". . . rock fish, cod, halibut, flounders, red and blue fish, yellow tail, mackerel, sardines and shell fish . . . which are split

open, salted and dried in the sun." In 1874, just prior to the completion of the railroad which brought Genovese fishermen to Monterey to compete for the catch, the Chinese fishing colonies were booming:

> A visit to Chinatown will convince anyone that they are doing a land office business. Fish are strewn from one end of their town to the other and all the fences in the vicinity are draped with them.

Though the Chinese did not actively pursue any of the region's sea mammals, if an opportunity arose to capture one, the Chinese would do so and then sell it to the sealers or whalers in the area. Sea lions which clambered onto the rocks adjacent to the fishing villages were sometimes shot, and evidence suggests that the Chinese at Monterey purchased the genitals of male sea lions, which they dried and ground into an aphrodisiac. The Chinese did not actively hunt whales, but if a dead whale washed ashore without a harpoon to indicate ownership, the Chinese

*Left*: Point Alones Fishing Village, c. 1890. Flounder hanging by the tails on drying rack at right.
ROY CHRISTIAN

*Right*: Point Alones Fishing Village, c. 1890. Objects drying on racks appear to be sea lion testicles which were dried and used as an aphrodisiac.
PAT HATHAWAY

Point Alones Village, c. 1890. Sea
urchin shells. Sea urchin and roe were
eaten directly out of the shell with a
spoon.     MONTEREY COUNTY LIBRARY

*Opposite*: Point Alones Village, c. 1895.
Woman is cutting and cleaning sharks
on the beach. Note that fins, a delicacy, have already been removed.
BANCROFT LIBRARY

would claim it and then sell it to the shore whalers. While the
whaling companies operated in Monterey, the Chinese sometimes bought the whale sinew which remained after the blubber
was cut from the whale carcass, paying as much as sixty dollars
for the sinew from one large whale: "They ship [the sinew] to
China for some purpose not clearly understood by anybody.
They tell the whalers they are an article of food."

The Chinese also made good use of the forests of seaweed
which surrounded the Monterey Peninsula, and during particular seasons of the year, they harvested a particular variety of
brown kelp, spread it on the ground to dry, and then shipped it
in bundles to San Francisco and China. Dried kelp had long been
used by the Chinese to make soup, and dried kelp from the
Monterey Peninsula had an excellent reputation throughout the
Chinese community in California and was harvested well into
the twentieth century. Sea urchins were eaten raw out of their
shells, and sea slugs were a highly-prized delicacy. Eventually

Near Lighthouse Point, c. 1895. Fisherman is spreading seaweed to dry. Dried seaweed was a highly-prized product of Monterey Chinese fishing village.      BANCROFT LIBRARY

the task becomes one of finding a sea plant or creature that the Chinese at Monterey did *not* use in some way or another, and though there must have been some, it is difficult to list them.

The diversity of Chinese fishing harvests undermines the argument that Chinese were extremely hard on the resources. The eclecticism which the Chinese brought to the Monterey Peninsula ensured that the burden of supporting the community was spread evenly across the animal and plant kingdom.

# CHINESE BOATS AND FISHING PRACTICES

Despite the exaggerated claims of residents of Santa Cruz and Monterey, neither side of Monterey had a natural harbor of refuge; Monterey was exposed to winds from the northwest and Santa Cruz to winds from the south and southwest. To make matters worse, the waters around the shore of the bay were too shallow for deep-draft vessels, so piers and wharves were necessary wherever cargo was to be loaded or unloaded. Until the erection of breakwaters in the twentieth century, fishermen in the bay either had to be ready to move their boats from one side of the bay to the other for shelter or have a means of removing their boats from the water when bad weather threatened. Traditional Chinese fishing boats were ideally suited for Monterey Bay as their flat-bottomed design made it possible for the Chinese to fish close to shore and to haul their boats from the water at day's end. Chinese boats were not built to standard specifications; there was no set length or configuration as each Chinese boat builder worked from memory and experience, not plans. The boats constructed by the Chinese in the Monterey Bay Region were built of redwood:

> The redwood boards for the main part of the vessel were heated and bent, then fastened together with the old-style, headless iron nails. The fishermen were so skillful in their building that when they were finished, the nails were completely covered with wood and thus hardly liable to deteriorate by rust. The outside of the craft was normally painted black, with eyes at the prow to enable the boat to see where it was going.

In 1875 the three Chinese fishing villages near Monterey had a total of thirty boats between them, most of them made in the villages.

The largest vessel associated with the Chinese fishing villages was a twelve-ton junk used to transport fish and supplies. Too

Point Alones Village, c. 1900. Shows
wide variety of boats used by Chinese
fishermen.          PAT HATHAWAY

large to be pulled out of the water, the junk migrated between
Pescadero and Point Alones depending on the weather. During
the late 1880s and 1890s, the junk was a common sight along the
coast, raising suspicions of smuggling among local law enforcement officials. In 1889 a United States officer staged a dramatic
raid on the junk as it lay off Point Alones, and with visions of a
hold full of opium, the officer stormed down into the junk's hold
only to find strong-smelling dried fish.

The workhorse of the Chinese fishing fleet was the locally
built twenty-one-foot fishing sampan. The flat-bottomed sampan relied on a single lateen sail or was sculled by a single fisherman standing near the stern, facing forward, and pushing a
single sweep oar. To most observers unfamiliar with Chinese
boats and seamanship, the sampans and their Chinese sailors
looked ungainly and awkward. Professor Jordan called the boats
"broad, flat and clumsy," and a reporter for the *Monterey Weekly
Herald* said they were "odd-shaped and lumbersome-looking

Point Alones Village, c. 1885. Sampans on the left; trawl lines on the right. Trawl lines were coiled in baskets and usually had upwards of two hundred hooks per line. Lines were baited prior to departure and then spread out on the sea bottom.
ROY CHRISTIAN

Point Alones Village, c. 1890. Shows distinctive arched keel of Chinese sampan. All sampans were constructed by Chinese fishermen in the region.
PAT HATHAWAY

Point Alones Village, c. 1890. Two Chinese fishermen baiting trawl line hooks prior to going fishing. Boxes in foreground were used to ship fish by rail.     BANCROFT LIBRARY

craft that float over the billows, when lightly loaded, with both ends in the air." Yet years of observation diminished this skepticism about Chinese boats and their sailors, especially when storms wreaked havoc with all but the Chinese boats which could be pulled safely out of harm's way. The row of sampans resting on the beach like crocodiles basking in the sun were not only picturesque but eminently practical.

The fishing equipment used by the Chinese on the Monterey Peninsula was also traditional and straightforward in its design. The abalone fishermen used a short, flat iron bar for prying the abalone from the rocks, while set lines, trawl lines, and gill nets

44

were used for catching the swimming fish. One fishing technique used in the surf at Monterey was quite unusual in California, and Professor Jordan noted that he had not seen the technique used elsewhere along the Pacific Coast:

> The gill-nets are placed among the kelp-covered rocks, not far from shore, and the boat goes around among the nets to frighten the fish into them. The old man plies the oar, sculling the boat. The young man stands in the bow, with a long pole, which he throws into the water at such an angle that it returns to him. The woman sits in the middle of the boat, with the baby strapped on her back. She is armed with two drum-sticks, with which she keeps up an infernal racket by hammering on the seat in front of her. This is supposed to frighten the fish so that they frantically plunge into the nets.

This fishing technique further evinces the difference between Chinese fishermen at Monterey and their counterparts elsewhere in California. The family nature of the fish-driving operation combined with the sophistication of the technique lends further weight to the idea that these were fishermen from China, not just Chinese laborers who had decided to enter the fishing business.

## COMPETITION FOR THE FISHING GROUNDS

The Monterey and Salinas Valley Railroad was built by Salinas Valley landowners who hoped to avoid the high shipping fees charged by the Southern Pacific Railroad. They planned to ship wheat from the Salinas Valley to Monterey by rail and then by sea to San Francisco and points beyond. The railroad also provided the first dependable land connection between Monterey and San Francisco, making it possible to travel on the narrow gauge from Monterey to Salinas and then on the Southern Pacific to San Francisco in seven hours.

Fish could also be shipped by train to San Francisco, and two weeks after the Monterey and Salinas Valley began operation in 1874, a small company of Italian fishermen arrived in Monterey to begin catching fish and shipping it fresh to San Francisco, ending the monopoly of the Chinese. The Italian company set its headquarters within a half-mile of the railroad depot in some small shacks on the beach adjacent to the old United States Customs House, and by the summer of 1875 it shipped up to a ton of fresh fish on the railroad each day. The fresh fish business was so good that in the fall of 1875 a second Italian company joined the first, for a total of a dozen Italian fishermen working off the beach at the Customs House. In November 1876 the *San Francisco Chronicle* described the Italian fishing companies at Monterey:

> The Italian Fishing Companies have since the opening of the railroad supplied the San Francisco markets with very large quantities of fresh fish, such as mackerel, halibut, pampinos [pompano], sardines, albicores [*sic*], salmon, smelts, flounders, rock cod and turbot. Some mornings they have shipped as many as 40 boxes averaging more than 100 pounds apiece. For the last four months the shipments have exceeded 100,000 pounds. During the month of August, the catch amounted to 40,000 pounds.

The word "fresh" is somewhat misleading when describing fresh fish shipping during the nineteenth century. Usually a morning's catch was put aboard the afternoon train (without cleaning and without ice) and arrived in San Francisco for sale at the fish market almost twenty-four hours after it was caught. Professor Jordan estimated that at least one-half of the catch was rotten before noon, and the fish were not cleaned until after the customer had purchased them: "In general no attempt of any kind is made to prevent the fish from undergoing decomposition." Jordan found the San Francisco fish market to be one of the poorest large markets in the United States, and he laid the blame for the poor quality of the market at the feet of the Italian and Portuguese fishermen who controlled it: "As a rule the Latin fishermen [Italian and Portuguese] are careless and wasteful." Jordan wryly suggested that the waste was at least partly an intentional effort to keep the price of the fish artificially high. The Chinese were not the only ethnic group targeted for a "wastefulness" that most likely was prevalent throughout the industry.

As the Italians settled in at the Customs House, the size and scope of the Chinese fishing villages on the Monterey Peninsula grew impressively. An informal census published in 1875 in the *Monterey Weekly Herald* counted sixty adult Chinese fishermen (forty-nine men and eleven women) organized into eight companies. Six of the companies were at Point Alones: Man Lee Company, Sun Sing Lee Company, Hek Lee Company, Yee Lee Company, and Man Sing Company. Sun Choy Lee Company and Boo Lee Company were at Pescadero, and Yee Lee Company was at Point Lobos. The Chinese companies also took advantage of the new railroad connection, but with the San Francisco market controlled by Italians, they concentrated on shipping a small amount of their catch fresh to smaller towns along the railroad line such as Salinas, Gilroy, and San Jose. The Chinese at Monterey continued to dry most of their catch and ship it out of Monterey aboard steamers and junks.

The small expansion into the fresh fish market was accompanied by a sizable reduction of the fishing grounds available to the Chinese, however. Operating from the Customs House beach, the Italians shouldered the Chinese fishermen west toward Point Pinos, and within a year of their arrival, the Italians controlled the bay waters; the Chinese fished "almost entirely outside the bay between Point Pinos and Point Lobos." The Chinese fishermen did not surrender the fishing business in the face of Italian competition, however, for in January 1876 they built several new boats and redoubled their fishing efforts at Carmel Bay. By the close of the second season, the arrangement was set—the Chinese fished for abalone and rockfish in Carmel Bay, shipping most of the catch, dried, to San Francisco by steamer, while the Italians fished directly off Monterey and shipped their catch fresh to San Francisco by rail. The Chinese and Italian fishermen were able to make such an adjustment at Monterey because the peninsula was still relatively isolated and there was enough room along the coast to accommodate both groups. In 1876 Monterey was the exception; elsewhere, Chinese who competed with whites met with mobs and violence.

## FISHING ON THE NORTH SIDE OF MONTEREY BAY

Ernest Otto placed a Chinese fishing colony on the Santa Cruz County coastline in the 1850s. The fishing camp must have been temporary as no Chinese fishermen are listed in Santa Cruz in either the 1860 or 1870 census. Fishermen from Pescadero and Point Alone often sailed across the bay to fish for mackerel and anchovies off the mouths of Soquel and Aptos creeks, and a reference in the *Santa Cruz Sentinel* in 1862 noted that a number of Chinese were fishing for mackerel off Soquel. As in Monterey, the fresh fish industry, except for the local market, had to await the arrival of a railroad connection in 1875.

When a narrow-gauge railroad similar to the Monterey and Salinas Valley was built between Santa Cruz and the Southern Pacific station just outside Watsonville, a company of Italian fishermen (together with some Californios already living in Santa Cruz) developed a fresh fish business centered at the railroad's terminus in Santa Cruz. Where the Monterey and Salinas Valley left Monterey and went directly inland to Salinas, the route of the Santa Cruz Railroad hugged the coastline for most of its length; stations such as Capitola and Aptos were relatively close to the beach. Soon after the railroad was completed, a company of Chinese fishermen set up a permanent fishing camp on the beach just east of Camp Capitola and began shipping boxes of fresh fish which were loaded at the Capitola and Aptos stations. By 1878 over half of the fish caught in Santa Cruz County were caught by the Chinese near Capitola. In 1879 the 139,000 pounds of fresh fish put aboard the railroad in Santa Cruz were joined by 177,000 pounds of Chinese-caught fresh fish loaded at Capitola and Soquel. The Chinese were able to load their catch on board the train without coming into direct competition with the Italians and Californios at Santa Cruz.

The Chinese also had an advantage over the Italians in the design of their boats. The Santa Cruz County coastline was much more exposed and shallow than that at Monterey, and the keeled *feluccas* used by the Italians were too unwieldy to beach. During their first winters at Santa Cruz, the Italians took their boats across to Monterey. In the late 1870s the Italians at Santa Cruz developed a solution to their problem—they rigged davits to the wharf at Santa Cruz, and when bad weather threatened, they hoisted the boats out of the water and hung them like lifeboats along the top of the wharf. But the Italians still did not have the mobility which permitted them to move very far from a wharf, and though they eventually put davits on the wharf at Camp Capitola in the late 1870s, they did not yet compete with Chinese fishing on the beaches east of the Capitola bluff.

The 1880 manuscript census lists thirty-two non-Chinese fishermen at Santa Cruz and twenty-nine Chinese fishermen on the beach around the corner from Capitola. The Chinese fishermen ranged in age from sixteen to forty-eight, and no women or families lived in the fishing camp. The fishing camp resembled a topsy-turvy apartment building, built of driftwood and shakes, leaning back against the bluff as far as possible from the surf.

Chinese fishing village near Capitola, c. 1880. Shows the recycled nature of the village's construction. Village was on the beach at the base of the bluff in what is now New Brighton Beach State Park.

Framed against the bluff, the shaggy camp had a certain charm: "The houses were about six feet above ground and the bluffs were picturesque with [their] growth, especially when the evening yellow primroses were in bloom."

The fishermen used equipment similar to that used by the Chinese at Monterey (seine, gill net, and trawl line), but the broad, flat beach made the task of seining easier than it was at Monterey. When the seine was full, the net was towed back to the surf adjacent to the village; then, using the same windlasses with which they hauled the boats out in the evening, the fishermen inched the seine onto the beach. Sometimes the net was so heavy with fish that it broke, scattering fish all over the beach. The Chinese caught a little of everything in their nets:

> The catches included smelt, sardines, anchovies, herring, many king fish, and some flat fish such as sole, petrolli sole, rex sole, turbet, flounders, skates, violin fish, sting rays, and once in a while an electric fish.

50

The Chinese also caught three types of anadromous fish as they migrated up Santa Cruz County streams: steelhead trout, salmon, and shad. When the spawning runs began, the Chinese stretched nets across the mouths of Soquel and Aptos creeks to catch the fish. Sportsmen had complained of this practice to the California legislature, and by the late 1870s it was illegal to catch trout with a seine. In 1877 nine Chinese were arrested and fined ten dollars each for catching steelhead trout in Aptos Creek with nets. Eventually a legal compromise was reached, and the Chinese were allowed to use nets at the creek mouths if they blocked no more than one-third of the waterway at any one time, permitting some of the fish to reach their spawning grounds.

Eastern shad had been introduced into the Monterey region in the 1870s, and during their migratory runs in early summer, they were caught by both Chinese and Californio fishermen and sold fresh on the Santa Cruz streets; in 1879 fresh shad ten inches long sold for six cents apiece. During the decade that Chinese fishermen worked the beaches near Aptos, Chinese fish peddlers were a regular sight on the streets of Santa Cruz, Capitola, Soquel, and Watsonville, their fish baskets swaying on bamboo shoulder poles.

Political forces drove the Chinese out of the fishing business in Santa Cruz. Organized the same year that the railroad and Italian fishermen arrived in the county, the Santa Cruz County anti-Chinese movement was particularly strong. Non-Chinese fishermen had political allies in the Santa Cruz Workingmen's Party, which pressured Chinese fishermen constantly. Though the Italian and Portuguese fishermen were prevented by their dependence on wharves from competing with the Chinese near Aptos, they urged political leaders to push the Chinese off the beaches with regulations and laws. The myriad fishing regulations passed in California during the anti-Chinese frenzy of the late 1870s were rigorously enforced in Santa Cruz County,

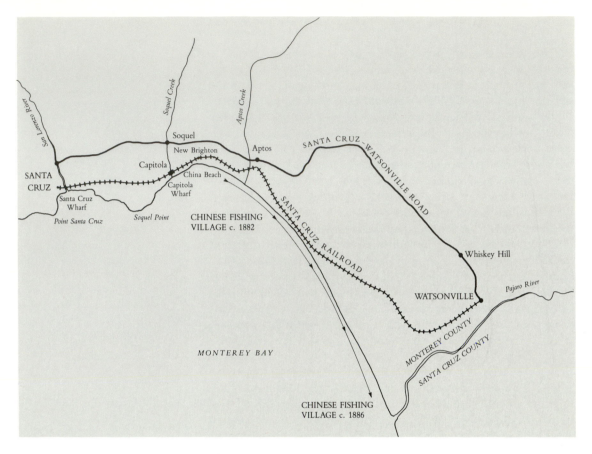

Map 2-1

SANTA CRUZ COUNTY, c. 1876

The Santa Cruz Railroad, completed in 1876, opened up the Santa Cruz County coastline between Watsonville and Santa Cruz. Chinese fishermen camped just east of Capitola shipped their catch on the railroad at New Brighton and Aptos. Development and fishing restrictions pushed the Chinese village east along the beach, forcing them to leave the county by 1888.

52

though often ignored in Monterey. In May 1880, the moment the 1879 constitutional provision prohibiting Chinese from fishing California's coastal waters went into effect, the Santa Cruz County sheriff arrested three Chinese fishermen near Aptos for violating the provision. A month later the three were released when the provision was declared unconstitutional.

The railroad which brought the fishing industry to Santa Cruz County also spurred the area's fledgling tourist industry, and the long, wide beaches became a primary attraction for visitors. Coastal development moved east from Santa Cruz along the railroad line, and in 1878 Camp San Jose opened on the bluff above the Chinese fishing camp at China Beach. The manager of the campground forced the Chinese to abandon their fishing camp and move east down the beach toward Aptos. The Chinese fishermen seem to have had no formal rent or lease arrangements with the landowners along the bluffs, making them particularly vulnerable to harassment from law enforcement officials and neighboring landowners. Each year the pressures of tourism and competition forced them farther east. When a neighborhood grew uncomfortable, the Chinese picked up and moved down the beach, retreating slowly, until they ran out of beach. In 1887 the Chinese made their last fishing camp in Santa Cruz County at Camp Goodall near the mouth of the Pajaro River, and the following year, when W. A. Wilcox of the United States Fish Commission toured Santa Cruz County, no fish were shipped from Aptos station, and no Chinese fishermen remained in Santa Cruz County. Chinese fishermen in the county lasted only a decade, with Californio, Portuguese, and Italian fishermen replacing them after 1888. Evidence suggests that Chinese driven from the county joined the burgeoning Point Alones village in Monterey, where Chinese did not have to combat such vociferous opposition.

## SQUID FISHING

The Point Alones village was not entirely free from the problems besieging Chinese fishermen elsewhere. Its prosperity depended on resolving increasing disputes with Italian fishermen
and Portuguese whalers. Though the Chinese fishermen kept the
unwritten agreement that relegated most of their fishing activity
to Carmel Bay, the number of confrontations over fishing territory rose each year. In 1880 the issue came to a head, and the
combatants fought in the court room. The Portuguese whalers
had taken to running their whale boats into the nets of Chinese
fishermen and cutting them to shreds with their knives. After
suffering the indignity in silence for some time (partly because
they believed the incidents to be beyond the jurisdiction of the
local courts), the Chinese fishermen decided to set a net for
the whalers. In March 1880 the Chinese took a white American
out with them, and while this potential witness hid in the bottom
of the boat, the Chinese spread their nets and began to fish. Right
on cue the Portuguese whalers sailed up and began cutting
the fishing gear; the witness then stood and formally observed
the entire incident. The Chinese sued the Portuguese whaling
company, and when the suit came to trial the witness testified
that he saw the Portuguese cut the nets. The attorney for the
whalers was able to argue successfully that the witness was
biased, and the suit was thrown out of court. As in many other
cases, Chinese who took legal action found that justice was
rarely the result.

Although the willingness of the Chinese to pursue their legal
rights ended the harassment, it seemed only a matter of time before the Italians, Portuguese, and anti-Chinese proponents in
Monterey might join forces and drive the Chinese fishermen off
the Monterey peninsula as they had done on the Santa Cruz
County coast. The Chinese needed to develop a new focus for

their operation if they hoped to remain at Monterey. When the solution finally came it was so ingenious and so logical that it has been taken for granted by all who have written about it. Just when the script called for the Chinese to be driven away, they found a new resource in the translucent squid which migrated by the millions into Monterey Bay, prolonging the life of the Chinese fishing village at Point Alones.

Each spring, from locations still not entirely known, millions of squid come to Monterey to spawn. The squid had been ignored as a commercial product by Portuguese and Italian fishermen, though both included squid in their traditional cuisine in

Point Alones Village, c. 1890. Squid drying. Note squid-draped rock in foreground. Squid were split, salted, and placed on the racks (called flakes) to dry.

CALIFORNIA HISTORICAL SOCIETY

Europe. China offered a huge potential market for dried squid as the fish was highly prized in Chinese cuisine. The small (about eight inches long) mollusk required little cleaning and was ideal for the Chinese method of open-air drying. The major drawback to the development of the squid industry was the fact that though a small portion of the squid spawned in Carmel Bay, the bulk of the squid spawned in Monterey Bay, in waters which were considered the fishing province of the Portuguese and Italians.

Fishermen in China had discovered years before that some species of fish were attracted to lights suspended over the water at night, like moths to a flame. Squid would eventually swim to the surface and surround the light; all the fishermen needed to do was scoop the mesmerized squid into their boats. While the Italian fishermen were home in bed sleeping, the Chinese caught squid and returned to Point Alones by daybreak to unload the squid and spread them to dry. This complementary use of the bay's resources gave new life and energy to the Point Alones village at a time when many Chinese fishing villages in California were dying out.

The squid usually arrived off Monterey in late April, remaining in the bay for two months before the spawning cycle was complete. Sometimes a second, smaller spawning run occurred in the fall, but the spring run was larger, its beginning usually heralded by a phalanx of sea birds, large fish, and whales intent on partaking of the feast. During squid season the satellite fishing villages closed, and all Chinese came to the Point Alones village to work in the squid harvest. Once the season ended, the Chinese resumed bottom fishing south of Point Pinos, and the Chinese families returned to the village at Pescadero.

The Chinese squid fishermen were organized into three boat teams. In one boat a single fisherman lit a torch or small pitch fire and suspended it in a pan or wire basket over the water, sculling slowly until a school of squid answered the summons of the light. As the squid formed an attentive circle "hovering just

beneath the surface, in the glow of the light that flares and spar-
kles in the wind," the other two boats quietly encircled the squid
with a purse seine. When the net was drawn tight, the Chinese
filled all three boats with squid, using small scoops or dip nets,
and returned to the Point Alones village.

Each morning the previous night's catch was split, salted, and
spread on drying racks or rooftops or draped on fences and over
rocks; the village looked as if it had rained squid during the
night. The larger squid (destined for markets in China) were
split, cleaned, and laid out on drying racks (called flakes) to keep
them off the ground. The smaller squid were spread out on the
ground without being split or cleaned. In the early years of
the squid industry at Monterey, women and children provided
much of the labor for the drying process, but during the 1890s
many of the single men who had moved to Monterey provided
the labor. The squid were turned at least once during the three-
day drying period, and when sufficiently dry they were packed
into 130-pound bundles and shipped by steamer to San Francisco.
In the 1888 squid season, the Chinese shipped 230,000 pounds
of dried squid from Monterey, a harvest valued at $12,500. Mon-
terey was the only place in California where the squid run was
large enough to support extensive squid fishing, and each year
Monterey provided over 90% of California's production of dried
squid.

Interviews with Chinese descendants of the fishermen explained the difference between the split and cleaned squid which
were dried on flakes and the whole squid which were dried on
the ground. The whole, poor-quality squid were packed in barrels in alternating layers of squid and salt. The barrels of salted
squid were then shipped to China. During the late nineteenth
century, the Chinese government had a monopoly on salt production and levied an extremely high tax on it. The squid were im-
ported as fertilizer, but the Chinese who bought the squid were
really purchasing the salt in which it was packed; the squid were

Point Alones Village, c. 1890. Squid
boats. Note wire basket hanging from
pole on boat in center of photo. Fire to
attract squid was burned in the basket.
PAT HATHAWAY

used as fertilizer after they were separated from the precious salt.
Salt might well have been listed alongside squid as a major commodity being shipped out of the Point Alones village.

Residents knew the squid season was underway when the
odor which rose above the drying squid drifted on the wind into
Monterey or Pacific Grove. Complaints from local residents
about the odor became as regular as the migrating squid. Objections to industrial odor are extremely subjective, as residents are
often willing to put up with noxious smells if they are related to
employment and the economic well-being of their community.
The residents of Watsonville never complained about the odor of
the sugar beet factory which carried the community through the
depression of the early 1890s. Thus, during the late 1880s and
early 1890s, the communities around the Point Alones village
grumbled, complained, and even passed petitions, but ultimately permitted the Chinese to continue to dry their squid because
the economic benefit of the Chinese fishery outweighed the

"abominable stench." As the first canneries moved into Monterey in the late 1890s, however, the scale began to tip, and the odor of the drying squid became less and less tolerable. The canneries brought just as noisome a stench to Monterey as did the squid yards—the difference was that the cannery odor was neutralized by the sweet smell of money. When the canneries displaced the economic value of the drying squid, objections to the odor reached a peak and eventually caused the end of Chinese squid fishing.

Yet residents along the coast at Monterey and Pacific Grove could also admire the lights of fires on the Chinese boats dotting the bay off Pacific Grove on moonless spring nights. Bobbing like fireflies over the water, "the lights of eleven Chinese boats formed a straight line far out into the bay." As tourism became more and more important to Pacific Grove, the lights became an integral part of the tourist sights. When pressure from Pacific Grove and Monterey citizens forced the Chinese to stop catching and drying squid by 1905, the citizens of Pacific Grove instituted the Lantern Festival to perpetuate the tradition of the lights. The first Lantern Festival was held in July 1905, and several Chinese and Japanese fishing boats were rented from the fishermen to carry the lanterns out onto the water. Lanterns were also lit in the windows and on the porches of all the Pacific Grove houses facing the ocean so they would "resemble a bit our Chinatown by swinging globes and fanciful designs in barbaric colors." The Pacific Grove Lantern Festival became an annual affair, and sometime in the early years, a story about a search for a Chinese Empress was attached to the event to give it mythical justification. The Lantern Festival actually duplicates the lights of those ingenious Chinese squid fishermen and as such is a fitting monument to the memory of the Chinese fishing pioneers on Monterey Bay.

Another branch of labor in this valley, is weeding sugar beets, done by Chinamen, who work on their knees, which become so sore that blood is left as they move along.

*Watsonville Pajaronian*, 1878

# 3

# Agriculture

THE CHECKERBOARD OF TEXTURES and colors which characterizes the Salinas and Pajaro valleys represents an astonishing variety of agricultural products. In the 1980s the top ten cash crops of the region included broccoli, strawberries, apples, cut flowers, wine grapes, cauliflower, and mushrooms. It is difficult to believe that in the 1850s and 1860s the region was dominated by a single crop—wheat. When the first crews of Chinese farm laborers entered the region in the summer of 1866, they brought the same resourceful attitude toward working the land that they brought to harvesting the abundance of the sea. From 1866 to 1900 the Chinese farm laborer was the mainstay of agriculture in the Monterey Bay Region, providing his labor to plant, tend, and harvest crops and reclaim land and his experience to show Yankee farmers the vast agricultural potential of the region.

The Franciscan missionaries introduced agriculture to the Monterey Bay Region in 1770. Surrounded by fields planted in wheat, corn, beans, and peas, with a vineyard and orchard usually planted adjacent to the mission buildings, each of the region's missions was worked by an Indian labor force. In each mission friars took annual tallies of livestock and produce. In 1832 the missions San Antonio, Soledad, San Carlos (Carmel), Santa Cruz, and San Juan Bautista owned a total of 23,700 head of cattle, 31,000 head of sheep, and 2,100 horses. From 1770 to 1832 the same missions had produced a staggering 1,321,000 tons of wheat. When the missions were secularized in the mid-1830s, the Indian labor supply dispersed, and raising livestock became the dominant industry during the late 1830s and 1840s. With neither an adequate source of labor nor an extensive market for agricultural products, the initial diversity of the Franciscans narrowed to beef and beans.

In 1850 the United States census enumerator made the following assessment of the agriculture of the Monterey Bay Region:

> Ranching is the principal interest of the country. Ranches of unknown extent, even to the owners, are covered with vast herds of cattle and horses whose number also, is generally unknown with [the] proprietors. The extent of agriculture is the raising of a small patch of beans—hence the chief articles of food are beef and beans . . . Labor is almost unknown, hence no production.

A brief, heady flirtation with potatoes in 1851 and 1852 ended in a catastrophic collapse of the market which made Yankee farmers in the region extremely wary of growing specialty crops. They returned to planting dependable wheat. When the drought of 1863–64 broke the back of the livestock industry, cereal grains emerged as the number one agricultural product in California. In 1881 King Wheat reigned over 3 million acres in California which produced 1.5 million tons of wheat each year. Wheat fields covered the Salinas, Pajaro, and San Juan valleys in the Monterey Bay Region. The reliance on a single crop began to strain the fecundity of even the rich alluvial soils of these coastal valleys, but two major obstacles stood in the way of diversification: poor shipping facilities and an absence of dependable agricultural labor.

During the 1850s and 1860s, the region's produce was shipped by sea off landings located at creek and river mouths around the bay. Piers were built at each landing, but winter storms battered them mercilessly and most of the piers lasted but a season or two before the ocean swept them away. Where there were no piers, the sacks of wheat were transferred from the beach to schooners anchored off-shore by surf boats which were winched back and forth through the breakers. When the Southern Pacific Railroad entered the region in 1872 and extended its San Francisco line to Salinas, the farmers had a welcome alternative to shipping by sea. The welcome wore off quickly, however, when the farmers learned that the rates charged by the railroad could be just as capricious as Pacific storms. During the 1870s the region's farmers helped build several competing lines in an effort to keep shipping rates down. The advent of the railroad removed one of the major obstacles to agricultural development.

The absence of agricultural laborers was more difficult to solve. From 1770 into the 1860s, most of the field labor in Northern California was provided by California Indians. As late as the 1860s, white labor contractors herded bands of dispirited Indians (known derisively as "Diggers") through the valleys each summer to harvest the grain, but their number dropped sharply each year because of disease. White harvest hands sometimes supplemented the Indians, but they were expensive and undependable. What the farmers needed was a supply of relatively inexpensive but dependable farm laborers.

## THE FIRST CHINESE FARM LABORERS IN THE REGION—SUMMER, 1866

During the summer of 1866 farm laborers were in such short supply that the few Indians available to harvest demanded two dollars per day. Beleaguered farmers in the Monterey Bay Region arranged contracts with Chinese labor contractors in San Francisco, and Chinese farm laborers were used extensively in the region for the first time in the 1866 harvest. Each year following the summer of 1866, the number of Chinese harvest hands in the region increased as the farmers found that they had the one vital trait which neither whites nor Indians had demonstrated—reliability: "They [the Chinese] make excellent hands and can be depended upon to go to work on *Monday mornings*."

Many of the Chinese working in the 1866–68 harvests had been miners in the Sierra Nevada, coming down from the mountains as the mining boom played itself out. This pool of laborers swelled in May 1869 when the Central Pacific Railroad released its Chinese construction crews. So many Chinese farm laborers flooded the Pajaro Valley during the summer of 1869 that they were willing to extend credit to the farmers, waiting for payment until after the crop was harvested and sold. This patience with regard to payday further endeared them to the region's farmers. The willingness of the Chinese to work under adverse conditions, their dependability, and their relative cheapness (when compared to white laborers) made it possible for the region's farmers to expand their wheat production.

By the summer of 1870 crews of Chinese farm laborers were working throughout the Monterey Bay Region, and the federal census taken that summer counted 120 Chinese farm laborers in the region (though the actual number was probably higher), with the largest concentration being around Castroville (32). The San Juan Valley had the next highest number (29), followed by the Pajaro Valley (28), and the Carmel Valley (14). The largest crew of Chinese farm laborers (14) worked on the Flint-Bixby Ranch outside San Juan Bautista. The farm laborers were all male and all China-born and averaged 27.5 years of age.

The availability of both shipping and dependable farm laborers in 1872 resulted in an increase in wheat and barley grown in the Monterey Bay region, particularly in the Salinas Valley. In October 1873 a Watsonville newspaper editor exclaimed that the warehouses were "crammed" with grain:

> Crops are excellent, freights low, and prices good; what more could be desired in a farming community we cannot imagine. Immense

quantities of grain have already been shipped and there is still an immense quantity stored which has not been sold.

At that moment, however, a random collection of agricultural experiments was taking place throughout the region. Inspired by a dependable supply of Chinese laborers, farmers introduced crops that were much more labor-intensive than wheat. By the 1880s wheat was displaced as the area's most important crop.

## TOBACCO AND HOPS

Tobacco had been introduced as a crop in the Pajaro Valley during the Civil War by James D. Culp, who had patented an innovative process for curing tobacco leaves. In 1864 a small cigar and chewing tobacco factory in Watsonville processed the small amount of tobacco grown there. By the late 1860s it was clear that the cool, foggy summers in the Pajaro Valley were not as suitable for drying tobacco leaves as was the weather in the southern Santa Clara Valley, and Culp moved his operations to Gilroy.

When Chinese laborers became available in large numbers after the completion of the railroad in 1869, the tobacco industry, particularly cigar making, boomed. In 1873 Culp built a huge three-story brick cigar factory (reputedly the world's largest at that time) on Monterey Street in Gilroy. Culp's factory employed 370 Chinese who rolled 1.5 million cigars each month. Tobacco acreage spread south from Gilroy toward Hollister, and eventually another huge cigar factory was built on San Felipe Road north of Hollister, employing over two hundred Chinese cigar makers. Virulent lobbying against Chinese-made cigars and competition from higher quality producers finally put the two Central California cigar factories out of business in the 1880s, but not before area farmers had a glimpse of the enormous potential of labor-intensive agriculture in the Monterey Bay Region.

One of the primary ingredients in the brewing of beer, hops demanded much more care and attention than tobacco; the hop vines had to be trellised, tied to the strings by hand, harvested by hand, and kiln-dried. The first hops in the region were planted in the Pajaro Valley in 1870, and though several attempts were made to grow hops near Natividad in the Salinas Valley, the Pajaro Valley became the area's primary hop-growing region. From the outset Chinese provided the tender loving care which the hops required. An 1870 article noted that Orin Smith's hop yard near Watsonville was being operated by Chinese, "four of whom are busily engaged in hoeing and plowing." In 1871 Smith's small hop yard required one hundred Chinese workers to harvest the crop. In 1877 Owen Tuttle, the man credited with pioneering successful hop cultivation in the Pajaro Valley, had planted fourteen acres of hops east of Watsonville and employed forty Chinese in his hop fields.

Though not a major crop in the Pajaro Valley, hop growing continued into the 1890s with most of the hop acreage located east of Watsonville in what is called the Lake District. In 1895, on thirty-nine acres adjacent to Tynan Lake, James Tynan's widow Margaret entered into a typical lease with the Chong Wo Company in which the Chinese agreed to sharecrop hops on the property. Lam Ho and Low Kew, partners in the Chong Wo Company, agreed to cultivate, "harvest, pick, dry and cure" the hops, and deliver the hops to the railroad depot in 190-pound bales. During the five year duration of the lease, the Tynans were to receive one-third of the crop as rent, and in exchange they gave the Chinese the use of the land and the hop-drying and bale-pressing equipment. Hop acreage steadily declined after the turn of the century, and hop cultivation ended with Prohibition. Both tobacco and hop cultivation succeeded due to Chinese labor, and this encouraged other experiments with labor-intensive crops during the 1870s and 1880s, with farmers hoping to find a substitute which might bring a higher return per acre than wheat.

## MUSTARD—CHINESE GOLD

The Chinese provided more than just muscle to the fledgling agricultural revolution against wheat. With their wide experience of more intensive farming in a crowded land, the Chinese brought a wider vision to California than did the Yankee farmers. If you had asked a Yankee farmer how many uses he could name for the land and plants in the Pajaro Valley, he might be able to list six; had you asked a Chinese the same question, he would have been able to cite dozens. Without question, raw Chinese labor was extremely valuable to the development of California agriculture, but the gift of vision and inspiration was priceless. It was the Chinese who transformed the mustard weeds which grew wild throughout the Monterey Bay Region into agricultural gold.

The mustard was probably introduced during the Spanish era. One legend has it that the Franciscan friars scattered mustard seeds along the trails which linked the missions so they would be tied together with a network of yellow blossoms in the spring. Whether planted intentionally or by accident, the mustard proved to be an aggressive guest, quickly crowding out the native grasses. By the mid-1850s the region was covered with the plant:

> . . . the most sublime scene I ever saw was one June following a wet winter, and the entire Salinas Valley from the Pacific Ocean to Paso Robles was covered with mustard, some of it reaching ten feet in height. I saw this vast yellow blanket being fanned into ripples by the wind from the foothills . . . The ground was so fertile and the mustard grew so high that it furnished wonderful protection to all kinds of game and animals that they came down out of the wooded mountains to make it their home during the summer.

Ranchers and farmers considered mustard a nuisance that crowded cultivated crops and could not be eaten by livestock.

Picturesque to travelers, a nuisance to farmers, the fields of mustard were seen as an opportunity by the Chinese who entered the region in the 1860s. Mustard seed contained an oil highly valued as a seasoning both in Europe and China, and according to a local story, the first Chinese to exploit the value of the wild mustard was "Poison Jim." Jim earned his living by poisoning ground squirrels for San Juan Valley farmers; besides their voracious appetites, ground squirrels were extremely hazardous to horseback riders—a mis-step in a squirrel hole could break a horse's leg. One spring, following a wet winter when the mustard crop threatened to crowd out the entire grain crop in the San Juan Valley, Jim went to each of the farmers in the valley and offered to cut down the mustard in exchange for the mustard seeds. Since mustard is an annual, the seeds were the culprits, and if Jim cut down the plants and removed the seeds, he would break the cycle and the mustard would not reappear in the fields. The farmers eagerly agreed to Jim's offer. Jim then went to San Francisco and contracted several dozen fellow Chinese. Working as a crew, they cut the mustard, spread it out on canvas, and beat it with flails to remove the seeds. Jim was able to sell enough of his mustard seed to a San Francisco broker to pay his workers, but most of the seed was bagged and stored. That same year the mustard crop failed in both Europe and South Africa, and European mustard brokers began to scour the world for mustard seed. Eventually a French mustard buyer heard of Poison Jim's mustard cache near San Juan Bautista and sought him out. After spirited negotiations Jim sold the mustard for an astounding $35,000 in gold.

The story of the mustard-turned-into-gold spread quickly through the Monterey Bay Region, and farmers began to hire Chinese farm laborers to harvest the mustard. In 1865 Dodge and Millard of Moss's Landing employed a crew of twenty Chinese to harvest wild mustard growing nearby. By the 1870s it was not unusual for upwards of 400,000 pounds of mustard seed to be shipped from the Salinas Valley each fall. The Chinese harvesters received from two to three cents per pound for harvesting, flailing, and bagging the seeds. By 1882 wild mustard had become scarce enough to require the *intentional* planting and cultivation of mustard in the Salinas Valley; the plant had made the full evolution from a nuisance weed to a valuable crop:

> The yellow mustard fields of the Salinas Valley are very beautiful . . . It is cultivated mainly by Chinese. During the past nine months of the present year [1882] about 250,000 pounds were shipped from this city [San Francisco] . . . There is a brisk demand for mustard in Eastern [United States] markets.

An opportunity to make money was never lost on David Jacks, a wealthy Monterey landowner, and in 1887 he cultivated mustard on hundreds of acres of his Chualar Ranch under the careful attention of sharecropping Chinese farmers: "Yellow mustard on David Jacks' ranch . . . farmed by the Chinamen, is turning out 25 sacks to the acre."

In the 1890s the Monterey County Assessor often listed mustard seed on his unsecured property tax rolls. Sam Sing, the Salinas merchant, paid taxes on 17 tons of mustard seed in 1890, and in 1894 Charley Mack, the Castroville labor contractor, paid taxes on a healthy 26 tons. The year 1895 appears to be the high-water mark: Sam Sing had 34 tons of mustard on hand, while Sam So Chong had a whopping 68 tons of mustard seed. Chinese continued to grow and harvest mustard into the early twentieth century, but as the Chinese population in the Monterey Bay Region declined, so did the commercial mustard industry. Mustard is no longer commercially harvested in the Monterey Bay Region, but it is often used by farmers between crops as a ground cover because the plant's roots help break up the soil. It is also planted between rows of fruit trees in orchards for the same reason.

Poison Jim became famous in San Juan Bautista for his philanthropy. During a serious drought he bought several wagons of provisions which were distributed to the needy in San Benito County; later in his life he enjoyed treating children at Christmas:

> A prosperous San Juan Mongolian, named Jim Jack, distributed one hundred pounds of candy among the school children of San Juan on Christmas day. [The Hollister newspaper] says he is of quite a benevolent nature, and has expended several hundred dollars in charity during the past year.

The people of San Juan Bautista knew him as "Jim Jack," the kind old Chinese who gave candy to children, but few knew that he was also a famous alchemist who had taught an entire region how to turn weeds into gold.

## THE BEET SUGAR INDUSTRY

Crops such as tobacco, hops, and mustard seriously threatened the reign of wheat, but sugar beets finally revolutionized agriculture in the Monterey Bay Region. Sugar beets came into their own when the largest beet sugar factory in North America began operating in Watsonville in 1888. The industry brought profound changes to the economic, political, and social fabric of the region, including the establishment of an essential Chinese labor force. The California Beet Sugar Company began when the first successful beet sugar plant in the United States was built in 1870 on the east side of San Francisco Bay at a place called Alvarado (now Union City) in Alameda County. The mill was operated under the guidance of two experts from Fon du Lac, Michigan, while the capital came from several California investors, including Benjamin Flint of San Juan Bautista. Some of the beets processed at Alvarado were grown near the factory with the remainder coming from Flint's rich bottom land in the San Juan Valley. The crew of Chinese farm laborers listed on Flint's ranch in the 1870 federal census probably worked that first crop of sugar beets.

The mill's investors planned to shift all the beet acreage to the Monterey Bay Region and ship the beets to Alvarado for processing. The first season was successful (the first successful season for a beet sugar factory *ever* in the United States), and in 1871 Flint distributed sugar beet seed to thirty Salinas Valley farmers to experiment with the crop throughout the valley. Before the plan to extend the beet acreage into the valley could be realized, the company went bankrupt in 1872. The soil around Alvarado proved unsuitable for beet growing, and the cost of fuel (coal was burned to power the steam plant) was prohibitive.

This brief experience with sugar beets in the region demonstrated that the soil was excellent for raising the beets and that sufficient Chinese labor was available to support the labor-intensive beet cultivation on a large scale. The first order of business, however, was to cut the cost of fuel and move the factory closer to the beets. In 1874 the company re-capitalized and moved to Soquel on the north side of Monterey Bay.

The boilers, graters, desiccators, and separators were moved from Alvarado to Soquel in the spring of 1874, and a new three-and-one-half-story factory was constructed just upstream from Camp Capitola on the east bank of Soquel Creek. The Soquel site of the California Beet Sugar Company was superior to Alvarado because firewood and water were plentiful; lime, used extensively in the sugar process, was manufactured in Santa Cruz; the nearby Soquel Landing facilitated shipping, and the route of the Santa Cruz Railroad (under construction in 1874) passed within one hundred yards of the factory. Most important, the factory could draw from hundreds of acres of rich alluvial soil, both in the Soquel Creek flood plain and in the Pajaro Valley to the east.

The first beet crop was planted on the alluvial plain surrounding the factory site (present-day Capitola), and while assisting in the construction of the factory, Chinese farmers cultivated, thinned, and weeded the sugar beets. Chinese workers thinned the beets by crawling along each row on their hands and knees. In fall the Chinese dug up the beets, cleaned and topped them (the tops were used for cattle feed), and loaded them in wagons for the short trip to the factory. The 1874 campaign (the French term still used in the sugar beet industry to describe the processing season) ran through the fall of 1874, and Chinese factory workers cut and loaded firewood for the boilers, lifted and moved the 180-pound syrup cans, and packed the four tons of sugar processed each twenty-four hour day. Of the 200 men employed by the California Beet Sugar Company, 145 were Chinese. A reporter for the *Santa Cruz Sentinel* visited the plant during that first season:

> Here we are in the field. We see half a dozen Chinamen filling a cart with beets and we will follow it to yonder large three and a half story building with a wing. We meet empty carts returning to the field to be re-loaded from the piles of beets, with tops all cleanly cut away, lying thickly all over fifty acres . . . They [the company] have nine hundred acres of their own land in beets, besides large quantities on rented land.

The company extended its beet acreage eastward for the next two seasons, and by 1876 over half of the beets processed at Soquel were grown in the Pajaro Valley and shipped to Soquel on the narrow-gauge Santa Cruz Railroad. A newspaper reporter traveling from Watsonville to Castroville in 1877 described the influence of sugar beets on the Pajaro Valley:

> One can scarcely help but be surprised at the number of wagon loads of beets he will meet on their way to the [Pajaro] depot for shipment

to the Soquel Beet Sugar Factory. Almost every farmer in the lower Pajaro Valley set apart a small portion of his land for the cultivation of this article. . . .

Slowly the beet acreage began to drift south and east, away from the factory, setting a pattern of growth which continued through the nineteenth century.

To encourage farmers to grow sugar beets and to guarantee that there would be beets to crush each fall, the company offered contracts to the farmers before the crop was planted; the contracts guaranteed the farmer a per-ton price based on the sugar content of the beets. This helped revolutionize the region's agriculture: for the first time farmers actually sold their crop before it was even planted. This contract system is still in use in the sugar beet industry.

In turn the farmers sub-contracted the actual growing of the beets to Chinese labor contractors. The farmers provided the land, seed, and water while the Chinese planted, thinned, harvested, cleaned, topped, and loaded the beets for shipment. In a contract between Ah Dong and John T. Porter signed in 1879, Ah Dong agreed to raise the beets for seventy cents per ton, while Porter contracted with the California Beet Sugar Company at Soquel to sell the beets for four dollars per ton. Deducting the shipping costs of less than a dollar per ton, the sugar beets were "quite a source of revenue." This three-level system of contracts established a tripod of factory owner, grower, and Chinese beet contractor, each essential to the industry. Though neither the growers nor factory owners ever treated the Chinese as equals in the arrangement, they grudgingly admitted that without the Chinese to raise the beets and work in the factory, the system would collapse.

At the height of the anti-Chinese movement in California and Santa Cruz County, the anti-Chinese proponents prowled the area protesting the number of Chinese employed in the sugar beet operations. A Soquel observer noted in 1876 that the owners of the company "persist in employing a good many 'heathen Chinese' to do the work, to the exclusion of so many naturalized citizens." A Watsonville farmer responded to those complaints by explaining that work in the sugar beets "was of such a nature that only Chinamen could be obtained to do it." The weeding of the sugar beets, he continued, was done by Chinese "who work on their knees which become so sore that blood is left as they move along." The thoughtful farmer declared that if whites were unemployed (there was a depression in California at the time), it was because labor-saving machinery had been introduced into Pajaro Valley agriculture, not because the Chinese had put them out of work: "It would be impossible to obtain white labor to do this work."

The California Beet Sugar Company tottered in 1878 when the price of sugar dropped as a result of increased competition from Hawaiian cane sugar. (Ironically, Claus Spreckels, the importer of Hawaiian cane sugar into the United States, had a summer home in Aptos, only a few miles east of Soquel on the Santa Cruz Railroad line along which beets were transported to the factory.) The company was unable to pay its largest beet supplier, John T. Porter, for the beets delivered; Porter sued and, after a court judgement in 1879, took over the company. During the company's last campaign in 1879, Yep Yak and a Chinese crew ran the entire operation. Competition from Hawaiian cane sugar diminished the profit margin in beet sugar manufacturing, and Porter decided to close the factory. In December 1880 the factory buildings and equipment were sold at a sheriff's sale, ending the Soquel beet sugar operation. But the Soquel experience with sugar beets cemented a strong relationship between John T. Porter, the largest supplier of beets to the Soquel factory by the late 1870s, and the Chinese beet contractors and laborers. Porter later owned the largest Chinatown in the Monterey Bay

Region and championed the Chinese cause both socially and politically.

The Soquel beet sugar operation left several other legacies to the Monterey Bay Region. First, regional farmers, particularly those in the Pajaro Valley, learned from experience that sugar beets, and potentially other crops, offered a sizable, guaranteed profit each season that made them preferable to wheat. Second, the farmers understood that the key to the profit in any labor-intensive crop was the dependable, hard-working Chinese who were willing to crawl through the fields and give the beets the necessary care and attention. By 1880 the revolution against King Wheat was well under way in the Monterey Bay Region, though the failure of the sugar beet experiment obscured this fact. Later Watsonville would become the sugar capital of Northern California, thanks in large part to the Chinese workers willing to bloody their knees in the fields.

## STRAWBERRIES

The Santa Cruz County strawberry industry began in the 1850s in fields north of Santa Cruz, and during the early years the Santa Cruz–area strawberry fields were contracted out to Chinese market gardeners. The first sizable and successful commercial planting of strawberries in the Pajaro Valley came late in the 1870s, and by 1881 a fledgling forty-two acres of strawberries had been planted in the valley. The introduction of irrigation, together with the surplus of Chinese farm laborers freed up by the collapse of the Soquel beet sugar factory, caused the strawberry acreage to jump to 268 acres by 1885. By the spring of 1886 the Watsonville newspaper estimated that three hundred Chinese were working in strawberry fields around Watsonville.

The year 1886 saw a number of Pajaro Valley farmers enter

Pajaro Valley, 1890s. Chinese strawberry farmers. Rare photograph of
Chinese farm workers.

FLORENCE WAUGAMAN

into leases with Chinese berry contractors. The landowners furnished the land, plants, water, and boxes while the Chinese
furnished the skilled labor to plant, cultivate, pick, and pack
the berries. The Chinese strawberry contractors split the proceeds from the season evenly with the landowners. Perhaps one
of the largest sharecropped berry farms, the Lake Farm north of
Watsonville owned by Thurber, Buckley, and Steward cultivated
one hundred acres of strawberries and forty acres of raspberries
and blackberries:

> The method of conducting this farm is to let it to Chinamen on
> shares, the owner furnishing everything, the Chinamen performing
> the labor and receiving one-half. On Lake Farm during the busy
> season from three to four hundred men are employed, while in
> the winter about sixty are kept busy. These Chinamen represent a
> number of companies, and work under bosses. They live by them-
> selves, mixing with Caucasians only to the extent which necessity
> compels them in business relations.

Chinese farm laborers preferred to be paid a piece-rate rather
than a daily wage, and sharecropping arrangements were even
more desirable. But the most highly prized working arrangements for the capital-poor Chinese were leases under which they
reclaimed the land in exchange for its free use for four or five
years. By the late 1880s the Chinese were clearing the willows
and tules out of the slough country west of Watsonville and
bringing marginal land into berry and vegetable production.

In the Struve and Hansen sloughs, the standard reclamation
lease ran for four years, and a number of success stories attested
to the fertility of the land as well as the ability of the Chinese to
clear and work it. In 1890 a Chinese crew planted one acre of
raspberries on reclaimed land and sold the berries for $1,300.
Another piece of reclaimed slough land produced 200 sacks of
potatoes (one hundred pounds per sack) to the acre in 1888 and
180 sacks to the acre the following year. The crop of choice seems
to have been berries:

Pajaro Valley, 1890s. Chinese cultivating strawberries.

FLORENCE WAUGAMAN

Wherever Chinamen have cleared land in the slough district they have put in raspberries, and they have leased desirable tracts of land in different parts of the valley, paying cash rent in advance to cultivate blackberries.

When the reclamation leases expired, landowners rarely renewed them on a long-term basis with the Chinese farmers, preferring instead to follow the example of the Chinese and grow berries or vegetables themselves.

By 1890 the diversification of agriculture in the Pajaro Valley had drastically diminished cereal grain acreage:

Acreage in orchards is increasing every year, [with] beet and other crops [taking] much of the acreage of the [Pajaro] district . . . It will not take many years before a threshing outfit will be an unusual sight in the [Pajaro] valley.

Each year the transformation of the region's agriculture moved south and east, and by the turn of the century, the Salinas Valley was undergoing a similar shift from wheat to more specialized crops. Chinese farm laborers were the catalyst for transforming a vast wheat field into the "salad bowl of the world."

A person passing on the SPCRR train the other day said he counted thirty-two graves by the wayside of the Chinamen that were killed at the recent explosion in tunnel No. 3.

*Santa Cruz Sentinel*,
November, 1879.

# 4

# Railroads

Iт тоок one hundred years for the heroic feats of the
Chinese who worked on the Transcontinental Railroad to be included in the historical accounts written about the building
of the Central Pacific Railroad through and over the Sierra Nevada; the image of Chinese railroad workers hanging over cliffs
in baskets as they drilled the blasting holes has finally become
part of the history of the American West. When the Central Pacific and Union Pacific Railroads joined in Utah in 1869, the Central Pacific released an estimated five thousand Chinese railroad
workers who provided the labor for a decade of railroad building
throughout California. In 1870 there were no railroad tracks in
the Monterey Bay Region, but by 1880 Chinese railroad builders
dug cuts, laid ballast, drilled tunnels, built trestles, laid track, and
risked death to build almost one hundred miles of track, bringing
Santa Cruz and Monterey counties into the industrial age.

Isolated by natural barriers, fragmented by difficult terrain
such as sloughs, swamps, and mountains, the Monterey Bay Region was unified by the railroads and connected with the outside
world. The region was a microcosm that exemplified the transformation worked by the railroads and their builders, and two
important themes stand out. First, the transformation was made
possible by the courageous Chinese railroad workers risking life

and limb to build the roads under seemingly impossible conditions—drilling over two miles of tunnels through the Santa Cruz Mountains during the construction of the South Pacific Coast Railroad or pushing a standard-gauge railroad through the tortuous Aptos Canyon for the Southern Pacific. Second, numerous challenges to Southern Pacific's power sprang up in the region during the 1870s; nowhere was the Southern Pacific challenged as often as in the Monterey Bay Region and nowhere was the victory of the giant corporation so complete—by 1886 the Southern Pacific owned all the region's railroads and most of the Monterey Peninsula.

No one location in the Monterey Bay possessed all the requirements for an excellent harbor. Harbors at Santa Cruz and Monterey were exposed to seasonal gales. Nineteenth-century ship captains berthed in Monterey Bay were constantly on the alert for a gale which might necessitate raising anchor and running for the opposite shore to avoid shipwreck. Treacherous fog often obscured the points and rocks, and all these factors persuaded ship captains to lay over in San Francisco whenever possible.

Most businessmen and developers in the region quickly recognized the need for a dependable rail connection with San Francisco and the outside world. In the 1860s numerous public meetings were organized to explore this option, but capital in the region to support such a major undertaking was insufficient. During the Civil War Chinese railroad crews had pushed a railroad south from San Francisco to San Jose; opened in January 1864, the San Jose Railroad covered half the distance from the Monterey Bay Region to San Francisco. Entrepreneurs around the Monterey Bay anxiously awaited continuation of the railroad south of San Jose, but it was not until the San Jose Railroad was taken over by the owners of the Central Pacific Railroad and renamed the Southern Pacific Railroad in 1869 that the line was extended to Gilroy, where once again, construction was halted.

Communities served by steamers (Santa Cruz, Monterey) wanted to supplement and eventually replace shipping with the more dependable railroad service. Communities serviced only by expensive freight wagons (San Juan Bautista, Salinas City), saw the railroad as the difference between economic survival and disaster. San Juan Bautista was close enough to Gilroy to pin its hopes on the eventual extension of the San Jose line south into the San Juan Valley, but the restless leaders in the Salinas Valley could not wait; the freight being paid on the growing wheat crop each summer was strangling the town.

A series of citizens' meetings in Salinas and Monterey in 1867 and 1868 led to the incorporation of the Monterey and Salinas Railroad (M&SRR) in 1869. The M&SRR was to be a twenty-one-mile railroad connecting Salinas with a wharf in Monterey, replacing the freight wagons which carried the ever-increasing wheat crop to Moss's Landing for shipment. Surveyors quickly moved along the route, and for a fleeting moment, the M&SRR seemed all but built. But capital did not materialize quickly enough, and while the M&SRR hesitated, the Southern Pacific made its move.

With the completion of the Transcontinental Railroad in May 1869, the owners of the railroad wanted a route south from San Francisco and Sacramento that would give them a monopoly on rail traffic within California. Keeping their plan to extend down the San Joaquin Valley a closely guarded secret, the Southern Pacific made two feints that suggested it planned to locate its north-south main line along the coast. The first line went south from Gilroy to Hollister, and the company seemed intent on connecting Gilroy with Bakersfield and Los Angeles through Hollister. Chinese railroad crews quickly laid the tracks through the Bolsa district into Hollister by January 1871, but the Hollister branch eventually stopped at Tres Pinos, five miles south of Hollister. Undoubtedly inspired by the efforts of Salinas City to connect with the coast using the M&SRR, Southern Pacific made its second probe down the coast from Gilroy in April 1871. Bypassing San Juan Bautista (and effectively killing any hopes the town had to become a county seat or railroad center), the Southern Pacific pushed through the Pajaro Gap and into the Pajaro Valley (missing Watsonville by a mile), reaching Salinas City in November 1872 to tap the wheat-rich Salinas Valley. Observers became suspicious of the Southern Pacific's avowed intention to continue on to Southern California after the railroad stopped in Soledad in 1873. (The route was not extended beyond Soledad until 1886.) The few extant descriptions of the construction of the Gilroy-Salinas extension provide a sketchy picture of over five hundred Chinese building grade and laying track at a furious rate. Most of the Chinese working on the Salinas extension were veterans of the Transcontinental, and laying down rails through the Pajaro Valley and into Salinas City was easy by comparison.

Largely due to the arrival of the Southern Pacific Railroad in Salinas in November 1872, Salinas had wrestled the Monterey County seat away from Monterey by 1874. But the boom the Southern Pacific Railroad brought to the Salinas Valley quickly lost its luster. With its extortion of rights-of-way and depot acreage, decisions about routes and schedules shrouded in secrecy, and a cavalier attitude about the setting of rates, the Southern Pacific Railroad aroused animosity throughout the region. Salinas City, the city which had hailed the Southern Pacific Railroad as a savior in 1872, was ready to slip out of the corporation's embrace in early 1874 by reviving the plan for that direct rail connection to Monterey and the sea.

## THE MONTEREY AND SALINAS VALLEY RAILROAD

The Monterey and Salinas Valley Railroad was the first of several proposed Granger railroads constructed in central California. The Grange (Patrons of Husbandry) was founded in the Midwest in 1867 as a farmer's protest against railroad abuses, and by 1874 a unit of the organization was active in Salinas. The term *Granger railroad* referred to a railroad built with private funds rather than public subsidies or public funds, on a narrow gauge, to serve a community's shipping needs. Some railroads, such as the Santa Cruz Railroad, were mis-labeled Granger railroads even though they received public subsidies and had no connection with the Grange, because they brought relief from the monopoly of Southern Pacific.

The M&SVRR probably deserves the appellation of Granger railroad more than any other, as the inspiration for the railroad came from Salinas Valley farmers who belonged to the Grange, and the railroad's Board of Directors was dominated by men who belonged to the organization. Encouraged by Salinas Valley farmers eager to find a cheaper alternative to the $4.50 per ton rate charged by the Southern Pacific to ship wheat to San Francisco, two influential Monterey property owners, Carlisle Abbott and David Jacks, organized the M&SVRR in 1874, connecting Salinas with a wharf in Monterey. One-third of the $300,000 capital used to construct the road came in the form of a loan from Santa Cruz lime producer Henry Cowell.

Cheap rates could only come with cheap construction, so the route of the narrow gauge was laid out to avoid obstacles (though the major obstacle, the Salinas River, could not be avoided) and most of the right-of-way was donated to the railroad. As surveyors moved across the Salinas Valley in April 1874, scrapers, wheelbarrows, and a steam donkey arrived in Monterey by steamer, and the first major competitive threat to the Southern Pacific was under way. Leland Stanford came to Salinas late in April (ostensibly to check his holdings there), and he scoffed at the idea that the little railroad could compete with his Southern Pacific. The first Chinese railroad workers for the project arrived by steamer right behind the steam donkey and wheelbarrows.

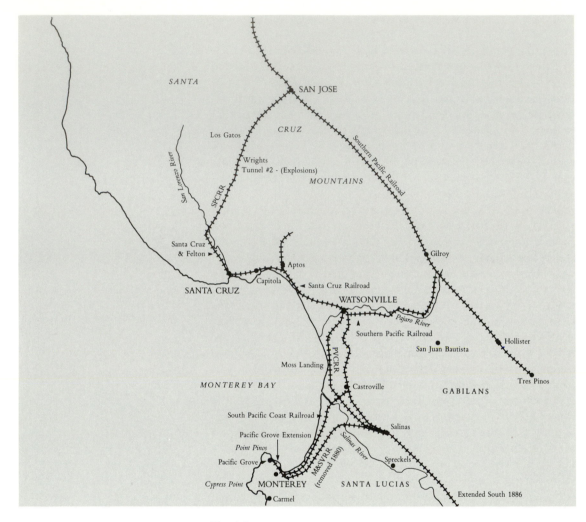

Map 4–1

MONTEREY BAY REGION RAILROADS

Map shows railroads constructed in the region between 1872 and 1900. All the railroad lines were constructed by Chinese railroad workers.

84

By May 150 Chinese were cutting the grade between Monterey and the Salinas River. Throughout the next seven months, the M&SVRR tried to supplement its construction crews with white laborers, but few white workers came forward for the arduous work, so the Chinese provided the bulk of the labor on the road's construction.

The M&SVRR faced two obstacles during its construction. The first came in June 1874, when the wheat harvest began in the surrounding valley. Many of the horse teams used to pull the scrapers had been hired from neighboring farmers, but once the wheat harvest began, the farmers took back their horses and also lured Chinese workers away from the railroad to harvest their wheat. By the end of June 1874, only fifty Chinese continued to work on the railroad grade. The M&SVRR raised its wages to keep the last Chinese from bolting to the wheat harvest, and grading continued slowly toward the Salinas River.

The Salinas River was the second obstacle faced by the railroad. A tent village of Chinese railroad workers marked the end of the graded line by mid-July, and the M&SVRR spent the next two months driving piles for a trestle across the river. The level of the Salinas River was very low in August, but it had a reputation for rising and wandering in the winter, so Chinese crews took extra care to shore up the approaches at each end of the trestle. Meanwhile track was being laid on the grade from Monterey east, and once the trestle was completed in late August, it took just three weeks to complete grading the line to Salinas; while one Chinese crew laid track, other Chinese crews moved along the right-of-way putting the finishing touches on the cuts and fills and ballasting the road along the beach just east of Monterey.

The M&SVRR's 18.5 miles of track were completed October 9, 1874, in just under seven months. As the first Granger railroad, the M&SVRR became celebrated throughout California:

> Monterey county has solved the problem of how to cut loose from the grinding extortions of Railroad monopoly. Their little narrow-

Monterey, c. 1876. Monterey and Salinas Valley Railroad Depot and end of the tracks at Monterey. Photo shows simplicity of depot for the narrow-gauge railroad. Railroad was constructed by Chinese railroad workers.
ROY CHRISTIAN

gauge railroad has taken the kinks out of a small section of Stanford's line, and made the people of that locality no longer dependent upon the will and pleasure of the Railroad King.

The completion of the M&SVRR forced Southern Pacific to drop its rates from $5.50 per ton to $3.75 per ton to be competitive with the M&SVRR rates of $1 per ton to the wharf at Monterey. When the ship *H. L. Richardson* came alongside the railroad's wharf at Monterey to take on a load of grain bound directly for Liverpool, the victory over railroad magnates, middlemen, and shipping gougers in general seemed assured. The railroad created stronger ties between Salinas and Monterey and established a healthy industry in fresh game (fresh fish, venison, quail, and rabbit were shipped within a day to San Francisco), but it never achieved the dreams of independence from the Southern Pacific. The railroad failed to show a profit over the next four years.

The Salinas River trestle proved to be the railroad's undoing. A flood in January 1875 swept it away, and it took Chinese crews two months to get the road running again. The trestle went down again the following January, this time for six months, and public support for the road began to dwindle along with its dependability. The Southern Pacific lowered its rates and waited as the M&SVRR staggered through the depression of 1877–78. When the railroad was unable to make the payments on the $100,000 construction loan in December of 1878, Henry Cowell foreclosed on the railroad, driving it into bankruptcy. Leland Stanford and the Southern Pacific Railroad paid their final respects not by scoffing, but by buying the M&SVRR at auction.

The speed with which the Southern Pacific moved in to take over the M&SVRR testifies to the vision of local developers and promoters. Ironically, when the M&SVRR was completed in October 1874, the influence and presence of the Southern Pacific Railroad in Monterey were non-existent. The modest success of the M&SVRR spurred the Southern Pacific (and its other tentacle, the Pacific Improvement Company) to action, and by 1881 the Southern Pacific owned a large part of the Monterey Peninsula, a huge resort hotel east of Monterey, and the only railroad in Monterey. The first railroad to compete directly with the Southern Pacific in the Monterey Bay Region, the M&SVRR was also the first to be crushed and absorbed by the corporation, a fate which met all the other competing Granger railroads born during those heady 1870s.

## THE SANTA CRUZ AND FELTON RAILROAD

If nineteenth-century Monterey County owed much to the coming of the railroads, Santa Cruz County owed everything, for railroads constructed during the 1870s tied together the isolated communities along the north coast of Monterey Bay and launched an era of unparalleled development. Until the mid-1870s the tiny settlements along the coastal terrace were temporary beachheads, isolated by a beautiful but convoluted landscape. Winter storms often trapped residents of Santa Cruz between impassable creeks and mountains on one side and southwesterly gales and mountainous seas on the other. In the 1860s it was not unusual for the county to be out of contact with the outside world for weeks at a time. The road between Santa Cruz and Watsonville was so precarious that during the smallpox epidemic of 1868 some Santa Cruz citizens attempted to isolate the disease in Watsonville by destroying the bridge across Aptos Creek.

It took no imagination to see the economic potential in the redwood forests covering the mountains to the north, but each treasure-filled basin was carefully guarded by a narrow, steep-sided canyon. Lumbermen could hike into the canyons to reach the trees, but once they cut the trees into lumber, each piece had to be wrestled down out of the mountains, across a rickety wharf, and onto a steamer docked in the shallow water alongside. Limestone-related industries (lime, blasting powder) had been moderately successful in the 1860s, shipping their products out by sea, but until the first railroad locomotive fired up in 1875, development of the county's resources was piecemeal and fitful. Chinese railroad workers turned the quarter-century-old dream of Santa Cruz developers into reality. Between 1875 and 1880 the Chinese built three separate railroads, laid forty-two miles of track, and drilled 2.6 miles of tunnels to stitch Santa Cruz County together and attach it permanently to the world beyond the Santa Cruz Mountains. The Chinese contributed not only their muscle and sweat, but their lives. At least fifty Chinese were killed in accidents while building those railroads. For every mile of railroad, one Chinese died.

The first railroad on the north side of Monterey Bay was a tenuous little narrow gauge connecting the San Lorenzo River Valley and its redwood and lime deposits with the wharves at Santa Cruz eight miles away. Construction on an earlier railroad into the mountains had been stopped in 1870 by a suit brought by Henry Cowell. In 1874 the Santa Cruz and Felton Railroad was incorporated, and in just eight months Chinese railroad workers built the eight-mile line between Santa Cruz and Felton. The line was engineered around rocks and large trees to avoid the cost of removing them. The light rails were draped on the canyon walls like Christmas tree tinsel, and the railroad crews held their breath each time they brought a loaded train down the canyon after the line opened in July 1875. Lumber cut in the canyons beyond Felton was loaded onto an amazing fourteen-mile flume which shot each board to the Felton railhead to be loaded on the narrow gauge and sent to Santa Cruz. Though the entire operation resembled a large Tinker-toy contraption, the Santa Cruz and Felton brought millions of board feet of redwood out of the mountains.

The railroad's policy of avoiding natural obstacles failed in Santa Cruz. When the Santa Cruz and Felton proposed to loop out around Mission Hill and run its locomotive down Pacific Avenue, the town council required the railroad to use horses to pull the loaded cars through the heart of the business district. As badly as Santa Cruz businessmen wanted the railroad connection with Felton, they did not want railroad locomotives (even tiny narrow-gauge ones) rumbling down the main business street. The arrangement was unsatisfactory for the railroad, so in 1876, while the horses quietly pulled the car loads of lumber through town, the railroad began drilling a nine-hundred-foot tunnel through Mission Hill at the north end of Pacific Avenue.

The Mission Hill tunnel was the only nineteenth-century railroad project not constructed by the Chinese. The anti-Chinese movement was running at full steam in 1876, and Santa Cruz could not tolerate a large crew of Chinese working in the heart of town. Working in shifts around the clock, thirty-two Cornish miners took six months to dig the tunnel, and in the process both Santa Cruz and the railroad learned that intolerance was expensive—the tunnel cost a whopping $20,000. The *Santa Cruz Weekly Courier* crowed that, "not a single Mongolian raised a pick in [the Mission Hill tunnel's] prosecution."

## THE SANTA CRUZ RAILROAD

Santa Cruz businessmen had been peering over the Santa Cruz Mountains for years, monitoring the progress of the railroad from San Francisco to San Jose and then to Gilroy. Early efforts to coax the railroad over the Santa Cruz Mountains failed, and in 1872 the businessmen watched with disappointment as the Chinese crews working for Southern Pacific came through the Pajaro Gap and turned south into the Salinas Valley rather than north into Santa Cruz County. The Santa Cruz railroad boosters then invited Southern Pacific to build an extension from Pajaro to Santa Cruz, but Southern Pacific engineers estimated that it would cost $16,000 per mile to build a railroad across that washboard terrace, and the railroad politely declined the invitation. Finally a group of Santa Cruz, Soquel, and Aptos businessmen (including Claus Spreckels and Frederick Hihn) organized their own railroad and, with the aid of a subsidy approved by county voters, began construction of the Santa Cruz Railroad in December 1873. Most railroads were built from both ends toward the middle, doubling the rate at which track was laid, but because the voters of the Pajaro Valley had opposed the subsidy for the railroad, the line was built east from Santa Cruz, giving

Santa Cruz the advantage of rail contact with Soquel and Aptos but not Watsonville. Despite the anti-Chinese movement which gripped Santa Cruz at the time, most of the construction of the Santa Cruz Railroad was done by Chinese.

The Chinese railroad workers lived in a cluster of tents on the railroad right-of-way about a mile east of Santa Cruz, riding to work each morning on the construction train as construction moved east: "The village is empty during the day, but at night all the characteristics of Chinese life are in full blast." Few (if any) of the Chinese railroad workers lived in the established China-towns in Santa Cruz or Watsonville, though they would often travel into those towns on their day off in search of gambling, opium, prostitutes, or companionship. On work days China-town took its wares out to the tent village, providing the camp cooks with fresh vegetables, fish, and rice. Even the lotteries sent salesmen out to the railroad workers, and the lottery agent ran along the tracks collecting tickets and money which he would tie up in a red bandanna and carry back to Santa Cruz for the drawing each evening. Should one of the railroad workers be lucky enough to win, the agent would return the next day with the winnings. This was the origin of the lottery runner, an institution which survives in today's Keno runner at gambling casinos in Nevada.

Chinese railroad workers on the Santa Cruz Railroad worked six ten-hour days a week and were paid one dollar a day. Two dollars per week was deducted from their pay for food, while expenses such as clothing and recreation chipped away at the remaining four dollars so that they averaged three dollars per week profit. During the road's construction the lotteries in Santa Cruz and Watsonville hummed with activity, the lure of a winning six hundred dollar ticket making further inroads into the crew's pay. Luck played startlingly contrasting roles in the daily life of the

Chinese railroad workers; good luck might bring a winning lottery ticket, while bad luck could bring injury or even death in an accident.

Even on the relatively straightforward Santa Cruz Railroad, railroad work was dangerous business. In April 1876, a month before the railroad was completed, the brakes failed on the construction train and it plowed into a group of Chinese working on the grade, killing one and injuring two others. The next month the bank of a railroad cut fell on two Chinese, breaking their legs. The most melancholy accident on the Santa Cruz Railroad, however, occurred in January 1876, when a construction train ran over a Chinese railroad worker, mangling his legs. Doctors in Santa Cruz amputated both his legs, and against all odds the man survived. The Santa Cruz Railroad paid all the Chinese railroad worker's medical expenses and promised to provide living expenses for the man once he left the hospital.

With the railroad's completion in May 1876, Santa Cruz could connect with the Southern Pacific in Pajaro by changing trains. From 1876 to 1880, the Santa Cruz Railroad enjoyed a nominal financial success, with freight providing most of the railroad's revenue. The plaintive whistle of the small locomotives (the Betsy Jane, the Jupiter, and the Pacific) sounded the beginning of a manufacturing boom in Santa Cruz County.

## THE SOUTH PACIFIC COAST RAILROAD

The dream of a railroad over the Santa Cruz Mountains to San Jose had tempted Santa Cruz businessmen since the early 1860s, but with the Santa Cruz Railroad connection to the Bay Area via Pajaro and the Southern Pacific after 1876, a trans-mountain railroad seemed redundant. Construction costs for a railroad through the mountains would be extremely high, and once the railroad was completed, it would be in direct competition with the Southern Pacific Railroad, a risky proposition. Senator James Fair, multi-millionaire and visionary, was not awed by the challenges posed by either the Southern Pacific or the Santa Cruz Mountains. He saw (correctly) that the economic potential of the mountains could make the railroad economically self-sufficient once it was completed; the construction costs could be mitigated by using less expensive Chinese railroad workers. With his briefcase filled with Comstock mining money, Fair incorporated and began construction of the South Pacific Coast Railroad in 1876.

The SPCRR route began on the east side of San Francisco Bay (which was not already locked up by the Southern Pacific), came south along the bay to San Jose, then to Los Gatos and over the mountains to Felton. Construction of the Dumbarton–to–Los Gatos segment went quickly as the route was relatively straight and level. The Los Gatos–to–Felton segment was another matter.

Compared to the soaring, majestic Sierra Nevada, the Santa Cruz Mountains are small and round, covered with redwood and Douglas fir. On closer inspection, however, the Santa Cruz Mountains are dark, brooding, mean little mountains, twisted and gnarled by the faults which run their entire length. For railroad and road builders the mountains offered their own peculiar challenges, as it was necessary to crisscross canyons and ridges to cross them. Fair decided to go through the mountains rather than over them, and the SPCRR route included a 6,243-foot tunnel at the summit, a 5,325-foot tunnel between Laurel and Glenwood, and six smaller tunnels through ridges along the line. The key to Fair's plan, the tunnels, leveled out the grades so that the narrow gauge would be able to operate safely and efficiently.

The first year of construction was devoted to laying track

from Newark south through San Jose and into Los Gatos canyon. Once the rails reached the forbidding Summit ridge, tunneling began while track was laid north from Felton. In August 1878 the SPCRR employed seven hundred men, six hundred of whom were Chinese. Chinese did all the grading, tunneling, track-laying, and ballasting, while whites built trestles and supervised the construction. By 1879, when the tunnels were being drilled and track was being laid in the canyons, approximately one thousand Chinese railroad workers laid track in the Santa Cruz Mountains.

Most of the Chinese working on the SPCRR were experienced railroad crews who had worked on other railroads in the West; many were probably veterans of the Transcontinental Railroad. When the SPCRR needed Chinese railroad workers, they contacted the Ning Yeung Company (one of the Six Companies of San Francisco); most of the railroad workers in the region were hired through the Ning Yeung Company. The Chinese crews of twenty to thirty men were supervised by a Chinese contractor who took his orders from a white supervisor and acted as paymaster for the Chinese workers. The Muir brothers, supervising construction for the SPCRR, paid the crews' wages directly to the Ning Yeung Company, which in turn paid the laborers. In 1878 the railroad paid 77.5¢ per day for each Chinese laborer and furnished wood and water for cooking. Later, as the depression of the mid-1870s eased, the rate rose to $1 per day; following the explosions in the Summit tunnel, Chinese tunnel workers were lured back to work for $1.25 per day. We do not know how much the Six Companies deducted from each worker's salary for meals, but it was estimated that each laborer might clear $15 per month working six days a week. The Muir Brothers employed thousands of Chinese railroad workers during the four years it took to build the railroad, and by the end of the project the white contractors praised the Chinese as hard-working, honest, and "possessed of retentive memories." Both the Muirs and other whites found that the Chinese were not docile, however, for when the Chinese railroad workers felt they were being mistreated or abused, they responded quickly and, on occasion, violently.

Sometimes local tax collectors tried to make deductions from the crew's wages in the form of road taxes, but they took great risk in doing so. When the railroad was working up the Los Gatos Canyon in July 1878, Fred Farmer, Santa Clara County's Deputy Assessor, heard that a payday was scheduled and drove his wagon to the railhead just as the money was being distributed. He stood next to the paymaster and began collecting the two dollar road tax as each Chinese worker was paid. When one crew insisted on being paid off further up the road, Fred followed, collecting sixty dollars and issuing thirty receipts. At that point the Chinese surrounded the tax collector, screaming at him in Chinese and brandishing their picks and shovels. Farmer drew his gun and retreated back to his wagon, threatening to shoot. He and the white supervisors were badly outnumbered, however, and had he pulled the trigger he would probably have been killed. Farmer bravely visited other Chinese camps and eventually collected $525 (of which he received a percentage). At the day's end Farmer had to return along the same route, and "with Chinamen to the right of him, Chinamen to the left of him, Fred drove bravely on through a parting volley of rocks."

The key to Fair's daring dream of a railroad over the mountains was the use of the tunnel to level out the grades, and the tunnels at Wrights and Laurel proved to be the most costly for everyone involved. The two tunnels eventually cost $400,000 to drill, and no construction project in the region cost more human lives. The Wrights tunnel was begun in December 1877, with a crew of forty-five Chinese working at the north (Wrights) end. During the two-and-one-half years that the tunnel took to complete, several camps were established near the tunnel mouth and cabins were built to house the Chinese tunnel workers:

> Beside the tunnel's portal are ruins of a Chinese town; two cabins are stuck on the steep hill-side above the opening . . . [nearby] there is a Chinese camp that, for picturesque arrangement and beauty of situation, could not be surpassed. It is located on two sides of a triangular gulch, through the apex of which tumbles a mountain spring in a succession of clear, cool pools. The tents are pitched directly into the steep hill-side facing out, with a broad terraced walk running in front of them all, and crossing the stream at the intersection on a bridge of logs.

The site may have been lovely, but the experiences the Chinese had in the Wrights tunnel were not. By mid-1878, as Chinese crews worked at both ends of the tunnel, a pocket of coal gas was struck at the north end of the tunnel. Oil seeped from the walls of the tunnel, collecting in pools on the tunnel floor, while gas mixed with the air in the tunnel, creating an extremely volatile and dangerous situation. The oil was scooped up and removed in tins while the gas was burned off ("flashed") every ten minutes so that the Chinese could work at the tunnel face. When the crew changed at the end of a shift, the supervisor of the next crew had to crawl into the tunnel pushing ahead of him a lighted rag on a pole which burned off the accumulated gas. The Chinese crews and their white superintendents grew increasingly apprehensive about the danger in the tunnel, but by February 1879 they had drilled almost one-half mile into the mountain from the north end.

On February 13, 1879, during a routine burning of the coal gas, some oil caught fire and a sheet of flame roared through the tunnel. The Chinese fell to the floor of the tunnel to avoid the fire, but the intensity of the heat burned everyone in the tunnel.

The tunnel acted like a huge cannon, and railroad cars and equipment standing outside the tunnel were blown about like toys by the force of the explosion. Those who heard the explosion believed that the entire powder magazine for the railroad had exploded. Amazingly, none of those in the tunnel were killed in the initial blast, but many were thrown violently against the tunnel wall and badly burned; a dozen blackened and moaning Chinese were brought out of the tunnel:

> O. B. Castle carried one [Chinese] out and laid him on the bank, the breathing mass leaving the fleshy imprint of a human being in the rescuer's arms, the body breathing through its side as if it had been thrown against some solid substance with great violence.

A San Jose doctor got to the tunnel within hours of the explosion, but despite his ministering, five of the injured Chinese died, and a number of the survivors had to be taken to San Francisco for further treatment.

Wrights Tunnel, c. 1890. Chinese crews are repairing a slide on the face of the notorious Wrights tunnel. Dozens of Chinese were killed during the construction of this tunnel.
BRUCE MACGREGOR

97

The company installed pipes in the Wrights tunnel and pumped fresh air into it so that work might resume, but the Chinese were not eager to go back into the tunnel. Apprehension about the entire project spread to other crews of Chinese workers on the line, and the usually hard-working, punctual workers dragged their feet when asked to go into the other tunnels. Several days after the explosion, foreman Patrick Daily fired a Chinese working in the south end of the tunnel for "being lazy." A brawl broke out between the Chinese crew and their supervisors, resulting in assorted scalp wounds, broken teeth, and bruises. Following the brawl, the Chinese refused to resume work in the Wrights tunnel, and the company vowed to replace them with white tunnel workers. During the next two months, the South Pacific Coast experimented with white laborers in the Wrights tunnel, but by May 1879 the non-Chinese tunnel workers had so "utterly failed" that the company sought out a new Chinese crew and lured them into working in the tunnel for $1.25 per day.

Gas and oil continued to seep into the tunnel, and the Chinese workers were not enthusiastic about working there. In June foreman Nick Borrosey, frustrated by a Chinese who seemed to be shirking his work, told the laborer to leave the tunnel. When Borrosey tried to forcibly eject the man, the crew charged the foreman, and amid "a shower of picks and drills," Borrosey ran back toward the mouth of the tunnel. As he did so, he turned and fired several shots at the crew, killing one of the Chinese. Several days later all work stopped when gas and oil in the tunnel ignited and burned steadily for two weeks. The suspicion grew that the Wrights tunnel was cursed.

It was. Despite the precautions of new fresh air pumps and routine removal of the accumulated oil and gas, pockets of gas still collected at the tunnel face. On the night of November 17, 1879, twenty-one Chinese and two whites were working at the tunnel face 2,700 feet into the mountain when a small dynamite charge ignited some undetected gas. With a "roar and shock that shook the mountains from base to summit," a sheet of flame roared out of the tunnel. Hearing the explosion, twenty Chinese rushed out of their tents and into the tunnel to rescue their comrades. When they were 1,500 feet into the tunnel, a second explosion occurred, followed by "a sheet of lurid flame which the great mountain belched forth, consuming everything before it." Of the 41 Chinese in the tunnel, 24 were killed outright and the remaining 17 were badly burned:

> The stench of burning flesh, combined with the escaping gas, is almost overpowering anywhere near the portal. The cabins are filled with mutilated Chinamen, some shrieking with the excruciating pain they are undergoing; others praying in their native tongue to their countrymen to kill them and put an end to their sufferings, or beseeching the God of Fire to have mercy upon them and cease his torments. In most of the cabins tapers are burning, the perfume from which serves somewhat to temper the sickening odor of roasted flesh.

Rescuers removed the bodies of the Chinese from the tunnel, laid them in a row alongside the tracks, dressed them in clean clothing, and put them into rough-hewn redwood coffins. An incense taper was placed at the foot of each coffin to ward off evil spirits, and after a small ceremony most of the bodies were buried on a flat a mile north of Wrights.

Some of the wounded were taken to Chinatown, San Francisco, for treatment, but despite the efforts of Chinese and white physicians, seven of the burned Chinese died, bringing the death toll of the explosion to thirty-one. Though badly burned, the two white supervisors who had been in the tunnel eventually recovered.

With but seven hundred feet remaining between the two tunnel faces, the South Pacific Coast Railroad pushed ahead to complete the project. An electric light was placed in the tunnel to decrease the threat of an explosion ignited by an open flame, and

Wrights tunnel, c. 1890. Chinese resident of town of Wrights. The Chinese believed the tunnel to be cursed.
BRUCE MACGREGOR

the air pumps which had been destroyed in the explosion were replaced. A new crew of Chinese was hired to work in the north end of the tunnel, but when they arrived in January 1880, they would not occupy the tents of their dead countrymen nor enter the tunnel until "the devils they asserted were in the tunnel" were driven away. Incense was burned and lucky red papers were plastered on the portal of the tunnel. Finally, after two Chinese who "shook like aspens" were coaxed into the tunnel to show that it was safe, work resumed.

The morale of the Chinese working on the cursed north end of the Wrights tunnel was so poor that the company finally hired a crew of Cornish miners to replace them, while the remaining Chinese worked on the south end of the tunnel. In competitions reminiscent of the Union Pacific/Central Pacific track-laying contests, the Cornish crew challenged the Chinese crew to see who could do the greater work in a week. The Chinese won easily, averaging eight feet per day to the Cornish men's four, but observers complained that the Chinese had an unfair advantage because they were smaller and more of them could work at the tunnel face.(!)

The wind which blew through the Wrights tunnel helped keep gas from accumulating once the tunnel was completed in late April 1880. The railroad company also installed several gas lamps on the walls of the tunnel to help burn off the gas which continually seeped from the mountain. With the completion of the railroad, the summer season of 1880 promised to be a busy one for Santa Cruz. But a week after the SPCRR began operation, an excursion train returning from a day at Big Trees derailed, killing thirteen passengers and casting a gloom over what otherwise might have been a joyful spring in the seaside city.

Bad luck also continued to haunt the Chinese working for the South Pacific Coast. In February 1881 a huge mud avalanche swept down a mountain above Felton and buried a camp of Chinese railroad workers. A dozen bodies were eventually recovered, but it was not known how many others might have been swept down the rain-swollen San Lorenzo River and into the ocean.

The Chinese never received any public recognition for their enormous contributions to the construction of the South Pacific Coast Railroad; they were not mentioned in the railroad dedication speeches. The only reminders were at Wrights: the thirty-one Chinese grave markers beside the tracks, the tattered red good-luck papers fluttering in the wind on the portal beams, and the ever-burning gas lights deep inside the tunnel.

## THE SOUTHERN PACIFIC TAKES OVER

Taken separately, the four narrow-gauge railroads built in the Monterey Bay Region between 1874 and 1880 are not impressive. The thin, light rails, teetering trestles, and diminutive locomotives look like toys in the old photographs. Yet a map of the region reveals that the four lines created a network which paralleled and challenged the Southern Pacific: the Monterey and Salinas Valley to the southwest, the Santa Cruz railroad in the northwest, and the South Pacific Coast punching through mountains to the north.

The Southern Pacific Railroad took the challenge of the narrow-gauge railroads seriously. Colis Huntington may have snorted derisively when the Monterey and Salinas Valley Railroad began construction in 1874; five years later the competitive network threatened the Southern Pacific's hegemony, and as the Chinese tunneled through the Santa Cruz Mountains, the Southern Pacific made its first move to counter the network of narrow-gauge railroads.

When the Southern Pacific bought the Monterey & Salinas Valley Railroad in September 1879, it immediately began to survey a new route from Castroville to Monterey; the direct line between Salinas and Monterey was replaced by a route which jogged north through Castroville. Chinese crews tore up the narrow-gauge tracks between Salinas and Monterey, and Southern Pacific sold the rail and rolling stock to the Nevada Central Railroad. Even before David Jacks signed the final papers transferring the Monterey & Salinas Valley to the corporation, a crew of fourteen whites and two hundred Chinese began grading a broad-gauge line from Castroville to Monterey with seventy horse-drawn scrapers. Under Superintendent James Strowbridge, the veteran railroad builder, the fourteen-mile line was completed in early spring. But the Southern Pacific had not taken into account the temperament of the Salinas River, and in April "not a vestige of this bridge [the new trestle], in which everybody had such great confidence, remains to be seen." The company rebuilt the trestle soon enough to have the line completed for the grand opening of the Del Monte Hotel in June; in less than a year the Monterey Peninsula had fallen completely under the control of the Southern Pacific Railroad.

As the Del Monte Hotel was being built, Duncan McPherson, editor of the *Santa Cruz Sentinel*, analyzed the significance of Southern Pacific's move to the Monterey Peninsula in an editorial. McPherson saw the move as an effort to develop a tourist spot to compete with Santa Cruz, but the Santa Cruz editor termed the move one of the "poorest [Stanford] ever made." McPherson predicted that once the novelty of the Del Monte wore off, the shorter trip "over one of the most varied grand and picturesque routes in the known world" to Santa Cruz would lure most travelers to the South Pacific Coast Railroad.

McPherson's analysis was sound for March 1880, but he could not have predicted the sequence of events which found the Southern Pacific Railroad in Santa Cruz within the year. Just as its sister Granger railroad had been done in by a fallen trestle, the Santa Cruz Railroad went under when its San Lorenzo River trestle was knocked down by a flood in February 1881. The Santa Cruz Railroad did not have the resources to reconstruct the trestle, and in a Sheriff's sale in the spring of 1881, much of the railroad's stock passed into the hands of Southern Pacific Railroad.

Thus, the Southern Pacific arrived in Santa Cruz in 1882, cow-catcher to cow-catcher with its competition, the South Pacific Coast. In three short years the Southern Pacific had encircled Monterey Bay, and could run tourists to both Monterey and Santa Cruz while carrying manufactured and agricultural products out to San Francisco. In 1883 Southern Pacific brought hundreds of Chinese railroad workers into Santa Cruz County to broad-gauge their new line and bring it into the fold. Crews of Chinese pulled the short ties and laid down new track between Santa Cruz and Watsonville, until in October 1883 the final section of track along the beach was broad-gauged.

Taking its cue from the South Pacific Coast Railroad, the Southern Pacific Railroad built a broad-gauge spur line from Aptos into the Aptos Canyon to tap one of the largest stands of first-growth redwood timber still standing in Santa Cruz County

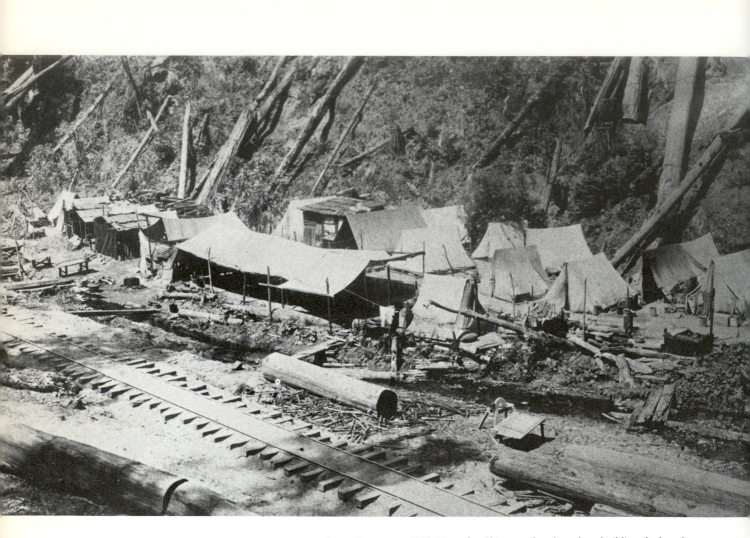

Aptos Canyon, c. 1890. Tents for Chinese railroad workers building the broad-gauge line for Southern Pacific up the treacherous Aptos Canyon.

Aptos Canyon, c. 1890. Chinese railroad workers who constructed the broad-gauge railroad up the Aptos Canyon. China Ridge was named for these Chinese railroad workers.

RICK HAMMAN

in the 1880s. If the South Pacific Coast railroad was a model of adaptation to local conditions and ingenuity and economy in the face of difficult terrain, the Southern Pacific branch into the Aptos Canyon was a model of arrogance and power. Rather than drape a narrow-gauge railroad up the twisting canyon, the Southern Pacific used cuts, fills, and trestles to force its heavy, broad-gauge railroad north from Aptos. And, as always, the railroad relied on crews of Chinese laborers. The construction of the broad gauge began in the summer of 1883, and 225 Chinese railroad workers cut, filled, and laid track into the canyon. In a rare instance of dishonesty, a Chinese contractor who acted as paymaster "made himself scarce" with six hundred dollars intended for his crew; the crew went after him, but records do not tell us whether they caught him. For the next three years, as the railroad extended up to and through a narrow, vertical stretch of canyon called Hell's Gate and into unbelievably steep country,

Valencia Creek, c. 1885. Chinese railroad crew building the narrow-gauge
line from Aptos to Frederick Hihn's
mill on Valencia Creek.
PAJARO VALLEY HISTORICAL
ASSOCIATION

the Chinese continued to straighten turns and level the bumps;
to keep the grade the Chinese sometimes worked on cliffs several hundred feet above the creek. By 1888 the Southern Pacific
decided to stop construction at Monte Vista, seven miles from
Aptos, and for the next ten years the line carried millions of
board feet of lumber from the Aptos Canyon.

The South Pacific Coast Railroad finally fell to the Southern
Pacific Railroad. Although it was one of the few narrow-gauge
railroads in California to operate at a profit and James Fair had
rebuffed offers from the Southern Pacific to buy the road, in
1886 financial difficulties not related to the SPCRR made it necessary for him to pass control of his railroad to the Southern Pacific through a lease arrangement. The Southern Pacific then
turned its attention to the railroad line which had extended south
down the Salinas Valley and stopped at Soledad in 1874. In 1886
hundreds of Chinese laborers moved into the Salinas Valley to
push the line south through new towns called Greenfield, King
City, San Ardo, and Bradley. In scenes reminiscent of those in

the Sierra Nevada twenty years before, gangs of Chinese blasted and cleared rock and graded the line: "Six miles out of Soledad we pass close to the Chinese graders who look like swarming bees on the edge of the bluffs, shoveling and blasting for several miles." Later that year, as the line passed San Miguel and approached the San Luis Obispo County line, the hundreds of Chinese swelled to over one thousand as the Chinese who dug the reservoir west of Pacific Grove were transferred to the Salinas Valley. By the end of 1886 the line had passed beyond Paso Robles and out of Monterey County, but did not reach Los Angeles until more than a decade later. The extension of the Southern Pacific helped open up the southern Salinas Valley to intensive agriculture, and when farmers began planting sugar beets in the valley in the early 1890s, the crop from King City was shipped north to Spreckel's sugar factories on the railroad.

In 1888 the Southern Pacific surveyed a route west of the Monterey depot through Pacific Grove and around the point to the sand deposits, and for a time rumors flew that the line would be extended to the Carmel Valley and the coal deposits there. (There were several unsuccessful efforts to mine coal in the Carmel Valley beginning in the 1870s, and a short narrow-gauge, horse-drawn railroad was built by Chinese in the valley in 1878.) It took the corporation a year to negotiate a right-of-way through the United States government's land at the Presidio, and in May 1889 construction began just west of Monterey: "Mongolians as busy as bees with their large bamboo hats, dump cars and the inevitable mule running to and fro, foretells that the road will be at Pacific Grove before the month is out . . ." The extension forced the removal of the Chinese cemetery at the Point Alones Chinese fishing village because it lay in the right-of-way. A crew of Chinese moved the cemetery out to Point Almejas where it remained until the Chinese left the Point Alones village in 1907. By July 1889 the line reached the sand deposits where it stopped,

Pacific Grove Extension, 1889. Chinese railroad workers building the Southern Pacific extension from Monterey, past Pacific Grove.

and despite periodic proposals to extend the line to Carmel, it never went farther. The sand which brought $2.50 per cubic yard more than paid for the construction of the extension.

## THE PAJARO VALLEY CONSOLIDATED RAILROAD

Claus Spreckels built a narrow-gauge line from his Watsonville sugar mill into the Salinas Valley to avoid Southern Pacific shipping charges. In 1890 the line was extended eleven miles to Moss Landing by crews of primarily Chinese railroad workers so that Spreckels could ship processed sugar to San Francisco by steamer. The following year the line was extended to Salinas, again using Chinese laborers. Though extension of the line both north of Watsonville and south of Salinas was discussed, the line

Pacific Grove Extension, 1889. Chinese railroad workers riding construction car somewhere between Monterey and Pacific Grove.     CALIFORNIA STATE LIBRARY

Pacific Grove Extension, 1889. Building the railroad between Monterey and Pacific Grove. Remarkable photograph shows Chinese tamping powder into blast holes and standing on boxes of explosives.

never covered more than the twenty-three miles between Watsonville and Salinas. Though Spreckels had built the road mainly to spite the Southern Pacific, it turned a profit during its early years of operation.

The Pajaro Valley Consolidated Railroad was the last railroad project in the Monterey Bay Region in which Chinese railroad workers bore the primary responsibility for construction. The restrictions passed on Chinese immigration in the 1880s had done their work, and the aging, diminishing Chinese population in California was replaced by the younger Japanese immigrants.

Crucial to the development of the Monterey Bay Region in the nineteenth century, the railroads had a beneficial impact on agriculture, manufacturing, and tourism. Whether shipping lumber out in flat cars or bringing tourists in parlor cars, the trains came through cuts and tunnels and over grades built by the Chinese. The economic successes of the nineteenth century were built on the sweat and blood of Chinese railroad workers.

PART TWO

# THE CHINATOWNS

In civility, complaisance, and polite manners [Americans] are
wholly wanting and are very
properly styled barbarians.

Chung Sun, Watsonville, 1871

# 5

# The Anti-Chinese Movement

Perhaps the single most important influence on the make-up and durability of Chinatowns in California, the anti-Chinese movement made it particularly difficult for Chinese to make the transition from seasonal laborers and "sojourners" to established residents and participants. In the Monterey Bay Region the strength of the anti-Chinese movement varied according to the degree of each community's dependence on Chinese labor and the state of the economy, but everywhere it curtailed the lives of Chinese in Chinatowns.

The Chinese were not the first ethnic group to wear the horns of the scapegoat in the Monterey Bay region, nor would they be the last. The depression of 1876–77, which marked the beginning of a full-scale anti-Chinese hysteria in the region, also marked the end of a quarter-century campaign against the Hispanic residents, and the seam which separates the two is almost invisible. A brief review of the Hispanophobia which gripped the Monterey Bay Region from 1850 to 1877 will help give a context to the Sinophobia which followed.

When immigrants from the United States and Europe finally trickled into the Monterey Bay Region after the discovery of gold in 1848, they found the region thinly populated by Mexicans and Californios. Most of the arable land was in the hands of a few *rancheros*, and though the ranchers made good use of the land, in the eyes of Yankees fresh from the Atlantic states, the land was not being used at all. The Yankees viewed the California dons who owned the large Mexican land grants as obstacles to progress: "If the grants were just cut up and sold as small farms," moaned the *Pacific Sentinel*, "progress would surely come to the region." In 1850, with the help of legislation passed by the United States Congress, the Yankees began a campaign to separate the rancheros from their land, and in the process of discrediting their land titles, the Yankees also discredited their culture. The poised, proud, almost regal dons of the Mexican era became known collectively as "greasers," and their relaxed way of life became "lazy" and "degenerate." The conflict over land titles became a culture clash between Protestant Yankee values and Catholic Latin values, and by the mid-1850s the scene was set for a violent confrontation between the two groups.

An economic slow-down in 1855, coupled with a drought and depression in 1856–57, exacerbated the frustration felt by the Yankees into a full-scale race war. Mobs of vigilantes roamed the Monterey Bay Region lynching Hispanic people at the slightest provocation. The usual excuse used at a lynching was that the victim was a horse thief. Hispanic bandidos exacted revenge for their people, striking at isolated Yankee settlements or ambushing travelers on lonely roads. In the Monterey Bay Region lynching of Hispanics peaked by 1860 and became sporadic during the more prosperous decades that followed the Civil War.

This quarter-century of Hispanophobia in the Monterey Bay Region left important legacies for the remainder of the nineteenth century. First, it legitimized scapegoating in response to complex economic problems, as Yankees in the region came away from their vendetta against Hispanics convinced that they had vanquished the "cause" of their economic difficulties. Second, the Hispanophobics had singled out a people who were culturally and physically distinct as their targets. Third, the use of direct mob action had become acceptable during the period, and though newspaper editors often chided people for taking the law into their own hands, the Yankee legal system rarely tried to apprehend or convict the members of lynch mobs.

In 1877, the very year that a mob broke into the Santa Cruz jail and hanged two Hispanic men from the Water Street bridge, California was hit again by drought and depression: a national depression reached California in 1876, and the winter of 1876–77 was the driest since the mid-1850s. Another highly visible scapegoat had entered the region in the form of Chinese laborers.

## ANTI-CHINESE LEGISLATION

National, state, and local governments wove a cocoon of legal restrictions around the Chinese immigrant during the nineteenth century. Chinese immigrants were ineligible to become naturalized American citizens, could not testify against whites in California courts, and had to pay special Foreign Miner's Taxes in the Sierra gold fields. Local governments followed suit with laws prohibiting Chinese from walking with poles on the sidewalks (known as pole ordinances), wearing queues, or exhuming the bones of their countrymen for shipment back to China.

The watershed event in the relationship between the Chinese immigrants and the United States government was the Chinese Exclusion Act signed into law in May 1882. The Exclusion Law suspended the immigration of new Chinese laborers into the country for ten years; Chinese teachers, students, merchants, and travelers could continue to enter the United States and Chinese laborers already here were assured of the right to leave and re-enter.

But in 1888 Congress passed the Scott Act, cancelling this right of re-entry, and tightened the Exclusion Law, which prohibited Chinese from leaving the country and re-entering unless they had a family in the United States or owned property worth at least one thousand dollars. In 1892 the Geary Act extended the Exclusion Law for ten more years, and Congress added the provision that all Chinese in the United States had to file for a certificate of residence or face deportation.

The State of California singled out Chinese women for particular legal scrutiny, passing the first of several laws designed to restrict their entry into the state in 1870. On the face of it, the "Act to Prevent the Kidnapping and Importation of Mongolian, Chinese, and Japanese Females for Criminal or Demoralizing Purposes" passed in 1870 was intended to protect Asian women. The law assumed, however, that all Chinese women who entered the state were prostitutes until they proved to the contrary. Similar acts were passed in 1893 and 1901, and all had the effect of further discouraging the immigration of Chinese women into California and making it more difficult for Chinese men to start families in California.

An unusual California referendum commissioned by the state legislature in 1879 provides some insight into the breadth and universality of anti-Chinese feelings in the three Monterey Bay counties. In September 1879 the voters of California were asked to vote for or against continued Chinese immigration into the United States. The results of the poll were tainted by the fact that the issue was worded in such terms ("Against Chinese Immigration") that to vote in favor of continued Chinese immigration, the voter had to erase the "against" and write in "for." Statewide, a staggering 94% (over 150,000) voted "against" further

Chinese immigration while fewer than 9,000 went through the trouble of putting "for." The referendum gave a clear message to politicians seeking public favor.

The results were even more astonishing in the Monterey Bay Region counties: of the 5,828 votes cast in the referendum, only 7 wrote in "for." The breakdown by county shows San Benito County—1,026 against, 2 in favor; Monterey County—2,345 against, 1 in favor; Santa Cruz County—2,450 against and 4 in favor. One could conclude from the referendum that anti-Chinese sentiment was universal throughout the region, but it must be noted that the issue was the general one of Chinese immigration, not whether the Chinese should continue living or working in the region. The voting reflected nearly universal opposition to Chinese immigration, but this opinion was translated into action in each of the major communities in the region in a variety of ways, as each community had to compromise its anti-Chinese feelings when dealing with its own Chinese community.

## THE ANTI-CHINESE MOVEMENT IN THE MONTEREY BAY REGION

Sporadic and isolated expressions of anti-Chinese sentiment coalesced into organizations in the mid-1870s. The Order of Caucasians was the first anti-Chinese organization to appear in the Monterey Bay Region, with chapters started in Salinas and Santa Cruz. The Salinas chapter formed in late 1875 to "protect white labor" and boasted of having fifty-two founding members. Formed in December 1877, the Santa Cruz chapter of Caucasians claimed fifty founding members, including the editor of the *Santa Cruz Sentinel*, Duncan McPherson, who regularly published the organization's proceedings. The Salinas and Santa Cruz Caucasians were modeled after a similar society in San Francisco, but where the San Francisco group often used violence and even publicly advocated murder of Chinese, the two Monterey Bay groups claimed to be "law abiding" and disavowed the use of violence.

The Workingmen's Party eclipsed the Order of Caucasians in 1878. Formed in San Francisco in the fall of 1877, the Workingmen's Party opposed monopolists, government corruption, big capital, and the root of all evil, the Chinese. The leader of the party was Denis Kearney, a naturalized Irish immigrant who had become a modestly successful San Francisco businessman; Kearney achieved considerable fame as a sandlot orator in the fall of 1877, and under the slogan "The Chinese Must Go," both he and the party leaped to statewide prominence in early 1878. Kearney was arrested several times for making inflammatory statements such as, "The dignity of labor must be sustained, even if we have to kill every wretch that opposes it." Combining the simplistic argument that the Chinese were the cause of all California's ills with shrill and intemperate rhetoric, the Workingmen's Party swept into the Monterey Bay Region during the winter of 1877–78.

The Santa Cruz Workingmen's Party, founded in February 1878, grew to an astonishing 266 members within a month, making it the largest branch of the party outside San Francisco. Under the banner "No Nationality! No Religion! . . . No Chinamen Need Apply," the Santa Cruz Workingmen's Party won four of the six seats on the Santa Cruz Town Council in April 1878. For three years the Santa Cruz Workingmen's Party met regularly and kept the issue of Chinese immigration and employment before the people of Santa Cruz.

The Order of Caucasians and the Workingmen's Party were led by some hard-driving, ambitious Santa Cruz men who by the late 1870s could hardly be classed as workingmen. The two

# Regular Workingmen's Ticket,

## SANTA CRUZ COUNTY.

### For

1. DELEGATE AT LARGE TO CONST'L CONVENTION, PAUL BONNET.
2. DELEGATE AT LARGE TO CONST'L CONVENTION, A. FISCHER.
3. DELEGATE AT LARGE TO CONST'L CONVENTION, J. W. JAMISON.
4. DELEGATE AT LARGE TO CONST'L CONVENTION, JAMES KIDNEY.
5. DELEGATE AT LARGE TO CONST'L CONVENTION, J. R. PICO.
6. DELEGATE AT LARGE TO CONST'L CONVENTION, J. R. SHARPSTEIN.
7. DELEGATE AT LARGE TO CONST'L CONVENTION, CHARLES TILLSON.
8. DELEGATE AT LARGE TO CONST'L CONVENTION, J. A. WHELAN.
9. DELEGATE AT LARGE TO CONST'L CONVENTION, P. S. DORNEY.
10. DELEGATE AT LARGE TO CONST'L CONVENTION, J. B. KELLY.
11. DELEGATE AT LARGE TO CONST'L CONVENTION, H. P. WILLIAMS.
12. DELEGATE AT LARGE TO CONST'L CONVENTION, H. L. McKELVEY.
13. DELEGATE AT LARGE TO CONST'L CONVENTION, JOHN GREENWELL.
14. DELEGATE AT LARGE TO CONST'L CONVENTION, L. J. MORROW.
15. DELEGATE AT LARGE TO CONST'L CONVENTION, G. THOM.
16. DELEGATE AT LARGE TO CONST'L CONVENTION, J. M. TODD.
17. DELEGATE AT LARGE TO CONST'L CONVENTION, W. F. STONE.
18. DELEGATE AT LARGE TO CONST'L CONVENTION, W. H. NORTHCUTT.
19. DELEGATE AT LARGE TO CONST'L CONVENTION, D. M. GLOSTER.
20. DELEGATE AT LARGE TO CONST'L CONVENTION, JOHN C. CRIGLER.
21. DELEGATE AT LARGE TO CONST'L CONVENTION, J. C. GARBER.
22. DELEGATE AT LARGE TO CONST'L CONVENTION, H. A. BOYLE.
23. DELEGATE AT LARGE TO CONST'L CONVENTION, JONAS SPECT.
24. DELEGATE AT LARGE TO CONST'L CONVENTION, W. M. THORP.
25. DELEGATE AT LARGE TO CONST'L CONVENTION, ISAAC BICKNELL.
26. DELEGATE AT LARGE TO CONST'L CONVENTION, D. A. DRYDEN.
27. DELEGATE AT LARGE TO CONST'L CONVENTION, WILLIAM VINTER.
28. DELEGATE AT LARGE TO CONST'L CONVENTION, B. PILKINGTON.
29. DELEGATE AT LARGE TO CONST'L CONVENTION, J. F. BREEN.
30. DELEGATE AT LARGE TO CONST'L CONVENTION, ISAAC KINLEY.
31. DELEGATE AT LARGE TO CONST'L CONVENTION, R. D. PITT.
32. DELEGATE AT LARGE TO CONST'L CONVENTION, O. T. CHUBB.
33. DELEGATE FROM SIXTH SENATORIAL DISTRICT, WM. F. WHITE.
34. DELEGATE FROM SANTA CRUZ COUNTY, DANIEL TUTTLE.

Workingmen's Party Ballot, 1879. Ballot has Workingmen's Party motto at the top and lists the party's delegate candidates to the California State Constitutional Convention of 1879.

SANTA CRUZ CITY MUSEUM

most prominent leaders were Duncan McPherson and Elihu Anthony. One of the original sub-dividers of downtown Santa Cruz in the early 1850s, Anthony owned a number of buildings and businesses in Santa Cruz by the time he was elected as president of the Santa Cruz Workingmen's Party. Duncan McPherson was owner and editor of the *Santa Cruz Sentinel*, and this otherwise erudite and reasonable man switched his attention from the Order of Caucasians to the Workingmen's Party in February 1878. Though others held office in the anti-Chinese organizations in Santa Cruz, Duncan McPherson kept the issue alive from the 1870s into the late 1880s. He regularly wrote editorials about the Chinese, their culture, employment patterns, and immigration, and his vivid and often scurrilous editorials were models of anti-Chinese vituperation. In an editorial just before the Santa Cruz Workingmen's Party was founded, McPherson stated:

> The Chinamen are an unmitigated curse to this state. They have done a thousand times more evil than good . . . Chinamen are not citizens in any sense of the word. They do not grant us the miserable boon of letting their heathen carcasses manure our soil, but ship the bones of their dead to the land of Confucius for final interment.

When President Arthur vetoed the first Chinese Exclusion Law, McPherson declared the veto to be "a calamity to this State a black Friday in our history and an outrageous insult to our people." Lamenting President Arthur's lack of fortitude, McPherson declared that "this prolific land by the broadest sea lies prostrate and helpless, the Chinese dragon standing on its throat and vomiting its degraded vermin into its gaping mouth." When the anti-Chinese movement surfaced again in California in the winter of 1885–86, McPherson flogged the issue so hard that he nearly persuaded the Santa Cruz city government to pass an ordinance banning the Chinese from living there.

Watsonville dutifully formed a chapter of the Workingmen's Party in early 1878, but the group appeared to be going through the motions, even though Watsonville was continually goaded by arch-rival Santa Cruz to demonstrate its anti-Chinese feelings. During the winter of 1885–86, Santa Cruz began a series of maneuvers to put pressure on Watsonville. The anti-Chinese leadership in Santa Cruz proposed an economic boycott of all businesses that employed Chinese directly or indirectly. Watsonville exploded:

> To drive [the Chinese] from town to town like hunted beasts, and to blacklist those who employ them, is something contrary to that spirit of broad humanity supposed to be characteristic of this great nation which has invited to its shores the poor and downtrodden of all countries . . . to invite people here and then drive them out is un-American . . .

The humanitarian argument obscured the economic motives; the effects of such a boycott in the Pajaro Valley would have been "depreciation of property value, loss of crops, foreclosures of mortgages." The debate on the boycott in the spring of 1886 exposed much more about the economic differences between Santa Cruz and Watsonville than it did about the Chinese or Chinese immigration. The economy of the Pajaro Valley depended on Chinese muscle in the fields, while the manufacturing interests in and around Santa Cruz used little if any Chinese labor. For Santa Cruz the loss of Chinese labor might mean a little inconvenience in terms of laundries and domestics, but for Watsonville the loss of Chinese labor portended economic ruin. Santa Cruz dubbed the Watsonville resistance to the boycott "The Strawberry Rebellion," and the Pajaro Valley soon gained a reputation for pro-Chinese sentiment throughout California. Chinese fleeing the boycott in Santa Cruz sought refuge in Watsonville's Chinatown. In May 1886 a representative of the California Non-

Partisan Anti-Chinese Association announced that the "most pronounced pro-Chinese sentiment to be found in this State exists in Watsonville."

In Salinas huge meetings and rallies demonstrated the town's support for the Workingmen's Party and Denis Kearney. In late 1876 a petition espousing a ban on Chinese immigration was circulated throughout Monterey County, and most of the nine hundred signatures on the petition came from the Salinas area. Salinas quickly acquired a reputation as the center of anti-Chinese activities in Monterey County. The Workingmen's Party did not fare well in the Salinas city elections, however. In the March 1878 election only one of the party's candidates was elected. When the party pulled out all stops during the 1879 elections, in which eight seats on the town council were vacant, it only captured two seats, despite a visit by Kearney just prior to the elections.

A Workingmen's Party was also formed in Monterey in late 1878, but it had neither the support nor the membership to sustain it, and within a year the organization folded. When Denis Kearney's aides canvassed the populace before his visit in March 1879, the only issue that seemed to concern most Montereyans was David Jacks. Kearney's appearance in 1879 did little to bolster the Workingmen's Party, and it ceased to meet by August of that year.

In March 1879 Kearney entered the Monterey Bay Region to campaign for the ratification of a new State Constitution. The proposed constitution contained several anti-monopoly, anti-capitalist provisions, but it was strongest in its antipathy toward the Chinese: it prohibited employment of Chinese by state, local, or county government, prohibited fishing in the coastal waters of California by aliens, and pledged the state to discourage the immigration of Chinese into the state. The region's reactions to Kearney ranged from lukewarm to passionate, but all illustrated the contradictions between the espousal of the anti-Chinese cause and the pragmatic need to co-exist with the Chinese community.

Kearney received a quiet and polite reception at Monterey, but Kearney was anything but polite in his speech there. Apparently primed by his aides to localize his remarks (something he did at each stop in the region), Kearney delivered a scathing denunciation of landowner David Jacks, calling him "Captain Jacks, the Chief of the Monterey Highwaymen." David Jacks might have been one of the most disliked men in Monterey County, but both the public and the local newspaper found Kearney's remarks intemperate and irrelevant to the issue of the constitution.

Kearney fared better in his speech in Salinas, though the editor of the *Salinas Weekly Index* noted a "general feeling of disappointment" when Kearney was finally seen in the flesh: "[Kearney] is of medium stature. His brow does not denote a high intelligence . . . his speeches are incoherent and destitute of logical arrangement." Editor Hill was particularly distressed with Kearney's use of "profanity, vulgarity, and obscenity," but concluded that Kearney was the most important man in California politics, "honest and true to the cause he advocates."

Evidence of opposition to the Workingmen's Party suggests that reasonable minds were at work in the Salinas Valley. For example, a letter in the local newspaper calmly refuted the arguments of Kearney and the Workingmen's Party. To the charge that the Chinese were foreigners, the writer asked, "Are there no other foreigners in our midst?"; to the claim that the Chinese did not assimilate, the letter pointed out that neither did Indians or Negroes. The letter answered the complaint that the Chinese were frugal and industrious by asking, "since when are frugality and industry a crime?" and to the complaint that all the Chinese were single males addressed the rhetorical question, "is it a crime to be single?" The writer concluded that if the workingmen of

California wanted concessions, they should earn them, and not be given them by hampering and restricting the Chinese. The letter, signed "Fair Play," was answered the following week by a writer who surmised that "Fair Play" was employed by the Chinese Six Companies.

Watsonville's reaction to Kearney was polite when he arrived to speak to the assembled Workingmen's Party chapter. He was received by a small group at the railroad depot, and four hundred attended his evening speech. The sixty Workingmen's Party members dutifully filed in to see Kearney while the remainder of the crowd attended "to see how a little Irishman could walk over the people," according to one observer. At his departure Kearney expressed disappointment with the reception he had received.

Kearney's last stop in the region was Santa Cruz, and there he spoke to his most enthusiastic audience. A crowd estimated at 3,500 jammed the street, sidewalk, store windows, and rooftops to hear Kearney speak. In the glow of two huge bonfires, Kearney lambasted the "railroad robbers and the political cutthroats of [California] who have pooled their issues to import long-tailed lepers from Asia."

Each town's enthusiasm for Kearney's cause failed to extend to organized action against the Chinese for a variety of reasons. The contradiction between the political idealism of the anti-Chinese movement and the economic reality of California in the late 1870s was most apparent in agricultural communities like Salinas where the strident cries of "The Chinese Must Go" were contradicted by the community's dependence on Chinese farm laborers. Many who espoused the "Chinese Must Go" philosophy did so out of fear of being branded "soft" on the issue, rather than a real desire to see the Chinese depart.

Most of the white leaders in Santa Cruz, where the movement was strongest, saw it as a springboard for their political ambitions beyond the county. Santa Cruz became such a flagship in the statewide anti-Chinese movement that several of the city's leaders, including Elihu Anthony and William T. Jeter, were catapulted into statewide politics. In a huge rally on the Lower Plaza (a half-block from the Front Street Chinatown) in 1886, a crowd displayed placards urging, "The Chinese Must Go," "No Chinese Need Apply," and "America Must Never Give Up to the Chinese Invasion." Some Chinese became so frightened that they purchased guns and ammunition to defend themselves. In the following day's edition of the *Santa Cruz Sentinel*, McPherson stated that the Chinese were "needlessly" frightened by the rally and that they were not the real objects of the anti-Chinese propaganda.

Some citizens did not distinguish between rhetoric and action, as the politicians did, making Santa Cruz the least hospitable home for Chinese in the region. Santa Cruz's Chinatown had the smallest number of women and families of the four major Chinatowns of the Monterey Bay Region. Sporadic violence against Chinese was most frequent in Santa Cruz; they were taunted, stoned, and chased back to Chinatown in numerous incidents. Most Chinese felt uncomfortable when they ventured beyond the protective confines of Chinatown. Santa Cruz's Chinatown atrophied before other Chinatowns in the region, and Santa Cruz still has the lowest percentage of Chinese people in the region's major cities.

The Chinese were indispensable to the increasingly labor-intensive agriculture of the Pajaro Valley, particularly after Claus Spreckels announced his intention to build a beet sugar factory there in 1887. Though Santa Cruz taunted Watsonville, the town, like Salinas, needed the Chinese too much to pay more than lip service to the anti-Chinese movement, and its Workingmen's Party, never strong, folded in 1878. Several of its more avid members had to join the Santa Cruz chapter. By 1879 Watsonville had amended the slogan of the anti-Chinese movement, and the local paper proclaimed, "The Chinese must go forth—to bind."

In Salinas, where the Chinese laborers played an increasingly important role in the burgeoning agricultural industry, the anti-Chinese movement could not survive the contradiction between its aims and the town's needs. When many California towns and cities staged protest demonstrations in April and May of 1882 over the initial veto of the Chinese Exclusion Law and later celebrated its passage, Salinas held no public demonstrations. The last flurry of anti-Chinese organizing during the statewide campaign in 1885–86 saw the Salinas Non-Partisan Anti-Chinese Committee, formed in February 1886, unsuccessfully attempt to force Chinese laundries in downtown Salinas to move to Chinatown. When the Scott Act was signed into law in 1888, Salinas held its last public anti-Chinese demonstration.

Even though the anti-Chinese sentiment in Salinas was not well organized, individual Chinese in Salinas were always candidates for practical jokes. In his memoirs, one white Salinas pioneer described a meeting with a Chinese in Salinas in the 1870s:

> One day when Dan Ragan and I were going home from town to the Abbott ranch we went down Abbott street. When about half way to where the I.O.O.F. cemetery is now we saw a Chinaman riding a white mare. I said to Dan, 'Hold on. There is a five-gallon can. I will get it. You ride up to him and love him up and I'll wire the can to the horse's tail.' So Dan put his arms around the Chinaman's neck and the Chinaman yelled, 'Whoa, whachtmalla.'' He asked Dan to let go. When he did I let the can go too, and the way that mare kicked and the Chinese hollered was a scream. Then up the road they went. I have no idea where or how far. A white streak was all I saw.

Monterey's multi-cultural nature hampered its anti-Chinese movement. Hispanic, English, Portuguese, Italians, and Chinese coexisted with very little friction, and when Portuguese whalers cut the nets of Chinese fishermen, they received little support from the town. The anti-Chinese movement had few grievances

in a town in which Chinese did not compete with white laborers for work and in which an international population made "scape-goating" difficult and risky. In addition, the Chinese fishing village at Point Alones was isolated from the town; the two rarely came into a conflict which might have inflamed anti-Chinese sentiment.

Manuel Ortins Store, Monterey, 1880s. White Labor Cigars signs, such as the one in upper left, were common during the 1880s. Manuel Ortins (on right) was a Portuguese immigrant.

## IMPACT ON THE CHINESE

Articles and books about the anti-Chinese movement in the United States reveal much about the majority community and its politics, but they rarely say much about the Chinese people, the target of those movements. In many studies of the issue, the Chinese are viewed through the eyes of the anti-Chinese protagonists, and these works may, in a subtle way, have encouraged the continued use of stereotypes which originated in the

129

anti-Chinese movement. An accurate picture of the Chinese cannot be gained through the window of the anti-Chinese movement. Anti-Chinese writers described the Chinese as mindless, faceless unskilled laborers who were all either railroad workers or laundrymen; they all smoked opium, gambled, visited prostitutes, and ran away at the slightest threat. Just as anti-Chinese proponents characterized the Chinese as villains, later studies characterized them as helpless victims—a fact not borne out by their responses to harassment.

The Chinese responded to the anti-Chinese movement with their feet. They did not have to take a referendum to determine the most and least comfortable places for them in the Monterey Bay Region during the nineteenth century—they showed their preference by their numbers. Monterey was the most comfortable, Santa Cruz the least, with Watsonville and Salinas varying according to the political tenor of the time. The constant racist pressures toughened the Chinese and taught them how to fight within the legal system. Chinatowns hired their own policemen (Watsonville's Chinatown had a security guard listed in the 1880 manuscript census) and their own attorneys (often the best attorneys in town). They actively pursued justice, as when they took the Portuguese whalers to court for cutting their fishing nets in Monterey. When need required, they called upon the legal and financial resources of the Chinese Six Companies and the Chinese Vice-Consul in San Francisco. (The Six Companies came into the region to investigate the murders of Tim Wong and Lou Sing.) The myth of the Chinese fleeing with their queues flying before the anti-Chinese forces does not fit the Monterey Bay Region. When push came to shove, they dug in and fought legally for rights to which they were entitled.

But the Chinese suffered greatly from legal restrictions against which they had no recourse. Immigration restrictions meant that most Chinese in California (as well as the rest of the United

States) were single men who had had to leave their families and had no hope of bringing them to the United States. The family was the primary focus of traditional Chinese culture. The Chinese character for the spoken word "alone" has as one of its two symbols the character for "orphan;" to be alone was to be an orphan, adrift. The overwhelming emphasis on male children and continuation of the family line was also a hedge against old age; Chinese children supported their parents in old age. More, it was a religious necessity; the ancestor worship common to China required that the spirits of the deceased be cared for, fed, and made to feel a part of the living world. The bond between the living and the dead and the seasonal festivals which strengthened it welded the family together. Those single men who came alone to the Golden Mountain might survive in old age without the aid of the family, but their spirits could not possibly be at rest after death without the ministrations of the family.

Trapped by economic realities and immigration restrictions, most of the single Chinese who had not founded families on the Golden Mountain faced a lonely death and an even more lonely existence as hungry ghosts, wandering uncared for and unfed through the spirit world. This relentless urge to die in the security of one's family goes a long way to explain the tenacity with which elderly Chinese men worked to get back to China. Misunderstood by whites, this was taken as evidence that the Chinese were mere transients, sojourners; where Chinese immigrants established families in the Monterey Bay Region, the urge to return to China to die was tempered by the knowledge that one's spirit would be cared for by children and grandchildren already born in America.

But for those who had no families, the Chinese organized Benevolent Associations to provide at least some of the missing familial securities and comforts—caring for the indigent and sick, holding funerals, tending graves, and shipping the bones of the dead back to China. In Chinese funerals in the region, a burial brick identifying the deceased and his village of origin was put in the coffin "for identification as later, the bones would be removed to be sent back to [China] for burial." Within a decade of burial, the body would be exhumed, placed in a box, and shipped back to the family village for final and permanent burial, to be cared for by the deceased's family—forever. The district associations took responsibility for sending the bones back to China, each of them employing two or three men solely to "travel over the State, [make] property calculations for decomposition, and gather up the relics of their late members." When a certain number of decomposed bodies had accumulated, the bone pickers would come to town and dig up the bodies:

> They [the bone pickers] . . . take the longest bone, say the leg, get a box made of that length, and 18 inches or 2 feet wide and deep, for the reception of all the bones. Each bone is then taken out of the [coffin] and dipped into a bucket of brandy and water. They are then polished with a stiff brush until they almost shine, and are then packed closely in the smaller receptacle. The polishers do not touch the bones with their hands, but handle them very dexterously with two sticks. They are very scrupulous in preserving every bone. The small box is then nailed up . . . and the bones of the Celestial, in due time, are laid in his native land as per agreement. . . .

All the cemeteries in the Monterey Bay Region underwent these periodic exhumations, usually at ten-year intervals. In 1913, for example, the bone pickers, under the direction of the Six Companies, came to Watsonville's Chinese cemetery and worked for two weeks to exhume 68 bodies of Chinese who had died over an eleven-year period. In the previous exhumation, 120 bodies had been shipped, making a total of 188 Chinese returned to China between 1902 and 1913 from Watsonville alone. A local observer estimated that eventually 10,000 boxes of bones would leave the United States for shipment to China during 1913.

Few of the cultural practices of the Chinese in California received such a strong reaction as did this practice of the exhumation of the dead for shipment to China. Non-Chinese watched in horror as the Chinese cemeteries were periodically turned over by the bone pickers and expressed their horror by enacting legislation to prevent the practice. In 1878 California passed a law titled, "An Act to Protect Public Health from Infection Caused by Exhumation and Removal of the Remains of Deceased Persons." After 1878 it was necessary for the bone pickers to get permits from county health officials before they could exhume the bones. The law at least partially reflected a belief on the part of the non-Chinese that the shipment of the dead back to China was another measure of the disdain the Chinese felt for America.

## A CHINESE VIEW

Very few first-person accounts by Chinese immigrants exist to counteract the prejudiced descriptions of Chinese customs and character. Few Chinese immigrants had the education or the leisure time to write an account of their experiences. For many Americans, it was easy to get away with the assumption that Chinese immigrants were relatively indifferent peasants who were dulled to the discrimination they experienced—language barriers effectively prevented them from being contradicted. But Watsonville briefly hosted a Chinese immigrant who sharply contradicted such misconceptions and articulated the suffering he shared with many others.

Chung Sun came to the United States in 1871 with six hundred dollars and a plan to start a tea plantation in Southern California. He arrived in Los Angeles at the height of the 1871 anti-Chinese riots in which at least twenty Chinese were killed by mobs. Chung Sun was beaten and robbed, apparently saved from death only by his ability to speak English and plead with his attackers. Soured on Southern California, he came north,

working as a laborer to meet his living expenses. In early November 1871 he found work as a ditch digger in Watsonville,
earning $1.50 per day as he helped to put in Watsonville's new
gas lighting system.

A mutual friend acted as go-between for Chung Sun and the
editor of the *Watsonville Pajaronian*, C. O. Cummings. Though
Chung Sun spoke and understood English, he did not write it
with confidence, so this mutual friend (who also read Chinese)
translated two of Chung Sun's letters for Cummings. The first
of the two remarkable letters was directed to Cummings and
conveyed Chung Sun's response to the treatment he and other
Chinese immigrants had received in America:

> *Unlearned as you may think us to be, we are not wholly ignorant of your
> history . . . we [Chinese] are taught to believe that the sublime teachings of
> our own Confucius and other sages of the East are [in the United States]
> reduced to a practical philosophy, regulating, governing, and harmonizing
> all your civil and political conduct; . . . that your government is founded and
> conducted upon principles of pure justice and that all of every clime, race, and
> creed are here surely protected in person, liberty and property.*

Chung Sun's belief in America was sorely tested by the events
in Los Angeles:

> *I left the loved and ever venerated land of my nativity to seek in [the United
> States] that freedom and security which I could never hope to realize in my
> own, and now after some months' residence in your great country, with the
> experience of travel, study and observation, I hope you will pardon me for
> expressing a painful disappointment. The ill treatment of [my] own coun-
> trymen may perhaps be excused on the grounds of race, color, language and
> religion, but such prejudice can only prevail among the ignorant . . .*

The letter concluded with the same note of optimism which
characterized the response of many new immigrants after their
first experience of prejudice in the United States:

> *. . . being a man of education and culture I am capable of other work than
> digging in the streets, but my philosophy teaches me, any useful [his em-
> phasis] work is more honorable than idleness. I shall therefore, with pa-*

*tience and resignation continue to dig with an abiding hope for something better . . . I shall try to be charitable as well as just to all mankind, but as a people will hardly correct their faults without knowing them, I write this in a spirit of kindness, notwithstanding my ill treatment, and ask you to publish it . . .*

And publish it Cummings did. Surprisingly, Cummings did not publish any responses the next week.

But he did publish another letter from Chung Sun. Having completed his work on the Watsonville gas ditch, Chung Sun went to San Francisco. Again through a common friend, the Watsonville newspaper editor received a copy of a letter Chung Sun wrote to a Chinese friend in Hong Kong. The fact that it was written to another Chinese helps explain the more direct tone the letter takes toward America and Americans. Chung Sun was puzzled by the contradictions he saw in American society:

*They have no purely national settlement in anything . . . there is no uniform mode of dress or manner of living; no system, regularity or order about anything, but all is a jumble of confusion and a labyrinth of contradictions.*

He saw the Confucian principles turned upside down in America, people without education becoming rich, and the learned starving. Finally, reluctantly, Chung Sun admitted that though Americans should be given credit for technological advances, their treatment of each other and the Chinese earned them, in his eyes, the most traditional of all Chinese judgments: ". . . in civility, complaisance, and polite manners [Americans] are wholly wanting and are very properly styled barbarians."

Apparently Chung Sun had acquired enough money to return to China, and a week or so after writing the letter, he took his realistic view of America back to China. Both letters have a feeling of patience and forbearance, as if the learned man from the centuries-old civilization had expected to find America a little rough around the edges. Had he remained, his experience would probably have confirmed what Chung Sun already knew— to a Chinese, most Californians were barbarians indeed.

The little colony of Celestials below town, steadily thriving upon the profits of dried fish, shark fins and abalones, contribute in no small degree to the business of the city.

*Monterey Gazette*,
January, 1864.

# 6

# Monterey

By the early 1870s the Monterey Peninsula had become the center of a regional Chinese fishing industry which fanned out along the coast from Año Nuevo south to Salmon Creek (beyond Point Sur). The industry flowered like a sea anemone during the summer; the Chinese probed into deserted coves and

Solitary Chinese fisherman and his camp, 1880s. Taken somewhere near the mouth of the Pajaro River, the photograph shows a simple, seasonal Chinese fishing camp.

BANCROFT LIBRARY

set up temporary fishing camps all along the coast, retreating in fall to one of the three permanent fishing villages near Monterey. Though at least one "China Camp" on the coast south of Point Lobos in the 1880s marked the site of an abandoned Chinese fishing camp (an 1888 map shows a "China Camp" at Salmon Creek), the seasonal camps rarely remained in one place long enough to be noted in the records. The three villages near Monterey, however, became permanent features on the Monterey Peninsula.

## THE VILLAGES OF CARMEL BAY

Carmel Bay is a small, rocky-bottomed bay two miles south of Point Pinos. Thanks to the upwelling of colder, nutrient-rich water from a submarine canyon just off-shore, the bay boasted a wealth of marine life; the abundant food, clear water, and rocky bottom provided year-round fishing. Flounder, rockfish, king fish, sharks, and smelt were abundant in winter and spring, while barracuda, yellow tail, halibut, pompano, and sea bass were caught there in the summer. The bay's reputation as a fishing ground was well established by the time the Chinese arrived in the 1850s—the north side of the bay was known as Pescadero (the fishing place) by the Spanish and Mexican residents of nearby Monterey. In the half-century of Chinese fishing activity in the region, Carmel Bay was a popular spot for the Chinese fishermen: "The little bay . . . is dotted with rocky islets covered with the nests of sea birds . . . the aulone [abalone] shells are very abundant here and it is a favorite resort of the Chinese fishermen." The points that frame the bay (Pescadero and Lobos) curve in to form small, protected coves, and on these coves the Chinese built fishing villages.

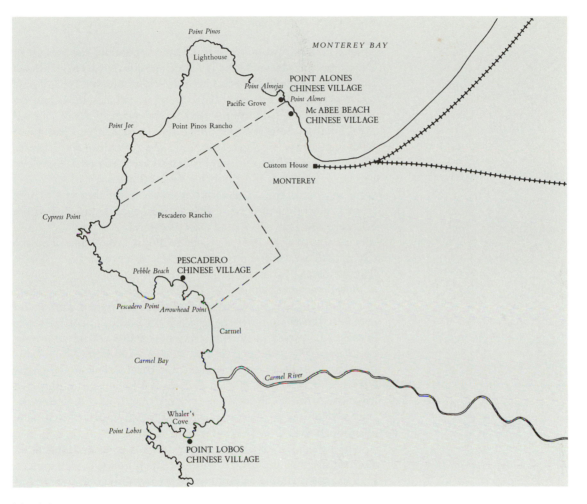

Map 6-1

MONTEREY PENINSULA AND THE
CHINESE FISHING VILLAGES

139

The first and most important village, possibly the earliest in the region, was located on a level terrace above the cove at Point Lobos, now called Whaler's Cove. It is possible that the Chinese had established a fishing village there as early as 1851, and by 1860 six Chinese fishermen lived there in a small village. In 1862 the Chinese fishermen were joined by a company of Portuguese whalers, and the two groups shared the cove until the Chinese left in the late 1870s. Though Whaler's Cove did not have a sloping sandy beach as did the other two village sites, there was a stone quay which had been built in the 1850s for shipping granite from a quarry on the point. The Chinese could ship their catch off the quay as well as pull their boats out of the water there when necessary. In 1874 a visitor to Point Lobos described the cove: "still as a millpond with its high stone wharf and quaint fishing vessels."

A traveler to Carmel Bay in 1875 walked across the white sandy bed of the Carmel River and "on to the quaint hamlet and romantic little bay under the lee of Point Lobos . . . [where] are located a company of Portuguese whalers and a Chinese fishing company." The most precise assessment of the Point Lobos Chinese fishing village was provided by the United States Coast Survey in 1876 which labeled a cluster of fourteen buildings on the cove as the "Chinese Fishery" (see map 6-2). Sometime between 1876 and 1880, for reasons still not clear, the Chinese abandoned their Point Lobos fishing village.

The fishermen's shacks remained for many years. During an 1892 smuggling incident involving the ship *Halcyon*, nineteen Chinese were landed at night at Stillwater Cove, and several of them took refuge in a "fisherman's shanty at Point Lobos" before finally being captured by the sheriff. A small cove just south of Point Lobos has retained the name China Cove, and local stories have it that a Chinese fishing village was also located there, though neither the Coastal Survey Maps nor the manuscript cen-

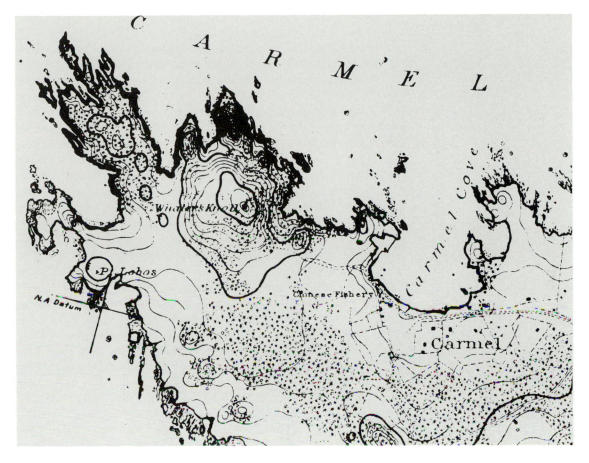

Map 6-2

POINT LOBOS

United States Coast Survey, 1876

Whaler's Knoll is on the left, while present-day Whaler's Cove is labeled as Carmel Cove. Chinese fishery is collection of buildings along fence line in lower left corner of Carmel Cove. Development labeled "Carmel" in lower right was an old subdivision that did not survive.

141

sus confirms it. It may have been a seasonal village where abalone hunters and rock fishermen spent the summer months before retreating to the more established villages to the north. After the Chinese Exclusion Act of 1882 was passed, the rocky coastline around Point Lobos offered good places to land Chinese immigrants smuggled in from Mexico or Canada, and the smuggling of Chinese is also associated with the place called China Cove.

On the north side of Carmel Bay, Pescadero Point also curves around to form a small bay sheltered from the open sea. Like the two hemispheres on the top of a heart, the bay is actually two distinct coves with a small peninsula jutting down to separate them. Pebble Beach is on the west side of the point and Stillwater Cove on the east. David Jacks acquired Pescadero, the coves, and the adjoining Pescadero Rancho at a sheriff's sale in 1862, and in January 1863 he built a short wharf on Stillwater Cove so that he could ship firewood, sand, and Monterey Pine tree seeds. In 1864 the cove had a "good wharf at which common-sized craft can lie in most weather to load and unload."

The first documented use of the Pebble Beach village site by Chinese fishermen is found in an 1868 lease between the China Man Hop Company and David Jacks. The lease, which specifies the fishing camp location as being the site of the "Old China House," hints at prior use by the Chinese. The China Man Hop Company leased the small site from Jacks for six dollars and "two dozen alones [abalone] each and every month." The 1868 lease marked the beginning of a permanent fishing village which remained at that spot until 1912. Though the Chinese were there to fish, they sometimes worked for Jacks and he would credit their labor toward the rent they paid for the village site. Jacks' ledgers list the Chinese fishermen burning brush, fixing fences, cleaning and repairing sheep troughs, and herding sheep.

A small oak-filled arroyo divided the terrace around Stillwater Cove, and the Chinese village grew along the bluff until it

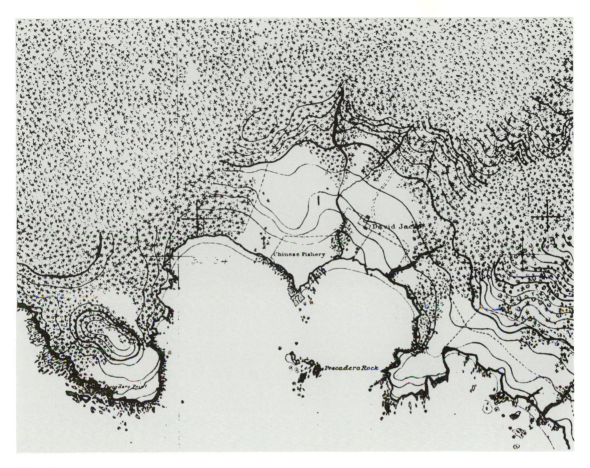

Map 6-3

PESCADERO POINT

United States Coast Survey, 1876

Pebble Beach is the cove on the left and Stillwater Cove is on the right. Chinese fishery was located along the gully to the right of the point between David Jacks' barn and Stillwater Cove. Seventeenth green of present-day Pebble Beach Golf Course is located at the site of the "Chinese Fishery."

143

Pescadero Fishing Village, looking east, c. 1890. Seventeen-Mile Drive passed through the Chinese fishing village. One of several road-side shell stands on far left. Jung San Choy's house and Stillwater Cove on right just beyond range.

straddled the ravine. It was a perfect fishing village site—protected sandy beach for pulling the boats out during bad weather, open terrace with southern exposure for fish drying, fresh water from nearby springs, and all of it facing the fish-filled, clear waters of Carmel Bay. The 1876 United States Coast Survey lists five buildings on the bluff above the beach and four more back in the oak trees below David Jacks' dairy barn (see map 6-3). In his 1879 visit Professor David Starr Jordan counted forty Chinese living in eight houses; the Pescadero fishermen had also built twelve boats. During calm weather the Chinese moored their boats to a heavy chain suspended between some off-shore rocks and the fishing village. The chain eventually rusted through, but short lengths of it dangled from the rocks for many years after the Chinese had left Pescadero.

Jacks sold the Pescadero Rancho and most of the Point Pinos Ranch to the Pacific Improvement Company in 1880 and then leased back the land so he could continue to graze his cattle and

Jung family shell stand, Pescadero, c. 1890. Photo taken looking east; Pebble Beach and Stillwater Cove can be seen in the distance. This may have been the first souvenir stand in Monterey Peninsula history.    BANCROFT LIBRARY

sheep. The Pacific Improvement Company specifically excluded from Jacks' lease all lands "occupied by Chinese for dwellings." In 1881 the Chinese at Pescadero began paying their rents to their new landlord, the Pacific Improvement Company.

The Pacific Improvement Company brought tourism to the Monterey Peninsula, and as part of their extensive development, they opened a scenic drive along the coast in 1881. Designed primarily for guests staying at their new Del Monte Hotel, the drive (eventually named the Seventeen-Mile Drive) offered sightseers striking views of rock, surf, surging ocean, and gnarled cypress trees. Where the drive skirted Pebble Beach and Stillwater Cove, it passed directly through the Chinese fishing village. Within a year of the drive's construction, the Chinese at Pescadero opened a roadside stand where they sold polished shells and souvenirs to the parade of tourists. This stand was one of the first souvenir shops in Monterey County, and the selling of shells and trinkets supplemented the income of the Chinese fishermen at Pescadero well into the twentieth century. In 1888 J. W. Collins noted the village for the U.S. Fish Commission:

> At Pescadero, on Carmel Bay, is another Chinese fishing camp, settled in 1868 and [it] has a resident population of some 30 fishermen; it is picturesquely situated on a road that skirts the shore, and is within easy reach of the fishing grounds in Carmel Bay.

Apparently the tourists of the late nineteenth century had just as short an attention span as their twentieth-century counterparts, for the Pacific Improvement Company found it necessary to spice up even the heart-stopping scenery along the Seventeen-Mile Drive with "exotic" sights. In 1890 the Company brought a herd of buffalo to the ranch lands behind Pebble Beach, and the buffalo became part of the "sights" listed along the drive. The Chinese villages along the drive also became one of the "exotic" sights. In spite of the endless stream of tourists during the 1880s and 1890s, fishing continued to be the primary focus of the Pescadero village, though the numbers of Chinese living there steadily declined. From the thirty inhabitants listed in 1888, the village dropped to twelve in 1900, with seven active fishermen.

After the fire at the Point Alones fishing village in May 1906, the Pacific Improvement Company reviewed all its leases with its Chinese tenants on the Monterey Peninsula and had its attorney redraw those which were deemed to be vague. In that process the Pacific Improvement Company created the most complete map of the Pescadero Chinese fishing village; though it was late in the village's history, the size and scope of the village was still close to what it had been in 1876 when the Coastal Survey mapped it. The 1906 map shows eight houses, but only four were occupied: "San Choy, Ge Wah, Tai Wo (Tom Wong) and Ah Tung (Foo Chung) were living in houses marked with their names."

The Chinese family most often associated with Pescadero was that of Jung San Choy (also called San Choy or Sun Choy). Jung

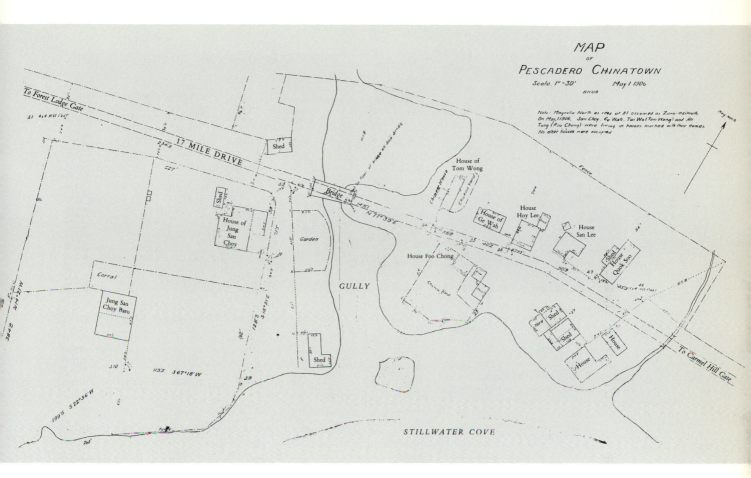

Map 6-4

PESCADERO FISHING VILLAGE, 1906

Special Collections, Stanford University

Map of Pescadero Chinatown made by the Pacific Improvement Company to confirm lease arrangements and property boundaries. Present-day Pebble Beach Beach and Tennis Club is located on left side of gully where Jung San Choy's house ("House San Choy"), garden, and shed were.

147

*Left*: Jung San Choy, c. 1890. Fisherman and abalone shell dealer Jung San Choy lived at the Pescadero fishing village until after 1900. Jung is not wearing a queue, an indication of his intent to remain in the United States.
PAT HATHAWAY

*Right*: Jung San Choy and family, c. 1890. All of the children in Jung's family were born on the Monterey Peninsula and were American citizens.
MONTEREY PUBLIC LIBRARY

San Choy and his older sons fished off Pescadero, while his wife, Ah Slow, and the younger children tended the souvenir stand. The 1900 manuscript census lists the Jung family as two parents and seven children, all of the children native-born Californians. Where Jung San Choy listed his occupation as fisherman in 1900, in the 1910 census he and his son Jung Loy Gum listed "abalone shell seller" as their occupation. At one time they had three shell stands, one at home on the point, another at Pebble Beach, and a third near the lunch tables at the Cypress Tree on the Seventeen-Mile Drive. The Pacific Improvement Company renewed Jung San Choy's lease on his home and the surrounding sheds and land in July 1906; the lease was to run for a year and Jung San Choy was to pay six dollars per year for the use of the property. The lease was renewed in 1908 and 1909.

Jung San Choy paid a visit to China in 1907, and upon his return to the United States was detained for several weeks at San Francisco while a number of Monterey Peninsula whites (including a local judge) went to San Francisco to testify on his behalf.

Jung San Choy and family, Pescadero, c. 1895. Jung on left, his wife beside him, and six of their children.

PAT HATHAWAY

*Below*: Old Chinese Fisherman, Pescadero, 1900. One of a handful of older Chinese fishermen who lived at Pescadero until the Pacific Improvement Company began developing the Pebble Beach Lodge and golf course.

CALIFORNIA STATE LIBRARY

Eventually, after the immigration officials came to Monterey to collect testimony, Jung San Choy was released and allowed to return home to Pescadero.

Age, immigration laws, and the dwindling role of Chinese in the fishing industry cut the numbers of Pescadero residents to five by 1910, with only two of those actually fishing. The Pacific Improvement Company began to subdivide the Pescadero Ranch into home sites in 1909, and the few Chinese living at the fishing village moved away. In 1912 Jung San Choy left his souvenir stand and moved out of the Pescadero village, ending Chinese occupation of the site which had begun in 1868.

## POINT JOE

Most of the solitary Chinese abalone shell and moss gatherers retreated to the Point Alones village during the winter months, but in the 1890s several Chinese lived year-round in a small

Point Joe, c. 1895. Using driftwood and recycled lumber, a Chinese shepherd built this house in the lee of the rocks just south of Point Joe.

bunker on a rocky point south of Point Pinos. In December 1896 the coastal steamer *St. Paul* wrecked on the point, and a newspaper reporter out to see the shipwreck wrote a description of the Chinese there:

> The proverbial thrift of the Chinese as a nation finds exemplification through the inmates of the little chipmunk hole of a shanty belonging to the Chinamen, at whose threshold, almost, the steamer *St. Paul* went to pieces. These human machines, have, with the usual stoicism characterizing their race, gathered fragment by fragment the bits of wood flung by the waves from the wreck to the beach, and afterwards hurled by the wind hither and thither, and stored it carefully near their home, where they are laboriously picking it apart for future use. Of the timbers from the wreck they have sufficient lumber to build a thousand shanties similar to the one they now occupy, and firewood to tide them over for a century . . .

After the turn of the century a solitary Chinese lived in the lean-to, tending a herd of goats and selling trinkets to travelers passing on the Seventeen-Mile Drive, which came within a dozen

yards of his home. Residents came to know him as "Chinaman Joe," and Ben Hoang remembers him walking from his wind-swept home into Monterey and back, selling trinkets and singing softly to himself. Whether Joe was named for the Point, or the Point named after Joe, is not clear, but in either case, Point Joe is linked with the solitary Chinese man tending his goats and collecting flotsam along the beach.

## THE POINT ALONES VILLAGE

The largest Chinese fishing village in the Monterey Bay Area was tucked between Point Almejas (Mussel Point) and Point Alones (Abalone Point) approximately a mile west of Monterey and just beyond the edge of Monterey city limits. Protected from rough seas by Point Almejas and from political storms by a one-mile distance from Monterey, the fishing village became not

Map 6-5

## POINT ALONES FISHING VILLAGE

United States Coast Survey, 1878

Original Pacific Grove Campground is on left of map and road to the lighthouse (Lighthouse Ave.) passes through the lower part of the map. Point Almejas (Mussel Point) is on right of map (now called China Point or Cabrillo Point), and Chinese fishing village is on the cove just east of the point. Point Alones, now the site of the Monterey Bay Aquarium, is the point to the right of the fishing village.

Point Alones village, Pacific Grove, 1880s. Looking toward Monterey, this photograph shows the extent of the fishing village. Boat ramp is on extreme right, and tall, white building just behind the village is the temple. Cypress trees on extreme left mark the boundary between Pacific Grove and Monterey.     PAT HATHAWAY

only the linchpin of the Chinese fishing industry in the area but the cultural capital for all Chinese living in the region. The first cove outside town, the Point Alones site met all the prerequisites of a Chinese fishing village—sheltered cove, sloping sandy beach, open ground for drying fish, and (during the early years) a small wharf.

The Chinese occupation of the cove probably began during the abalone rush in the spring of 1853, and some of the cabins built by the abalone gatherers were probably on the cove. Another account has the Chinese living on the cove in 1857, several years after Henry De Graw built a small wharf there to provide shipping facilities for the Point Pinos Rancho of which he was part-owner. Once the abalone rush ended, most of the Chinese men moved on to other projects, leaving a small group of Chinese families on the Monterey Peninsula, including Point Lobos and Point Alones. The 1860 manuscript census lists fifteen Chinese living at Point Alones in four separate households; two of the Chinese were adult females, while the remaining thirteen were adult male fishermen. The following year a newspaper account corroborated the size of the Point Alones village when it estimated that there were "fifteen or twenty" Chinese working and living there.

David Jacks purchased a part-interest in the Point Pinos Rancho in 1867, and in July 1869 he began collecting rents from the Point Alones Chinese village. Jacks charged the Chinese an annual rent of two hundred dollars for the village site, and the Chinese owned all the buildings. The annual rent (paid quarterly) entitled the Chinese to collect all the "dry fallen down timber" in the pine forest behind the village for heating and cooking.

Not until 1870 does the unique character of the Point Alones village begin to emerge as both the census and a lengthy description of the village published that year in the newspaper mention the women and children living in the village:

> The Chinatown of Monterey is located down the shore towards the Light House, the male residents occupying themselves exclusively as fishermen. Built of redwood shakes, their houses look nevertheless as old as a suburb of Canton and there proceeds from it a most ancient and fish-like smell. There are plenty of women in the village . . . and as a consequence a number of small specimens of the Mongol type, toddling about among pigs and poultry. The village grows all the while and the business this people is engaged in seems to thrive. Their catch consists mainly of sharks, of which they dry the tails and fins, but they do not neglect the scale fish found in the bay and collect besides numbers of aulones [abalones]. All are dried in the sun and then made up in bales like fodder and exported going by steamer to San Francisco for distribution.

Chinese women and children were unusual in the United States in 1870. The manuscript census lists fourteen distinct Chinese family units in Point Lobos, Pescadero, and Point Alones, and except for a Chinese family with one child living in Salinas, all the Chinese families in both Santa Cruz and Monterey counties lived in the fishing villages. A startling 43% of the 47 Chinese living in Point Alones were female, and compared with the

*Above*: Point Alones village, Pacific Grove, 1880s. Temple is white, two-story building in foreground. Fish drying racks can be seen surrounding temple. Point Almejas, now the site of Hopkins Marine Station, is on left.

PAT HATHAWAY

*Opposite*: Chinese fishermen with children, Point Alones, 1890s. The Point Alones village had an extremely high percentage of women and children, attesting to the intention of its residents to remain in the United States.

PAT HATHAWAY

average 7% in the nationwide Chinese population, the proportion of women in the Point Alones village was extremely high. Fifteen of the Point Alones Chinese were under eighteen.

The Chinese on the Monterey Peninsula in the nineteenth century did not fit the stereotype of Chinese men who left their families temporarily to come to California to work in the mines or on the railroads. The Monterey fishing industry was established by families of fishermen, and the fishing itself was pursued by the entire family, not just the men. When Professor David Starr Jordan visited Monterey in 1879, he noted particularly that the women also worked in the fishing industry: "Some of the women here go fishing with the men. Others stay at home and dress the fish, which operation is aided by a heavy hatchet-like knife." One of the most detailed descriptions of the Point Alones village published in the 1870s has the village organized into "companies," but most of the companies mentioned were actually families: "Man Lee Company, three men and three

Point Alones Village, 1890s. Photo shows boats, fishermen, and some of the many children who lived in the village.          CALIFORNIA STATE LIBRARY

women; Sun Sing Lee Company, three men two women and three children . . ." The presence of large families at Point Alones meant that the village had an America-born second generation very early in its existence, and from this second generation several vigorous young men emerged to provide the leadership for the fishing community.

Each Chinese community in the Monterey Bay Area had a go-between whose function it was to communicate between the Chinese and their non-Chinese neighbors. Usually a China-born merchant who learned to speak English during the course of his business, the go-between often came to be recognized as the "mayor" of the Chinese community, though the actual leadership of the community more often than not rested in a council of elders. The go-between for the Monterey fishing villages was a bright young America-born man named Wong Wah Foo, also called Tim Wong. Born in Sacramento, California, in 1853, Tim Wong moved with his family to Monterey during the 1860s. In

1870, at age seventeen, Tim caught the attention of a Monterey newspaper because he spoke Chinese, English, and Spanish fluently (he later added Portuguese to his repertoire, for dealing with the whalers) and because he was "very clever as a person of business." In his role as go-between, Tim collected the rents from the individual fishing families and delivered them to David Jacks each quarter. Over time Jacks grew to trust Tim well enough that he sometimes loaned Tim money, though he charged him 1½% monthly interest on the loans.

Tim quickly asserted his rights as an American citizen and was extremely active politically. In September 1875 he voted the Republican ticket and became what many local newspapers believed to be the first America-born Chinese to vote in the

Point Alones fisherman with family, 1890s. Family has not been identified, but its size is testimony to the permanent nature of the Point Alones Chinese community.

United States. Tim took his responsibilities as a citizen very seriously, and he often spoke out for the rights of the Chinese living in the region. In January 1876, after a trip on the steamer *Santa Cruz*, Tim took out an advertisement in the *Monterey Weekly Herald* complaining that Chinese passengers were required to pay full fare on the steamer but were not allowed to eat at the same tables with whites. He signed the advertisement as Ah Tim, "an American citizen claiming the equal rights vouchsafed by our constitution."

Sisters, Monterey, 1890s.
PAT HATHAWAY

Woman at Point Alones village, 1890s. Unusual photograph taken from inside the village shows a woman going about her chores. Note the duck cages in the foreground and the sampans at anchor in the distance on the left.

MONTEREY COUNTY LIBRARY

Point Alones Village, looking west, 1890s. The main street ran parallel to the shore, and the backs of the buildings on the right jutted out over the water. Fisherman on right is coiling trawl lines. Boxes on left were used to ship fish by rail.     ROY CHRISTIAN

Point Alones Village, main street, looking east, 1890s. Sign on left says, "Lum Gung Lee, Chines [*sic*] Intelligence Office." An intelligence office was an employment agency.                    PAT HATHAWAY

Point Alones Village, altar, 1890s. Outdoor shrine near center of village. Chinese calligraphy invokes peace, longevity, and felicity. Statement just above bowl with incense says, "Heaven preserve us people."  PAT HATHAWAY

163

## THE LEGEND OF CHINA'S WAR
## WITH MONTEREY—1875

According to local Monterey legend, Empress Dowager Tzu Hsi was angered by accounts of Chinese citizens being mistreated by anti-Chinese mobs in California, and vowing revenge, she dispatched a punitive expedition of seven war junks under the command of Admiral Tau to go to California and teach the barbarians a lesson. The fleet sailed into Monterey Bay in the fall of 1875.

Admiral Tau and his junks stood off Monterey, and when they discovered no reaction from the shore, the Chinese fired a warning cannon shot which fell harmlessly in the water, short of the shore. The cannon shot attracted a crowd, but Monterey did not return fire, and after several hours of waiting, Admiral Tau and some of his troops went ashore to investigate the situation. The Montereyans welcomed Tau with flowers and a fiesta, and faulty translation led the Admiral to believe that Monterey (and all of California) had surrendered to his forces. At the conclusion of the parties, Tau and his soldiers returned to their junks to await the formal surrender documents.

Days turned into weeks, and as the time passed Admiral Tau's forces began to defect, slipping overboard and swimming ashore. Finally, when the surrender did not seem forthcoming, and a return trip to China seemed impossible, Admiral Tau took all the valuables from his junk and deserted. The junks swung at anchor for awhile until they were finally broken up and used for building materials in the Point Alones fishing village.

The war junks are not mentioned in any of the contemporary newspapers in the region, and since the alleged attack occurred at a time when such an event would have been recorded, *somewhere*, it appears doubtful. The only reference to a Chinese fleet attacking Monterey appeared in the *Monterey Gazette*, February 19,

1864, when the editor made a vague reference to ". . . the rumored approach of a hostile fleet from China."

## SOUTHERN PACIFIC COMES TO MONTEREY

While the Chinese fishermen were retreating from Santa Cruz County, a series of events strengthened the position of the Chinese fishing villages on the Monterey Peninsula. By 1888 the fishing villages at Point Alones and Pescadero were both thriving and secure because the Chinese squid-fishing industry enabled them to fish while avoiding direct competition with the Italians on bay waters. But the Chinese villages also benefited from the arrival of a new landlord on the peninsula in 1880—the Southern Pacific Railroad Corporation. The arrival of the Southern Pacific as a major landowner around Monterey was not only a major event in the history of the Chinese fishing villages, it was one of the most important events in the history of the entire peninsula.

During its two-hundred-year history, the Monterey Peninsula was influenced most by two major powers—the Spanish/Mexican colonial regime which established and maintained Monterey as a provincial capital, and the Southern Pacific Railroad. When California became a state and the capital moved to San Jose in 1850, Monterey went into suspended animation. Newspaper editors and visitors often referred to Monterey as "Rip Van Winkle," the town that went to sleep. When Robert Louis Stevenson visited Monterey in 1879, he found the town "essentially and wholly Mexican" with Spanish the language of choice. That slumber suited the Chinese fishermen just fine, and while Monterey slept, the Chinese worked hard to establish the varied and successful fishing industry. The arrival of the railroad and Italians in 1875 roused Monterey, and if events had taken their normal course (as they did on the Santa Cruz side), development would have soon been pressing in on the Chinese villages.

With little commercial activity from 1850–1880, there had been no pressure to subdivide the large parcels of land on the peninsula (some said that the large parcels *caused* that inactivity), and in 1880 David Jacks owned two ranches on the peninsula which were almost exactly as they had been when granted to the original owners during the Mexican era. When the Southern Pacific Railroad began looking for a location to develop as a tourist destination, the Monterey Peninsula beckoned. Part of the inspiration for the Southern Pacific's move to Monterey came from the burgeoning tourist industry at Santa Cruz and the imminent completion of a competing railroad (the South Pacific Coast Railroad) which would bring San Francisco Bay Area residents directly into Santa Cruz through the Santa Cruz Mountains. In 1880, in one bold stroke, the Southern Pacific Railroad bought over six thousand acres of undeveloped land on the Monterey Peninsula (including both the Pescadero and Point Pinos ranches from Jacks), and laid out a major tourist development. They built the vacation area from scratch; in a six-month frenzy the Southern Pacific laid a broad-gauge railroad extension from Castroville to Monterey, built a major first-class hotel (the Del Monte), and began to advertise the Monterey Peninsula as the Newport of the Pacific.

The Southern Pacific Railroad and its land development branch, the Pacific Improvement Company, were noted employers of Chinese laborers, and they brought a number of Chinese to Monterey to work in the Del Monte Hotel and to provide the labor for laying out the scenic drives through their property on the peninsula. All this activity had little effect on the Chinese fishing villages, but the long-range impact of the arrival of the Southern Pacific on the fishermen was major.

Where the Chinese fishermen on the Santa Cruz side had been squatters, camping furtively along the high-tide line, the Chinese fishing villages at Pescadero and Point Alones not only had formal rental agreements for their village sites, but beginning in 1881, their landlord, the Pacific Improvement Company, was the most powerful political and economic entity on the Monterey Peninsula. Because the Pacific Improvement Company intended to keep the huge parcels intact (except for continuing the subdivision of Pacific Grove which was already under way), the villages were spared the piecemeal encroachment of coastal development which plagued the fishermen on the Santa Cruz side of the bay. The huge fiefdom set up by the Pacific Improvement Company at Monterey may have frustrated other developers looking for opportunities, but for the Chinese, the situation was ideal.

The Southern Pacific Railroad often listed the Chinese villages as exotic sights along the Seventeen-Mile Drive, making their presence valuable to the tourist industry. Poets, painters, photographers, and just plain tourists were charmed by the villages and their Chinese inhabitants. The Del Monte Hotel eventually bussed hotel guests to Point Alones to watch the Chinese New Year celebrations and later, in the 1890s, the Ring Games. The Del Monte Hotel was geared to the upper-class tourist, and the rich, famous, and (sometimes) educated visitors from the East coast found the Chinese villages to be curiosities, like the twisted cypress trees and crashing waves. Though there may have been something patronizing, almost zoo-like, about the relationship between the Del Monte guests and the Chinese villages, being set upon by finger-pointing, gawking visitors from Boston was certainly better than being set upon by a group of disgruntled fishermen as sometimes happened to the Chinese near Santa Cruz.

Point Alones Village, looking east toward Monterey, 1890s. Fence and trees in distance are Monterey/Pacific Grove boundary. Present-day Monterey Bay Aquarium is located on that site.   CALIFORNIA HISTORICAL SOCIETY

168

The list of properties which the Pacific Improvement Company bought from David Jacks in 1880 included the Pacific Grove Retreat which was a short distance west of the Point Alones fishing village. Established by the Methodist Episcopal Church in 1875, and originally called Ocean Grove after the summer Chautauqua center at Ocean Grove, New York, Pacific Grove was a small collection of cottages and tents when the Pacific Improvement Company bought it. Pacific Grove was designed as a summer community, and after 1880, under the direction of the Pacific Improvement Company, lots sold briskly; by 1886 the company had sold 1,500 lots for summer residents. More important for the future of the Chinese fishing village, however, was the growth of year-round residents in the grove; by 1884 the grove had one hundred full-time residents, despite the strict Methodist Episcopal regulations (no whiskey, wine, or cider; no dancing or carousing; all public places closed by 10 P.M.). Chinese vegetable peddlers and fish peddlers sold their wares in the campground during the summer, and the Pacific Improvement Company hired Chinese to burn brush, work on the streets, and clean out the seasonal cabins.

The Methodist Episcopal church established a Chinese mission at the Point Alones village in 1883. The energy and leadership for the mission came from Mrs. Eunice L. Wilson of Pacific Grove; the mission lasted until her death in January 1894. From 1883 to 1890 classes were held in a small school building on the coast just west of the fishing village, but after the building's lease expired in 1890, Mrs. Wilson moved the school into Pacific Grove. The mission school was the only educational opportunity available to the children of the Point Alones fishing village, and enrollment averaged twenty or more students, including the children of Jung San Choy who came to the mission from their Pescadero home.

170

Chinese Mission, Point Alones, late
1880s. Mrs. Eunice Wilson, the
founder of the mission, is seated in
right foreground surrounded by children. Several of Jung San Choy's children are in the photograph, including
a daughter standing just to the right of
Mrs. Wilson. Run by the Methodist
Episcopal Church, the mission was located at the village until 1890.

CALIFORNIA STATE LIBRARY

Chinese Mission, Pacific Grove, early
1890s. The mission moved into Pacific
Grove in 1890. Mrs. Eunice Wilson,
seated in the center of the group, died
in January 1894, and the mission foun-
dered after that.

CALIFORNIA STATE LIBRARY

Jung San Choy's children, 1890s. These children walked to the Chinese mission from Pescadero each day.
PAT HATHAWAY

The mission dropped into "inocuous quietude" after Mrs. Wilson's death; none of the other Protestant missionary organizations could be induced to take over the mission because it was located in the midst of a Methodist Episcopal community. Impatient with the delays in resuming the school, the Point Alones Chinese approached the Pacific Grove school trustees and asked that their children be allowed to attend the Pacific Grove elementary school. The trustees allowed the children to enter the school, but on the condition that "they present themselves clean and under the same conditions as white children;" apparently children attending Mrs. Wilson's mission school brought "their dogs, parents and minor brothers and sisters with them to look on."

Perhaps the most illustrious product of Mrs. Wilson's mission school was the first male student to enroll in the school in 1883, Leong Qui Pak (Len Puk). Len Puk showed so much promise that the Methodist Episcopal leadership sent him on to school in London for two years. Upon his return to the United States, Len

172

MONTEREY

Robert Leon Park (Leong Qui Pak), early twentieth century. The first male student at the Chinese Mission in Pacific Grove, Robert L. Park was one of the founders of the Chinese American Citizen's Alliance, and later worked for the United States Immigration and Naturalization Service.

CALIFORNIA STATE LIBRARY

Puk moved to San Francisco where he completed grammar school and high school and enrolled at the University of California at Berkeley. In 1894 he returned to visit the Pacific Grove Chinese mission:

> Few, upon casually meeting this handsome, well bred, well dressed young gentleman would think of his being a Chinaman, still less that he ever belonged to our own despised Chinatown.

It was just such judgments about his community that Robert Leon Park (the name he used after his baptism as a Christian) began to fight. In 1895 he was one of the founders of the Native Sons of the Golden State, dedicated to championing the rights of Chinese communities in California. In 1896, when he was President of the Native Sons of the Golden State, he was interviewed by the *San Francisco Examiner* on the eve of the 1896 presidential election. The newspaper interviewed fifteen America-born Chinese to determine their preferences in the coming election.

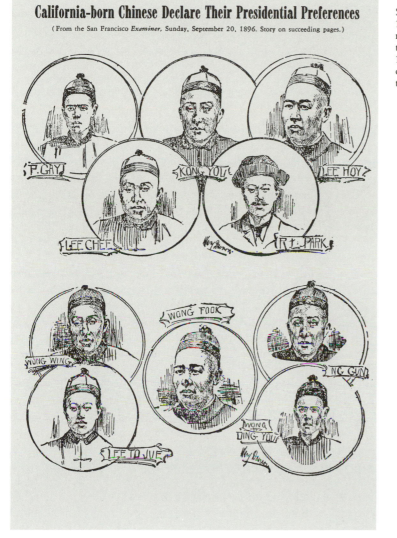

**California-born Chinese Declare Their Presidential Preferences**

(From the San Francisco *Examiner*, Sunday, September 20, 1896. Story on succeeding pages.)

P. GAY
KONG YOU
LEE HOY
LEE CHEE
R.L. PARK
WONG WING
WONG FOOK
NG GUN
LEE TO JUE
WONG DING YOU

Sketch from *San Francisco Examiner*, 1896. Shows ten America-born Chinese who were interviewed for an article on the presidential election of 1896. Robert Leon Park, second row on right, was the only one not wearing traditional Chinese clothing.

CHINESE HISTORICAL SOCIETY

Robert Leon Park was the only one of the fifteen who had completely discarded his Chinese-style clothing:

> A natty young man is [Robert] Leon Park, President of the Native Sons of the Golden State—not "Golden West." He gave up Chinese clothes long ago, but it is a noteworthy fact that he is the only one of all the fifteen voters who has doffed the Oriental garb. He is now a special student at the University at Berkeley . . .

After several unsuccessful efforts at a career in journalism, Robert Leon Park became an inspector for the United States Immigration and Naturalization Service, a career that often fell to educated Chinese, who had few alternatives at that time.

The Chinese mission was an exception to the usual relations between the Point Alones fishing village and Pacific Grove, which were distant, sometimes testy. During the 1880s and 1890s, the small Chinese world and the small Methodist world orbited each other with little interaction.

In addition to developing Pacific Grove, the Pacific Improvement Company also undertook several major construction projects on the Monterey Peninsula during the 1880s, employing its enormous resources. Monterey had always been plagued by the lack of a dependable fresh water supply. In 1882, dissatisfied with the municipal water system, the Pacific Improvement Company drilled its own well at the Del Monte Hotel, but the ground water there proved insufficient for the hotel's needs. The company bought the six-thousand-acre Los Laureles Rancho in the Carmel Valley and, using a number of Chinese laborers, built a pipeline down the Carmel Valley, around Cypress Point and Point Pinos, through Pacific Grove and finally to the Del Monte Hotel, a distance of twenty-three miles. That water system, as good as it was, was unable to prevent the destruction of the hotel by fire in 1887, so while the hotel's Chinese crew was running the ashes through a sluice box to recover jewelry and money for the hotel guests (perhaps the largest Chinese gold-mining operation in Monterey's history), the Pacific Improvement Company planned the construction of a new hotel and an improved water system to serve it.

During the summer of 1888, after the dedication of the second Del Monte Hotel, the company began the construction of a reservoir to increase the storage capacity of their Carmel Valley water system. The reservoir was to be located in a small ravine in the forest above Point Joe on the site of an old clay pit. In August 1888 trainloads of Chinese laborers began arriving in Monterey, and the company marched them to the reservoir site where they burned brush, cleared trees, and blasted stumps. Under a pall of dust and smoke, they dug a lake with picks, shovels, and horse-drawn scrapers. The 100 Chinese at the reservoir site in August grew to 1,300 by early October, and by the end of the month,

Del Monte Hotel burning, 1887. Jewelry abandoned by hotel guests was recovered for them by Chinese staff members who "mined" the hotel ashes by running them through a makeshift sluice box.　　PAT HATHAWAY

1,700 Chinese and 640 horses worked on the reservoir. The Chinese lived adjacent to the site in "long rows of white tents dotted through the pine woods almost as far as the eye can reach."

While the reservoir was being dug, President Cleveland signed the Scott Act which further restricted Chinese immigration into the United States. A small celebration in Monterey commemorated the signing of the bill, but the editor of the *Monterey Argus* noted that the white supervisors working with the Chinese at the reservoir site did not celebrate the signing; with over one thousand Chinese in the vicinity, "it wouldn't be healthy policy."

On December 4, 1888, just as the first winter rains began to fall in the Carmel Valley, and a miraculous three months after construction had begun, the flood gates were opened, and one thousand gallons of Carmel Valley water flowed into the thirty-acre lake each minute. The 140 million-gallon reservoir was thirty-seven feet deep at its deepest point and had cost the company $175,000. As the reservoir neared completion, the Pacific Improvement Company began pulling Chinese off the project and sending them to the terminus of the railroad line which they were extending south through the Salinas Valley.

## THE MURDER OF TIM WONG

When the Pacific Improvement Company bought the Point Alones village site in 1880, the fishing village had a population of thirty-six Chinese living in nineteen households. Families still dominated the village, but there had been a marked increase of single male Chinese fishermen, from two in 1870 to fourteen in 1880. The families were clustered at the west end of the village, while the single men each lived alone in cabins along the narrow lane which served as the village's main street. Until the village was destroyed in the 1906 fire, the pattern of families on the west end, single men on the east, was maintained. Most men who moved into the Point Alones village during the 1880s and 1890s were fishermen who had come to Monterey from areas such as Santa Cruz, where Chinese fishermen were no longer welcome, but a few, such as a group of ex-cooks, came from other professions. Most found work in assisting the fishermen in the village. The adjustment from a village of families to this new mix of laborers and families did not come without friction, and as the village began to change, Tim Wong faced his greatest challenge as spokesman for the original fishing families.

The first hint of difficulty came in 1876 when a Chinese entrepreneur named Go Ti announced his intention to open a house of prostitution in the Point Alones village. Up to that time, recreational businesses (opium, gambling, prostitution) had been restricted to the small Chinatown on California Street (now Munras) in downtown Monterey. This small Chinatown primarily served other Chinese, particularly the large staff of the Del Monte Hotel and the Chinese laundrymen and cooks who worked throughout Monterey. Go Ti owned a laundry and a small house of prostitution in the California Street Chinatown, and he asked the leaders of the Point Alones village for permission to expand his prostitution business to their village. The leaders refused the request, and when Tim Wong delivered the decision to Go Ti, Go Ti vowed to kill Tim Wong. Later that same day Go Ti and several companions went looking for Tim Wong in the fishing village with guns drawn. Tim fled, hiding in the Pescadero fishing village until the sheriff intervened and arrested Go Ti and his companions for attempted murder. Charges were eventually dropped, and the dispute died down.

As the number of single men living in the fishing village increased, so did the pressure to introduce recreational businesses there, and Tim often expressed the fear that disgruntled Chinese wanted to kill him. In July 1885 his fears came true—his body

was found hanging from a tree in the pine forest behind the
Point Alones village. Thirteen wounds were found in Tim's
body.

> There were no holes in his clothing, and it is supposed that after kill-
> ing him his murderers changed his clothing and hung him to the
> tree, thinking, perhaps, that it would be considered a case of suicide
> and no investigation would be made, as he was "only a Chinaman."

The local newspapers expressed outrage at Tim's murder, and
one editor suggested that, if caught, his murderer "could be
strung up without the intervention of judge or jury." The Chinese Six Companies offered a six hundred dollar reward for
Tim's murderer in a curiously graduated system of payments:

> The above reward ($600) will be paid for the arrest and conviction of
> the murderer of Wong Foo (Ah Tim) two months after he [the mur-
> derer] shall have suffered the death penalty. Four hundred dollars will
> be paid if the murderer be sentenced to imprisonment for life; two
> hundred dollars if he be sent to prison for 30 years.

No arrests were ever made, but Tim was probably murdered by
disgruntled Chinese who were trying to open the Point Alones
village for recreational businesses.

Tim Wong's death marked the transition from a smaller,
family-oriented village dominated by fishing families to a larger, heterogeneous Chinese village complete with gambling,
opium, and prostitution. Brilliant, energetic, and opinionated,
Tim Wong was a decade ahead of his time. Had he been born ten
years later and acquired the advantage of a formal education, he
probably would have risen to state-level leadership in the Chinese community in the 1890s, as did fellow Montereyan Len
Puk. Instead he used his talents to fight for the rights of fellow
Chinese and to preserve the integrity of the Point Alones fishing
village, no less noble a cause. He died in the attempt, and though
Tim Wong's position as public leader of the Point Alones village

was eventually filled by other California-born Chinese, the Point Alones village was poorer without him. Tim's widow and four children continued to live on the peninsula, and one of his sons was still living in Monterey in 1910. A Chinese saying best summarizes Tim Wong's life: "The tallest tree catches all the wind."

As the Point Alones village moved into the 1890s, it was as secure as any Chinese community in California could be. Relations with the Italian and Portuguese fishermen had stabilized, the supply of squid was dependable, and the Pacific Improvement Company was a powerful and stable landlord. The Point Alones village was the senior Chinese community in the region, and by the mid-1890s it had grown to be the largest, a vibrant, prosperous village which looked, sounded, and smelled like a village in China.

A large number of Chinese will be required this year in this section, as it will be impossible to gather the immense crops without them.

*Watsonville Pajaronian*,
June, 1869.

# 7

# Watsonville

Watsonville has a no-nonsense air about it; the rows of two-story buildings along Main Street are as functional and un-adorned as the fields that surround the city. From the town's origins in the 1850s, agriculture has been its primary reason for being. Watsonville's business district grew up along the single Main Street, and until the 1860s the stores, saloons, and shops were confined to a strip on either side of that street. Only a handful of Chinese laundrymen and cooks, scattered in several wash houses along the southern part of Main Street, lived in Watsonville before the summer of 1866.

In 1865 Joseph Ordish opened a new street which branched perpendicularly off Main Street to the east; he named the street Maple Avenue for the trees he planted in boxes along both sides. Main Street was the commercial riverbed of the town, while Maple was just a quiet eddy where exposure, traffic, and rents were all low. The intersection of Maple and Union (parallel to Main Street) became the site for Watsonville's first Chinatown. By 1869 at least one Chinese laundry had opened on the south-east corner of the intersection. By 1870 most of the Chinese businesses in Watsonville were located there.

Both the land and the buildings on the southeast corner of Maple and Union were owned by John T. Porter; in 1880 the land was appraised at nine hundred dollars and the buildings at two thousand dollars. As the region's largest sugar beet grower in the 1870s and part-owner of the sugar beet factory at Soquel in its last season, Porter had come to depend heavily on Chinese beet contractors. Porter owned extensive farm acreage from Watsonville to Castroville, and he was one of the first farmers in the valley to make extensive use of Chinese farm laborers.

Watsonville and the Maple/Union Chinatown pulsed in a seasonal rhythm, busy during the summer and fall and quiet during the winter and spring. Until Pajaro Valley agriculture began to diversify in the 1870s, most of the Chinese went back to San Francisco after the grain harvest was completed. The Maple/Union Chinatown provided services to the farm laborers in the summer and then shrank to a dozen or so laundrymen and cooks in the winter. The 1870 manuscript census shows a Chinese community which primarily provided service to fellow Chinese. Five businesses straddled the corner, including a Chinese store, laundry, and two boarding houses. The boarding houses contained eight Chinese cooks, three farm laborers, and a Chinese labor contractor, and all were men. The remainder of the Chinese farm laborers listed in the Pajaro Valley lived outside Watsonville's city limits in camps on the farms where they worked. A fifth household contained a single Chinese male and four unmarried Chinese females aged 21, 23, 24, and 28, with no occupation listed. Based on complaints published in the local newspaper in 1871, this fifth household was probably a house of prostitution: "It is a well-known fact that there are several disreputable Chinese houses right in the center of town; the inmates stand at the door and invite customers. . . ." Although common in the Pajaro Valley, prostitution had been restricted by custom to Whiskey Hill, a small town north of Watsonville, until the early 1870s; the complaint about Chinese prostitutes on the corner of Maple and Union had to do with their location, not their existence.

Newspaper accounts in the 1870s give glimpses of a Chinese island in the center of Watsonville. The sounds of firecrackers heralding the New Year or a funeral, the gongs and drums of a Chinese band, the shouts of Chinese playing *fan tan*, the "soul harrowing" squeal of hogs being slaughtered, the smell of incense, opium, roasting chicken, and pork, Chinese men in their pork-pie hats swaying along Maple Avenue, their loads bouncing in slow motion at each end of their carrying pole, an entire lacquered hog twisting and glistening in the sun, laundry flapping from racks built above the flat roofs, and butterfly-shaped kites dancing high over the town in the April breezes might have characterized any Chinese village.

By 1874 Watsonville's Chinatown had grown to ten buildings, with the addition of a slaughter house, several gambling houses, and at least one opium den. As the acreage of labor-intensive crops such as hops and sugar beets expanded in the Pajaro Valley, the Chinatown also grew and the Chinese population became less transient and more permanent.

The 1880 census records that from the five households and twenty-seven Chinese in 1870, the Maple/Union Chinatown grew to a total of seventy-nine Chinese residents and twenty-two households. Since Chinatown was hemmed in on all sides by white-owned businesses, growth was accommodated by adding second stories to existing buildings and wedging new two-story buildings between existing ones. By 1880 six retail grocery stores, one Chinese restaurant, one Chinese barber, and one Chinese labor contractor had been added to the community, and the census taker also counted one gambling hall, one opium den, and three houses of prostitution. Ah Kee and Ah Flen gave their occupation as "opium sellers," while E. Fawn and Kee Worn listed their occupation as gamblers. Ah Kan is listed as a policeman, probably hired by the Chinese merchants to provide security after a series of incendiary attempts were made on the Chinese community in 1876 and 1877.

Though ten Chinese women lived in Watsonville in 1880, no Chinese children under the age of eighteen years were recorded, and only three married couples were listed: 50-year-old Ah Kan and his 28-year-old wife Ah Run; Ah Lee, a 38-year-old cook and his 36-year-old wife Ching; and 44-year-old laundryman Ah Long and his 30-year-old wife Ah Law. The seasonal nature of the farm labor and the bachelor-oriented social milieu of the Maple/Union Chinatown were not conducive to raising families, and it was not until Chinatown moved across the river in 1888 that Chinese children first appeared in Watsonville.

## THE MOVE—1888

Legend has it that one dark night in 1888 a mob drove the Chinese in Watsonville "across the river" and into Monterey County. Both whites and Chinese in Watsonville re-tell the story today, with conviction. But the story remains glaringly inaccurate, out of place, a piece that will not fit the puzzle. The truth is almost exactly the opposite: following a series of delicate meetings, the Chinese voluntarily agreed to move across the river. Hardly a mob action. Yet both parties chose to alter the truth, and they continue doing so almost one hundred years later. We will first examine the historical record and then consider the versions of the myth kept alive by whites and Chinese.

Over the years periodic grumbling about Chinatown in the editorials of the Watsonville newspapers had focused primarily on the poor sanitation there. The Chinese often responded by cleaning up Chinatown. One such exchange occurred in 1874, beginning with a graphic editorial complaint about the Maple/ Union Chinatown:

> This delectable sink hole of barbarism and multitudinous stinks . . . poisons the balmy breeze for twice its area around with opium, hog

flesh, dead fowls, (the smell being) only second to the howling, and wrangling, and fighting of Chinamen and the lowest greasers and Indians. . . .

Stung by public opinion, the Chinese retaliated by piling all their trash in the center of Maple Street and setting it afire:

> . . . when the green, and black, and oily smoke rolled up toward the starry vault of heaven and the evening zephyrs gently wafted it to all parts of our beautiful town, people gasped and clawed at their hand-kerchiefs, and remarked 'whew' and thought of suicide. The stench was fearful, and in less than four minutes the streets were deserted even by the dogs, and a few belated buzzards, flying but a short distance over town, caught a breath of it and with dispairing [*sic*] squawks fell dead upon the earth.

The relationship between whites and Chinese in Watsonville often resembled a friendly joust, rarely reaching the viciousness and stridency which characterized white-Chinese relations else-where in the county and the state.

Events in 1888 brought into question the status of the twenty-year-old Maple/Union Chinatown. The announcement that Spreckels would locate his huge sugar beet processing plant in Watsonville meant that a large number of Chinese sugar beet workers could be expected to move into the Pajaro Valley, swell-ing an already bulging Chinatown and forcing the Chinese com-munity either to expand along Maple and Union Streets or to begin a second Chinatown elsewhere in Watsonville. Spreckels' announcement also touched off a healthy building boom in Wat-sonville, and a large tract just east of Chinatown, known as the Peckham and Hawkins tract, was ripe for development if the Chinese could be moved.

At a meeting of interested property owners held on February 11, 1888, a committee composed of J. W. Gally, H. S. Fletcher, N. McLean, A. B. Chalmers, and B. M. Bockius was formed to investigate the possibility of moving Chinatown to another site.

John T. Porter. Owner of the Maple/
Union Chinatown site and Brooklyn,
Porter was one of the first to recognize
the importance the Chinese would
have in Central California agriculture.
He championed the rights of the Chinese in Watsonville and in the courts of
San Francisco.          NANCY TALLEY

Citing both sanitary and business considerations, the committee
set out to find a solution which "would be mutually satisfactory
to all concerned." After several weeks of research the committee
presented its proposal to the Chinese community's leaders. The
plan was simple: Chinatown would be moved from the corner of
Maple and Union to a site just across the Pajaro River, owned by
John T. Porter. Most of the old buildings would be moved to the
new site, and all moving expenses plus the first three months'
rent for each Chinese making the move would be paid by the
Watsonville committee.

The Chinese responded by suggesting that an outside party be
invited to arbitrate the agreement. They asked Vice-Consul F. A.
Bee, the representative of the Chinese Imperial government in
San Francisco, to arbitrate and agreed to abide by his decision.
With the sinking feeling that once again they had been outmaneuvered, the town's leaders wrote a letter inviting Vice-
Consul Bee to Watsonville. "The Chinese are cunning and crafty,"
moaned the newspaper, "as the representative of the Chinese
government, the Consul's feelings will naturally incline to the
side of the [Chinese] whose interests he represents. . . ."

Vice-Consul Bee, accompanied by the head of the Chinese
Six Companies and a secretary, made an unprecedented trip to
Watsonville (it was the first time he had left San Francisco in five
years) to look over the arrangements and confer with the Chinese community. Bee and his companions viewed both sites and
observed that the new site was spacious and had better drainage.
After conferring with the Chinese community and convincing
several of the merchants that the move was in their best interest,
Bee extracted a unanimous vote of approval for the plan.

Porter quickly set to work laying out the main street for the
new Chinatown, letting contracts to build new buildings and
move old ones. Over the summer buildings were put on skids

and hauled down Union Street and across the river and placed in rows facing the new street. One story has it that several of the elderly Chinese actually rode to the new Chinatown in the buildings. "The old Chinese quarters look desolate since the removal of the Mongolians . . ." said the *Watsonville Pajaronian* in August, and on September 10 the last Chinese left the Maple/Union Street Chinatown.

The *Watsonville Pajaronian* described the move as "the first time in the history of the Pacific slope where Chinese have been removed from a community of their own consent. . . ." In the annals of nineteenth-century Chinese-white relations in California, no similar arrangements are recorded. Certainly, the event was unique in the Monterey Bay Region. Why did it happen in Watsonville?

First, John T. Porter, the owner of the Maple/Union Chinatown, owned an acceptable site large enough to accommodate the new Chinatown. That the site was close to Watsonville yet in another county was an added plus, for the new Chinatown would be outside the jurisdiction of either the Watsonville town council or the Santa Cruz County Board of Supervisors. Over the years Watsonville had passed dozens of ordinances attempting to control activities such as gambling, prostitution, opium smoking, and even kite flying, but usually enforcement was half-hearted. Now the burden of law enforcement shifted to Monterey County, and Watsonville had a clear conscience when the activities increased.

Second, a precedent for the move was set in 1885. Frustrated by the open cesspools behind the Chinese laundries, and inspired by anti-Chinese laundry ordinances in other cities, the Watsonville town council adopted an ordinance prohibiting Chinese from washing clothes within the town limits. Porter offered the laundrymen a site across the river to do their washing, so the

Chinese took in the laundry in Chinatown, washed it in temporary laundries set up in Pajaro, and then brought it back to Chinatown where it was ironed and returned to the customers.

Third, John T. Porter's leadership during the move was pivotal, for the Chinese trusted him; when the Chinese first heard of the committee's proposal to move Chinatown, they met with Porter to discuss it. As a landlord, Porter had a large financial stake in Chinatown, and the reliable income provided by his Chinese tenants motivated him to find a site on his property. But Porter was motivated by more than economics—he set this huge Chinatown within fifty yards of his own home. Porter had a history of aiding the Chinese, from testifying on their behalf during habeas corpus proceedings in San Francisco to attending Chinese weddings and funerals. His willingness to publicly befriend the Chinese took political courage as Porter was becoming increasingly involved in statewide Republican party politics in the 1880s. (When Porter's son, Warren R. Porter, became involved in state politics in the early twentieth century, his father's close relationship with the Chinese handicapped him; Warren was elected lieutenant-governor despite being branded a "Chinaman-lover.")

Fourth, Chinese Vice-Consul Bee's instrumental role as negotiator smoothed what could have been a very awkward situation. In later years Bee and Porter continued to act as arbiters. In 1891, when the Watsonville town council again began to harass the few Chinese laundrymen still operating on Main Street in Watsonville, Bee asked Porter to intercede on behalf of the Chinese. In a letter written April 16, 1891, Bee included a clipping describing a new Watsonville anti-laundry ordinance and asked Porter to inform the town council that the Chinese government would take the matter to court if the ordinance was not rescinded. "I am sorry to be compelled to go to war with my friends in Watsonville," Bee concluded. The town council backed down and "war" was averted.

Finally, the Chinese community in Watsonville had clout. Watsonville had hitched all its hopes and dreams to the success of Spreckels' sugar mill, and only with Chinese in the beet fields could the mill be supplied with sufficient sugar beets. By the late 1880s Chinese farm workers were the mainstay of California agriculture. The Watsonville situation was unique in that the Chinese were able to use their advantage because Watsonville needed the Chinese, and the Chinese knew it.

But the boast of Watsonville whites that they had "driven" the Chinese across the river persists to this day. Beginning with the first newspaper article heralding the arrival of Chinese farm laborers in the Pajaro Valley in 1866, Watsonville farmers had found themselves apologizing for the presence of the Chinese, explaining that it was "necessary" to bring them into the valley because no one else was available to do the work. In the beginning it was only necessary to defend the use of Chinese farm laborers to other Watsonville residents, but when the anti-Chinese movement swept through California in the 1870s, Watsonville became increasingly embarrassed about the extensive use of Chinese laborers in the Pajaro Valley.

While arch-rival Santa Cruz fired salvo after anti-Chinese salvo in its strident and bitter newspaper, the *Santa Cruz Sentinel*, Watsonville's anti-Chinese guns remained mute and feeble. Watsonville knew just how valuable the Chinese were to the Pajaro Valley economy. When Workingmen's Party clubs were formed throughout California in 1878, Watsonville also formed a chapter. But members were required not to employ Chinese labor in their businesses. Thus, in July of 1878, the Watsonville Workingmen's Party passed a rule making it acceptable for members to employ Chinese labor. Santa Cruz sneered.

The citizens of Watsonville disliked the idea of continued Chinese immigration just as much as their Santa Cruz counterparts—only one Watsonville citizen voted in favor of Chinese immigration in the 1879 referendum. The farmers would have employed others to do the work in the fields, but they could find no one else willing to pick the berries, thin the beets, or pick the hops. And Watsonville's long-standing rivalry with the manufacturing town of Santa Cruz strengthened the farmers' opposition to the anti-Chinese movement. When Watsonville opposed the Santa Cruz campaign to boycott Chinese laborers (which would have crippled the Pajaro Valley) in the "Strawberry Rebellion" of 1886, it gained a reputation for being pro-Chinese.

But the Watsonville newspaper supplied other motives for the opposition to the boycott:

> The Pajaro Valley does not want the Chinese any more than does any other section, but the people of this community believe that . . . in this free country no body of men should tell their fellow citizens what they should or should not do.

As noble as it may sound, the freedom of action argument obscured Watsonville's real feelings. Watsonville found it necessary to explain its need for Chinese laborers continually and to reassure neighboring communities (and itself) that it disliked the Chinese just as much as the next town. This embarrassment of need, in the eyes of white Watsonville, illustrated a fundamental weakness in the economic and social fabric of California agriculture.

The watershed year of 1888 provided Watsonville with two opportunities to restore some of its civic pride. First, it had captured the largest sugar beet factory in North America, and second it had "solved" its Chinese "problem." As the Chinese moved across the river in July, the *Watsonville Pajaronian* puffed, "Watsonville will be the first town in the country to effect a peaceful removal of the Chinese." "Removal" implies that Watsonville had forced the Chinese to leave town, and in later years the story grew to include a mob chasing the Chinese into Monterey County. In Phil Francis' *Beautiful Santa Cruz County*, published in 1896, the Chinatown in North Monterey County was described as an "undesirable lot of being" which was once in Watsonville until, by ordinance, it "was made to move out." In 1964 a Monterey writer claimed that Watsonville "passed an ordinance to the effect that 'The Chinese Must Go. They Must Leave Watsonville.'"

Watsonville went to extremes to obscure the fact that it had treated the Chinese as equals during the negotiations and that it needed the Chinese to maintain its sugar beet industry. Given the anti-Chinese feeling throughout the state, the town dared not admit the truth. Embarrassment of need continued to affect policy in the Pajaro Valley during each successive wave of farm laborers, whether they were from Japan, the Philippines, Oklahoma, or Mexico.

The Chinese embellished the myth much later, when Japanese farm laborers began coming into the Pajaro Valley in the 1890s. The new immigrants lived for a brief time in Chinatown before boldly moving across the river into Watsonville and establishing a vigorous Japantown on south Main Street. To save face and explain their presence in the Chinatown across the river from Watsonville, the Chinese began repeating the story that whites had been telling all those years—the myth of the mob became a convenient explanation. Explaining and posturing aside, the move across the river benefited the Chinese. There was room to grow in the new Chinatown, and far from being embarrassed about their new quarters, the Chinese exhibited considerable cultural and community pride during the decade from 1888 to 1898.

## BROOKLYN'S EARLY YEARS

The Watsonville Chinese moved across the river in the summer of 1888 imbued with a new sense of confidence and optimism: they had been dealt with as equals by Watsonville's political leaders; they had been important enough to warrant the special attention of Vice-Consul Bee; and they were confident that Spreckels' new sugar beet factory would provide employment in the sugar beet fields for all who wanted it. At a time when horizons were narrowing for many other Chinese communities in California, the Watsonville Chinese community faced a secure and exciting future. The Chinatown that moved across the river was primarily a labor camp designed to service the needs of seasonal Chinese farm laborers. Where the Point Alones fishing village began with families and added a single-male population later, Watsonville began with single males, and only in the 1890s did children and families make their appearance there.

An interesting collection of merchants, laborers, and gamblers moved across the river and into Monterey County during the summer of 1888, and perhaps as a fitting symbol of its rough-edged quality, the Chinatown was nicknamed Brooklyn. The explanation most often given for the origin of the name Brooklyn was that the relationship between the new Chinatown and Watsonville was similar to that between Brooklyn and Manhattan—the rough, ethnic neighborhood across the river from the heart of the city. The name Brooklyn was applied both to the entire Chinatown and the main street which John T. Porter had laid out in the summer of 1888; both white and Chinese old-timers in Watsonville still refer to the Pajaro Chinatown as Brooklyn. When the Chinatown was subdivided and sold in 1933, the name Brooklyn was officially given to the main street and it survives to this day.

Brooklyn began as a wide dirt street beginning just south of the Pajaro River bridge, with a row of buildings on each side of the main street. Later development east along San Juan Road turned the Chinese community into something of an inverted L, but the heart of the community was always the main street. In

September 1888, the first month that the Porters collected rents in the new town, sixteen buildings lined the east side of the street and twenty lined the west side. Over the years several buildings were added at the south end of the street until the street reached its maximum size of forty-two buildings just prior to the fire in 1924.

Approximately fifty yards south of Brooklyn stood the John T. Porter family home, a large hodgepodge of early Californian and Victorian architecture which eventually grew to be a three-story, twenty-three-room mansion. Some of the optimism felt by the Chinese as they moved into Brooklyn in the fall of 1888 resulted from the security they felt as tenants of the Porters. Though the flavor of the manor and the serfs characterized the relationship between the Porters and the Chinese, the strong bond of mutual respect was genuine. Porter had been something of a distant landlord when Chinatown was on his Maple/Union

Brooklyn Chinatown, c. 1900. Looking north on Brooklyn Street towards the Pajaro River and Watsonville. Chee Kong Tong temple is on far left. Wooden crossing planks on the street kept Chinese occupants dry when the street turned to mud in the winter.

PAJARO VALLEY HISTORICAL
ASSOCIATION

193

*Left*: Frances Cummins Porter. Mrs. Porter collected the rents from the tenants of Brooklyn and was regarded fondly by the Chinese living there.
BERNICE PORTER

*Right*: A page from the Brooklyn Ledger Book, January 1889. Mrs. Porter wrote each resident's name, the date, and the amount paid each month until the fire of 1924.      BERNICE PORTER

194

lot in Watsonville, but after 1888 the Chinese lived almost in his yard. Porter, the owner of both the land and the buildings, constructed the newer buildings to the specifications of the Chinese tenants. The return on his investment included rents from the thirty-six buildings ranging from three to ten dollars per month depending on their size; the rents were collected each month by John T. Porter's wife, Frances Cummins Porter. Porter family tradition has it that Mrs. Porter was allowed to keep the Brooklyn rents for her personal spending money, which would help explain the devotion she showed to her task; for thirty-six years, Mrs. Porter toured Brooklyn each month, entering the name of the tenant and the rent collected in her personal ledger book.

Mrs. Porter's monthly rent-collection trip through Brooklyn in a black carriage is still a vivid part of the memories of Chinese who lived there.

In addition to a practical interest in having Chinatown close to his extensive farm holdings in the Pajaro Valley, John T. Porter had a mutually affectionate relationship with the Chinese. Porter often testified for the Chinese in their frequent brushes with the immigration officials. Mrs. Porter kept two buildings on Brooklyn's main street as rent-free hostels for older single men who were unable to pay their rent, and over the years she developed many close ties with the Brooklyn Chinese. Her death inspired an outpouring of affection from her Chinese tenants, and even today, older Chinese who grew up in Brooklyn remember her with respect and affection. The Porters were partially responsible for Brooklyn's growth into one of the largest Chinatowns in California.

Because Brooklyn was located on the far-flung northern border of Monterey County, the county's law enforcement officials tended to overlook many of the illegal activities going on there. But the county also overlooked the border when it was allocating funds for improvements to bridges and roads or for levees for flood control. The Pajaro River bridge was often in good repair from Watsonville to its center span but shabby from there to the south bank; at one time the bridge was covered on the Santa Cruz County side, but open to the elements on the Monterey County side. Funds were short for bridge repair and non-existent for flood control. Brooklyn experienced the first of many floods in January 1890, when four feet of water flowed through the town, and the main street became a torrent. Floods became part of Brooklyn's seasonal rhythm (as they did in Chinatowns in Santa Cruz and Salinas), and just as their counterparts in China watched the Yangtze and Hwang rivers with apprehension, the Chinese in Brooklyn always kept a weather eye on the Pajaro River during winter rains; when the river reached flood

Key to House No. 32- Chinatown- Pajaro Monterey County

A key from Brooklyn.

BERNICE PORTER

Brooklyn Chinatown, Flood, 1911. Looking south on Brooklyn Street (Chee Kong Tong temple at far end of row on the right). Brooklyn flooded almost every winter, and most residents moved their belongings to the second floors of the buildings until the water subsided. There are two people standing on second-floor balconies halfway down the row of buildings on the right.

stage, the Chinese moved their belongings to the second stories of the town's buildings and moved them back when the waters receded.

Thus, the responsibility for providing most of the municipal services in Brooklyn fell to its owner, John T. Porter. Fire was a much more serious threat to the town than flooding, and in 1890 Porter moved to protect the town by forming a volunteer fire department. Since Brooklyn was in Monterey County, the Watsonville Fire Department could not be counted on to cross the bridge into another county to fight a fire. Porter purchased an old tournament fire cart from the Watsonville department, and after buying hose and equipment to go with it, he turned the cart and the organization of the fire department over to Hop Yick, one of Brooklyn's leading merchants. Hop Yick scheduled the fire department's first fire drill to coincide with the 1890 lunar New Year festivities, but the flood delayed the drill until early February 1890. Word of the scheduled fire drill spread quickly

196

Brooklyn Chinatown, 1906. Photo taken at the intersection of Brooklyn Street and San Juan Road looking east down San Juan Road. Crack was caused by the May 1906 earthquake.
GEORGE RIDER

through Watsonville, and hundreds of spectators came across the bridge to watch the new Chinese fire company in action. When Hop Yick saw the size of the crowd, he called off the fire drill, much to the disappointment of the assembled spectators. The *Watsonville Pajaronian* grumped that the modesty of the Chinese fire department "spoiled a good show."

When the Brooklyn fire department was called out to fight its first fire in June 1892, it quickly put out a fire in a burning barn, saving the barn (and perhaps the entire town) from destruction. The newspaper observed, "John T. Porter made a good investment when he purchased the hose cart for them."

Porter also provided security in the form of two security guards, George and Allen Riley. The Rileys patrolled Brooklyn at night and saw that neither the peace nor the law was violated. The Rileys developed an early reputation for rousting vagrants and keeping opium smoking and prostitution confined to Brooklyn.

## ORGANIZATION OF WATSONVILLE'S CHINATOWN

While Porter attempted to provide at least some of the municipal services the Chinese had lost by moving onto private property, the Chinese created an internal organization to replace the traditional family system which they had left behind in China. Dozens of organizations within the Chinese communities in California were organized along a variety of social, political, and economic lines, and though Watsonville had its own bewildering collection of societies, it was based on a three-tiered organization.

The individual Chinese represented the first tier. The second tier included a variety of societies, some based on Chinese districts-of-origin, some based on politics, and others organized around recreational activities such as gambling and prostitution. The individual Chinese usually belonged to at least one and often several of these societies, most of which were headquartered in San Francisco. A representative body composed of elected delegates from each of these societies composed the third tier of organization, most commonly called the Chinese Association, or Chinese Benevolent Association. This Association settled disputes between the various societies and attempted to represent the entire Watsonville Chinese community to the outside world with a single voice.

Beyond Watsonville the Chinese Consolidated Benevolent Association (commonly known as the Chinese Six Companies) in San Francisco acted as representatives to the United States government for the Chinese throughout California. This intricate spider web of organizations and societies yielded to prevailing political winds, and the evolution of Watsonville's community structure and its relationship with the Chinese Six Companies provide some insights into the workings of a rural Chinese community in California.

During its early years on the corner of Maple and Union, the Watsonville Chinatown was under almost direct control of the Six Companies and had little internal organization or strength. However, in the mid-1880s the need for a strong voice to represent the interests of the Watsonville community became apparent, and a Chinese Association was formed to represent the needs of the community, particularly during the negotiations surrounding the move in 1888. At the time of the move, the Watsonville Chinese community went directly to the Chinese Vice-Consul for advice, rather than to the Chinese Six Companies.

Once Chinatown moved across the river, the recreational activities increased, and the tongs that controlled gambling and prostitution grew in influence. The most influential society within the Chinese Association in the early 1890s was the Chee Kong Tong. Also known as the Chinese Freemasons (it had no formal connection with the Masons), or the Triads, the Chee Kong Tong began as a secret political organization in China but evolved into a more broadly based recreational society in America. In a Chinatown composed almost exclusively of single Chinese males, tongs such as the Chee Kong Tong dominated the Chinese Association.

The struggle over the implementation of the Geary Act during 1893–94 sheds light on the network of relationships between the tongs and the Chinese Six Companies in San Francisco. Signed into law by the President in May 1892, the Geary Act extended the Chinese Exclusion Act of 1882 and placed further restrictions on Chinese already in the United States. The most onerous of the Geary Act's new restrictions required that all Chinese laborers residing in the United States register with the United States government by May 1893 and obtain certificates of residence. The government intended to sharpen the distinction between laborers and merchants so that the Chinese could not move easily from one category to the other or circumvent the immigration restrictions against them. Chinese laborers failing to register faced deportation. The Chinese Six Companies felt the Geary Act was unconstitutional and immediately challenged it with a test case; the Six Companies advised all Chinese laborers not to register until the case had been tried.

In the spring of 1893, as the deadline for registration drew near, the *Watsonville Pajaronian* observed that pressure from the Six Companies on local Chinese had resulted in their "not rushing for the registration office." Underscoring the importance of the Chinese to the Pajaro Valley economy, the newspaper also noted that their deportation would have left the valley "considerably crippled for some time." Chinese labor contractors faced the loss of lucrative sugar beet and berry contracts if the unregistered laborers were deported, and they tried to convince the laborers to register before the deadline. The Chee Kong Tong led the group pushing for registration, while the Six Companies in San Francisco led the effort against. Caught between these two organizations, the Chinese laborers asked for a meeting to help clarify the issues.

On Monday, April 10, a mass meeting was held in Brooklyn. John T. Porter was invited by the Chinese to present his views, and he encouraged the Chinese to consider the large financial stake they had in staying in the Pajaro Valley (not to mention his own interest) and the losses that would result should they be deported to China. As a result of the meeting, the Chinese Association sent a delegation composed of Porter, Quong Yuen Lung, and Lum Sang to San Francisco to discuss the registration issue with Vice-Consul Bee and the Chinese Six Companies. The wishes of the Six Companies prevailed, and despite the exhortations of Porter and the Chee Kong Tong, few of the Watsonville Chinese registered.

The Six Companies' position was partly based on the belief that the Geary Act would be held unconstitutional, but in a decision that surprised almost everyone, the United States Supreme

Court upheld the constitutionality of the Geary Act in May 1893. "Great big hunks of gloom" settled over Brooklyn on hearing news of the decision, because most of the Chinese had been confident the act would be overturned. A new deadline was set for registration in the spring of 1894, and this time the Six Companies encouraged Chinese laborers to register. Charles E. Peckham was appointed Registrar of Chinese for Santa Cruz, San Benito, and Monterey counties, and beginning in January 1894 he toured his district and registered an estimated 1,100 Chinese laborers as required.

The political struggle over whether to comply with the Geary Act demonstrated that the Watsonville Chinese community, perhaps strengthened by its negotiating experience in the move, did not simply obey the tongs or Porter, whose influence it had respected enough to send him as one of its representatives to San Francisco. The Chinese Six Companies were tarnished by the Geary Act episode, while the Chee Kong Tong became the single most important society within Watsonville's Chinese Association.

## THE TONGS IN BROOKLYN

In the popular mind the tongs were sinister organizations dedicated to violence and evil, yet in practice they resembled guilds. Most tong members merely worked for the organization as professional gamblers and bookkeepers. The Chee Kong Tong, or the Triads, probably exerted the greatest influence in nineteenth-century Brooklyn. Though this tong sometimes dabbled in gambling or prostitution, its primary objective was political and ceremonial. In most communities the tong had a fraternal hall which also doubled as a temple, or "joss house," and this secret society conducted highly ceremonious rituals. (Note: "joss" is a

202

Sign which was posted by the Porter family in Brooklyn.

BERNICE PORTER

# WARNING

## TO WHOM IT MAY CONCERN:

Brooklyn, Chinatown, is PRIVATE PROPERTY. And warning is hereby issued that all persons not having business herein with the residents thereof, will be regarded as TRESPASSERS.

This warning applies to persons not tenants, and those not patronizing stores or restaurants. Loitering around Chinatown will not be tolerated under any circumstances.

### L. J. LAWRENCE
Constable Pajaro Township, Monterey Cou

corruption of the Portuguese word *deus*, used by Portuguese in China to refer to God or God Houses.) Non-Chinese observers, struck by the obvious similarity between the Chee Kong Tong and the Masonic order, dubbed it the Chinese Freemasons.

Active in Brooklyn's 1893–94 debate over registering for the Geary Act, the Chee Kong Tong consolidated its growing influence by building a temple in January 1895. Mrs. Porter did not collect rent for the new Chee Kong Tong headquarters (#44 Brooklyn Street—see map 7-2) so it is likely that the Chee Kong Tong paid for its construction. (Mrs. Porter did not charge rent to any group, such as missionaries, using a building for religious purposes.) Hop Yick returned from China that fall with the temple "trimmings," and the temple was dedicated to the God of Literature, Kuan Kung, who was also known as the God of Peace and War.

Like most Chinese temples in California, the Brooklyn temple was a two-story building with the sanctuary located upstairs.

The temple was tended by a retired Chee Kong Tong member who lit incense to the deity each day and maintained the building. Chinese might come to the temple to seek advice from the deity or make an offering to him, but other than the primary lunar calendar festivals, or the festival of Kuan Kung's birthday in June, the sanctuary was generally deserted. Downstairs, particularly during the busy summer season when Brooklyn was filled with farm laborers, the tong kept a hostel where members might stay if they had no other place.

In contrast, "highbinder" tongs (so called to distinguish them from regular fraternal societies such as the Chee Kong Tong) represented a small but noisy percentage of the tong membership. These tongs controlled gambling, prostitution, and opium traffic. From their San Francisco headquarters, the tongs exercised much more direct control over these activities in rural Chinese communities than did the Six Companies. The two highbinder tongs which seemed to have had the most influence in Watsonville were the Suey Sing Tong and the Bing Kong Tong, and before World War II most of the Chinese-operated gambling halls were controlled by one of these two organizations.

When rival tongs came into conflict in San Francisco, those conflicts were often mirrored in small towns like Watsonville. But the infamous "tong wars," which have been exaggerated out of proportion to their real importance, only rarely spilled over into Brooklyn. In July 1890, for example, the newspaper noted that "Little Pete," a famous highbinder from San Francisco, was visiting Brooklyn. In October 1892 five San Francisco highbinders came into Brooklyn and fired eight shots at a Chinese resident. All eight shots missed (one put a hole in the intended victim's cap), and in the resulting scuffle, three of the highbinders were arrested and held over for trial. Because no one in Brooklyn would testify against the three, the charges were reduced to simple assault, resulting in a fifty dollar fine and their release. Until the 1890s, when they shifted their attention to the social and ceremonial activity befitting a family community, the tongs catered to the vices of the male laborers quartered in Brooklyn.

## GAMBLING, PROSTITUTION, AND OPIUM SMOKING

In the traditional Chinese view of the universe, fate's hand was at the tiller and life was a gamble. For most nineteenth-century Chinese it was better to be born lucky than clever. The Chinese courted fate through astrologers, soothsayers, geomancers, and gambling. The Chinese in the Monterey Bay Region were no exception, and one of the earliest institutions to form in each of the area's Chinatowns was the gambling hall. Wherever a large group of Chinese laborers congregated, somewhere, somehow, gambling went on. Any event could be bet on, but the most attractive bets (and games) revolved around randomness rather than skill. Nothing could substitute for luck.

For the Chinese laborer facing weeks, months, and even years of hard work before he would accumulate enough money to go into business or return to China, the lure of gambling proved irresistible. Possibly more than any other single factor, the agricultural laborer's gambling losses kept him tied to the labor contractors, money lenders, and field work. As the foremost American expert on Chinese gambling, Stewart Culin, noted in 1891, "the mass of the people . . . are often compelled to stay on far beyond the time they would otherwise remain in this country." The only sure winner in the gambling games was the house.

The two most popular Chinese gambling games in California in the nineteenth and early twentieth centuries were *fan tan* and *pok kop pew*. These simple games were based on predicting a number which was selected by chance. In *fan tan*, which translates as "repeatedly spreading out," the bettor tried to guess how many objects (beans, coins) would remain from a pile after groups of four were removed:

> The expressionless Oriental . . . would take a handful of white buttons from a jar at his side, cast them in a heap upon the table, and slide a bronze or copper cup over them. The gamblers would then make their bets, placing their money upon whatever numeral they would—and "fannin" it or not, as they pleased. The [dealer] would lift the lid and silently begin counting the buttons in groups of four, this by means of a piece of thin, curved bamboo. Those whose bets tallied with the last number of buttons won.

While *fan tan* was generally a low-stakes, steady game requiring a streak of luck to win a large sum, in the lottery a single stroke of luck meant winning hundreds and even thousands of dollars. The bettor attempted to guess which of twenty numbers would be drawn from a pool of eighty. The lottery's Chinese name, *pok kop pew*, or the "white pigeon ticket," derived from an original Chinese game played with racing birds. The lottery (the predecessor of the Nevada gambling game called Keno) had a great appeal for the non-Chinese, because it was extremely straightforward:

> The lottery, perhaps, was the most colorful and alluring game for the stranger. Here one placed his money, marked out a given number of Chinese characters on the lottery ticket and awaited his doom or his making. His doom or making was contained in the sing-song voice of an Oriental, who read the winning tickets. As he read, another would punch out the holes on the lottery tags. Those whose numbers corresponded with the punched holes, won. Those whose numbers differed, swallowed hard and went out for a breath of air.

Gambling had been widely practiced in Watsonville's Chinatown before 1888, but when the town moved into the legal

Lottery ticket from Brooklyn, *c.* 1920. Gamblers bet on the characters they believed would be selected in a random drawing of twenty. The symbols are the first eighty characters from a classical Chinese poem. The poem was read from top to bottom, right to left. "Capital $2,000" refers to the aggregate limit of the pay-offs for the particular game, and "N. T." stands for night ticket to help dissuade counterfeiters. Called *pok kop pew* (white pigeon ticket), the lottery evolved into present-day Keno which is played in Nevada.                BETTY LEWIS limbo of northern Monterey County, the number of gambling halls increased until Brooklyn gained a reputation as a major gambling center, perhaps second only to Chinatown, San Francisco. It is difficult to measure just how many gambling halls operated in Brooklyn at any given time, because games were often set up in stores and boarding houses at a moment's notice and lasted only until someone broke the bank. An observer recalled, "In those [early] days gambling games were conducted in little rear rooms. Many thousands of dollars in gold passed hands—often from the white hand to the yellow—and often, too, from yellow to white."

The tempo of gambling in Brooklyn was tied to the seasonal rhythm of agriculture in the Pajaro Valley. During the summer months when many of the laborers lived in the country near the fields, they spent their one day off each week in Chinatown: "Brooklyn is deserted except on Sundays. The lottery and gambling games are quiet, and the Mongolian quarter bustles but once a week." After contracts were paid off in the fall, the games increased until they reached a crescendo in the weeks before the lunar New Year celebration. After the New Year the gaming pulse slowed until the flow of early summer cash speeded it up again.

The New Year gambling frenzy was caused in part by the Chinese tradition of settling outstanding debts before the year's end. Bettors hoped that the next game, the next draw, would bring the luck to pay off the debts, but luck rarely paid the bills. They then had to turn to Chinese money lenders, and many Chinese laborers found themselves working the next year to pay off the money lender. The laborers' contracts in the sugar beets or berry fields made them a good risk, but the 10% per month interest rates (120% annual interest rates!) charged by the moneylenders were excruciating, and each year the laborers became further entangled in the financial web, getting farther and farther

behind. The farther behind the Chinese laborer fell, the more attractive the gambling tables became, as they offered an instant
solution.

*Fan tan* and lotteries were illegal in California in the 1890s, but
suppression of the Brooklyn games was intermittent. If most patrons at the tables were Chinese and the violence was minimal,
the authorities in Monterey County ignored the gambling. But
if the number of Watsonville whites going into the gambling
halls increased, then the alarm went up in the editorial pages of
the newspaper, and a crackdown followed. In 1893, an observation by the *Watsonville Pajaronian* that "the Chinese lottery games
across the river are being well patronized at present by Watsonville people," was followed within the week by a raid on Brooklyn. A week later the games reopened. Occasionally Chinese
who felt they were being cheated in the games would call in the
law, and on at least one occasion, Chinese merchants who felt
that the games were cutting into their legitimate grocery business complained publicly. Generally, however, Brooklyn was
treated as a pleasure island, beyond Watsonville's legal and moral
horizon, but conveniently reached by the Pajaro River Bridge.
The periodic clucking by the newspaper did little to stem the
flow of Watsonville residents back and forth across the bridge
under cover of darkness.

Prostitution was common in most California Chinatowns,
and one Chinese-American historian has estimated that 1,452 of
the 1,769 Chinese women in San Francisco in 1870 were prostitutes. Although less prevalent than gambling, prostitution was
endemic in Brooklyn. Fights over prostitutes would sometimes
break out and bring public attention to the houses, but for the
most part, the houses did not draw comment unless white women
were found working there. In 1897 "a number of white women
were openly cohabiting with the Chinamen," and the constables
swooped down and drove them out of Brooklyn. Once the

white prostitutes had been driven away, the editor of the newspaper suggested that the six lotteries operating in Brooklyn should also be closed down, but his suggestion was not followed. Chinese who grew up in Brooklyn in the early twentieth century remember the houses of prostitution, and at least one interviewee claimed that prostitution was common there even after the second Chinatown fire in 1933.

Opium smoking was also common in Brooklyn, though most interviewees believed that it was confined mainly to the older Chinese men living out their lives alone. As with prostitution, Watsonville did not complain about the practice unless whites were involved. Soon after the 1888 move the Riley brothers made a concerted effort to keep the "fiends" from crossing the bridge to smoke opium. The Chinese opium peddlers responded by setting up a system of sentinels around Brooklyn to warn of approaching law officers. The editor of the *Watsonville Pajaronian* applauded the Riley brothers' effort, but few arrests were ever made.

## BROOKLYN IN THE MID-1890s—FROM LABOR CAMP TO COMMUNITY

Reconstructing Brooklyn from the archival record is like making a rubbing of a coin on a piece of paper—each stroke gives a little better definition, but the image is always vague. It is possible to partially reconstruct the businesses active in Brooklyn in the mid-1890s using assessor's records and Frances Porter's ledger book. At least fifteen grocery and general merchandise businesses lined the main street, including Bow Ching Chong Co., Fong Lee Co., Gee Lee Co., Hop Yick, Quong Chong, Sue San Lung, Sun Wy Kee, Sun Yuen Co., Tong Hop Chong Kee Co., Wing Wo Lung Co., and the Yuk Kee Co. There were two drug-

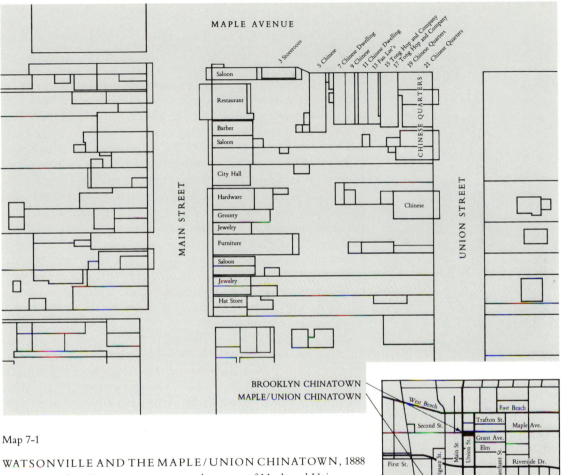

MAPLE AVENUE

3 Storeroom
5 Chinese
7 Chinese Dwelling
9 Chinese
11 Chinese Dwelling
13 Fan Lee's
15 Tong Hop and Company
17 Tong Hop and Company
19 Chinese Quarters
21 Chinese Quarters

Saloon

Restaurant

Barber

Saloon

City Hall

Hardware

Grocery

Jewelry

Furniture

Saloon

Jewelry

Hat Store

CHINESE QUARTERS

Chinese

MAIN STREET

UNION STREET

BROOKLYN CHINATOWN
MAPLE/UNION CHINATOWN

Map 7-1

WATSONVILLE AND THE MAPLE/UNION CHINATOWN, 1888

Watsonville's first Chinatown grew up on the corner of Maple and Union soon
after Maple Street was opened in 1865. The property and buildings were owned
by John T. Porter. The community grew as the region's agriculture diversified,
and by the mid-1880s, the corner was no longer large enough to accommodate
the Chinatown. After some delicate negotiations, the community moved across
the Pajaro River in the summer of 1888. Map derived from Sanborn Map Company maps, Map Library, UCSC.

stores (Bow Tie Wo Co., Yuen Him Co.) and one restaurant (Sun Yin Bi).

When Chinese residents of the United States returned after visits to China, immigration officials assumed that they were illegal immigrants until they proved otherwise. Upon filing a writ of habeas corpus, the Chinese went into United States District Court and submitted to lengthy cross-examination by government prosecutors in which they had to prove that they had been in the United States before and that they had been neither laborers nor laundrymen. The government interviewed the Chinese to the benefit of historians, and though the process was discriminatory and dreadful for the Chinese returning from China, the resulting records document, sometimes in minute detail, the Chinatowns of California. We are fortunate to have one such habeas corpus case involving a Watsonville merchant, Ng Yee Yick (also known as Ng Men Ngim), and the testimony he gave in 1894 provides a glimpse of the operation of a Chinese store in Brooklyn and the relationship of the Chinese merchants to the Watsonville white community.

Born in China, Ng Yee Yick came to California in 1876, and for the first eight years of his residency in the United States, he was a farm laborer. In 1884 Ng Yee Yick and a partner, Ng Moon Kai, set up a business in the Maple/Union Chinatown in Watsonville which Ng Yee Yick characterized as a "general merchandise" store. The two partners moved the store across the river to Brooklyn in 1888, and by 1890 Ng Yee Yick had enough financial security to make a return visit to China. He began preparing for his journey in November 1890, wishing to get back to China in time for the lunar New Year festivities in early 1891. Knowing that he had to have a certificate attesting to his previous residence in order to be re-admitted into the United States, Ng Yee Yick had L. D. Holbrook, a Watsonville notary, prepare

Ng Yee Yick, 1890. Partner in the store Yee Yick, Ng visited China in 1890 and was allowed to re-enter the U.S. in 1894 after submitting to a rigorous habeas corpus hearing in San Francisco.                    NATIONAL ARCHIVES

a document which stated in part that "We the undersigned hereby certify that we have known Yee Yick . . . for the last ten years . . . and that he is a merchant doing business in Pajaro." Ng Yee Yick then had A. T. Dresser, the town's Wells Fargo Agent, John T. Porter, Julius Lee, a prominent attorney, and Cyrus Short, Deputy Sheriff, sign the certificate. The cross-section of signators selected by Ng Yee Yick represents the most trust-worthy men in Watsonville at that time. Before departing for China, Ng Yee Yick also had his certificate countersigned by King Owyang, the Chinese Vice-Consul in San Francisco.

All those gilt-edged signatures meant nothing upon his return in June 1894. He was confined onboard ship until he could hire attorney T. D. Riordan, a specialist in Chinese immigration pro-ceedings. On June 6, 1894, Ng Yee Yick was questioned through a translator and under oath by W. G. Witter, the Commissioner for the United States government. After establishing that his name was Ng Yee Yick and that he had traveled to China in 1890, Ng Yee Yick described his business in Watsonville:

Q.  Does the firm of Yee Yick engage in any other business than the business of provisions and general merchandise?

A.  Well, we deal in Chinese merchandise, provisions, sell liquors and sell cigarettes, and so forth.

Q.  Is there any other business besides merchandise conducted in the same building or store occupied by the firm of Yee Yick?

A.  No, sir.

Q.  How many Chinese stores are there in Watsonville?

A.  Well, I should say between thirty and forty.

Q.  You consider every building occupied by Chinese a Chinese store?

A.  They are stores.

Q.  Do you know any white people in Watsonville?

A.  Yes, sir.

Q.  Who do you know there?

A.  Mr. Holbrook, Mr. Short, Mr. Julius Lee and Mr. Porter.

Q. Do you know any persons down there except those who signed
   your paper?
A. Well, I do not know any others because I had to keep the books
   of the firm and did not go out a great deal.
Q. What is the name of your partner?
A. Ng Moon Kai.
Q. What are the names of the two men you employ?
A. Yee Ah Gong and Ng Cheung.
Q. They have no interest of any kind in the store?
A. No, Sir. They only work there for wages.

What begins to emerge from the testimony is a picture of the
narrowness of the Chinese world in Brooklyn and its nearly
complete separation from the white world in Watsonville. Later
that day, Ng Yee Yick's partner was called to the witness stand,
and during his session of cross-examination, he explained that
the company also provided room and board for Chinese farm
laborers:

Q. And you board them there in the store, do you?
A. Well, the people that stop in our store buy their stuff from us
   and do their own cooking.
Q. How many people lived there at any one time in your store?
A. Sometimes three or four and sometimes ten or so.
Q. Did you ever have more than ten on hand at any one time?
A. Sometimes we have more.
Q. How many did you have at the most?
A. Fourteen or fifteen.
Q. Who did you contract labor with?
A. All kinds of ranches and farms.
Q. Do you remember any men to whom you contracted your la-
   bor out to?
A. Mr. Carson.
Q. Any one else?
A. Mr. Porter.
Q. What labor do you furnish him?
A. He hired sometimes—according to how his crops are. He hired
   lots of our men to stack hay.

Later testimony from Ng King, the manager of a Chinese wholesale business in San Francisco, revealed that Yee Yick & Co. purchased upwards of one thousand dollars worth of goods per month from the wholesaler, most of it Chinese merchandise. Ng Yee Yick was allowed to re-enter the United States and he returned to Brooklyn to continue his business.

The 1890s saw several of the established residents of Brooklyn marry and begin families; as some of the older, China-born pioneers returned to China or died, a new generation of Brooklyn-born Chinese children were born to take their place. In 1896 the newspaper noted "a small army of Chinese children" in Brooklyn, and the first Chinese boy began attending public school in Watsonville in 1897. Watsonville's Chinatown did not become a community of families until a good twenty-five years after the Point Alones fishing village, primarily because of the transitory

Skeptical Chinese boy, Brooklyn Chinatown, c. 1895. One of the first photographs of a child in Brooklyn. Photo taken looking north toward Pajaro River bridge and Watsonville.

PAJARO VALLEY HISTORICAL
ASSOCIATION

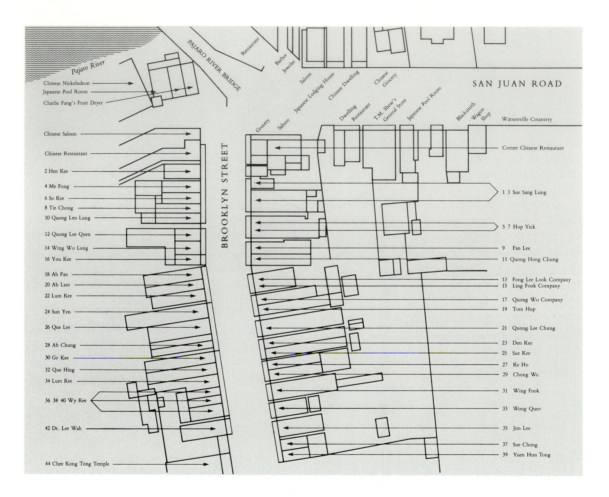

Pajaro River

PAJARO RIVER BRIDGE

Restaurant

Barber
Jeweler
Saloon
Japanese Lodging House
Chinese Dwelling
Chinese Grocery

SAN JUAN ROAD

Chinese Nickelodeon →
Japanese Pool Room →
Charlie Fang's Fruit Dryer →

Grocery
Saloon
Dwelling
Restaurant
T.M. Shew's General Store
Japanese Pool Room
Blacksmith
Wagon Shop
Watsonville Creamery

BROOKLYN STREET

Chinese Saloon

Chinese Restaurant

2 Hen Kee

4 Me Fong

6 So Kee

8 Tie Chong

10 Quong Len Lung

12 Quong Lee Quen

14 Wing Wo Lung

16 You Kee

18 Ah Fan

20 Ah Lam

22 Lum Kee

24 Sun Yen

26 Que Lee

28 Ah Chung

30 Go Kee

32 Que Hing

34 Lum Kee

36 38 40 Wy Kee

42 Dr. Lee Wah

44 Chee Kong Tong Temple

Corner Chinese Restaurant

1 3 Sue Sang Lung

5 7 Hop Yick

9 Fan Lee

11 Quong Hong Chung

13 Fong Lee Look Company

15 Ling Fook Company

17 Quong Wo Company

19 Tom Hop

21 Quong Lee Chung

23 Den Kee

25 Sue Kee

27 Ke Ho

29 Chong Wo

31 Wing Fook

33 Wong Quen

35 Jim Lee

37 Sue Chong

39 Yuen Hun Tong

Map 7-2

BROOKLYN CHINATOWN, c. 1900

Watsonville's Chinese community thrived after moving to this site in 1888. The names on the buildings were taken from Frances C. Porter's rent receipt books. Map derived from Sanborn Map Company maps, Map Library, UCSC.

214

nature of agricultural work in the Pajaro Valley before 1888. Not until the move to Brooklyn and the construction of Spreckels' giant sugar factory, which promised the Chinese a future, did Brooklyn have a temple (the temples in Salinas and Monterey pre-date Brooklyn's by at least a decade) or a mission school.

Brooklyn's growth in the late 1890s was also spurred by another development in the Pajaro Valley's agricultural industry—fruit packing and processing. With their homes secure under benevolent landlords Frances and John T. Porter, with their economic base secure in the growing apple industry, land reclamation, berry and vegetable cultivation, the Brooklyn Chinese launched their first America-born generation. Brooklyn's movement into this second stage of development challenges (as did the early Monterey fishermen) the label of "sojourner" which has been attached to the Chinese in America. When hostile conditions improved enough to offer the Chinese some hope for the future, they behaved as all other immigrant groups did, making the United States their permanent home. But many Chinese were never offered this hope; Brooklyn boomed in the 1890s at a time when most rural Chinatowns in California had atrophied and their residents had drifted to San Francisco or returned to China.

## SUGAR CITY

Claus Spreckels, the man most responsible for putting the Soquel beet sugar factory out of business in 1880, revived the business by bringing the world's largest beet sugar factory to Watsonville in 1888. Spreckels had been processing raw cane sugar in San Francisco since 1856, and had experimented with the manufacture of beet sugar in the 1860s. He had also been the leading grower and processor of Hawaiian cane sugar as well as the most influential man (next to the King) in the Hawaiian Kingdom.

But he pushed too hard, and the King and some of his supporters forced Spreckels out of Hawaiian politics and off the islands in 1886. Spreckels traveled to Austria to study the latest advances in beet sugar processing and returned to California in 1887 to announce his intention to build North America's largest and most advanced beet sugar refinery.

Spreckels traveled throughout northern and central California making his standard everyone-ought-to-raise-sugar-beets speech and assessing the amount of interest shown by farmers for raising beets. He demanded that the city he selected as the site of his new refinery donate land for a mill as well as commit a minimum of 2,500 acres of beets for the 1888 sugar campaign. Salinas and Watsonville scrambled to fulfill his demands, but Watsonville moved more quickly, and in December 1887 Spreckels announced that he had chosen Watsonville. Spreckels' choice was certainly influenced by his knowledge of the region, for he owned a summer home and hotel in Aptos and had witnessed the rise and fall of the Soquel beet sugar factory.

The Western Beet Sugar Company factory became the economic flagship of the Pajaro Valley, spreading an estimated $50,000 each month throughout the valley. The factory cost $350,000 to build (equal to one-third of the assessed value of the entire town). The Loma Prieta Lumber Company (John T. Porter was a major stockholder) delivered a staggering two million board feet of lumber (140 railroad cars) from Aptos for the construction of the factory, and the lime for the sugar process came from the hills near Santa Cruz. Sugar beet by-products also spawned several secondary industries: Spreckels shipped the lime residue to Hawaii where it was used as fertilizer, while the pulp was fed to cattle on a large feed lot just south of Watsonville. The new factory had a gargantuan appetite of 350 tons of beets per day (compared to the Soquel factory's 60 tons per day).

Western Beet Sugar Company Factory, Watsonville, c. 1890. Built by Claus Spreckels in 1888, this factory tied together Watsonville and Chinese sugar beet contractors for the next decade. After carrying Watsonville unscathed through the depression of the mid-1890s, the mill was closed in 1898 when Spreckels moved his sugar processing plant to a site just outside Salinas.                                ROY CHRISTIAN

The magnitude of the sugar beet crop was conveyed in an accounting of the number of horses and teams lined up to deliver beets to the factory on a Saturday morning in December 1896: 91 wagons in line, "33 two-horse teams, 45 four-horse teams, 5 five-horse teams, and 8 six-horse teams totalling 319 horses in line." Watsonville wore its title of Sugar City proudly, and the town named its professional baseball team the Sugar Beets.

The sugar factory insulated Watsonville from the chilly effects of the depression which followed the Panic of 1893. While unemployment and foreclosures were commonplace in Salinas and Santa Cruz, Watsonville showed no ill effects: "There is no record of (business) failure here. The courts show no foreclosures of mortgages . . . the Pajaro Valley and Watsonville have come through the years of panic without a failure. The success of this community and our people has come from the beet factory." In his book *Beautiful Santa Cruz County*, Phil Francis likened the sugar factory to a "Pandora's horn, monthly shaken above Watsonville," concluding that "Watsonville always finds trade active and money plenty, even when neighboring towns are in the throes of business depression."

The picture was not entirely rosy. By May 1888, as the first beet crop began to demand its almost daily hoeing and thinning, the Pajaro Valley found itself short-handed: "Men, women and children—anyone who can handle a hoe and who can thin out growing beets can find employment here . . ." Crews of Chinese beet workers were ordered from San Francisco and daily wages rose to $1.75 as the farmers anxiously tried to fulfill their obligations to Spreckels, who had made it clear that if enough beets weren't produced to keep the mill in operation, he had no qualms about moving the factory elsewhere. From the first season some Pajaro farmers had difficulty producing the labor-intensive crop; when the contracts for the 1889 season were signed, the acreage of beets committed to the factory by the Pajaro Valley actually declined.

The appearance of white faces in the Pajaro Valley's seasonal farm labor force has always been an excellent barometer of the health of California's economy—the more whites willing to do field work, the worse the economy. Chinese control of sugar beet contracts slipped from a monopoly of 98% in 1890 to 70% in 1895, reflecting the increasing competition from non-Chinese. In an ironic reversal of roles (the Chinese had always been labeled "cheap labor"), the white beet contractors undercut the rates charged by the Chinese for raising beets. During the years they had control of the contracts, the Chinese had steadily driven the rate for raising a ton of beets from 70¢ to over $1. In 1895, when the Chinese offered the landowners contracts at $1.06 per ton, whites offered to do the work for $1.04.

Several of the white sugar beet crews in the Pajaro Valley during the 1895 season were organized along distinctly ethnic lines. A group of Italians took beet contracts at one dollar a ton in the southern Pajaro Valley, while along San Juan Road a group of Portuguese worked over five hundred acres of sugar beets. In the vicinity of Chittenden's (present-day Aromas), a group of "Spaniards" (probably Californios or Mexicans) worked the beets, and white laborers also began picking hops, which had heretofore been a Chinese monopoly.

A decade earlier the Chinese, who had much more experience raising and harvesting sugar beets, would have successfully competed with the white beet workers. The consequences of the 1882 Exclusion Law, the 1888 Scott Act, and the 1892 Geary Act became apparent by 1895. All three cut deeply into the Chinese population in California and prevented a new wave of immigrants from China. Hundreds of Chinese laborers fled to Canada and Mexico during the Geary Act Registration in 1893, and this exodus immediately affected the Pajaro Valley: "There is a shortage of berry pickers and the Chinese bosses appear to be unable or unwilling to get more men . . . It is supposed that the surplus laborers are being sent to Mexico or British Columbia." By 1895 the Chinese work force was not only dwindling, it was aging.

Still fewer Chinese were available to work in the sugar beet fields in the Pajaro Valley because many had signed long-term leases to grow berries and vegetable crops. The trend to leases began in the mid-1880s when several Chinese farmers signed sharecropping leases in the Pajaro Valley, and many Chinese also held long-term leases for land reclamation. In the face of competition from other sugar beet contractors during the mid-1890s, this trend toward the potentially more lucrative leases was not surprising.

As each year passed the Pajaro Valley became more dependent on farm workers, and with the number of Chinese available to do seasonal farm labor decreasing, the valley faced a potential shortage of laborers when the economy improved and whites were reabsorbed into the economy. In the mid-1890s a group of young, vigorous farm laborers from Japan entered the Pajaro Valley. The first mention of Japanese offering contracts to work sugar beets appeared in 1895 when a group of them offered to grow and harvest the beets for an astonishingly low ninety cents per ton, sixteen cents below the price offered by the Chinese. Undoubtedly the willingness of the Japanese to work the beets for ninety cents per ton further discouraged the Chinese beet

contractors who were used to receiving a dollar or more per ton.
In 1900 a Watsonville newspaper observed:

> Chinese labor is rapidly becoming scarcer. The exclusion act has
> kept out the immigration of young Chinese, and most of those who
> were in California when the exclusion act was passed have reached
> an age where they are unable to give a full day's labor.

The 1900 census caught the transition perfectly—a crew of nine
Chinese strawberry pickers with an average age of fifty-one
years alongside a crew of eight Japanese strawberry pickers with
an average age of twenty-one.

The Pajaro Valley farmers were never completely comfortable
with the large amount of labor demanded by sugar beets, and
within the first two seasons of the Watsonville sugar factory's
operation, the acreage of sugar beets began to creep south into
the country around Castroville. To ensure that he had enough
beets to process in the 1889 season, Spreckels (in partnership with
W. V. Gaffey) leased several thousand acres on the Moro Cojo
Ranch near Castroville, adding to the southward shift of sugar
beet acreage. Spreckels built the Watsonville–Moro Cojo narrow-gauge railroad from his Watsonville factory to Moss Landing in 1890 to ship the beets to and from the factory and to avoid
the high shipping rates charged by Southern Pacific. (Spreckels
had a running feud with Southern Pacific.) The processed sugar
was transported by rail to Moss Landing and shipped out to San
Francisco on Spreckels' own ships. Spreckels renamed the railroad the Pajaro Valley Consolidated Railroad (though only 10%
of its tracks were actually in the Pajaro Valley) and extended the
line into the Salinas Valley. The 1893 season was the last campaign in which Pajaro Valley sugar beets made up over half of the
beets processed at Watsonville, and in 1894 more beets were
shipped into the valley from Castroville and Salinas than were
grown there.

It was simply a matter of time before the cost of shipping the beets back to Watsonville would force Spreckels to act, and in 1896 when the cost of shipping the beets reached one dollar per ton, Spreckels announced that he would build a new sugar factory in the Salinas Valley. Watsonville's civic leaders tried to convince themselves that there was room in the region for two factories, but it was not to be. When the new Salinas Valley plant became operational in 1898, the Watsonville plant was closed, and Watsonville's decade as Sugar City came to an end.

When the rumors of Spreckels' move began to circulate through Watsonville in 1896, many observers feared the consequences. Phil Francis described the factory as "the heart which pumps the life blood of the city's trade through every artery and vein of the whole community. Remove the factory and Watsonville would be struck a staggering blow." But the factory protected the city during the depression in the mid-1890s and inspired Pajaro Valley farmers to shift from cereal grains to a wide variety of labor-intensive crops. When Spreckels' factory closed in 1898, Watsonville's economy barely stumbled, because the decade of sugar production in the valley had brought tremendous agricultural diversification. Raspberry, blackberry, strawberry, potato, and hop acreage had increased during the 1890s, and the number of fruit trees had jumped astronomically. Some farmers continued shipping beets to Salinas on the Pajaro Valley Consolidated Railroad.

Watsonville matured during its decade as Sugar City, changing from a little town passively watching the fluctuations of wheat prices to a sophisticated and diversified agricultural community in which discussions of sugar trusts, beet contracts, and sugar percentages were commonplace. The local newspaper featured editorials on international trade, and the community watched with interest (and opposition) as United States involvement in Hawaiian affairs threatened to make cane sugar once again a competitor.

No person upon any sidewalk shall carry a basket or baskets, bag or bags, suspended from or attached to poles across or upon the shoulders.

Santa Cruz City Charter,
Section III, 1880.

# 8

# Santa Cruz

OF THE FOUR MAJOR CITIES in the Monterey Bay Region in the nineteenth century, Monterey was the senior community, a town of adobes, serapes, fandangos; the Chinese fishermen lived in fishing villages to the west and were a distant but important part of Monterey's economy. Founded after statehood, both Salinas and Watsonville shared the common economic base of agriculture and, not surprisingly, the Chinese communities in each were grudgingly given a certain status, because they were essential to the economy of the towns.

Santa Cruz, though it had roots in the Spanish era, had developed as a vigorous manufacturing center, a town of mills, factories, and white church steeples—a feisty, Protestant Yankee town. In contrast to the other major Chinese communities in the region, the Chinese never established a permanent niche in the Santa Cruz economy or achieved the security that provided. The Chinese in Santa Cruz worked and lived as if balancing on a tightrope, always vulnerable to the social and political winds that swept through the community. In other communities in the region the Chinese rarely worked in close proximity to whites, but in Santa Cruz the Chinese were much more intimately involved in the non-Chinese community's lives, for the contribution they made was a most personal one—domestic service.

Santa Cruz in the early 1870s. Ships, wharves, and factories attest to Santa Cruz's early manufacturing. Cowell and Davis lime wharf on left, California Powder Works wharf in center of photograph. Absence of Santa Cruz Railroad tracks along beach places this etching before 1875.                                         ROY CHRISTIAN

But the first Chinese in Santa Cruz worked in manufacturing. Rich in resources such as limestone and lumber, Santa Cruz drew manufacturers because the San Lorenzo River offered both water and power. Lime kilns, tanneries, and lumber mills began to sprout alongside the river in the 1850s. When the Civil War cut off California's supply of explosives (vital to all types of construction), the California Powder Works was established on the San Lorenzo a mile up-river from Santa Cruz. The large bend in the river between the factory and Santa Cruz shielded the town from the inevitable accidental explosions. The factory manufactured its first blasting powder in 1864, and by the 1870s the California Powder Works was one of the largest and most dependable industries in Santa Cruz.

In September 1864 a dozen Chinese laborers arrived at the powder factory, the first sizable group of Chinese ever seen in the Santa Cruz area. The newspaper believed that the Chinese were "throwing honest, hard working white men out of employment," and declared, "If they get blown up in the powder mills . . . it will not be much loss to the community." A month later a group of masked and armed vigilantes stormed the powder factory, tied up the night watchman, and herded the Chinese back toward Santa Cruz; the Sheriff intervened before anyone was hurt, and the Chinese returned to the powder works. Relatively insignificant in the history of California's anti-Chinese movement, the event set the tone which pervaded Chinese-white relations in Santa Cruz until the twentieth century. The threat of mob action and violence lurked just below the surface in Santa Cruz, and for most Chinese life in and around Santa Cruz was like living in a mine field.

The Chinese performed a variety of duties at the powder factory, grading roads, building retaining walls, and cooking for the factory population which lived in company bunkhouses. Their most valuable contribution to the factory, however, was as

coopers, manufacturing the heads, hoops, and stays of the barrels in which the blasting powder was stored: "The dexterity
with which the ingenious Chinamen manipulate the several parts
is truly remarkable." The 1870 manuscript census listed nine
Chinese men working at the powder mill, averaging a youthful
nineteen years of age. By the early 1870s the number of Chinese
employees at the California Powder Works had grown to thirty-
five men, most of whom worked in the cooperage and earned
one dollar per day plus room; the seventy whites who worked in
other areas of the powder plant were paid from $2.50 to $3.00
per day:

> The Chinese cook their own food, which is principally rice and fish,
> with an occasional chicken or piece of fresh pork thrown in . . .
> They are employed by the company because they are a necessity to
> do the work most white would not do, and working such rates as to
> allow the California Powder Company to compete successfully with
> Eastern manufacturers . . . Instead of paying to each individual
> Chinaman his wages, the sum total is given to a Chinese foreman
> who disburses it among his countrymen.

From the mid-1860s to the mid-1870s more Chinese lived at
the powder works than in the small Chinatown in Santa Cruz.
The Santa Cruz Chinese would hire the Pacific Ocean House's
large carriage and join their fellow countrymen at the powder
works to celebrate the lunar New Year and the June birthday of
the primary god in their temple, Kuan Kung. The temple was
probably the primary reason that the Santa Cruz Chinese traveled up to the powder mill to celebrate their holidays. It had a
distinctive balcony which projected beyond the face of the building, decorated in dark blues and reds, and from the flagstaff atop
the building flew a triangular yellow silk flag with the imperial
dragon emblazoned across it. In June 1875 eighty Chinese gathered at the powder works for a picnic and celebration. "Firecrackers were in order, and the general hubbub of Chinese jollity

disturbed the quiet inhabitants of Powder-burg." When a newspaper reporter inquired about the identity of the god whose birthday was being celebrated, a Chinese cooper compared Kuan Kung to George Washington and the upcoming Centennial: "You sabee, he one great man allee same Georgie Washingman; we make big time allee same you on Centennila Day."

The Chinese worked in the cooperage at the California Powder Works until the height of the anti-Chinese movement; in July 1878 the company finally bowed to local pressure and fired all its Chinese employees. Other than the Chinese who worked in the Soquel beet sugar factory between 1874 and 1880, the Chinese coopers were the only Chinese participating directly in manufacturing in the region.

## THE FIRST CHINATOWN—1862–1877

Santa Cruz's first Chinatown developed in the mid-1860s on the west side of Willow Street. Initially consisting of two or three laundries housing less than a dozen men, the small cluster of single-story buildings eventually expanded to take up most of the block between Lincoln and Walnut streets. Willow Street (present-day Pacific Avenue) was a secondary street in the 1860s, and the rents on south Willow were probably quite low. The Chinatown included a temple, one or two stores, and a collection of laundries. The only business which served whites was a small cigar factory owned by Ung Yah, where Chinese rolled several thousand cigars each week in view of pedestrians on the dirt sidewalk outside.

Like all subsequent Chinatowns in Santa Cruz, this Chinatown provided a haven of refuge to those Chinese who washed dishes, cooked, made beds, and waited on tables elsewhere in Santa Cruz. Even before the Santa Cruz economy began to

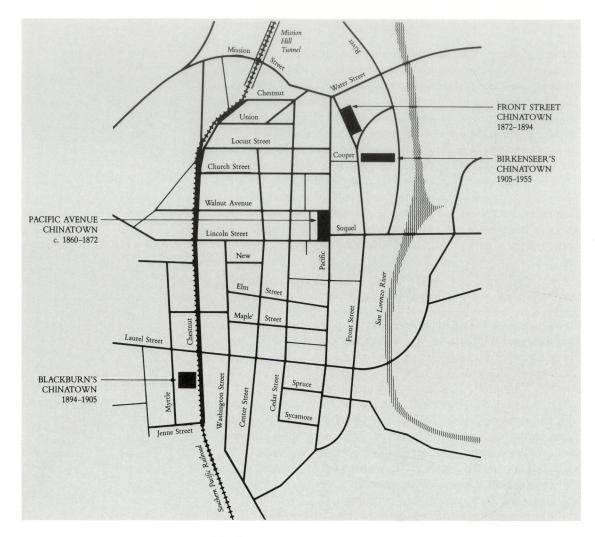

Map 8-1

SANTA CRUZ AND ITS CHINATOWNS

Map shows the location of Santa Cruz's four Chinatowns.

228

boom, whites of respectable means in Santa Cruz employed a Chinese houseboy or cook. Santa Cruz families who had Chinese servants in 1870 included Amasa Pray, retired merchant; Fred Barson, retired grocer; Dr. Frederick Bailey, physician; John Chase, butcher; Edwin Heacock, lawyer; Edward Beasley, teacher; and Bernard Peyton, superintendent of the Powder Works. Santa Cruz had more Chinese servants than any other town in the Monterey Bay Region because, as a manufacturing town, it had a much more substantial middle class than any of its counterpart towns in the region.

Usually, between the afternoon and evening meals, some of the Chinese would walk back to Chinatown and touch base, lapsing into soothing, familiar Cantonese. The work they performed was arduous, the hours long, the tasks often demeaning, but that all paled before the pressure of trying to speak English and function in what was, to them, a topsy-turvy white world.

A subtle paternalism characterized Santa Cruz's attitude toward its Chinese residents from the 1860s to the 1950s. In the middle distance of Santa Cruz's consciousness, the Chinese went quietly and efficiently about their work, appearing at the elbow of white Santa Cruz when called. To whites the Chinese were of a uniform age and appearance, all wearing denim coats, pants, slippers, and black felt hat. All Chinese were "John" or "Charlie," and male servants were "houseboys," and Santa Cruz often talked of "our Chinese." Although treating the Chinese as anonymous servants smoothed the point of contact between them and whites, this attitude objectified the Chinese—"our" Chinese could be manipulated at will, they had no faces and no personalities. In torchlight parades through Chinatown at the height of the anti-Chinese movement in Santa Cruz, the crowd's chants were couched in general terms—"The Chinese Must Go." The crowd never confronted an individual Chinese and told him, "*you* must go." While in Watsonville, Salinas, and Monterey the Chinese gained the grudging respect of whites because of the valuable contribution they made to agriculture or fishing, in Santa Cruz, no matter how hard or faithfully they served, they were still just servants or peddlers.

Chinatowns did not have a life of their own; they reflected the economic and social climate of the communities in which they were located. The unusual nature of Santa Cruz's Chinatown resulted, at least in part, from the majority community's unusual attitudes toward the Chinese. The percentage of Chinese women in Santa Cruz was the lowest in the Monterey Bay Region, and in most years the number of Chinese families in Santa Cruz could be counted on one hand. If the Point Alones village was a remarkable exception to the stereotype of the transient sojourner applied to the Chinese in California, the Chinese in nineteenth-century Santa Cruz were a confirmation of that stereotype, always on their guard, never able to carve a permanent niche. While the Point Alones fishing village remained in the same location for over fifty years, Chinatown Santa Cruz had five different locations, circling around the periphery of the community, moving from one low-rent district to another.

During the 1870s surveying and realignment of the Santa Cruz streets prompted the first move. Expansion of the Main Street (now Front Street) business district was limited on the east by the San Lorenzo River and on the south by a dead end, so in 1866, during the belated incorporation and survey of the town, Willow Street was renamed Pacific Avenue and designated the primary business street, while Front Street was declared a secondary street. Where south Willow had been off the beaten path in 1865, by the early 1870s businesses began to relocate on the new Pacific Avenue and the rents there began to rise. During the early 1870s the Chinese began to move to the vacant buildings on Front Street, and in 1877 the last of the Chinese moved from the old Willow Street Chinatown.

# THE FRONT STREET CHINATOWN

The Front Street Chinatown was Santa Cruz's largest, lasting from the late 1870s until April 1894, when it was destroyed by fire. Eventually, the Chinese community occupied most of the east side of Front Street between Cooper and Water Street, and several buildings across the street on the west side of Front Street. Here the Chinese community matured, dug in, and stood off several eviction efforts by the white community.

The 1880 manuscript census provides the first good assessment of this new Chinatown. The Chinatown consisted of ten buildings housing thirty-seven men, one woman; thirty-one of the men were laundrymen, two were cooks, one was a domestic, and one a merchant. The woman, Tom Sue, a thirty-six-year-old laundress, was listed as living alone in a separate household. Wing Sing, who later became an influential member of the Chinese community, was the only merchant listed.

Less than half of the ninety-eight Chinese living in Santa Cruz in 1880 lived in the Front Street Chinatown. A few lived in laundries, one near the new South Pacific Coast Railroad depot and another at the south end of Pacific Avenue. But scattered throughout Santa Cruz society were twenty-six Chinese domestics, servants, and cooks. The brewer Henry Rausch had a Chinese houseboy as did attorney C. B. Younger. Robert Thomas, the Wells Fargo agent, had a nineteen-year-old Chinese servant; C. S. Levy, a merchant, J. E. Butler, owner of a flour mill, and Dr. P. B. Fagen each had houseboys. Richard and Georgianna Bruce Kirby employed Fong, a twenty-year-old Chinese cook. Ah Hoon, the servant noted in the 1870 census as living in the Delamater residence, still lived there ten years later, demonstrating a longevity of employment commonplace for Chinese cooks and servants.

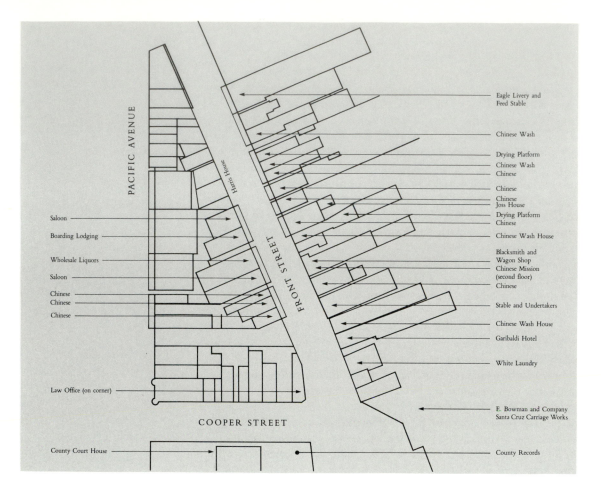

Map 8-2

FRONT STREET CHINATOWN, SANTA CRUZ, 1892

Front Street Chinatown had its back to the San Lorenzo River and most of the buildings were up on stilts to prevent flooding. Entire Chinatown was destroyed in the 1894 fire. Map derived from Sanborn Map Company maps, Map Library, UCSC.

232

The Chinese cooks and domestics in the Monterey Bay Region during the nineteenth century should never be dismissed as "the help." A bond often developed between the Chinese cook and the employing family which went far beyond that of employer-employee. Stories about the loyalty and dedication of Chinese household servants abound. The Chinese immigrants brought a strong background of family-centered tradition to California—in fact, for many of them, coming to California was itself an act of devotion to their family, to whom they often sent a good part of their wages. Sometimes, cut off from their own families back in China, the love which they would have lavished on their own children, nieces, and nephews overflowed onto the children in the houses where they lived and worked: "They [the Chinese] were the most loyal to the families where they were employed and that meant every member of the family, especially the children." The "adoption" of the Chinese servant by the white family manifested the paternal relationship Santa Cruz had with the Chinese, and though many stories tell of the loyalty of Chinese cooks for their employers, we have little evidence of how this feeling was reciprocated. Yet when death or a return to China separated the Chinese from his adopted family, both the family and the servant grieved.

To those who think that Chinese houseboys and cooks were common in Santa Cruz because they worked for less than white domestics, it should be noted that Chinese servants were prized so highly that they were paid higher salaries than their white counterparts. A white domestic in Santa Cruz in 1884 earned an average of fifteen dollars per month, while Chinese servants commanded twenty dollars. In San Francisco a good Chinese cook or servant could earn as much as forty dollars per month. Just like his counterparts working in the fields and on the railroads, the Chinese servant had a reputation for dependability and devotion which made him a welcome addition to the household that could afford him.

Chinese cooks were also valued by logging companies and ranchers as the quality of the food served in bunkhouses often determined the quality of the hands one could attract. A good Chinese cook was worth much more than the twenty-five to forty dollars per month he was paid. Santa Cruz County logging camps, dairies, lime kilns, and petroleum mines employed Chinese cooks during the later nineteenth and early twentieth centuries. The 1880 census lists six camp cooks scattered around the county, including Sam Ho, cook at the Comstock Mill behind Soquel. The 1910 census lists six Chinese camp cooks, including two at the petroleum mines near Bonny Doon, two at the Newell Creek logging mill, and Ah Sing, a forty-five-year-old cook at the Rincon Station lime kilns in the San Lorenzo River gorge.

The Chinese cook worked long, hard hours. In a 1967 interview John Dong, who had been the cook at the Cowell Ranch cookhouse, described cooking for fifteen hands. John began his fourteen-hour day each morning before 5:00 A.M. and had breakfast on the table by 6:00 A.M.: "You're just cleaning up and then you start lunch. After lunch, I'd take about an hour off. That was all. Then I'd start dinnertime. I'd have dinner at five-thirty or six o'clock." John was paid fifty-five dollars per month.

The relationship between the Chinese camp cook and the loggers or ranch hands was somewhat different from that between the Chinese household cook and his family, as a firmer hand was required to keep the loggers and ranch hands in line. The stereotype of the cleaver-wielding Chinese cook is partially rooted in the Chinese camp cook who often ruled his kitchen with a combination of Cantonese invective and threats. But beneath the bluster ran feelings of devotion and affection just as strong as those in a household in town. William Baird, superintendent of one of the Loma Prieta Lumber Company's logging camps, employed Mock Get as his camp cook for fifteen years. In March 1905, while supervising a logging operation in Hinckley Basin,

William Baird died. Mock Get, devastated by the loss, went into the cook house that evening and hanged himself. The Chee Kong Tong staged an elaborate funeral for Mock Get in Watsonville, and its members acted as pallbearers. Most of the people attending Mock Get's funeral, however, were the loggers and their wives, who followed the funeral procession to the Pioneer Cemetery in several large wagons, attesting to the strong bond which had developed between Mock Get and his extended family.

San Vicente Lumber Company, c. 1900. Loggers were always white, but third from right in center row is the company's Chinese cook whose regal bearing in the photograph suggests the great influence Chinese cooks had in the region's logging camps.

ROY CHRISTIAN

## THE MARKET GARDENS

The anti-Chinese sentiment which pervaded Santa Cruz during the nineteenth century made it a difficult town for Chinese who wished to branch into business for themselves. When the Chinese eschewed their "traditional" roles as domestics or laundrymen and attempted to gain employment in other fields or start a new business, they were quickly reminded of their place in the community. The one industry which they developed and dominated in nineteenth-century Santa Cruz was the growing and selling of fresh vegetables—the market gardens. Chinese market gardens were common throughout California in the nineteenth century and they supplied fresh vegetables to Watsonville, Salinas, Pacific Grove, and Monterey. But in Santa Cruz they seem to have been particularly well developed.

Generally, the Chinese market garden was run in partnership by Chinese (usually three or four) who pooled their resources and labor to lease a plot of land and grow vegetables for sale in town. Each partner had a specific function (bookkeeper, peddler) but all partners shared in the labor of planting, cultivating, and harvesting the vegetables. One of the first market gardens in the Santa Cruz area was on the outskirts of Felton. In 1876 George Treat leased five acres of land to Ah Hop and Ah Foo for "purposes of growing vegetables;" the six-year sharecrop lease stipulated that Treat received one-third of the vegetables and the Chinese the remainder.

That same year a group of Chinese leased six acres in Santa Cruz from Judge Rice to establish one of the first market gardens in Santa Cruz; the Chinese rented the land for five years, paying around twenty dollars per acre per year. When the lease expired in 1881, it was extended for another five years at a rent of twenty-three dollars per acre. The census of 1880 records two market gardens in Santa Cruz, one on Mission Street and one on Branciforte, each with a half-dozen Chinese residents.

By 1900 Santa Cruz was encircled by Chinese gardens, one on Harriet Blackburn's property near Neary's Lagoon, several on Garfield Avenue above the lagoon, four on King Street, one in the San Lorenzo River bottom behind Front Street, several across the river on the flats below the Branciforte bluff, and several up Blackburn Gulch in the warm belt along Branciforte Creek.

The Chinese gardeners usually built a small shack in the garden's center, living where they could guard their crops from eagle-eyed schoolboys. Dressed in denim trouser and blouses and often straw hats, the Chinese rose before dawn each day, filled their carrying baskets with fresh produce, and walked the early morning streets, their distinctive call matching the rhythm of the baskets swaying at each end of their shoulder poles. The call of the Chinese peddler was a familiar part of a Santa Cruz morning, and depending on the season, the baskets brimmed with cabbage, lettuce, okra, yams, raspberries, gooseberries, and blackberries. A section of each garden was set aside for Chinese delicacies such as water lily bulbs, Chinese lettuce, and water chestnuts to be sold in Chinatown.

An early specialty of the Rice market garden and other early Chinese market gardens was fresh strawberries. The appearance of fresh strawberries as early as February always astonished the transplanted New Englanders with their memories of shoulder-deep February snow. The price they were willing to pay for the season's first strawberries was also astonishing—seventy-five cents per quart, close to an entire day's wages. The high profits afforded by the early season berries made them worth the risk of unexpected frosts, unseasonal rains, insects, gophers, and small boys. When reliable railroad service came to Santa Cruz in 1876, crates of fresh strawberries were shipped on the early morning train to San Francisco.

Because the Chinese peddlers brought the fruits and vegetables through the streets each day, they made it possible for households to obtain fresh produce before the advent of refrigeration: "Last Monday Chinamen were selling green peas in the streets of Santa Cruz—three pounds for twenty-five cents—fresh and crisp, from the basket." In 1881 customers could purchase a day's fresh produce from a Chinese vegetable peddler for between five and ten cents.

The peddlers were much more than salesmen and many formed strong bonds with their customers. Many of the Chinese gardeners became known in Santa Cruz by nicknames such as "Doc," "Judge Rice," and "Joe Frey"—the names of the owners of the property the Chinese leased. "Doc" became well-known throughout Santa Cruz:

> He had one large protruding sharp tooth. He liked his patrons and if one would become sick or infected, he would want to prescribe for them. He used local as well as herbs from far away Cathay and according to the patrons, lots of his treatments succeeded where others had failed. Some of the poultices were none too good to look at. He could read the palms especially the girls who would seek him to read the lines in their hands and tell their fortunes.

During the early twentieth century, when the number of Santa Cruz Chinese began to decline, the market gardens passed into the hands of Italian gardeners. The Chinese market garden can be viewed as the forerunner of the twentieth-century Chinese-owned market. Its patterns of partnership, divided labor, and bond with the customer also characterized the markets. When refrigeration became reliable and cheap enough, the pattern reversed, and the customers came to the market.

## LAUNDRIES

Chinese laundries are probably the most misunderstood and least appreciated of all the businesses associated with the Chinese

in America. The stereotyped pidgin-speaking Chinese laundryman has so dominated popular American literature that even serious historians of the Chinese in America have dismissed the
role of the Chinese laundryman as peripheral to the more dramatic exploits of the railroad builders or fishermen. Yet the Chinese laundryman personified the persistence, adaptability, and
ingenuity of the Chinese immigrant. Often the first to establish
a Chinese business in a community, the laundryman skillfully
adapted to the shifting political and economic currents in the

Chinese laundryman, Felton, 1875.
One of the earliest photographs of a
Chinese taken in the Monterey Bay
Region, this photograph had a sarcas-
tic caption which said "California's
Washerwoman." Chinese laundrymen
were usually the pioneer Chinese set-
tlers in the region's communities.
MATTHEWS COLLECTION

community. There was no more hard-working Chinese immigrant than the laundryman, who worked twelve-hour shifts every day of the week in cramped, hot quarters.

Nor should it be overlooked that the Chinese laundryman acted as the Chinese community's front line during the anti-Chinese campaigns in the 1870s and 1880s—anti-Chinese mobs usually focused their incendiary attacks on Chinese wash houses (as in San Francisco during the "sand lot" riots in 1876), and local governments singled out Chinese laundries for discriminatory licensing and restrictions. The law books are filled with the names of Chinese laundrymen who returned fire through legal channels, standing their ground and challenging the ordinances in court; several major legal precedents granting equal protection under the law to Chinese immigrants were set in cases involving Chinese laundrymen. The hard-working and polite Chinese laundryman was also on the front line of social contact with the majority community, for he was often the only Chinese with whom most whites had any personal contact (which ironically led to the notion that all Chinese were laundrymen).

In contrast to popular opinion, no special tradition led Chinese to establish laundries in the United States. Rather, the Chinese went into the wash house business because it required little capital investment and a lot of manual labor, and no one else was doing it. From Wah Lee's first laundry in San Francisco in 1851, the institution of the Chinese laundry spread quickly throughout the West—heretofore clothing had either been laundered by Indians or sent to the Hawaiian Islands, an expensive proposition which often took many months. The Chinese wash house was the first Chinese business mentioned in Salinas, Watsonville, and Santa Cruz records. Dramatically underscoring the fact that the Chinese laundry was established to serve the white community, the largest and oldest Chinatown in the region, the Point Alones fishing village, never had a single Chinese laundry.

The Chinese laundry was the first foray into the community; Chinatowns grew up around these establishments. In Salinas and Watsonville the laundries were surrounded by boarding houses and recreational businesses for the Chinese farm laborers. In Santa Cruz, where the Chinese were not employed in agriculture or manufacturing, the wash houses attracted more wash houses as the community grew. In 1880 more Chinese laundrymen lived in Santa Cruz than in all the rest of the Monterey Bay Region combined; Santa Cruz had become the Chinese laundry capital of the Monterey Bay Region. From the early 1850s Santa Cruz had tried to cultivate an air of New England respectability, and as we have already seen, one manifestation of that veneer of gentility was the Chinese house boy. The Chinese laundryman helped extend that respectability by making it possible for women to avoid the drudgery of washing and ironing, "menial" labor beneath the dignity of most Santa Cruz whites. This posed a problem during the anti-Chinese flurries in the 1870s and 1880s; as hard as they might try, the local newspapers were unable to convince a non-Chinese laundry (usually called a "white laundry") to locate in Santa Cruz, so the shirts worn at anti-Chinese rallies were often washed, starched, and ironed at a Santa Cruz Chinese laundry. The biggest boost to the Chinese laundries, however, came from the tourist industry which began in earnest with the completion of the South Pacific Coast Railroad in the spring of 1880.

The census taken one month after the completion of the railroad counts all but one of the ten buildings in the Front Street Chinatown as laundries, the exception being a store operated by Wing Sing. The heads of the nine laundries included Louie Kee (known in town as "Louie"), William Ah Foy, Quong Chong (later a merchant), Henry Chong, and Wong Su; Jim Kee operated a laundry on Pacific Avenue. The ten laundries in Santa Cruz served a total population of 3,898, a ratio of 1 laundry for every 389 residents. Laundries also served boarding houses and small hotels which catered to the burgeoning tourist traffic brought by the railroad.

Watsonville, on the other hand, had a ratio of 1 Chinese laundry for each 560 Watsonville residents, while Salinas had a ratio of 1 to 500. Either Santa Cruz had inordinately clean shirts, or the other communities didn't. Most of the smaller communities in the region had at least one laundry; Spreckels' Aptos Hotel had a small Chinese laundry on the grounds; and the Mansion House Hotel in Watsonville had two Chinese laundrymen on its live-in staff. In 1878 David Jacks sold Charley Hop Kee, a Chinese laundryman, the laundry concession at the Pacific Grove Retreat, and for a seasonal fee of $125, the Chinese had the exclusive franchise to operate a laundry. The arrangement was renewed in 1879 and again in 1880, though Jacks apparently tried to induce other Chinese to come to Pacific Grove for a smaller fee.

In large urban Chinese communities like San Francisco, the Chinese laundries were organized in guilds which regulated the laundries and prevented unnecessary competition between them. Since the Chinese had a monopoly on the laundry business, they quickly organized to take advantage of their leverage, setting up territories of operation and fixing prices. In San Francisco, for example, the guilds ruled that there had to be at least ten doors between laundries, and laundries run by non-members were "quickly put out of business by threat, or, if necessary, by force." In smaller communities such as Santa Cruz, the rules were probably not as elaborate, but the laundrymen did set prices and lobby the town council when it singled out Chinese laundries for a special business license.

Santa Cruz newspaper reporter Ernest Otto wrote a detailed account of the interior workings of a turn-of-the-century Chinese laundry in Santa Cruz. The typical Chinese laundry occupied the ground floor of a thin, narrow, wooden two-story Chinatown building; a dozen ironing boards lined the side walls, and the wash tubs stood at the rear of the room. When the clothes were washed and the water pounded out of them, they were strung on lines outside at the rear of the building or on lines strung on the roof. During the rainy season clothes were dried on lines hanging inside near the ceiling. Hand irons were kept heated on a charcoal stove in the middle of the room, and when the iron he was using cooled down, the laundryman returned it to the stove and took another. With both hands occupied in holding and ironing the clothes, the Chinese used an unusual method to dampen the clothes while ironing them:

> At the side of each [Chinese] engaged in ironing was a sauce bowl filled with water, on top of a starch box. The Chinese, wearing a white cotton blouse, would bend over to fill his mouth with water and then spurt a spray over the clothes to dampen them.

When Duncan McPherson discovered the Chinese were spitting on the clothes, he warned his readers about the practice:

> Ulcerated tonsils and throats are common among Chinese laundry-men, hence the water squirted is often impregnated with germs of diseases, which are ironed into the clothes and thus scattered universally into all classes of society. Either the squirting or the patronage given to the Chinese laundries should be stopped.

Patronage of Chinese laundries in Santa Cruz continued despite McPherson's warnings, and there was never any documented case of disease being spread by the Chinese laundries.

Pressed clothes were then put in a large basket and delivered throughout Santa Cruz. An entire family's washing "seldom cost more than a dollar" in the nineteenth century; in 1884 the average Chinese laundryman made a profit of sixteen dollars per month, working twelve hours per day, seven days per week. Laundrymen usually slept beneath the ironing board while the second shift ironed above them.

Chinese laundrymen in Santa Cruz had a reputation for producing clean, well-ironed clothing: "There were no stiffer shirt bosoms, cuffs, or collars than those produced by a Chinese washerman;" the charcoal stove and ever-present incense in the laundry also gave the clothes a distinctive odor. The Chinese also gave their regular customers very personalized service, and on Chinese New Year women customers received a Chinese lily bulb, and the children either candies or firecrackers. Otto summed it up well when he concluded, "No one was kinder or more generous than your Chinese laundryman."

Sometimes the relationship between a long-established Chinese laundryman and his customers grew extremely close. In Pacific Grove, for example, the Chinese laundryman was known to his customers as "Jim Jim," and over the years he became a beloved figure in the community. During the lunar New Year festivities (usually, the only three days a Chinese laundryman took off each year were the three days before the New Year), Jim Jim's laundry was a center of hospitality punctuated by the "pandemonium" of firecrackers. In December 1900 Jim Jim decided to marry in a ceremony held in Pacific Grove on Grand Avenue in front of his laundry:

> The event of the week *par excellence* was the wedding yesterday afternoon of Jim Jim, Pacific Grove's popular Chinese laundryman, to an almond eyed belle of Santa Cruz. The bride arrived on the afternoon train and was met at the depot by the PG band who escorted her up town. The ceremony was held on Grand Avenue in front of Jim's place of business, his brother Jim Len, acting as master of ceremonies. The function was conducted in true Chinese style, regardless of expense, with firecrackers galore. It was witnessed by nearly the entire population of the grove.

Jim Jim was well loved in Pacific Grove, but not immune to the anti-Chinese sentiment that preoccupied the community in 1906; when Pacific Grove passed an ordinance prohibiting any Chinese laundries from operating inside the town limits, he was forced to move his laundry outside Pacific Grove to Lighthouse Avenue.

Anti-Chinese proponents in Santa Cruz continued to emphasize the potential danger to public health posed by the laundries on Front Street. The open cesspools beneath the laundries became an issue each summer when the San Lorenzo River run-off was insufficient to carry the sewage out to sea. The laundry effluent gathered in "stagnant pools and sink spots" issuing "fetid exhalations." Public health inspectors toured Chinatown periodically and ordered a load of gravel to be poured into the pools to dissipate the odor. Santa Cruz's Chinese laundries were never driven from the city, and in 1886 Duncan McPherson surrendered, admitting that the Chinese laundryman controlled the laundries because he had become "a skilled workman, instead of a low grade drudge, as formerly."

The advent of modern steam laundries and the restriction of Chinese immigration eventually put most of Santa Cruz's Chinese laundries out of business. In the 1900 census the number of Chinese laundrymen in Santa Cruz had dwindled to 11 men working in four different laundries, and their average age was 43. By 1910 only 10 laundrymen with an average age of 58 were left, and the Japanese began to replace the Chinese.

## CHINESE MERCHANTS

Wing Sing was the first Chinese merchant in Santa Cruz's Chinatown, and by the mid-1880s he had been joined by three other storekeepers in the Front Street Chinatown—Quong Chong, Wong Kee, and Ah Moon. The difficulty posed by the variability of Chinese names and titles often meant that the business name became attached to the storeowner; Ham Git, for example, was known as Wing Sing, the name of his business. Quong Chong was also a business name, and the surname of the owner is not clear. The four Chinese stores sold a variety of Chinese goods:

> . . . dried oysters always attached to a rounded bamboo circle, dried abalones, dried fish of many varieties, dried sea weed, dried shark's fins, roasted ducks, frequently roast pork from San Francisco, eggs from China, Chinese vermicelli, cases of peanut oil, then called Chinese nut oil, all the varieties of Chinese candies, including candied melon, cocoanut, ginger, dates, water lily roots, lichee nuts and other Chinese fruits . . . okra, yams, lily bulbs, Chinese lettuce, sugar cane.

The stores also sold Chinese slippers, water pipes, "ill smelling" Chinese tobacco, and opium. The Wing Sing Company specialized in Chinese medicines—"herbs, sea horses, horned toads, sea weed, deer horn and reptiles"—and was run by Ham Git with partners Ham Tung, Ham Yin, and Ham On. Since the store served an almost exclusively Chinese clientele, none of the partners had a good grasp of English, and Wing Sing (Ham Git) himself practiced traditional Chinese customs into the 1890s. Most whites only went into Chinese stores during the lunar New Year festivities when the merchants would hold an open house and dispense free treats to all who came to pay their respects.

Quong Chong always wore the finery of a Chinese merchant and was a distinctive sight on Chinatown's streets:

> [Quong Chong wore a] brocaded silk blouse of a plum color and in winter, one lined with fur. He wore the black horse-hair skull cap with a red coral top knot and the velvet shoes . . . he was fleshy with round face and when young was especially good-looking.

During the 1880s Quong Chong brought his wife to Santa Cruz from China and raised a family of five children; he maintained a traditional Chinese household, and at mealtime "he would proudly sit at the natural finish redwood table, alone, and be waited on by his wife. After eating, he would arise and the table would be taken over by the wife and the children." The

Quong Chong and his two sons, 1890. Quong Chong was one of the leading Chinese merchants in Santa Cruz. He staged large public parties to announce the birth of his sons. Quong Chong was noted for the careful attention he paid to his clothes.

SPECIAL COLLECTIONS, UCSC

birth of each of Quong Chong's children was marked by a large celebration in the Front Street Chinatown, and when his first son was born in October 1886, "flags were flying and firecrackers exploding in honor of Quong Chong's son and heir, who lately made his appearance into Chinatown."

Ah Moon had operated a laundry on River Street during the late 1860s and early 1870s, and when the Pacific Avenue Chinatown moved to Front Street, he abandoned his laundry and opened up a general merchandise store in Chinatown. Ah Moon's wife was the first Chinese woman (and one of only four during the nineteenth century) to live in Santa Cruz, and the appearance of the merchant, his wife, and child on a Santa Cruz street in the late 1870s was newsworthy enough to be mentioned in the newspaper.

The leading merchant and unofficial "mayor" of the Santa Cruz Chinatown, Wong Kee, operated a store in the only brick building in the Front Street Chinatown. Above the ground-level grocery store he ran a gambling parlor and opium den, and the Chee Kong Tong lodge headquarters and temple were attached to the rear of his store. The Chinese Six Companies' representative in the Santa Cruz Chinatown as well as the leader of the local Chee Kong Tong, Wong Kee often acted as the go-between when conflicts between whites and Chinese occurred. Wong Kee was also married, but in 1887 his wife died, and for the remainder of his life he kept a photograph of his wife in his store with a candle burning before it.

Once again, the testimony given during a re-entry habeas corpus case reveals much about Chinese business as well as the isolation of Chinatown. Ham Tung, a partner in the Wing Sing Chinese store, visited China in 1890, and when he returned to San Francisco in early 1894, immigration authorities detained him. Ham Tung filed a writ of habeas corpus to gain a hearing. Under the Scott and Geary Acts, he had to prove that he had been a resident of Santa Cruz and had not been a common laborer or be deported. Richard Thompson, the Wells Fargo agent in Santa Cruz, and his son, William, both testified on behalf of Ham Tung's re-entry into the United States, as did Wing Sing's business partner, Ham Git. Ham Tung had left the United States in 1890 without a certificate of identification, and only at the end of his stay had he asked his partners in Santa Cruz to put identification papers together (which the Thompsons signed) and send them to China so he could return. The government set out to prove that the Thompsons were in error about Ham Tung's identity. Richard Thompson testified first, identifying Ham Tung as the business manager for Wing Sing: "[Ham Tung] used to bring the money over to my office with the money book. He never did talk very good English. What made me recollect him is, that I used to cuss him a good deal." Thompson went on to indicate that the Wing Sing store was in the only brick building on Front Street, and that it sold Chinese goods and had "an opium smoking lay out." William Thompson corroborated his father's testimony. Ham Tung then took the stand and testified through an interpreter that he had originally come to the United States in 1880, had returned to China in 1890, and was attempting once again to return to Santa Cruz to work at his place of business, the Wing Sing Co.:

Ham Tung, 1894. Partner in the store known as Wing Sing, Ham Tung was detained by immigration authorities after a visit to China. Based on his inability to answer questions about Santa Cruz's Front Street Chinatown, Ham Tung was deported.

NATIONAL ARCHIVES

Q.  Do you still retain your interest in that store?
A.  Yes, sir.
Q.  What do you come back for now?
A.  To attend to my business.
Q.  What is your interest [in the business]?
A.  $1,000.00.
Q.  How many partners have you?
A.  Four.

Q.   What are their names?
A.   Ham Git, Ham Yin, Ham On and myself; four altogether.

In cross-examination, the government honed in on the question of the belated certificate:

Q.   When you went to China why did you not take a certificate of identification with you?
A.   I went away hurriedly.
Q.   Is it not a fact that when you went to China in July, 1890, you went to China without the intention of returning to the United States?
A.   I intended to return.
Q.   Why did you not then take some means of identifying yourself here upon your return to this country?
A.   I started away very hurriedly—suddenly.
Q.   Do you know that all Chinese who return here have more or less difficulty in landing, do you not?
A.   I know that, but I did not have time to get a certificate.
Q.   What was the reason of your haste for your departure to China?
A.   My mother was very sick in China and wanted me to come home immediately.
Q.   And when did you have this paper sent you to China?
A.   In the latter part of last year.
Q.   Who else do you know in Santa Cruz besides these two white men [the Thompsons]?
A.   I only know the two that signed my paper.
Q.   Did you work for Mr. Thompson in Santa Cruz?
A.   No, sir; I done Chinese business.
Q.   What street is your store situated on?
A.   Front Street.
Q.   What place of business was there right opposite your store?
A.   When I went to China, there was a red brick building right opposite my place and there used to be a liquor dealer. What there is now there I do not know.
Q.   What kind of goods did you sell?
A.   Drugs and general merchandise.
Q.   What did you do in carrying on the business of the firm?
A.   Bookkeeper.

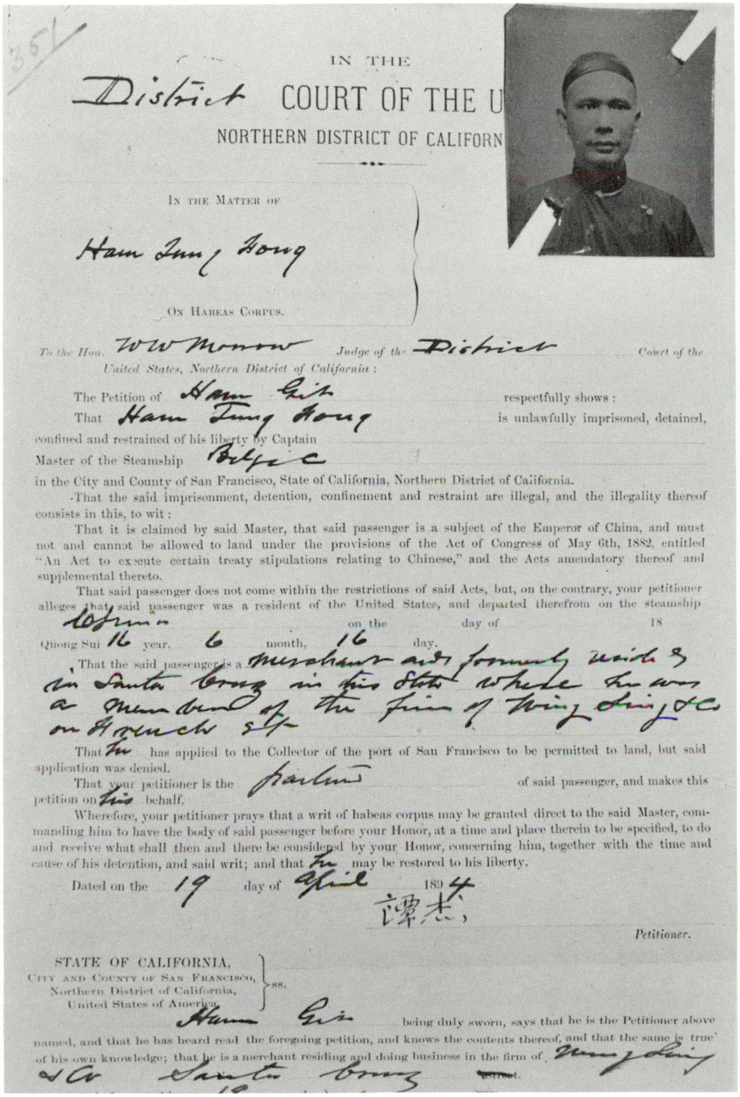

IN THE

District COURT OF THE U

NORTHERN DISTRICT OF CALIFORN

IN THE MATTER OF

Ham Tung Hong

ON HABEAS CORPUS.

To the Hon. W W Morrow Judge of the District Court of the United States, Northern District of California:

The Petition of Ham Git respectfully shows:

That Ham Tung Hong is unlawfully imprisoned, detained, confined and restrained of his liberty by Captain Master of the Steamship Belgic in the City and County of San Francisco, State of California, Northern District of California.

That the said imprisonment, detention, confinement and restraint are illegal, and the illegality thereof consists in this, to wit:

That it is claimed by said Master, that said passenger is a subject of the Emperor of China, and must not and cannot be allowed to land under the provisions of the Act of Congress of May 6th, 1882, entitled "An Act to execute certain treaty stipulations relating to Chinese," and the Acts amendatory thereof and supplemental thereto.

That said passenger does not come within the restrictions of said Acts, but, on the contrary, your petitioner alleges that said passenger was a resident of the United States, and departed therefrom on the steamship China on the day of 18 Quong Sui 16 year, 6 month, 16 day.

That the said passenger is a merchant and formerly resided in Santa Cruz in this State where he was a member of the firm of Wing Sing & Co on French St.

That he has applied to the Collector of the port of San Francisco to be permitted to land, but said application was denied.

That your petitioner is the partner of said passenger, and makes this petition on his behalf.

Wherefore, your petitioner prays that a writ of habeas corpus may be granted direct to the said Master, commanding him to have the body of said passenger before your Honor, at a time and place therein to be specified, to do and receive what shall then and there be considered by your Honor, concerning him, together with the time and cause of his detention, and said writ; and that he may be restored to his liberty.

Dated on the 19 day of April 1894

譚杰

Petitioner.

STATE OF CALIFORNIA,
City and County of San Francisco,
Northern District of California,
United States of America, } ss.

Ham Git being duly sworn, says that he is the Petitioner above named, and that he has heard read the foregoing petition, and knows the contents thereof, and that the same is true of his own knowledge; that he is a merchant residing and doing business in the firm of Wing Sing & Co Santa Cruz Street.

Ham Tung's writ of habeas corpus, 1894. Certificate describes Ham Tung as a "merchant and formerly resided in Santa Cruz in this state where he was a merchant of the firm of Wing Sing & Co on French [*sic*] St."

NATIONAL ARCHIVES

At this point the government prosecutor began to question Ham Tung about the physical layout of Chinatown, Santa Cruz, and the testimony is an excellent example of the kind of grilling given each Chinese when he returned to the United States.

Q. How many bridges are there that cross the river at Santa Cruz, in the town, or near the town, wagon bridges?

A. I know there are bridges, but I do not know how many.

Q. When did you first go into the firm?

A. In 1880.

Q. Have you been in the firm engaged in the store carrying on the business of the store, ever since you went into the store until you went to China?

A. Yes, sir.

Q. Now is there any bridge across the river above your store?

A. I don't remember.

Q. Is there any bridge across the river below your store?

A. I don't remember, I never went out around town much.

Q. Where was the Court House from your store?

A. Not very far.

Q. Which way?

A. I don't remember.

Q. I will draw myself a little plat of Santa Cruz, including the Wing Sing store, with which I am perfectly familiar. I have marked upon this little plat I have drawn, Front Street, Ocean Avenue and Cooper Street and I will state to you, to give you an idea, that your store according to your testimony and Mr. Thompson, is about there, where I have marked it. Where did the Court House stand?

A. I don't remember.

Q. Do you remember a Court House at all?

A. I remember there was a Court House there, but I never went there. I know there is a Court House.

Q. Was there any large stream of water?

A. I do not remember.

Q. To the Ocean, salt water, was there any quite large stream of water in the town of Santa Cruz and if so, where was it?

A. You went right down the straight street, the white man's street, runs right into the water.

Q. Do you mean Front Street upon which your store stood, runs to the water?

A. The street that runs down is a large street, that runs down to the wharf there.
Q. What is the name of the river, the stream of water?
A. I do not know, I never knew anything about the name.
Q. Was there any large Hotel anywhere within 350 feet of your store, that was upon the same level with your store, a white man's hotel?
A. Right near my place there were two saloons.
Q. Where was the stream of water, if any there was, in Santa Cruz, which is in the winter time a very large stream?
A. I do not know anything about it. I never went out much. I always done Chinese business.
Q. As you would stand in your store, the door fronting upon Front Street, with your face to Front Street, which way was the Ocean from you, the salt water, which hand, the right or left?
A. I cannot remember now, I have been over a few years in China now.
Q. Was it level around your store, in the rear of it, and for 200 feet distant from it, or was it hilly?
A. I don't remember exactly.
Q. Don't you remember in the rear of your store, there is something there that any one would know that had been there for one year, much less than 10?
A. Well, right around the store is level and back 200 feet is kind of steep.
Q. Anything else there besides kind of steep?
A. I don't remember.
Q. You don't remember?
A. No, sir.

That ended Ham Tung's testimony, and the obvious landmark the government examiner was trying to get Ham Tung to remember was the San Lorenzo River which ran directly behind (and during the winter beneath) Wing Sing's store. Ham Tung's partner was then called to the stand and he too was asked about the rear of the Wing Sing Store:

Q. Is there any stream near your store, and if so, where is it?
A. It is in the rear of the store.
Q. How far from it?

A.   It is right back there. There is a yard between that and us.
Q.   And that is all?
A.   There is a yard and then a small vacant space.
Q.   Is it 400 feet away?
A.   I should say maybe two blocks distant.

Ham Git then quickly identified the Court House and the location of the ocean in relation to Wing Sing Store, and the examiner wondered why Ham Tung had forgotten so much:

Q.   Why is it that this man does not know anything about Santa
     Cruz?
A.   Well, he has been sick ever since he has been in China.
Q.   That would not affect his mind, would it?
A.   Well, sometimes a person that is sick, his mind is confused.
Q.   Or his memory, it would not affect that would it?
A.   He had no memory.
Q.   This man does not remember anything about the streets, of the
     hills of the mountains or anything about Santa Cruz?
A.   He does not speak English and another thing, he does not know
     anything about Santa Cruz much.
Q.   How could he live in Santa Cruz ten years and not know any-
     thing about Santa Cruz?
A.   He has been away for several years.
Q.   He would certainly know about the river in the rear of his store
     would he not?
A.   Well, I don't know.

   Ham Tung's inability to answer the questions about Santa
Cruz resulted in his being refused entry into the United States
and he was returned to the ship *Belgic* which eventually took
him back to China. The Thompsons were not overlooked in the
final decision as the Commissioner noted, "I have no doubt of
the honesty and conscientiousness of the two white witnesses,
the first one of whom I have known for 25 years, but they are
simply mistaken as to the identity of this Chinese."
   We will probably never know whether the man claiming to be
Ham Tung was an imposter or not, but the above testimony

gives us a good sense of the rigor of the re-entry hearings and suggests how the Chinese viewed Santa Cruz from Front Street. The most telling reference, to "the white man's street," Pacific Avenue, indicates that those who spoke little or no English and worked in a capacity which required no contact with the white public might never venture beyond the confines of the Front Street Chinatown.

## CHINESE CULTURE

Ironically, the most vivid and detailed accounts of the cultural life of the immigrant Chinese in the Monterey Bay Region were recorded in Santa Cruz, the town that had the most strident antipathy for them. In order to condemn the habits of the Chinese, the anti-Chinese proponents had to describe them, and the result was a number of derogatory but detailed descriptions of Chinese New Year, funerals, and the temple. While Duncan McPherson and his newspaper colleagues in Santa Cruz were writing of the perils and evils of Santa Cruz's Chinatown, the boy Ernest Otto played there, wandering through the buildings, peeking into the temple and filing away a storehouse of impressions. During his long newspaper career in Santa Cruz, Otto drew on his boyhood memories to reconstruct the Front Street Chinatown. Reading those columns, written during the 1940s and 1950s under the title of "Old Santa Cruz," is like visiting Santa Cruz in the 1880s in the company of an anthropologist who sees everything from table height. As an adult Otto made a daily walk through Chinatown, visiting his friends and writing of their lives; everyone who grew up there in the 1930s and 1940s remembers Ernest Otto with fondness and affection. The Santa Cruz Chinese had no greater friend than Ernest Otto, and it is as if the spirits placed him there to balance the strident defamation that had been written earlier. Combining Ernest's memories with contemporary newspaper accounts, we can get a feeling for the traditions practiced by the Chinese in Santa Cruz.

The Chinese calendar is an agrarian one based partly on the solar cycle and partly on the lunar. The beginning of the year is calculated according to the winter solstice, but the first day of the new year falls on the second full moon after the solstice. The traditional Chinese calendar lists twenty-four celebrations throughout the year, but most of the minor festivals did not survive the trip across the Pacific. The festivals most often celebrated in California (and those that were the most public) were the lunar New Year, the beginning of Spring (Ch'ing Ming), and the Autumn festival (Spirits' Festival). That many of the Chinese in the Monterey Bay Region worked in some form of agriculture made the calendar quite appropriate. In some Chinese communities, special holidays commemorated the birthday of a particular deity, such as the Festival of the Ring in Monterey, which became an important event.

The New Year Festival highlighted the beginning of the Chinese year, a time of renewal and celebration, a time to clear accounts, placate the evil spirits, and win the favor of the good spirits. Traditionally the Chinese New Year celebration lasted two weeks, but in Santa Cruz the festival was condensed to a more practical three-day period. The one time that whites were welcome in Chinatown, Chinese New Year celebrations drew mixed crowds of whites and Chinese to the Front Street Chinatown as they did elsewhere throughout the region.

The traditional Chinese New Year celebration involved a complicated series of steps and observances, but these can be reduced to two phases, the private at-home rituals and the public open-house phase beginning on New Year's day. At year's end, Chinese cleaned up stores and houses: "Windows never washed during the year were [washed] at this season. It was also important to remove the old papers and hieroglyphics back of the 'stove god.'" Each house had a kitchen or stove god, and this deity delivered the year-end report to the officials in heaven. Much of the New Year festival revolved around preparing him for the journey and welcoming him back.

Each store also had at least one other shrine with an "ever-burning light" before it. Some shrines were elaborately carved, others were only "gold spattered red papers" with the name of the deity written on them in black Chinese characters, and each of these shrines was also cleaned and given a new set of good luck sayings written in gold on red (for good luck) paper. New good luck papers were also pasted onto door frames, and the sign over the door of the store or house was freshly painted. Interior doorways were protected with strips of red perforated papers which screened out the evil spirits who were unable to wriggle through the holes. Several months before the new year, the Chinese would put Chinese lily (*sui sin fa*, sometimes called Chinese narcissus) bulbs in dishes filled with rocks to bloom just before the festival: "If [the lilies] were in full bloom when New Year's arrived they would be placed on the altars and given to friends—their failure to bloom was [a] symbol of bad luck."

During the afternoon of the last day of the year, the Chinese followed a tradition of settling outstanding debts that often drove individual Chinese into the arms of money lenders. Otto recorded Chinese going "from house to house with sacks of silver dollars" paying off their debts. Families then gathered together (the few families there were in Santa Cruz) for a midnight feast and welcomed the kitchen god back from his celestial journey.

The public phase of Chinese New Year (and all other Chinese celebrations) was heralded by the firing of thousands of firecrackers. The firecrackers were used to frighten away the evil spirits while the kitchen god was away on his journey:

> At three o'clock a skirmish attack was made on the evil spirits with a small fusillade of firecrackers. Fifteen minutes later a grand attack was made on the devils, which the [Chinese] believe are always

around to bring ill luck. On Yiq Wau's porch was a Chinaman who held a pole from which hung a long string of firecrackers. For ten minutes the explosion of firecrackers, punctuated now and then with the noise of exploding bombs, was heard.

On the first day of the new year, Chinatown held an open house, and visitors were welcomed into stores and homes. Otto remembered the tables piled high with "grapefruit, piles of oranges and lacquer boxes of sweetmeats." Each store owner and merchant put on an open house, and Wong Kee gained a reputation for the most elaborate table of treats for his visitors, while Quong Chong was somewhat more reserved in his hospitality.

During the New Year open house, visitors were able to enter the temple, and Otto had vivid memories of the New Year ritual in the Chee Kong Tong temple behind Wong Kee's store:

> . . . in the center of the altar was an alcove for the picture of the gods, a group of several . . . the picture was a couple of feet back from the frame of the alcove of green with carved letters, with a touch of an oriental finish. Hanging from the center of the shrine was the ever burning light held in a brass holder. A pewter holder in front of the picture was filled with burning incense, punks or red candles made of grease. On each side of the alcove were tall, pewter holders for large decorated red candles and the tall punks.
> A couple of feet in front was a table-like altar. On this was a large pewter bowl for the burning of the fragrant smelling sandal wood by the worshiper [sic]. The altar cloth hanging along the front was of brightly embroidered red silk on which were many circular mirrors.
> Along the front was a piece of white matting on which the worshipper knelt and in his hands had the incenses and candles which were placed in the bowl. He would pour out libations of wine and burn paper representing the next world, money and clothes.

On New Year's day a roast pig, red paper wrapped around its feet, was set on a table in the center of the room, and Chinese music—cymbal, drum, and gong—was played during the day. The music, like the exploding firecrackers, was intended to

Interior of the Santa Cruz Chee Kong Tong temple, c. 1900. Shows ornate decorations in the temple. Photo probably taken at New Year's celebration as the altar is covered with offerings and Chinese lilies which were put in dishes and forced to bloom early for the occasion.

SPECIAL COLLECTIONS, UCSC

drive away the evil spirits. The exuberance of the firecrackers at New Year acted as an economic indicator for the previous year in Chinatown—less money meant fewer firecrackers at New Year's. The ability of Chinese to repay their debts also reflected the economy; in 1886, for example, Wong Kee (one of the first Chinese to invest in the fledgling apple industry) claimed that not only had he lost $1,500 speculating in apples, he expected to lose the $2,000 owed him by other Chinese because times were hard.

Ernest Otto left more observations about the Chinese in Santa Cruz than we have space for, but two subjects particularly fascinated him—Chinese barbers and opium smoking. The barber shop in Santa Cruz had the sign "Sing Lee—Front Street" over the door, and the barber had six fingers, "an extra finger which protruded from the bottom of a thumb." Young Ernest Otto would take newcomers to Chinatown to show them this wondrous sight, and at the same time he observed the ritual of maintaining the queue.

Queues, Point Alones Village, 1890s. Queues were worn by Chinese males until the Chinese Revolution of 1911. Most Chinese in California wore them tightly wound on top of the head and covered with a hat when they went outside Chinatown. Since this photograph was taken in the Chinese village, the men are wearing the queues exposed.     PAT HATHAWAY

The queue had been imposed on Chinese men by the Manchus when they conquered China in 1644, and it was considered a crime not to wear the queue in China. Thus the queue might be used as a measure of acculturation, because if a Chinese removed his queue, it meant he was not planning to return to China (though he could buy a false queue if he changed his mind). In the early days only two Chinese men in Santa Cruz did not wear the queue—Tong, a laborer at Hall's dairy, and the fisherman who worked for Fred Perez at the wharf. The traditional queue required that the forehead be shaved back to the middle of the head and the back part of the hair be worn in a long braid. Otto watched with fascination as the barber prepared the queue:

> The customer sat on a small, hard, wooden bench. First the barber unbraided the customer's queue . . . next came the shaving. A porcelain bowl was set in a spindle-legged stand trimmed with the usual Chinese red paint. In his hand, the barber would take a razor, made of roughly hammered steel. The razor, which was very sharp, was triangular in shape. The barber would hold a board below the head, since

about half the head was shaved. The hair was dipped in very hot water before it was shaved off. The hair then dropped onto the board. No shaving soap was used. The customer's ears were also cleaned and the barber's final act was to scrape the skin between the eyes.

The queue was often worn wound about the head beneath a black slouch hat.

When Otto was a young man, opium was sold openly in Chinese stores. The merchants kept the "sticky mass, like deep black molasses" in delicate brass boxes and measured it carefully on special ivory scales. Stores set aside a special area for opium smoking, usually a platform in a corner with a small lamp at its center:

> On the tray were the lamp and opium pipes. The opium pipe at each end was tipped with ivory and in the center was a large clay bowl. The smoker would remove with a long needle the drug from the small receptacle in which the opium was kept, form it into a pellet and then bake it over the small hole of the bowl and then inhale it and finally he would go into the land of dreams.

Otto noted that though opium smoking was common in Santa Cruz in the nineteenth century, it was rare in the twentieth.

## CHINESE FUNERALS

Evil spirits, as essential to the Chinese spirit world as good spirits, had to be placated and deluded through elaborate rules and ceremonies. Perhaps the individual's greatest moment of vulnerability came between the moment of death and the moment that the mortal remains were interred in the earth. The traditional Chinese funeral relied on a sequence of rituals to distract or ward off the evil spirits during this extremely defenseless time. Much of what we know about Chinese funerals in the Monterey Bay Region comes from Ernest Otto.

Chinese funeral, Watsonville, c. 1890. Mourners are dressed in white, and the hearse is just visible behind the tree on far left. Angle and nature of photograph suggests that it was taken surreptitiously by a bystander, as Chinese did not care to have photographs taken of their funeral processions.

SPECIAL COLLECTIONS, UCSC

The size and elaborateness of the Chinese funeral in Santa Cruz was directly proportional to the deceased's stature in the Chinese community. During the years of the Front Street Chinatown, an altar would be built on Front Street and piled high with food ranging from chicken and sweetmeat to the red-paper-footed roast pig. The gift of food was never a mere gesture in the Chinese community, as nothing was held more dear than food, particularly the specially prepared roast pig used for ceremonial occasions. Residents of the Chinese community would pay their respects to the deceased at this altar, and then, when the day of burial arrived (sometimes selected by a numerologist), a hearse would be hired for the funeral procession.

The Chinese funeral procession began with the required firecrackers to frighten away the ever-present evil spirits. The firecrackers sometimes frightened the horses more than the evil spirits. With Chinese band, mourners, and white school boys following close behind, the funeral procession wound up and over Mission Hill to the Chinese section of Evergreen Cemetery:

> The hearse would be preceded by numbers in line bearing banners and figures. The gongs of the orchestra would sound loudly. On each carriage would be posted red paper upon which would be the Chinese hieroglyphics. Likely at the school ground a score of boys would follow the ceremony. In the early days a transfer wagon would carry all the clothing, bedding, etc. of the deceased.

Somewhere in the funeral procession would be a man trying to confuse the evil spirits by scattering slips of perforated red papers along the funeral procession route. Evil spirits were single-minded to a fault, only capable of traveling in straight lines; a blizzard of hole-filled paper created a labyrinth that would slow them up. If the perforated papers were successful, the evil spirits ricocheted harmlessly off to the side and away from the deceased. Family members present dressed in the official costume of mourning white and followed the hearse. A 1906 newspaper account described Hock Kee's nephew following his uncle's hearse to Evergreen Cemetery:

> He [the nephew] followed . . . the hearse to the cemetery, his queue being braided with blue ribbon and band of white about his head, white and blue being the Chinese colors of mourning. He carried in his hands the entire distance to the cemetery a bowl containing the burning punks and candles.

The noise of the firecrackers, gong, and drums, like the scattering of perforated paper, was designed to keep the evil spirits at bay until the deceased could be buried.

The final act of the funeral was the ceremony which took place at the cemetery. The clothing, bedding, and belongings were placed in a pile and burned so that the deceased would have use of them in his new spirit world. In the early days the clothing was burned in the road next to Evergreen Cemetery, but during the 1890s, a ceremonial oven in which to burn the belongings was constructed. The mourners and pall bearers then burned paper money, lit incense and candles for the deceased, and left more offerings of food such as "roast pork, chickens, food and sweetmeats." The dead Chinese was buried in a simple pine coffin, and a redwood plank with the name, date, and village of birth was placed at the head of the grave. The mourners then filed past the grave and kowtowed to the deceased, ending the ceremony.

Similar funerals were re-enacted in each of the Monterey Bay Region Chinatowns. When a Chinese died in Brooklyn, the funeral procession crossed the river into Watsonville and went the entire length of Main Street to the Pioneer Cemetery on the hill just north of town. In Salinas the cemetery was located about a mile north of the Soledad Street Chinatown, on a hillside next to the public cemetery for county indigents, and the funeral processions also occasioned comment in the newspapers. At the Point Alones village the funerals occasioned less public comment, as the cemetery was adjacent to the village.

Once buried, the remains of the dead still required attention, and the surrogate families performed their duties on the two main cemetery holidays each year, Ch'ing Ming in the spring and Spirits' Day in the fall. Ch'ing Ming means pure brightness, and the holiday had its origins in celebrations in China which marked the beginning of spring. Using propitious willow branches, the senior family member swept the grave; food and drink were left for the spirit once the grave site was cleaned. This ritual reinforced the importance of filial duty as both the young and old members of the family fed and tended their ancestors.

The Associations and tongs also took over the responsibility of Ch'ing Ming for the family. Where Ch'ing Ming was a family affair in China, it became a community affair in towns like Santa

Cruz where the entire Chinese community went out to the cemetery to pay their respects to the spirits of their departed countrymen:

> An express wagon left Chinatown in the afternoon with a number of the older Chinamen. There was an entire roast hog done to a turn, cakes, liquors, rice and others of the choicest Chinese edibles, which were placed on the graves and on the altar at the Chinese plot in the Evergreen cemetery. Burning candles and punks were placed on the grave of each Chinaman buried, paper burned and prayers offered. The roast pork was brought back to Chinatown and divided among the Chinamen.

A similar ceremony occurred in the fall, on what is called the Spirits' Festival, with the family, or the surrogate family, returning to the cemetery to offer food and money to the spirits. This holiday did not usually attract much attention in the non-Chinese community, but in August 1881 the Salinas Chinese community left burning incense at the Chinese cemetery which set fire to the dry grass and burned many of the wooden grave markers before it was extinguished.

As the Chinatowns dwindled and their inhabitants dispersed, the associations found the funerals and celebrations more difficult to maintain. In 1915, for example, when Chin Sing died in Santa Cruz, he was destitute, and a collection of only forty dollars was taken up by the small Chinese community to ensure that he had a proper Chinese funeral. The numbers of Chinese in each community willing to assume the responsibility for burying the elderly Chinese pioneers grew smaller not only because the communities were getting smaller, but also because communities placed an increasing emphasis on the American way of doing things. Chinese who had converted to Christianity, for example, abandoned the old Chinese funeral rituals and would not support their continuation. Following the Chinese Revolution of 1911, many young Chinese felt increasing disdain for some of the traditional Chinese ceremonies, believing them to represent the old ways of the Chinese empire. All of these trends made it more important than ever for the older, traditional Chinese men either to return to China while they were still alive or see to it that their remains returned after they were dead.

Cemeteries can be extremely useful documents when reconstructing the social and economic history of a community. The arrangement of the graves, the absence of certain ethnic or religious groups, or the physical segregation of their graves within the cemetery often mirrors the relationships of the various groups during life. The easiest way to find the Chinese section of a California cemetery (except, of course, the large all-Chinese cemeteries at Colma outside San Francisco) is to walk the perimeter. In Santa Cruz, Watsonville, and Monterey, the Chinese sections are separate, on the edge, while in Salinas the Chinese cemetery is a separate section which originally was adjacent to the Salinas potter's field. Santa Cruz, where the Chinese community died out much earlier, is the only community which does not still hold memorial Ch'ing Ming services.

## THE CHEE KONG TONG IN SANTA CRUZ

Like the queues worn by the Chinese in Santa Cruz, the Chee Kong Tong harkened back to China and political issues there. As we noted earlier, the Chee Kong Tong (translated "Extend Justice Society") began as a secret society in seventeenth-century China. Formed to drive the Manchus out of China and restore the monarchy to the Chinese, the society was brought to California by the early immigrants from Canton.

The Chee Kong Tong came to Santa Cruz early in the 1860s (it had a temple at the Powder Mill in 1864), and the society

Chee Kong Tong temple, Santa Cruz, 1940s. Sign on the porch read "Chinese Freemasons Hall." Chinese in California accepted the title of Chinese Freemasons, though the Chee Kong Tong had no connection with the Masonic Order, because it helped keep anti–Chinese proponents from attacking the organization. This temple, located in Birkenseer's Chinatown, was demolished in 1950.

SPECIAL COLLECTIONS, UCSC

played an important role in the life of the Santa Cruz Chinese community, partly because the constantly harassed Chinese community in Santa Cruz needed more protection than elsewhere in the region. When trouble arose, the Santa Cruz Chinese summoned help from the Six Companies through the Chee Kong Tong.

Because the Chee Kong Tong was much more public in Santa Cruz than elsewhere in the region, much more is known about it. In Santa Cruz the Masonic Order was an extremely strong political force in the community, and the Chinese Chee Kong Tong exploited one of the strangest affinities imaginable. During the nineteenth century, the order of Freemasons adopted the notion that the Triad society was actually a branch of the Masons and referred to the Chee Kong Tong society as the "Chinese Freemasons." The Santa Cruz Chee Kong Tong was quick to exploit this unusual opportunity, adopting the name "Chinese Freemasons" and emblazoning it across the temple. Its members proudly wore Masonic emblems in their lapels: "Wong Kee would display his pin proudly and say it was that of a Master Mason. It did bear the square and the compass." As a branch of the Masonic order, the Chee Kong Tong was more accessible to whites, and several times white Masons were allowed to witness rituals generally never seen by non-Chinese. One of those to visit an initiation was Ernest Otto, and he estimated that before the 1911 Revolution in China (which rendered some of the tong's political purposes moot), 90% of the Chinese men in Santa Cruz belonged to the Chee Kong Tong; only the Chinese Christians did not join.

During the 1880s a representative of the Chee Kong Tong would come from San Francisco every fall to give instruction to candidates for membership; the instructional session lasted two days, and at its completion students were initiated into the organization. A party of white Masons visited such an instructional session in September 1883:

Here and there lay several Chinamen smoking, while on one side of the room an aged [Chinese], with a piece of bamboo in his hand, was talking to an eager group of listeners seated in a circle before him . . . In another part of the room a number of bowls were ranged on matting in which there were several kinds of meat, with cooked rice, thin strips of cocoanut and sweetmeats, the whole being placed before maps on which were depicted Chinese characters. Near these bowls were placed lights, and two large knives were crossed, and before the whole arrangement stood a number of Celestials chanting in a manner peculiar to themselves.

The white observers did not remain for the actual initiation; as they left they "heard the door slammed and bolted behind us."

The following year in the old Otto Hall in Santa Cruz, the Chee Kong Tong initiated twenty-eight new members before a crowd of over one hundred fellow members. Wong Kee estimated that there were five hundred society members in the Monterey Bay Region; the visitors at the initiation included members from Soquel and Watsonville. When the number of initiates and spectators was smaller, the initiation of new members was held in a small room adjoining the temple behind Wong Kee's store; a candle was always kept burning on a small altar:

There was also a circular steel rim and sword . . . [and] when the oath was taken the queue which was a sign of subjection to the Manchus, was unbraided, and the neophyte knelt with the circular hoop over him and the sword across his neck.

The Santa Cruz Chee Kong Tong offered refuge and strength for the Chinese living in the testy little town, and when called upon the Chee Kong Tong could flex impressive legal muscles. A good example of the power of the Chee Kong Tong, and the vulnerability of the Chinese in Santa Cruz, was an incident involving Lou Sing, a young laborer working at Vine Hill in the mountains above Santa Cruz. Two weeks after the initiation of twenty-four members into the Chee Kong Tong, Lou Sing, a seventeen-year-old Chinese laborer and society member, was found dead at the Kloss Ranch on Vine Hill. John P. Davenport, acting coroner, declared that Lou Sing had committed suicide. When the body was returned to Santa Cruz, the Chinese community determined that Lou Sing had a broken neck and whip welts on his arms. Davenport explained the broken neck by surmising that Lou Sing had taken the poison while standing up and had broken his neck when he fell unconscious. The Chinese believed that Lou Sing had been mistreated and murdered at Vine Hill; the Chee Kong Tong immediately contacted the Chinese Six Companies for help. Several days later the following advertisement appeared in the local newspaper over the signature of the Chinese Six Companies:

> We would like to ask, how could Lou Sing break his neck after he took poison? We say that he was hurt after he was leaving the stable with his hands tied behind his back . . . we have a witness to the whole proceeding, and will bring him forth when necessary. This witness took the rope off Lou Sing's hands. He says that one of the men told Lou Sing that if he did not leave in ten minutes he would shoot him; then a man took Lou Sing by the back of the neck and forced poison into his mouth. Another man stood guard outside and would not let the other Chinamen in. When the Chinamen asked what was in the spoon they were told it was milk. We intend to sift this case to the very bottom.

Lou Sing's funeral was delayed while Wong Kee, head of the local Chee Kong Tong, went to San Francisco to confer with the Six Companies. The Six Companies hired Dr. Charles Stivers, former police surgeon for the City of San Francisco, to do an autopsy on the body. The body was badly decomposed by the time Dr. Stivers arrived in Santa Cruz, and though he was able to determine that Lou Sing's neck had been dislocated through violence, he could not make a thorough examination of the contents of the stomach. Dr. Stivers then returned to San Francisco to give his findings to the Six Companies.

Lou Sing had been a member of the Kong Chow Company (one of the Six Companies), and that company, along with the local Chee Kong Tong, put on the most impressive Chinese funeral in Santa Cruz's history. Though Lou Sing died in poverty, he received a funeral of "pomp and magnificence":

> The coffin was placed on a pedestal in the street and each 'John', with a punk in hand, would make a bow before the coffin. The 'Freemasons,' to which he belonged, wore red and white ribbons, and took charge of the ceremonies . . . amid much noise and confusion the procession started for the old cemetery . . . punks and a bowl of incense were on the coffin in the hearse. A delegation of the deceased's brethren acted as pall bearers. A flag of the society was carried in front.

Though Lou Sing's murderer was never brought to justice, the Santa Cruz Chinese had demonstrated their defiance of the original coroner's verdict and left the clear message that they could call upon the extensive resources of the Chee Kong Tong and Chinese Six Companies when necessary.

## THE CHRISTIAN MISSION IN THE MONTEREY BAY REGION

Santa Cruz, which had the strongest anti-Chinese movement, ironically had the most active Chinese Christian mission in the Monterey Bay Region in the nineteenth century. Santa Cruz's strong Protestant roots plus the close contact between whites and Chinese domestics, cooks, and laundrymen help to explain the large number of Chinese who converted to Christianity. The Chinese Sunday school begun in the Santa Cruz Congregational Church in 1869 was the earliest recorded Christian institution dedicated to the conversion of Chinese in the Monterey Bay Region; missions in Salinas and Monterey both began in 1883, and the first one in Watsonville came in 1891, after the move across the Pajaro River. (The first mission in Watsonville, run by the Christian Church, had a membership of twenty and died out, to be replaced in 1894 by a Presbyterian Church mission.)

Protestant churches conducted most of the missionary work in California's Chinese communities, and most of their first missionaries had been to China; Dr. William Speer, a Presbyterian minister, opened the first Chinese mission in San Francisco in 1852. Dr. Speer's mission set the tone for most of the later, successful Chinese missions in California because it blended religious teaching with practical aid.

From the time of Confucius the Chinese have exhibited an impatience with other-worldly philosophies, preferring a much more practical, almost businesslike relationship with the deities who control affairs on earth. Dr. Speer and other Protestant ministers quickly learned that, for the Chinese who was busy trying to scratch out a living and survive in America, the missionary appeal had to be practical: "They [Chinese] believe in praying to the Christian God if such prayers will bring its rewards." Since Confucianism emphasized ethics, the missionaries concentrated on teaching the ethics of Christianity. The Chinese came to the Christian missions for companionship, for legal protection, for social mobility, and for the English lessons the church offered.

The Congregational Church led the missionary efforts among Santa Cruz's Chinese, beginning with a Sunday school class in April 1869. The first teacher was a woman, and the classes were conducted in English; the first class had a membership of twelve students and emphasized learning English: "Some could read the [English] alphabet, while others could not, but all manifested an industry and eagerness to learn." The difficulty faced by most Christian missions in California was that their students were mainly adults who spoke Cantonese while the ministers were whites who spoke only English. The Congregational Church's Chinese Sunday school continued through the 1870s, but not until 1881 was a full-fledged Chinese mission organized in Santa Cruz.

Congregational Chinese Mission, Birkenseer's Chinatown, Santa Cruz, c. 1896. Established by the Santa Cruz Congregational Church in 1869, the Santa Cruz Chinese Mission was relocated and rebuilt following the 1894 fire. Pon Fang, the leader of the Chinese congregation, is on the far left. Chin Ong is in the light coat, second from the right; On Chong is fourth from the right in the back row. The Reverend William H. Pond, leader of the Congregational missionary effort in the United States, is in the right foreground, while next to him is Mary L. Perkins of Santa Cruz, one of the supporters of the mission. This child in the front is Ah Yum. SPECIAL COLLECTIONS, UCSC

273

The Reverend W. H. Pond, one of the leading figures in the Chinese missionary movement (and a leader of the pro-Chinese immigration forces in California) authorized the establishment of the Santa Cruz Congregational Church's Chinese Mission in 1881. The Reverend Mahlon Willet had just taken over as pastor of the Santa Cruz church, and the Chinese mission was held in the rear of the Willet home under the guidance of Mrs. Willet. The daily routine at the mission was rigorous; the Chinese attended class each weekday evening until around nine o'clock, and Ernest Otto remembered seeing them returning to Front Street from the Walnut Street school. In addition to English lessons, each evening's class "closed with devotionals and Bible study and singing in Chinese and English." During the first year a Chinese minister named Wong Ock was assigned to the mission and his tenure from 1881 to 1883 certainly helped make the classes attractive; Otto (a member of the Congregational Church) estimated that forty baptized Chinese were members in the Congregational Church during the height of the mission's work.

Beginning in April 1882 the Chinese mission held a public recital to commemorate the mission's founding, and during the 1880s those recitals were extremely well-attended by the Santa Cruz populace. Reverend Pond would usually come down from San Francisco to officiate at the event, and it showcased for the public the progress that the Chinese students were making, much like a piano recital. Watsonville's Presbyterian Chinese mission held similar recitals, and Reverend Pond attended one in June 1897.

Perhaps the largest of the anniversary celebrations, held in April 1884, drew a standing-room-only crowd of whites to the Congregational church, many of whom were drawn there "to satisfy their curiosity and to be amused." Rev. Pond chaired the exercises, and each of the Chinese students, his "tight-wound queue . . . [reflecting] back the rays of the gaslights," went to the pulpit to demonstrate his skills at oratory or singing. Lem Sam

THIRTEENTH ANNIVERSARY

— OF THE —

# SANTA CRUZ CHINESE MISSION,

FIRST CONGREGATIONAL CHURCH.

## SUNDAY EVENING, MAY 12th, 1895.

### ORDER OF SERVICE:

VOLUNTARY............................................................

MUSIC.....................................................Choir

PRAYER...................................................Pastor

## EXERCISES BY CHINESE.

1. Chorus—"Up and Onward".....................By the School
2. Address—"Welcome"...............................Chin Wing
3. Bible Reading—"96 Psalm"...........................Chin Wah
4. Duet—"More About Jesus"...........Lem Sing and Pon Fang
5. Recitation—"All Things Bright and Beautiful".......Ah Ying
6. Song in Chinese—"Sabbath Home"..................School
7. Recitation—"He Will Gather the Wheat"...........George
8. Hymn—.......................................Congregation
9. Address—"Why I Came to California"............Joe Dun
10. Duet—"Give Me Jesus".............Pon Fang and Lem Sing
11. Recitation—"Gospel Banner"....................Pon Hong
12. Solo........................................Joe Dun
13. Address—"Freely ye Have Received, Freely Give"...Pon Fang

Address.................................................Pastor

Offertory...............................................

Hymn ...............................................Congregation

SURF PRINT.

Program from recital, May 1895. The Chinese Mission held a public recital each spring. The recital was extremely popular with the Santa Cruz public. Lam Sing (Lem Sing), who sang the duet with Pon Fang, later owned a market on Pacific Avenue in Santa Cruz.      LILLIAN MCPHERSON ROUSE described the difficulties he was having learning English, Lam Sing and Lam Poy recited from the Bible, and Dong Lung gave a talk entitled "These From the Land of China." Wong Ock and Rev. Pond then closed the celebration with short sermons. Pond noted that the mission cost approximately five hundred dollars per year, and a collection of seventy dollars taken up at the end of the ceremonies helped defray the costs. The newspaper account of the ceremony concluded:

> The exhibition on the whole, reflected credit on the teachers, and was a splendid example of patience and perseverance on their part, in being able to bring such an unlettered class to appear in public, and who seemed to 'sabe' all they said.

Pond often remained in Santa Cruz several days after the Chinese Mission celebration and usually gave at least one sermon to the general congregation the following Sunday. The Sunday following the 1884 anniversary, Pond gave a sermon in which he gave thanks that there were so many Chinese in Santa Cruz. That was too much for the editor of the *Santa Cruz Sentinel* (and Congregational Church member), Duncan McPherson, who blasted Pond in an editorial the following day:

> Mr. Pond is one of the most unacceptable preachers visiting Santa Cruz. If he thanks God for the presence of Chinamen in California, he is not sustained by the people of Santa Cruz. The people hereabouts are praying that the Chinese return speedily to the land of their nativity, there to dwell 'till life is over'. . . . Mr. Pond and all other worshippers of Celestials on this earth, can go with them, without leaving anything but a pleasant void behind.

McPherson's comments reflected the ongoing debate between church leadership and anti-Chinese proponents over Chinese immigration. Reverend Willet, responding to McPherson in a letter which McPherson published, declared that the responsibility for the missionary effort was not Mr. Pond's, but the Creator's:

> The men . . . who are intent upon enlightening the Chinese in our midst are . . . obeying 'marching orders.' If there is any fault found with that, let it be laid at the door of the great Captain of our faith—not upon the shoulders of his subordinates.

Willet went on to point out that nowhere in the Bible was there the phrase, "Thou shalt love a white man and hate a Chinaman." Reverend Pond continued to visit the Santa Cruz Chinese community into the twentieth century, and McPherson continued to attend church services.

Later in 1884 Wong Ock was transferred to do missionary work in Stockton, leaving the mission without a Chinese-speaking instructor. Not until the 1890s did a student at the Chinese mission become proficient enough in English to assume the bulk of the teaching duties at the mission. But the mission survived this and other changes. Sometime during the 1880s the mission moved from Walnut Street to a second-story location in the Front Street Chinatown. The recitals continued to be held in the Congregational Church, while the Front Street mission held an open house during the lunar New Year celebration. The Chinese leaders of the Congregational Church went to great efforts to entertain white visitors to Chinatown during the New Year festivities. In 1887 the mission had a "long table filled with Chinese confectionary, cakes and flowers," while hanging from the ceiling was "an air castle, which revolved around by the action of lighted candles, and displayed small paper figures of Chinese men and women." The success of the Santa Cruz Chinese Mission inspired the creation of the Chinese Christian Endeavor Society in 1892, the first in the United States.

The influence of the mission on the lives of the Chinese is well demonstrated by one of its most devoted members, Pon Fang, who rose from houseboy to successful merchant. Pon Fang, who came to California in 1878 at the age of fifteen, was employed by Santa Cruz physician P. B. Fagen as a houseboy. Fagen was a

Pon Fang (right), his wife, and son, Samuel, Santa Cruz, c. 1890. Pon Fang, leader of the Chinese Christian community, was also official Chinese-English translator for Santa Cruz County. He left Santa Cruz near the turn of the century to take a job with the Immigration and Naturalization Service as a translator.
VESTER DICK

member of the Congregational Church, and Fang began attending the Chinese mission where he learned to speak English well enough to become the official interpreter for cases involving Chinese in the Santa Cruz courts. Fang opened a store on Pacific Avenue, and in the evening he went to the Chinese mission where he "taught, sang, preached and was everything but an ordained minister." Pon Fang returned to China in the early 1890s, married, and started a family; he returned to Santa Cruz in 1894 and assumed the leadership of the Christian Chinese community just before fire destroyed the Front Street Chinatown.

A week following the fire, Pon Fang leased a new site for the Chinese Mission in the new Chinatown on land owned by Dr. Fagen and George Birkenseer. The new mission was located at 18 Bellevue Place, between Sing Kee and Yee Lung Kee. The twenty-year lease called for a monthly rent of twelve dollars, and Pon Fang agreed to paint the mission building and replace the wallpaper at least once every five years. The lease contained an interesting clause in which the Chinese agreed "not to let or underlet the whole or any part of said premises for laundry purposes . . ." The landlords agreed to maintain a plank sidewalk and electric street light and install fire hydrants.

The Chinese mission continued to operate at the new site well into the twentieth century, but as the Chinese population in Santa Cruz declined, so did the mission. Pon Fang eventually found work with the Immigration Service as an interpreter and moved away from Santa Cruz. Most of the few Chinese families who remained in town through the 1920s and 1930s were members of the Christian Chinese church.

## FRONT STREET CHINATOWN DESTROYED

Late Saturday night, April 14, 1894, a fire broke out at the north end of Chinatown on the east side of Front Street, and be-

Santa Cruz's Front Street Chinatown after the April 1894 fire. Taken looking west from river toward Front Street, photo shows the complete devastation of the Front Street Chinatown. Only a few pilings of the Chinese buildings remain.    SPECIAL COLLECTIONS, UCSC

fore it was over, it had burned the east side of Front Street between the Plaza and Cooper Street, the triangular block on the west side of Front Street, and the Court House on the south side of Cooper Street. The exact cause of the fire was never determined, but it destroyed the entire Front Street Chinatown, including Wong Kee's store, the temple, the Wing Sing and Company store, Quong Chong's store, and all the other Chinese businesses along Front Street. Quong Chong estimated his losses at $1,500. Some of the Chinese blamed Kuan Kung, the deity in the Chee Kong Tong temple, for failing to protect Chinatown as he had in the past:

> The Chinese mourn the loss of their Joss, blaming him for not protecting them from the fire. For years they have escaped, and the Joss was the recipient of much favor. When a move was made some years ago to make the Chinese go outside of the city-limits the Joss was given the credit of making the move a failure. As he was burned in the fire, the Celestials have no one to whom they can go for comfort.

Within a week the Chinese were rebuilding, and the Santa Cruz Chinese were quickly offered alternative sites upon which to rebuild. Dr. P. B. Fagen and George Birkenseer offered them an island in the San Lorenzo River known as the Midway, just a hundred yards downstream from the old Front Street site, while Mrs. Harriet Blackburn offered a new site next to Neary's Lagoon (off Laurel Street) on the west side of the Santa Cruz business district. Pon Fang and the Chinese Mission arranged leases with Fagen and Birkenseer and moved out to the island, but a small group led by Wong Kee moved to the Blackburn property. It is not clear exactly why the community divided after the fire, but the two groups may have contested leadership in the Chinese community. Ernest Otto only observed that "there was some disagreement among themselves." Another explanation for the division centers on a demographic shift in the Chinese population in the late 1880s and early 1890s. The 1900 manuscript census lists two dozen Chinese market gardeners on Santa Cruz's west side, and the Chinese merchants (Wong Kee and On Soon) who re-located to Mrs. Blackburn's property may have been following them.

Regardless of the cause, the Santa Cruz Chinese went into the last half of the 1890s divided, weakened by the fire, and lacking the unity which they had displayed in the 1880s. In 1895 the Santa Cruz Chinese community was still composed primarily of servants, cooks, and domestics who worked for wages and had little opportunity to accumulate sufficient capital to start families or return to China. Only the market gardens offered the kind of economic opportunity which might propel some of the Chinese to the second stage of the immigrant experience, but they were getting older, and time was beginning to run out. Sadly, during a decade (1895–1906) marked by pride and strength among the Chinese of the Monterey Bay Region, the Santa Cruz Chinese were weakened, divided, facing an uncertain future.

This land is Willow Land and in consideration of the premises said lessees agree to clear said land root and branch of all brush and trees thereon before November 1, 1883, and to have said land when delivered perfectly clear of brush and trees and in good farming condition.

Lease between Rafael Estrada and Jim Kee, 1882.

# 9

# Salinas and Castroville

DURING THE SPANISH and Mexican eras, Mission Santa Cruz, Mission San Juan Bautista, and Monterey formed the three corners of a triangle of commercial activity in the Monterey Bay Region. Watsonville lay at the opposite mid-point on the Santa Cruz–San Juan Bautista side, but because of the swamps and sloughs of the lower Salinas Valley, not until the 1860s did anyone attempt to locate a town on the other two sides. In 1864 Juan B. Castro established the town of Castroville on the Santa Cruz–Monterey side of the triangle; in 1868 Eugene Sherwood and Alanson Riker established Salinas City at a place called Halfway House, midway between Monterey and San Juan Bautista. The development of both Castroville and Salinas depended in large part upon the availability of Chinese laborers to reclaim and work the land. The inspiration for the Salinas Valley reclamation projects of the 1870s stemmed from a project in which Chinese laborers dug a large canal at the headwaters of the Salinas River in 1866.

The first major construction project in the Monterey Bay Region involving large numbers of Chinese laborers, the large diversion canal was dug for a gold-mining operation near San Antonio Mission (fifty miles up the Salinas River from the Salinas City site). Stories of gold in the Santa Lucias had abounded for years, and during the 1850s and 1860s prospectors wandered the mountains in search of that elusive strike. Chilenos and Indians willing to pan the gravel of the San Antonio River near the site of the old mission could make fifty cents a day, and prospectors believed that a Mother Lode waited somewhere nearby. But the gold-bearing gravels were some distance from the river, preventing extensive mining.

During the Mission period the Indians had constructed an elaborate system of irrigation canals to bring water to San Antonio Mission's crops, and in the 1860s Manuel Luco, the owner of the Milpitas Rancho, devised a plan to have Chinese miners divert the river and work the gold-bearing gravel. In March 1866 Luco signed an agreement with Ah Yuk, a representative of the Ning Yeung Company of San Francisco (one of the Chinese Six Companies) to dig a ditch from the San Antonio River to the Big Gulch. Luco and Ah Yuk agreed to divide both the water and proceeds from the mine equally, the Chinese building the ditch and doing the mining on Luco's property; the lease was to run for five years. Ah Yuk agreed to supply sixty Chinese laborers to the site within ten days of the signing of the agreement, and once the ditch was completed, he agreed to send a total of 550 Chinese miners to work the placers. The Ning Yeung Company's willingness to commit six hundred miners to such a speculative project reflects the surplus of Chinese miners (and laborers in general) that existed in California in 1866. The editor of the country's only newspaper expressed the hope that the Chinese miners would ". . . develop, perhaps, something that will be of lasting benefit."

The first group of sixty miners traveled by wagon from San Francisco to San Antonio with seven tons of equipment and food, arriving in early May. Monterey County's Deputy Assessor visited the site and expressed doubt that the scheme would work: "They won't be able to bring much water to the place they intend working." Within three weeks the Chinese miners came to the same conclusion, and they abandoned the incomplete project. Loading their equipment back on the wagons, the Chinese began the long walk back through the Salinas Valley to San Francisco. The *Monterey Gazette*'s editor met the "cadaverous looking" group of miners outside San Juan Bautista, and when asked why the project had gone "busted," the Chinese responded: "Sam Tonio no good, too muchee sand, too muchee workee, no ketchum gold." The editor cynically summarized the San Antonio Ditch scheme by observing, "Luco is the only one, we presume, who has made anything out of it, and if he had been sharp enough to salt the diggings liberally he might have made more."

Salinas City was the Monterey Bay Region's first successful instant town. Knowing that sufficient labor was available to overcome the natural disadvantages, Sherwood and Riker boldly violated the realtor's creed of "location" and laid their new town on hummocks which were bisected by sloughs and surrounded by swamps. Despite those disadvantages the gamble paid off; the developers sold Salinas City on the premise that it would be a town in which the American dream of opportunity and unrestrained growth could be realized. Many of the first businessmen came from Monterey, frustrated by the old established community and the lack of opportunities there. In 1866 the editor of the *Monterey Gazette*, frustrated by the slumbering community, declared, "We have no business, no commerce, no traffic." When a Sacramento Valley resident wrote a letter inquiring about the business opportunities in Monterey, the editor told him to stay away. "Don't come [to Monterey], at least with any business project on hand," he advised, "it would be an innovation, and our people do not look kindly on such things." Monterey slept on, content to savor its rich Mexican historical heritage; Salinas was filled with the hiss of railroad locomotives, the shouts of teamsters, and the promises of real estate speculators.

Though the population of Salinas literally exploded after the town was subdivided and lots offered for sale in 1868, the sloughs and slumps continued to plague the town's development; sewage festered throughout the town in summer and mud trapped wagons and horses during the winter. The row of lakes on the northeast side of Salinas was particularly troublesome during wet winters, so in 1875 the property owners in that area began a massive reclamation project to drain the sloughs and lakes.

Many of the landowners remembered the Chinese who had worked on the San Antonio Ditch and turned to the Chinese when it came time to clear and drain the sloughs of Salinas. Carr, Vanderhurst, and Sanborn owned the five-hundred-acre parcel of swamp land northeast of town, and in 1875 they hired twenty Chinese laborers to begin the laborious job of clearing and ditching the tule and willow swamp. Eventually over a hundred Chinese laborers slogged through the muck and grubbed out the brush and trees that choked the area—for one dollar per day. Cutting the peat soil "with huge knife-like spades and pitching it out . . . with steel forks and hooks," the Chinese dug six miles of ditches to drain the land. As a result, land worth twenty-eight dollars per acre in 1875 rose to one hundred dollars per acre by 1877. Other landowners, including James Iverson and C. D. Abbott, used Chinese crews to reclaim the land. When challenged by anti-Chinese agitators for using Chinese laborers, Abbott pointed out that "white men refused to work up to their knees in the water, slime and filth of the sloughs."

## EARLY SALINAS VALLEY AGRICULTURE

The Salinas Valley lagged one step behind the Pajaro Valley throughout the nineteenth century. When Pajaro Valley farmers planted potatoes and wheat in the 1850s, the Californios continued to graze livestock in the Salinas Valley; as Pajaro farmers diversified their crops, their Salinas counterparts were in the midst of their love affair with wheat. The legacy of Mexican land grants had left most of the land in large parcels more suitable to ranching than farming: in 1858 the Monterey County Assessor noted, "It is sincerely to be hoped that at an early day the . . . land titles will be properly segregated from the public domain, and patents [can] be issued for the land so that the laboring man can purchase under good and valid titles, and thus become more permanently settled." But the lag was also caused by the valley's inaccessibility, lack of a good harbor close by, a wide variety of soil types, and a bewildering array of rainfall patterns within the valley. (Two common Salinas Valley names which survived the Mexican era give clues to the dominant vegetation and landforms: one Mexican grant was named *Sausal*—"the willows"— and its southern boundary was *Sanjon del Alisal*—"slough of the alders.") In addition, sloughs connected over a dozen fresh water ponds and lakes, making it difficult to cross the northern Salinas Valley in summer and impossible to cross in a wet winter.

After 1866 Chinese labor made it possible to begin reclaiming farm land. An irrigation company was formed during the drought of 1876–77 to divert the Salinas River into an old channel (Alisal Slough) and irrigate the land between Salinas and Castroville. The company employed hundreds of Chinese to work on the irrigation ditches, but rain broke the drought and the project was abandoned. Whether bringing water or taking it away, the Chinese provided the muscle which turned the dreams and fancies of Salinas property owners into reality.

Until the end of the century, the Chinese slowly and steadily altered the face of the Salinas Valley, clearing vegetation and removing water to open the rich bottom lands to farming and development. In the early years the Chinese were day laborers, working either for Chinese labor contractors or directly for the landowners, but they preferred working for themselves; by 1877 they were negotiating reclamation leases with owners of willow and swamp lands. Just as in the Pajaro Valley, the Chinese farmed rent-free in exchange for reclaiming land and bringing it into production. Under this reclamation-lease system, much of the rich bottom land in the Salinas Valley came under cultivation.

Not surprisingly, one of the first landowners to see the advantages of the reclamation leases was David Jacks. In addition to owning most of the Monterey Peninsula, Jacks had extensive holdings along the Salinas River near Hill's Crossing (near present-day Spreckels) and at Chualar. Jacks arranged one of the first Salinas Valley reclamation leases with Sam Kee in 1877. In exchange for the five-year use of a one-hundred-acre tract of land along the Salinas River, Sam Kee agreed to "cut down and grub all timber and other trees and underbrush . . . and [to] burn all underbrush unfit for firewood." For his part, Jacks agreed to buy all the firewood Sam Kee could cut for $1.25 per cord. By 1880 Jacks had similar leases with Jim Kee, Ah Lee, and Charley Mack. The leases often stipulated what crops the Chinese farmers could plant (to assure that the soil was broken up) or required the Chinese to eradicate gophers and ground squirrels on the property: "Lessees will use all effectual efforts to effectuate the extermination of the squirrels and gophers that now or hereafter infest said premises." By the early 1880s Jacks had leased over one thousand acres of land to Chinese farmers in the Salinas Valley, and other land owners were quick to follow his example.

James Bardin, another Hill's Crossing landowner, arranged similar leases with several Chinese farmers. In 1888 Bardin signed a lease with Jim Sing on a small fifteen-acre parcel with the requirement that the Chinese grow either potatoes, pumpkins, beans, or mustard to help break up the soil. Rafael Estrada owned a one-hundred-acre section of land in a bend of the Salinas River which was covered with brush, tules, and willows. In July 1882 he signed a typical reclamation lease with Jim Kee and his partner Ah Pan in which the Chinese agreed to have the land "perfectly clear of brush and trees and in good farming condition" within sixteen months. That meant more than just cutting down the trees; the Chinese had to "clear said land root and branch of all brush and trees." In exchange the Chinese worked the land rent-free for a total of four years. Any firewood resulting from clearing the land belonged to the Chinese for their use or sale.

It might appear that Jim Kee and Ah Pan had full use of good farm land for a period of two and one-half years once the land was cleared, but the process of reclaiming land was more complicated than that. The Chinese lessees would hire Chinese crews to come in and clear the land, often using the firewood as partial payment. The clearing usually took at least a year. During the second year the land was drained and allowed to dry out. The third year the land was turned over and a crop with large roots (such as potatoes) was planted to help break up the soil. Finally, if everything worked according to schedule, the Chinese farmer would have the final year to recoup his three-year investment of time and labor before returning the land to its owner. The Chinese took all of the risk, while the landowner was ahead the moment the first tree was cut.

Despite the risks Chinese farmers entered into reclamation-lease agreements well into the twentieth century. There is no way of measuring just how many acres of prime farm land were brought into production by Chinese farmers over the years, but judging from the number of leases voluntarily registered with Monterey County (leases did not have to be registered with the county), they cleared and cultivated thousands of acres of bottom land.

As in the Pajaro Valley, perhaps the greatest contribution to

Salinas Valley agriculture was the inspiration the Chinese provided to the farmers. Before the 1870s most Salinas Valley farmers had focused their farming efforts on hilltops and hummocks, believing that sloughs were unsuitable for farming because of salty soil. (After all, Salinas means "salty" in Spanish.) But the Chinese knew that willow trees grow where the water is fresh, and they saw the agricultural potential of rich peat-bog soil. As with the abalone and squid, the Chinese saw the value in what others considered to be marginal or worthless. Every Salinas Valley landowner had a corner of "willow lands" somewhere on his property which he believed to be worthless, but the Chinese cleared the land and taught the farmer otherwise. Salinas Valley farmers were slow to learn the lesson, however, as other than the potatoes, beans, and mustard the Chinese grew in the bottom lands, wheat was the dominant crop in the Salinas Valley. If wheat was King in the Pajaro Valley, it was Emperor in the Salinas Valley—in 1881, of the 145,000 acres of land under cultivation, 140,000 were in wheat, barley, oats, or hay. The diversification of Salinas Valley agriculture was a slow, laborious process, accomplished only when the sugar beet acreage migrated south from the Pajaro Valley in the 1890s.

## EARLY SALINAS CHINATOWN

Since Chinese farm laborers were used extensively in the wheat harvest beginning in the summer of 1866, we can assume that Chinese were living in Salinas City soon after it was subdivided in 1868. The first reference to Chinese living in Salinas City appeared in a newspaper account of a shooting at a Chinese wash house in July 1869; the story does not indicate the exact location of the laundry, but it places the event in Salinas City. Most of the Chinese farm laborers working in the Salinas Valley in the late 1860s were seasonal laborers who came in for the wheat harvest and then moved on. Until the reclamation projects of the 1870s, the few Chinese living in Salinas were laundrymen and cooks.

The 1870 manuscript census gives the first clear view of the Chinese living in Salinas City. In July 1870 sixteen Chinese lived within the city, fourteen males and two females. Six of the men were cooks, two were laundrymen, one was a dishwasher, and the remainder were common laborers. One woman listed her occupation as seamstress (sometimes a euphemism for prostitute), while the other woman lived with her husband and their eleven-year-old son, constituting the only Chinese family in Salinas. (The census taker made no effort to transliterate the names of the Chinese, so we do not have any surnames for the 1870 census.) One of the Chinese households was a laundry located on Main Street near Central, with the other two Chinese households scattered elsewhere in the city. As with many Chinese communities in California, the early Chinese residents in Salinas City were dispersed throughout the town, and no clearly defined Chinatown existed as yet.

A special census taken in 1872 showed a ten-fold increase in Chinese population (113 men, 12 women), while Salinas City's total population doubled during the same period. The Chinese population grew to 8% of the total and 17% of the adult males. The sudden jump in Chinese population (occupations were not recorded) was probably due to the Southern Pacific Railroad's extension into Salinas, built by Chinese railroad workers.

Sherwood and Riker had centered the town on their common boundary, the Slough of the Alders which ran diagonally across the Salinas Valley. The Southern Pacific Railroad laid tracks along the same line, defeating the efforts of Sherwood and Riker

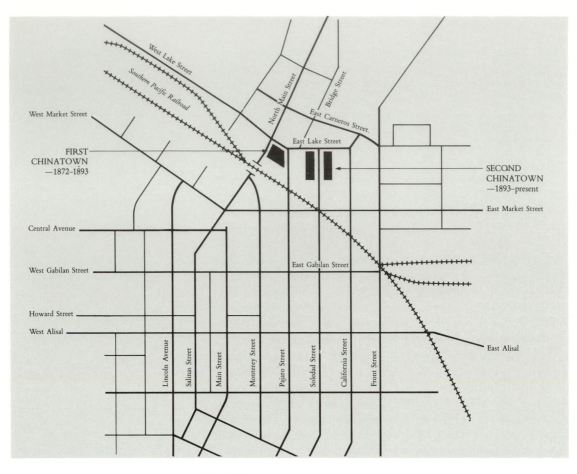

Map 9–1

## SALINAS AND ITS FIRST CHINATOWN, 1890

The location of Salinas' first Chinatown has been altered by the present-day underpass on Main Street. Note the beginnings of Japantown in the building at the upper tip of Chinatown. The triangular-shaped Chinatown was destroyed in a fire on June 13, 1983. Map derived from Sanborn Map Company maps, Map Library, UCSC.

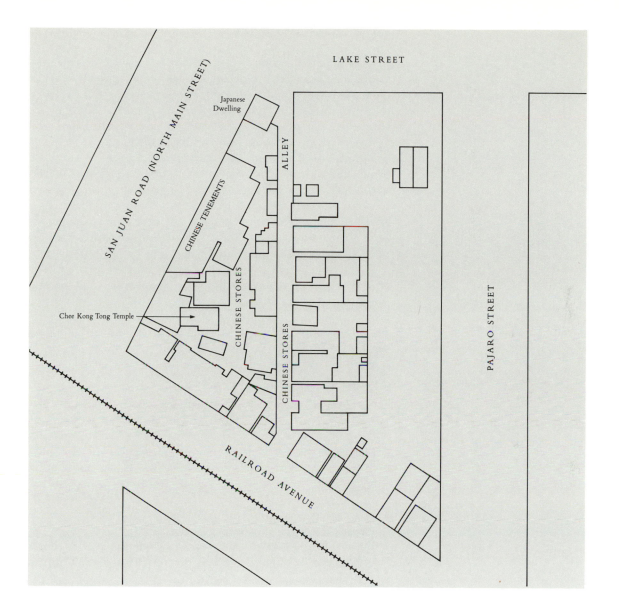

LAKE STREET

SAN JUAN ROAD (NORTH MAIN STREET)

Japanese
Dwelling

CHINESE TENEMENTS

ALLEY

CHINESE STORES

Chee Kong Tong Temple

CHINESE STORES

PAJARO STREET

RAILROAD AVENUE

to join the two sections of the town together. The town re-sembled an hour-glass, pinched together in the center by a single railroad crossing, and to this day the northern part of Salinas is divided from the southern by those railroad tracks. The diagonal cut of the railroad tracks intersected the north-south main street at an odd angle, creating some oddly-shaped city blocks. On a triangular block formed by San Juan Road (now North Main Street) and the railroad tracks on the south, Salinas' first China-town took root. Since the corner of Chinatown abutted the rail-road tracks, the Chinese probably began moving to the site soon after the railroad was completed in 1872. From the beginning Sa-linas' Chinatown was on "the other side of the tracks" from the main business district on Main Street.

The first mention of a Chinatown in Salinas appeared in an 1874 newspaper account of a fight "in Chinatown," and the next month an arsonist attempted to burn a house of prostitution which adjoined "the Chinese quarters." Fleeting accounts re-ported fires and fights in and around the Chinese quarter, but not until the 1880 census did Salinas' Chinatown receive more docu-mentation, which provided the basis for the table below.

| OCCUPATION | NUMBER | AVERAGE AGE |
|---|---|---|
| Laborers (inc Agri.) | 47 | 29 |
| Cooks | 21 | 30 |
| Merchants | 5 | 35 |
| Prostitute (all fem.) | 5 | 26 |
| Laundryman | 5 | 28 |
| Barber | 2 | 39 |
| Interpreter | 2 | 26 |
| Fisherman | 1 | 30 |
| Physician | 1 | 56 |
| Restaurant Owner | 1 | 41 |
| Labor Contractor | 1 | 19 |
| Total Number | 91 | Average Age 30 |

Perhaps the most striking feature of the Salinas Chinese community in 1880 was that there were no Chinese families, and all of the 103 Chinese were born in China. All but a dozen of them lived in Chinatown and all but one of the Chinese living outside Chinatown lived in laundries on Main Street. Only five of the Chinese were women, and all five gave their occupation as prostitute and lived in a single building in Chinatown. The occupational pattern in the preceding table clearly indicates that Salinas' Chinatown served the white community and the Chinese seasonal laborers who came into the Salinas Valley.

The Chinese laundries outside Chinatown on Main Street became a continual point of contention. After several unsuccessful efforts to prohibit Chinese from living outside Chinatown in the early 1880s, the Salinas Town Trustees passed a public health ordinance in 1886 prohibiting the Chinese from actually washing clothing in their buildings on Main Street. Clothes could be delivered and collected at the Main Street establishments, but the laundering had to be done across the tracks. After a brief protest the Chinese laundrymen agreed, and in July 1886 the laundry operations moved into Chinatown. The ordinance remained in force until March 1897 when it was repealed by the Salinas Town Trustees.

The Chinese rented their land and buildings in Salinas' first Chinatown. One of the landlords, Chama Zamora, signed a three-year lease with Chin Yik for a two-story building at the north end of Chinatown. Chin Yik agreed to rent the building, formerly a dance hall, for six years and pay eight dollars per month rent. Ten years later the building caught fire and burned to the ground, but Salinas firemen were able to contain the fire to that one building. The Chinese were so grateful that they treated the firemen to "hot coffee, biscuits and fine cigars," and gave each fireman a five-dollar gold piece. The newspaper noted that "want of gratitude is not one of the shortcomings of our Mongolian population."

During the early 1880s the cultural life of Salinas' Chinatown began to flower, and even though the town experienced a high turn-over in population from season to season, the Chee Kong Tong built the first temple in November 1882. The Chee Kong Tong's regular celebrations each Sunday brought complaints about the noise in the newspaper. "From early dawn on Sunday mornings until late at night the drums and gongs at the Chinese Joss House keep up a ceaseless beating. The discordant racket is a great annoyance to American residents in that vicinity." On balance, however, few complaints were made against the Chinese as they, like their counterparts in Watsonville, were vital to the agricultural economy of the Salinas Valley.

During the early 1880s Salinas Valley farmers needed farm laborers. In the summer of 1880 a Monterey newspaper noted that "harvest hands are exceedingly scarce in Monterey County, Indians, and Chinamen doing the most of the binding." The following summer farmers again complained that harvest hands were difficult to find. As in the Pajaro Valley, Chinese farm laborers were attractive to the farmers because they did "not get drunk and leave their employers in the lurch." After two summers of labor shortage, Salinas did not celebrate when the May 1882 Chinese Exclusion Law was signed. Salinas Valley farmers would have been unable to harvest their wheat without the Chinese in the 1880s, and however reluctantly they might admit it, they depended on the Chinese.

The one time each year that whites ventured into Chinatown with confidence was at the lunar New Year celebrations. The Salinas Chinese held an open house during the festivities, and whites came into the Chinese community to partake of the exotic sights, smells, and free delicacies. In a remarkable newspaper article published in the *Salinas Democrat* in February 1891, a reporter described in detail an evening in Salinas Chinatown, portraying a busy and exciting place. The buildings "nestled together as a brood of frightened chickens," and the helter-skelter arrangement of the buildings resembled "a western town after the advent of a tornado."

Charley Foo, a bilingual merchant who also worked as an interpreter, guided the reporter around Chinatown, introducing him to the community's leading merchants. At #13 Railroad Avenue was the Sam Sing Company, allied with the Hop Wo Association of San Francisco which handled Chinese imports; Sam Sing offered the reporter a cigar to commemorate the New Year. At #24 Railroad Avenue the reporter visited the Quong Sang Company, allied with the Ning Yeung Association in San Francisco. At #22 Railroad Avenue Wong Lee and Lin Yong gave the reporter another cigar. In the alley which ran off Railroad Avenue, the reporter visited Sam Wah's store (also allied with the Hop Wo Association) where a poker game was under way. He then visited Quong Wah at #17 Railroad Avenue, also allied with the Hop Wo Association. Charley Foo took the reporter to two barber shops (Chang Sing, Fong Kee and Lem Kee) where he was shown the tools that Chinese barbers used to clean their customer's ears: "Six very small and delicately made instruments are used—two swabs, a spoon, an ear-pick, and a pair of tweezers and a very small razor." (Chinese men had their ear-wax removed during a traditional hair-cutting, head-shaving visit.)

The buildings facing Main Street were primarily boarding houses for Chinese laborers, and Charley Foo introduced the reporter to Ah Sing and Yee Get, competitors in the boarding-house business. He also took him to a restaurant operated by Ah Kit, where the table was loaded with Chinese delicacies including Chinese donuts, Chinese vegetables, Chinese potatoes, and oranges.

The account gives a rare glimpse of a Chinatown dedicated primarily to the housing, barbering, and feeding of the Chinese farm laborers. The presence of the Ning Yeung Company (one of the Chinese Six Companies) indicates that most of the Salinas Chinese were probably from Toishan. Perhaps the most detailed description in the entire article, however, was devoted to the temple. Situated in the central alley, the temple was a somewhat rickety two-story structure with the statues upstairs:

> Here Confucius sits enthroned in regal splendor. He is surrounded by a large and beautiful frame of wood, curiously carved . . . Two brazen lions at the foot of the frame guard their kindly charge. In front of this god is a large stand holding five large lead vases. The front of the stand bears a wealth of carving, protected by a glass cover and strong wire screen. The carvings are illustrations of great men, like Washington, Foo explained, and also scenes in Chinese life, while the center is occupied by an illustration, showing Confucius dispensing justice. Here the faithful come and pray and make their offering of food and also money which is symbolized by the burning of a certain kind of paper. After each prayer the God is given a napkin in the shape of paper, as proper and necessary in connection with the food they gave him.

This account is remarkable for its sensitivity to Chinese culture as well as its extensive detail.

Two local anecdotes have survived which also give a rare glimpse of the humor of the hard-working Chinese farm laborers. Perhaps because both incidents recount practical jokes played on white people (dispelling the image of the timid Chinese), they were recorded by local newspapers as so many other incidents of Chinese humor were not.

In 1878 a rumor spread through Salinas that there was a haunted house located several miles south of town; people who had stayed overnight in the abandoned farmhouse told of having conversations with a spirit in the house. The people brave enough to spend a long night there were able to question the invisible spirit about past, present, or future and were answered with "Yes" or "No." The ritual required asking a question and then tapping the floor, and an answer would issue forth. Finally the Salinas newspaper sent a reporter to the house to spend the night and get to the bottom of the story. The reporter had an accomplice who stationed himself outside the house, and as the questions and floor-thumping began, the accomplice was able to determine that the voice was coming from beneath the house. While the reporter kept the "spirit" engaged in a dialogue about the future, the accomplice crawled beneath the house and found Ying Lou, a Chinese shepherd, answering to each thump on the floor. Ying Lou had been entertaining himself each evening by crawling beneath the floor and playing oracle to mystified visitors to the "haunted" house.

In another instance, Chinese farm laborers made extra money staging bar bets. One of the techniques many Chinese learned in China was to lift and carry enormous loads on their carrying poles. Combining strength, leverage, and balance, a slightly-built Chinese could carry a load many times his own weight. Not all whites in Salinas knew of this prowess, and the Chinese would periodically stage a demonstration not only to make a little money, but to demonstrate to the observing crowd that things are not always what they seem to be. In 1898 a group of men gathered outside a Salinas saloon to watch a challenge weight-lifting match between two Chinese. Eight fifty-pound sacks of rice were placed on the ground and one Chinese challenged the other to carry the entire load 150 feet. The crowd of whites observing the match (after several of them had tried unsuccessfully to lift the load) wagered with the Chinese men that the load could not be moved. The slightly-built Chinese deftly balanced the load on his carrying pole and walked the 150 feet and thirty feet further to make his point. The event had been staged by the two Chinese to make a little spending money on the "bar bet" and to gain a little respect.

## THE 1893 FIRE

Each Chinatown in the Monterey Bay Region was touched by a major fire at least once, and the fires might be viewed as an early form of urban renewal. Crowded Chinatowns were highly susceptible to fire; wood frame buildings were jammed together to make use of every available square foot of land. While there may have been some order to the streets and alleys when first laid out, as the community grew, buildings were erected at odd angles, making access for firemen impossible. For the Chinese, fires meant the loss of personal property, but people were rarely killed in fires as the Chinese seemed to sleep with one ear open for the fire alarm.

The big Salinas Chinatown fire broke out at 8:27 P.M. on June 13, 1893, and though the firemen arrived within minutes, they had difficulty finding hydrants, and it was not until 8:39 that they began putting water on the fire. By that time the fire was out of hand. "The hose companies worked heroically but found the water supply very deficient and the means at hand utterly inadequate to fight [the] fire."

The Chinese stacked their belongings in the street and ran back to save more. The scene was bedlam; "firecrackers, pistols and cartridges" exploded as the flames reached them, and pigs, ducks, and chickens fled into the streets. By 10 P.M. the fire was out and Chinatown was gone. About forty buildings went up in smoke, and the loss of buildings and belongings was estimated at between $25,000 and $40,000. It was believed that the fire began with the upsetting of a kerosene lamp.

The following morning, in a scene re-enacted in other communities in the region, whites picked through the ashes looking for valuables. Fred Gates, in a letter to the editor of the *Salinas Democrat*, wondered why guards were not posted to protect the property of the "unfortunate sufferers" of the fire: "In most civilized countries the authorities in places where large fires occur set a guard or guards to see that persons have no 'good finds' of those things which do not belong to them." The editor of the newspaper agreed that the Chinese "should have been protected."

Speculation about the rebuilding of Chinatown began almost immediately; the Cashier of the Salinas City Bank (owner of most of the property) indicated that the property had become too valuable, and unless the Chinese purchased the property from the bank, it would probably be put to other, more lucrative purposes. Many of the Salinas Chinese immediately moved to Castroville's Chinatown, and the Salinas newspaper speculated:

> Chinatown of Salinas will never again mar the perspective of Salinas . . . While all must deplore the calamity that brings loss to any class of human beings, there is a natural impulse of rejoicing that an unmoral excresence and an unsightly suburb has gone up in smoke.

At the very moment the *Salinas Index* was rejoicing, however, the owner of the property just east of the smoking ruins was offering the Chinese a new site for their Chinatown.

## THE SOLEDAD STREET CHINATOWN

Eugene Sherwood, co-founder of Salinas and owner of much of the land north of the railroad tracks, knew the value of Chinese laborers; he employed them on his ranch and leased farm land to them. Within four days of the fire he had approached some of the Chinese merchants and offered to lease them lots which faced Soledad Street, two blocks east of the old Chinatown site. On June 17, 1893, Sherwood signed agreements with Lee Saw, Gee Loy, Sam Sing, Sam Wo Chong, Wing Wah, and Sam Lung in which he leased lots for ten years at a monthly

Soledad Street Chinatown, Salinas, March 1911. The Salinas Chinatown was also prone to flooding. The odd-numbered side of the Chinatown faces the camera. Lake Street runs perpendicular to Soledad Street on the right.
MONTEREY COUNTY HISTORICAL SOCIETY

rental of five dollars; the leases were renewable. The length of the leases indicates that Sherwood meant for the new location to be a permanent one. Sherwood built no buildings, however, so the Chinese merchants erected buildings and leased them to Chinese tenants, an arrangement similar to that at the Point Alones village where David Jacks and the Pacific Improvement Company leased only the land to the Chinese. Thus, as in Watsonville and Monterey, one of the leading landowners in Salinas became the landlord for the Chinese. Within a month twelve new buildings had been erected on Soledad Street. Since the Chinese owned the buildings in their new Chinatown, they purchased 450 feet of fire hose which they stored in #16 to protect their buildings in case another fire should break out.

Several Chinese leaseholders became economic powers in Chinatown; Sam Sing and Sam Lung each leased the buildings on their lots, operated stores, and negotiated farming and reclamation leases throughout the Salinas Valley. Other names which appeared frequently in the assessor's personal property records in the 1890s were Hop Kee, Sam Wah Chung, Wah Lung, Hong Kee, and Tsue King Lum. The most famous Chinese in the Salinas Chinatown during the 1890s were Dr. James Lee Look, a Chinese physician, Charley Mack, a Chinese farmer and merchant, and Yee Shew (nicknamed "Finnegan"), a local businessman and eccentric. Part of Charley Mack's notoriety was due to his size—he was over six feet tall and weighed in excess of 250 pounds; he also became famous for developing several types of potatoes which were successfully grown in the Castroville area.

## THE CHINESE ECCENTRICS

Life on the Golden Mountain made pressing demands on the Chinese. As their absence from history books reflects, they were an "invisible" people, whose unacknowledged work laid the foundation for California's prosperity. Little is known about those Chinese who could not cope with the separation from family and tradition in China. Rare individuals who could not make the return to China or who were prevented by immigration laws from bringing their families over erupted in murderous rages or committed suicide. But perhaps the most poignant evidence of the difficulties Chinese faced is found in those few "eccentrics" whose behavior dramatically contrasted with the painful anonymity forced on their fellows.

Every Chinese community in the Monterey Bay Region harbored such people. An elderly Chinese dubbed "Joe," probably because he lived in a small driftwood shanty near Point Joe, became known as a hermit and walked the beach collecting driftwood or walked down Lighthouse Road into Monterey, a cat riding on his shoulder while he sang softly to himself. "Charley Lee," an elderly Chinese, begged from door to door throughout

Watsonville when he was not in the county jail on some kind of vagrancy charge. Charley Lee's Chinese name was Ung Gee, and to most Chinese and whites living in Watsonville in the early twentieth century, he was a familiar sight on the streets, shuffling along, talking to himself, his head wagging from side to side. He seemed to enjoy being arrested, a fact which was confirmed when the Santa Cruz County Sheriff went over the records after Charley died in 1922—of his twenty-nine years in Santa Cruz County, he had spent over nine in the County Jail. Charley died in the County Hospital after suffering a stroke, and the newspaper mused, "He was of a quiet nature and never seemed to make trouble, but when out of jail at the lower end of the county he would persistently keep up his begging from house to house."

In Salinas, too, lived a gentle soul who might be considered the archetype of the Chinese eccentric in the Monterey Bay Region. Yee Shew had been nicknamed "Finnegan" because of his effusive personality. He had operated a successful vegetable and market garden operation near Gonzales, and over the years he had made many friends among white customers as he drove his vegetable wagon around the roads of the Salinas Valley. He moved his business to Salinas in the 1890s and became a frequent sight on the Salinas streets, arguing with himself, shouting Cantonese phrases to no one in particular. He began to set fires, and after his second conviction for setting a fire in Salinas in 1894, he was sent to the state mental institution at Agnew where he died. Sam Sing, the successful Salinas farmer and merchant, also died at the state mental hospital. In December 1897, while preparing to return to China after many years, Sam went into a fit of raving and raging so severe that his friends had him taken to the mental hospital at Agnew for his own safety; Sam Sing died in the hospital later that month. When Charley Mack suffered a paralytic stroke soon after Sam Sing died, Chinese interviewed by the newspaper in Salinas' Chinatown believed that "the insanity and death of Sam Sing, soon followed by the paralysis of Charley Mack, are in the nature of a judgment." But a judgment for what was never made clear.

We will never know the full extent of the mental damage suffered by the Chinese immigrants living in the Monterey Bay Region, but for every one that went public with his "eccentric" or violent behavior, there must have been others who suffered quietly in Chinatown boardinghouses in the region. This is a subject that deserves much more attention that it has received, and perhaps in the enlightened 1980s we might come to understand just how fearsome the adjustment to the realities of the Golden Mountain must have been.

## SPRECKELS FACTORY TO SALINAS—1898

Though Watsonville reassured itself that Spreckels would never move his sugar mill out of town, the southerly march of the beet acreage into the Moro Cojo and beyond hinted otherwise. The extension of the Pajaro Valley Consolidated Railroad to Salinas in 1891 and the planting of sugar beets in the Salinas Valley in 1891–92 clearly indicated that the focus of the sugar industry was shifting into the Salinas Valley. In January 1893, the last campaign in which Pajaro Valley beets made up the bulk of the crop, the little narrow-gauge railroad shipped ninety-seven carloads of beets to the Watsonville mill from the Moro Cojo in a single day. When the 1894 season began, two hundred carloads of beets were shipped daily from the Salinas Valley to the Watsonville mill. As happened with the Soquel beet sugar factory in the 1870s, the beets were running away from the mill.

Spreckels carefully planned the move of his factory, taking advantage of the depression of the mid-1890s to purchase the Carr Abbott Ranch, the Spence Ranch, and part of the Buena Vista Ranch, all large, old-time landholdings in the Salinas Valley. Spreckels, now the owner of 7,000 acres of Salinas Valley farm land, made his first offer to the citizens of Salinas in August 1896: "If you farmers guarantee to grow the beets, I'll guarantee to turn 'em into sugar. I propose to build here at your door the greatest sugar factory and refinery in the world." But Spreckels' condition—a guaranteed 30,000 acres of beets under contract—met with astonishment. (Eight years before he had required a guarantee of a mere 2,500 acres of beets from Pajaro Valley farmers.) Salinas civic leaders spent the next two months exhorting farmers to sign contracts pledging the necessary acreage. Despite the obvious financial advantages of raising beets, wheat still held the Salinas Valley in its grip. Even James Bardin's sixty-dollar-per-acre clear profit on sugar beets did not convince farmers to switch to beets. As the manager of the Alvarado beet sugar factory put it, "The difficulty lies in changing the grain farmer into a vegetable grower. The average California farmer has gotten into a rut that is hard to get him out of." At times the editor of the Salinas newspaper resorted to doggerel to persuade the farmers to switch to beets:

> To banish hard times
> And increase our shekels
> Let's grow sugar beets
> And sell them to Spreckels.

Finally, though the commitments of acreage (19,000, including his own 7,000) were short of his goal, Spreckels announced that he planned to build the largest beet sugar factory in the world alongside the Salinas River at Hilltown, just south of Salinas City. Salinas finally had the mill—not exactly in town, but

Spreckels Sugar Factory under construction, 1898. Salinas is in the distance on the left, and the town of Spreckels is the white buildings in the distance on the right. When first constructed, the factory was the largest sugar beet manufacturing plant in the United States.                    GEORGE RIDER close enough to call its own. "From the edge of the Salinas river to Salinas the streets are clean, the people happy. Large fields that heretofore were devoted exclusively to cereal culture have been divided into smaller ones . . . and used for the cultivation of sugar beets."

As the rest of California climbed slowly out of the depression in the late 1890s, Spreckels and his sugar mill rocketed Salinas out of the doldrums; property values doubled by 1897, and construction was underway everywhere in Salinas. A streetcar line was built to connect Salinas with the new mill, and Spreckels tore down his Aptos hotel and used the materials to construct a small company town next to the new sugar plant.

Spreckels' biggest concern was maintaining a supply of beets to feed the mill once it began operation. There were not enough Chinese or Japanese laborers in the region to grow sufficient beets, but a number of unemployed whites in California might be induced to farm sugar beets. Several communal experiments were begun in the Salinas Valley in 1897, including one near Soledad run by the Salvation Army, a German colony near Natividad, and a colony of Kentuckians at Pleyto in southern Monterey County. Beets grown in 1897 and 1898 were still shipped back to Watsonville, but when the huge new sugar mill began crushing beets in the fall of 1899, the Watsonville mill remained silent, and the sugar mill finally found its permanent home. Like a huge magnet, the sugar mill pulled Chinese beet laborers from Brooklyn and Castroville into Salinas. Chinese beet contractors negotiated contracts in the Salinas Valley as they had in the Pajaro Valley and on the Moro Cojo. For example, Wing Tai Chung signed a lease with a landowner near the new sugar mill in which he agreed to farm 297 acres of beets. "All beet tops raised on said land shall belong to lessor and shall be left on the land . . . all beets raised on said land shall be delivered to the Western Beet

Sugar Company's factory at Spreckels." But two decades of im-migration restrictions had taken their toll, and Chinese beet con-tractors, limited by the shortage of Chinese laborers, did not dominate the sugar beet industry as they had in the past.

After Claus Spreckels moved his sugar mill to Salinas in 1899, many Chinese merchants who had fled to Castroville after the fire returned to Salinas. But Salinas Chinatown's population (in-cluding the laundries on Main Street) dwindled to 75 people (only one of whom was California-born) by 1900 at a time when the population of Brooklyn was 184 and that of Point Alones was 155. The absence of families and the dwindling numbers of men in Salinas attest to the fact that the Chinatown was primarily a camp for seasonal farm laborers.

## CHINATOWN, CASTROVILLE

When his factory was still in Watsonville, Spreckels built his own eleven-mile, narrow-gauge railroad from Watsonville to Moss Landing in 1891, both to ship raw sugar from the Watson-ville sugar factory to the harbor and to transport beets grown in the Moro Cojo area (in the vicinity of Moss Landing) back to the factory. The Moro Cojo became a new agricultural frontier pioneered by Chinese sugar beet contractors, as the sugar beet acreage slowly crept south to Salinas.

In the summer of 1891 hundreds of Chinese worked the land between Moss Landing and Castroville: "Over 1,000 acres of solid beet field stretches before the eye, and there is scarcely a spot where the solid mass of green is broken." The successful 1891 season precipitated a scramble for contracts in 1892 which might be termed a Sugar Beet Rush, as Chinese farmers and contractors tried to tie up as much acreage as possible in leases.

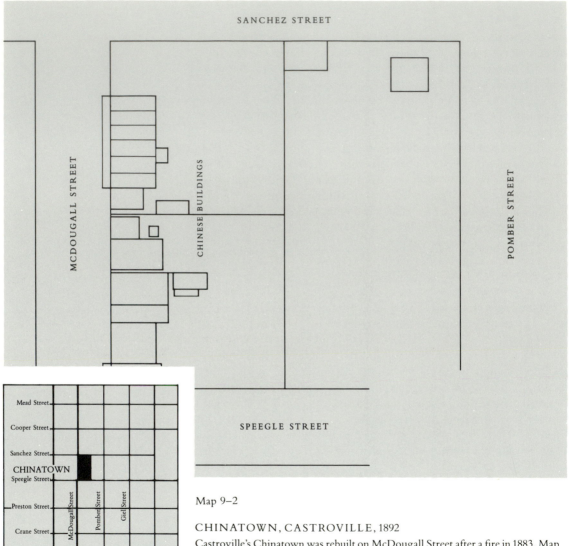

SANCHEZ STREET

MCDOUGALL STREET

CHINESE BUILDINGS

POMBER STREET

SPEEGLE STREET

Mead Street

Cooper Street

Sanchez Street

CHINATOWN

Speegle Street

Preston Street

Crane Street

McDougall Street

Pomber Street

Giel Street

Map 9–2

CHINATOWN, CASTROVILLE, 1892

Castroville's Chinatown was rebuilt on McDougall Street after a fire in 1883. Map derived from Sanborn Map Company map, Map Library, UCSC.

The Monterey County Assessor listed fifteen Chinese companies farming beets in the Castroville area, including Sam Kee, Sam Sung Sing, Tom Kee, Jim Wen, Jim Wing, Jim Bow, Chong Lee, and Jim Ming. A concomitant Chinese population explosion began in the small town of Castroville.

As early as the 1860s the token Chinese laundry had appeared in Castroville, but as agriculture began to intensify in the 1870s, a small Chinese section formed on Merritt Street on lots owned by John Manteufel. In 1878 Manteufel moved the tiny Chinatown to the corner of McDougall and Speegle streets. The entire Chinatown was destroyed by fire in 1883, and when rebuilt later that year began to fill almost the entire east side of Merritt between Speegle and Sanchez (see map 9-2).

The sugar beet boom helped swell the small Castroville Chinatown in 1891 until the Salinas newspaper claimed that it was the only part of Castroville that was growing:

> It is stated that the aggressive heathen have already fixed their longing eyes upon the Cooper residence, the finest in town, as an appropriate place for conversion into a 'joss house,' with a tan [fan tan] game in the second story. The influx of Chinese to Castroville finds a ready explanation in the fact that Chinese are hereafter to be employed exclusively on the sugar beet ranch, and the fellows with the buttons on their caps [Chinese merchants] follow in the wake of their countrymen to forestall the possibility of any of their earnings going into the coffers of the white race.

The Castroville Chinatown provided services as well as gambling houses, prostitutes, and opium to the hundreds of Chinese sugar beet workers in the area, and on days when Chinese beet contractors were paid, the place fairly jumped with activity:

> Castroville was a live town in its Chinese annex on Monday and Tuesday evenings, and the play was high at the fan tan and poker games. We are informed that one of the Chinese bosses lost $300 at one sitting . . . All the alluring games which prove so attractive to the Mongolian laborers and so destructive to his purse can now run

Jin Charley Den, Castroville, 1891. Jin Charley first came to the United States in 1881 and worked for Francis Blackie of Castroville. This photograph was taken for his return registration certificate when he visited China in 1891.

full blast for some time. The Mongolian colony has prospered this year.

As the beet acreage increased in the Moro Cojo and began to move further south and into the Salinas Valley, the Chinese population in Castroville continued to grow in size and influence. Perhaps the biggest boost to Castroville's Chinatown came after the Salinas Chinatown fire of 1893, when many of the displaced Chinese merchants gathered their belongings and moved to Castroville.

When Chinese merchant Jin Charley Den returned from a three-year trip to China in 1894, he underwent a hearing in San Francisco before he could re-enter the country. His habeas corpus case gives us some insight into the operation of a Chinese business. Jin Den (also known as Jin Charley Den) came to the United States in 1881, and in the mid-1880s he was employed by Francis Blackie, a Castroville farmer who testified at the hearing. Jin Charley Den became a buyer for Blackie's warehouse business, and in 1890 he formed the Wing Chong ("bright opportunity") company with three partners, Yee Tom, Yee Hin Wah, and Yee Lee. The Wing Chong Company sold both Chinese and American merchandise to Chinese customers and also acted as a labor contracting business, often housing the laborers in quarters above and behind the store. Wing Chong also sold potatoes, mustard seed, peas, and onions to white merchants such as Blackie and Patrick Jordan.

Castroville's Chinese community had one remarkable characteristic—part of the land it was built on came to be *owned* by Chinese. In 1891 Sam Kee and Jim Lee purchased a lot in Castroville and the Quong Chung Co. purchased another, causing the Salinas newspaper to comment that the Chinese were "buying up Castroville." The two lots were but a small part of the town, but their purchase by Chinese loomed quite large, for it was apparently the first time any Chinese had purchased property in the Monterey Bay Region. Although they negotiated many rental

313

Jin Charley Den's return certificate. Certificate was acquired prior to leaving for China so that he could return to the United States. Signatures attesting to his identity at the bottom of the certificate include F. Blackie and Stephen Castro of Castroville.

NATIONAL ARCHIVES

agreements and leases, Chinese had shied away from buying property until 1891. Nor did this purchase start a land rush by other Chinese. Once the Alien Land Law was passed in 1913, it became impossible for Chinese to purchase property unless they were citizens. The purchase of two lots in Castroville in 1891 by Chinese merchants expressed a rare feeling of confidence in the future.

Sam Kee, one of the property owners, reiterated his desire to settle in Castroville when he married a woman from San Francisco named Toy See; the ceremony was held in Castroville:

> The bride was met at the depot Saturday evening by a carriage from the livery stable, and was immediately driven to the business place of Chung Lee in Chinatown, where the ceremony took place amid great pomp at nine o'clock. A Chinese minister from Sacramento tied the knot in genuine Chinese style; the bride was gorgeously arrayed in jewelry and fine clothing. The value of the jewelry was $800 and of the clothing between $250 and $300 . . . Sunday morning the ceremonies closed a little after nine by a fusillade of bombs and firecrackers, lasting about fifteen minutes.

The transitory nature of the Castroville Chinatown (in spite of the purchases of land) became clear when the sugar beet acreage extended farther and farther south during the 1890s, beyond Castroville and into the Salinas Valley; many of the merchants returned to Salinas. Competition from Japanese beet contractors also made inroads on the Chinese population of Castroville. In 1896 a newspaper reporter noted, "Castroville was treated to the spectacle of a wagon load of [Japanese] which passed through town on Saturday last to work on the sugar beet ranches." By 1900 the population of Castroville's Chinatown, which had filled almost an entire block less than a decade earlier, had dropped to eleven.

The last manuscript census available for Castroville's Chinatown, taken in 1910, listed five Chinese households on McDougall Street. Merchant Quong Chong lived in #54; Gim Jee, another merchant, and his partner lived in #55, and Yee Mee, a grocery owner, lived with two cousins in #56. Two other buildings on McDougall Street were listed as boardinghouses for farm laborers; one housed five Chinese males (average age fifty-eight) and the other housed seven Chinese males (average age fifty-five). No Chinese women or children were listed in the last vestiges of Castroville's Chinese farm labor community. The last building closely identified with Castroville's McDougall Street Chinatown burned in the 1970s.

PART THREE

# THE DEMISE OF THE CHINATOWNS

The Chinese who is fortunate enough to obtain a ring gets a valuable trophy which insures him good fortune during the coming year.

Description of
the Ring Game,
*Monterey New Era*,
February, 1898.

# 10

# The Ring Game

THE DECADE SPANNING the turn of the century was the golden age of the Chinese community in the Monterey Bay Region. Watsonville's busy and prosperous Brooklyn Chinatown was expanding from sugar beet cultivation to apple drying. The Chinese in Santa Cruz, though split into two communities, were busy rebuilding their community after the 1894 fire. The Chinese in Salinas also were rebuilding after their 1893 fire, and the movement of sugar beet acreage into the Salinas Valley promised an economic boom. The dried squid industry on the Monterey Peninsula was securely established, strengthened by an arrangement with the Italian and Portuguese fresh fish industry. In terms of community pride and self-esteem, the period 1895–1906 marked the high point for the Chinese in the Monterey Bay Region.

This community pride focused on Chinese culture. On the one hand, the Chinese pointed with pride to things Chinese, and on the other hand, they made it clear that they had become part of the *American* scheme of things. This renaissance in Chinese culture within the Chinese community was in part due to a new appreciation and respect for Chinese culture on the part of the non-Chinese American public. With thousands of young American men journeying to Asia to help put down the Boxer Rebellion or to participate in the suppression of the Philippine revolution, Americans rediscovered Asian culture, particularly the arts

# THE RING GAME

of China and Japan. "Oriental" curios, interior decoration, and classical Asian art were popularized during the period, and though the Chinese immigrants in America still wore the label of "heathen Chinee," their art and culture grew in respectability. Chinese New Year celebrations became increasingly popular with the non-Chinese public. Chinese in America were often interviewed by newspapers and magazines about Chinese religion, festivals, arts, and even political events in China. The American public found that the Chinese laundryman, cook, fisherman, and gardener had a culture after all, and through their culture, the Chinese, for the first time in their experience on the Golden Mountain, gained a modicum of respectability.

The epicenter of this cultural renaissance in the Monterey Bay Region was the Point Alones village. The oldest and largest village in the region, it was also the only one which had not moved since the 1850s. The closest thing in California to China itself, the Point Alones village became a cultural lodestone for the Chinese in the Monterey Bay Region:

> [The Point Alones village] as seen in the afternoon from the bay, with [its] junks and lateen sailed fishing craft drawn up on the beach or coming in with their freight, the widespread nets, the children in red and yellow, the curious balconies projecting over the water, the flags, and high scaffolds and acres of drying fish, all [seemed] to be thoroughly Asiatic . . . the Asia of little fishing villages, such as travelers in China describe.

The Point Alones village became not only the cultural center for Chinese in the region but the capital of a regional Chinese community, because for the first (and last) time in the history of the region, the Chinese communities became more than just a scattering of distinct and separate Chinatowns; for this brief decade they became a true regional Chinese community.

This cultural and political upwelling is all the more remarkable in light of the continuing legal harassment directed at the

Point Alones Village, c. 1900. Village at its largest. Point Almejas on far left. Fenced area in distance was the cemetery which had been moved there when railroad tracks were put through the village in 1889.     PAT HATHAWAY

Chinese by the federal government. In 1892 the Chinese Exclusion Law was not only renewed but tightened by widening the definition of who was Chinese; Chinese was race, regardless of country of birth or place of origin. Further, the Chinese were required by the Geary Act to carry identification, a requirement they grudgingly met after a lengthy legal struggle.

## THE RING GAME

The annual celebration held on the second day of the second lunar month best symbolizes the maturity and pride of the region's Chinese. The festival became known as the Ring Game because of the contest held at the celebration's conclusion. Beginning in 1894, and each year thereafter until 1906, Chinese, like pilgrims to Mecca, came from throughout the Monterey Bay Region to the Point Alones village to participate in the festival. Though many non-Chinese observers believed the Ring Game to be the concluding event in the lunar New Year celebration, it was actually a separate festival in honor of T'u Ti, the God of Wealth.

Every village in southern China had a small statue of a god seated on his throne holding a golden ingot in his upraised hand. Most often called the earth god, the image was also known as T'u Ti, the god of wealth. The southern Chinese believed that T'u Ti had the power to confer good fortune and wealth. The festival honoring T'u Ti was a day-long affair which began with ceremonies and offerings to the god. Offerings of food were placed before the statue, and the image was covered with flowers. Later in the day Chinese men gathered for the festival's concluding event, a game which would decide who would have the blessings of wealth for the coming year.

The game required a combination of skill, strength, and, most of all, luck. A large wooden cannon mounted on a platform was loaded with a small charge of gunpowder, and a large rattan ball was fired from the cannon into the air above the assembled men of the village. When the ball came down, the men scrambled and fought to get it, for the one who possessed it would receive the smile of T'u Ti and would have wealth and good fortune for the coming year. The promise of good fortune and wealth had brought the Chinese to the Golden Mountain, and any advantage an individual Chinese might get in the pursuit of his elusive fortune was highly prized. The man who retrieved the ball after a fierce scramble exchanged it for a small gilt ornament which he took home and placed on the household altar to symbolize imminent success and wealth. In some southern Chinese cities, as many as thirty balls were fired into the air during the afternoon, each promising a degree of good luck; one of the balls (usually the first one fired) was, however, the most propitious.

The game made its first appearance in the Monterey Bay Region in 1894, and with a few minor alterations, the celebration was a faithful replica of that conducted in China. Instead of scrambling for a rattan ball, the Chinese in Calfornia fought for a ring of woven bamboo which was blasted into the air from a giant firecracker. (The firecracker gave the event its name—the Bomb Game—in Marysville, California, and Marysville still stages the game each year on the weekend closest to the second day of the second lunar month.) The men playing the Ring Game at Point Alones often organized into teams representing the various Chinese communities so that the man successful in wrestling the ring away from his competitors brought luck to himself and honor to his teammates. Thus the local press called the event the "Chinese Games," and each community's newspaper rooted for its local team.

The Ring Game, Point Alones, 1890s. Shrouded in the smoke of firecrackers, onlookers watch as the Chinese pay homage to T'u Ti prior to the scramble for the ring. Long string of firecrackers to the right of the pole was exploding as photograph was taken. Small altar to T'u Ti is behind the fence on the right. Note large numbers of white on-lookers. PAT HATHAWAY

324

The Ring Game, Point Alones, 1890s. Strings of firecrackers suspended from the poles were set off to frighten away evil spirits and mark the beginning of the festival of T'u Ti. Roast pig and other offerings can be seen at the base of the pole on the right.                                                                                     PAT HATHAWAY

The Ring Game, Point Alones, 1890s. Spectators are gathered around waiting as the men on the right prepare the firecracker which will send the ring into the air. Chinese men then scrambled for the ring; the one successful in getting and keeping the ring was destined to have a year of good luck and prosperity. Note the young white men in the group on the right. The games were often interrupted by whites who insisted upon joining the scramble.

PAT HATHAWAY

The Ring Game was no place for the frail or the faint of heart—it was serious and rough business. In describing the first game held in 1894, an observer noted: "As soon as a ring would descend hundreds of hands would make a grab for it, and in their mad effort to get it, Chinese would pile 15 or 20 feet deep in a heap." In 1901 "the ring flew skyward and mad scramble for its possession ensued, the Chinese jostling scrambling, scratching and fighting for the coveted trinket . . ."

Considering the intensity with which the Chinese participated in this celebration, it is surprising that so few were injured. In 1899 one of the bombs exploded prematurely, injuring the eye of the ordnance expert, and in 1900 one Chinese participant died from injuries suffered during the scramble.

As the depression of the mid-1890s gave way to more prosperous times, the annual Ring Game became more elaborate, and the number of Chinese attending the event grew. The contests held at Point Alones in 1899 and 1900 attracted the largest crowds, with Chinese delegations coming from San Jose, Gilroy, Salinas, Watsonville, and Santa Cruz. The expense of the celebration in 1899 was estimated in excess of five thousand dollars and the hundreds of Chinese participants were observed by over two thousand white onlookers.

The tide of cultural confidence and pride engendered by the Ring Games carried with it the surrounding Chinese communities, and though the other communities did not stage their own Ring Game festivals, the New Year festivals of the late 1890s were the most elaborate in each of the Chinatowns in the region. One institution which originated at the Point Alones Ring Game was transplanted throughout the region—the traveling culture show known as the Chinese parade.

## PARADES

Chinese delegations coming to the Ring Game would usually charter special railroad cars that brought all of them to Monterey on the day of the festival. A delegation of the Point Alones Chinese met the assembled delegations at the Monterey depot, and then they walked the mile to the Point Alones village. In 1898, rather than merely walk to the village, the Chinese staged their first parade:

> This procession was one of the most unique and brilliant spectacles ever seen here [Monterey]. Headed by the American flag and the great dragon flag of the Celestials, with fantastic banners, and dressed in fine silks of every color of the rainbow, the procession of about 150 Mongolians marched through the streets to the indescribable music of two Chinese bands.

Before the 1898 Ring Game, the Watsonville Chinese rented some costumes and finery for the parade. The morning of the Ring Games they suited up in their rented costumes, and before boarding the train, they marched across the bridge and into Watsonville, walking up and down Main Street. The response of the Watsonville populace to this dress rehearsal parade was very favorable, and after winning most of the rings at Point Alones that day, the Brooklyn Chinese decided to take up a collection and invest in their own parade regalia. An order for over three thousand dollars' worth of costumes was sent to China in early March 1898, and the Chinese waited expectantly for the finery which was "expected to surpass anything the Chinese societies have shown in this part of the State . . ."

The costumes arrived in June 1898. Unable to wait to show off their new regalia, the Brooklyn Chinese staged a grand celebration in early July. Beginning with an open house in Brooklyn, where the street was lined with decorations and tables in stores were laden with free food, the celebration culminated in a Chinese parade. Bow Ching Chong, the wealthy Chinese fruit grower and merchant, acted as the parade's Grand Marshal, and Chinese visitors as well as Watsonville residents lined Main Street to watch the Chinese parade with the American flag at the head of the procession.

Exactly ten years after they had moved across the river, three hundred Chinese came back across the bridge and paraded down Main Street Watsonville for all to see. The Chinese walked the entire length of Main Street before turning around and marching back to Brooklyn; over a thousand spectators lined the streets to watch "the variety and richness of costumes . . . shields and banners rich in colors. The women with bound feet were on horseback, and children had seats of honor in a wagon." Two Chinese bands provided the music and rhythm for "the most notable street parade ever witnessed in this city . . ."

Determined to get full use of their new parade costumes, the Brooklyn Chinese took to the streets again several days later, joining the Fourth of July parade, ". . . in full regalia, with their banner, bands, dragon, devil, joss house, and other features." In the span of one short week, the Watsonville Chinese had twice experienced the heady feeling of pride as they marched down Watsonville's Main Street; wrapped in the splendor of one of the world's oldest cultures, laborers, cooks, beet pullers, ditch diggers, and laundrymen celebrated their heritage.

The Ring Game parade in Monterey in March 1899 was the grandest parade of them all. Sixty Chinese from Salinas together with two hundred well-rehearsed paraders from Watsonville formed a procession replete with decorated horses, a dragon, and all the costumes imaginable. The dragon "wound its torturous way along the streets in the wake of a sedan chair which was made to do duty as a band wagon." And, at the head of the parade, the Chinese carried the "long silken folds of our glorious Stars and Stripes sweeping gracefully in the zephyrs." Appropriately, the Watsonville delegation again won most of the rings that day. Apparently T'u Ti was impressed with all the preparations that the Watsonville Chinese had undertaken in his honor.

The Ring Game parades continued in Monterey until the fire of May 1906. In 1902 the Chinese participated in the Monterey Fourth of July parade; their "Chinese vision with beautiful silken banners, headed by a Mongolian band, with a number of splendid floats" was the highlight of the parade. All this public adulation and praise was not for the Chinese people as they lived every day in their fishing village, but for the idealization of Chinese culture that their parade finery represented. After the 1906 fire in Point Alones, the celebration moved to the McAbee Beach Chinatown, but it lost momentum, and the final Ring Game was played in the 1920s. Today, the last ring caught at McAbee Beach resides in a place of honor in the home of Jack Yee, son of the Chinese merchant and squid drier Won Yee.

Parade, Main Street, Watsonville, July 1898. Parade began in Brooklyn at south end of Main Street and is shown here moving north toward the center of town. Building on left is the Pajaro Valley Bank (now Wells Fargo). Chinese residents of Brooklyn bought parade finery for the Ring Game in Monterey but could not resist the opportunity to show it off in Watsonville. Note American flag at the head of the parade.                                        FLORENCE WAUGAMAN

Parade, July 1898, Watsonville. Large banners were made of silk, and all the regalia was purchased in China by the community.                FLORENCE WAUGAMAN

331

332

Parade, July 1898, Watsonville. The traditional lion in front of the Pajaro Valley Bank. Note spectator standing in upstairs window.

FLORENCE WAUGAMAN

Parade, July 1898, Watsonville. Passing the Watsonville Plaza. Odd Fellows building is with tower in background. Several Chinese women with bound feet rode
horses in the parade. Long pheasant feathers adorn the headdress of the woman in
center of photograph.          FLORENCE WAUGAMAN

333

Parade, July 1898, Watsonville. Men dressed in traditional costumes carrying assorted fighting spears and pikes rest in front of the Pajaro Valley Bank. Chinese character on their tunics is the symbol for "courageous."

FLORENCE WAUGAMAN

*Opposite*: Parade, July 1898, Watsonville. The altar from the Chee Kong Tong temple was removed and placed on a wagon for the parade. Traditional Chinese music was played on the wagon, which was decorated in red, white, and blue.

FLORENCE WAUGAMAN

336

Parade, July 1898, Watsonville. The altar from the temple. Note the queue of the man on the right of the photograph.   FLORENCE WAUGAMAN

Parade, July 1898, Watsonville. The traditional band.    FLORENCE WAUGAMAN

Parade, July 1898, Watsonville. Parade returning to Chinatown. Parade members beginning to wilt in the July heat. Building to the rear was the Mansion House Hotel, which still stands, though it has been moved from the corner.

FLORENCE WAUGAMAN

*Opposite*: Parade, July 1898, Watsonville. Woman on horseback, riding sidesaddle; the toe of her bound foot can just be seen next to the stirrup.

FLORENCE WAUGAMAN

338

*Left*: Parade, July 1898, Watsonville. Large silk banner has an imperial dragon embroidered on it.                    FLORENCE WAUGAMAN

*Above*: Parade, July 1898, Watsonville. Leaders of the Chinese community in their traditional long-sleeved merchant clothes. They are shielding themselves from the hot July sun.                    FLORENCE WAUGAMAN

341

*Left*: Parade, July 1898, Watsonville. The lion returning to Chinatown. Mansion House in background.       FLORENCE WAUGAMAN

*Above*: Parade, July 1898, Watsonville. In full bloom, with American flag at the head of the procession, the Chinese return south on Main Street to Brooklyn. Note spectators crowded on the balconies of the Mansion House Hotel.
FLORENCE WAUGAMAN

344

Parade, July 1898, Watsonville. Two white women spectators lean together in conversation as the richly-costumed Chinese women pass them.

FLORENCE WAUGAMAN

## THE WELCOME WEARS THIN

Visitors to the Monterey Peninsula frequently toured the Point Alones village, and beginning in the 1870s, reporters, newspaper editors, and writers visited and wrote about the village. Robert Louis Stevenson visited the village in 1879 and wrote an often-quoted description:

> You will come upon a space of open down, a hamlet, a haven among rocks, a world of surge and screaming seagulls . . . And yet the boats that ride in the haven are of strange outlandish design; and, if you walk into the hamlet you will behold costumes and faces, and hear a tongue, that are unfamiliar to the memory. The joss-stock burns, the opium-pipe is smoked, the floors are strewn with slips of coloured paper—prayers, you would say, that had somehow missed their destination—and a man guiding his upright pencil from right to left across the sheet writes home the news of Monterey to the Celestial Empire.

Each year during the lunar New Year celebration, the Point Alones village held an "open house" where white visitors mixed easily with the Chinese as the latter made their New Year visits. In February 1870 the editor of the *Monterey Republican* visited the Point Alones village where he found many white visitors, "some [who] went to satisfy curiosity, many for free eatable delicacies . . ." Unfortunately, some of the visitors in 1870 also "took the occasion of the opportunity to mutilate and destroy property belonging to [the Chinese]."

Despite the periodic vandalism that occurred during the Chinese New Year celebrations, the Chinese continued to prepare special tables loaded with treats for white visitors. During the New Year celebration in 1889, for example, a long line of white visitors "could be seen winding through the narrow streets of the Chinese burg . . . many of them emerging from the quarter with handkerchiefs filled with candles, cakes and other oriental goody-goodies."

Over the years, the Point Alones village became an important part of the tourist's list of sights to see, and most tourist-oriented newspaper editions included the Chinese fishing village on the Monterey Peninsula's list of attractions. As one letter writer put it:

> Among the many attractions California offers to Eastern visitors, one of the most interesting is the Oriental element. The peculiar style of dress and manners is a great novelty. Even the Chinese fishing village in Pacific Grove, in spite of its mal-odoriferous smells, has its full quota of sightseers. To many it is simply curiosity that prompts the threading of its narrow street and peering into its open doorways.

The Ring Game attracted large crowds of sightseers to the Point Alones village, and vandalism against the Chinese increased dramatically. During the 1897 Ring Game, one observer noted that after a group of "well-dressed" young men climbed upon a drying frame to get a better view of the contest, "instead of standing quietly, they jumped up and down 'til [the frame] broke." The observer asked rhetorically, "If a Chinaman had done the same in an American yard, what do you think would have been the result?"

During that same day the custom of "peering into open doorways" escalated into outright rudeness. A group of white men and women stood watching a Chinese family through the open doorway of the house. When the family sat down to eat, one of the family members quietly closed the door. The crowd of onlookers then moved to a window to continue their observation, so the Chinese inside pulled the curtain shut. The group then moved to another window and so on until all the doors and windows of the Chinese home were shut and barred. A witness correctly observed that, to the onlookers, the desire of the Chinese family to eat in private "was of no consequence—they were only 'heathen Chinese.'"

New Year's crowd, Point Alones Village, c. 1900. The crowds of whites which descended upon the Point Alones village became more unruly each year, and the celebration was often punctuated by acts of vandalism against the property of the Chinese residents. Note the posturing of the men in the photograph.

MONTEREY PUBLIC LIBRARY

Each year the crowds grew larger and their behavior grew worse. After the 1898 Ring Game, the editor of the *Pacific Grove Review* (the same editor who was pushing for the removal of the Chinese village from Point Alones) declared that the behavior of some of the crowd was "a deplorable reflection upon the manners and decency of the young people who witnessed the ring contest . . ." Apparently a number of the young spectators pushed their way into the crowd of Chinese scrambling for the ring and began to wrestle it away from the Chinese who had won it. "Imagine," said the editor, "a band of lawless Chinese approaching one of our Fourth of July celebrations and jostling and fighting the prize winners." Particularly distressing to the editor, however, was that the lack of respect displayed towards the Chinese also reflected on the American flag which had headed the parade earlier in the day: "One would naturally think that the presence of the American flag at the head of the procession would have appealed to the innate decency of any boy born upon American soil . . ."

The bad manners displayed by some of the visitors at the 1898 game inspired several letters to the editor, all condemning the behavior of the rude spectators. One of the letters took a sarcastic tone when it concluded:

> Just think; on the 22nd of February, 1898, they never killed a single Chinaman . . . I suppose that in 1970, when all these boys [the white ruffians] have been converted and gone to a better land, a Chinaman with the American flag can march through the streets unmolested.

Many whites could not extend their admiration for Chinese culture as personified by the dragon, banners, and bands to the Chinese fishermen and their personal belongings. Incidents of vandalism were never numerous, nor did visitors ever do any physical harm to the Chinese, but the cumulative effect of the bad manners diminished the hospitality which the Chinese showed toward visitors. In Salinas Chinatown in 1891, a young white visitor to the New Year open house at Quong Wah's store dropped a firecracker in his kerosene lamp, starting a fire which came close to destroying both the store and Quong Wah. Quong Wah "bitterly deplored the want of sense in many white people" after the incident; his hospitality worn thin, he stopped having visitors in his store during festivals.

The renaissance of spirit which the Chinese in the Monterey Bay Region enjoyed was mirrored in other events in California. Perhaps most typical of the new spirit of American-Chinese cultural pride was the formation of the Native Sons of the Golden State in 1895. Members in the organization were primarily Chinese born in California, and the group was founded at least in part as a comment on the whites-only policies of the Native Sons of the Golden West.

Unfortunately, like the burst of sparks which comes just before the Fourth of July sparkler burns out, this Chinese cultural renaissance also marked the beginning of a decline in morale in the early twentieth century. The effects of the Exclusion laws began to be felt; with few women and children in the Chinese community, death and the return of some of the older men to China diminished the population. In some instances the populations of Chinatowns were cut in half by attrition between 1900 and 1910. With its high percentage of women and children, the only Chinese community in the entire Monterey Bay Region that had a chance to survive the demographic trough was the Point Alones village.

The only way to deal with Chinese is to impress them with your authority. A man with a shotgun is worth twenty men with books under their arms.

A. D. Shepard,
General Manager,
Pacific Improvement Company

# 11

# Monterey

CHINESE CAME to the Point Alones fishing village because it reminded them of similar villages they had left behind in China; whites came to visit because it was unlike any other Chinese settlement in America they had ever seen. Perched and propped on the rocks with drying racks hanging over the water, the village was a delight for poets, painters, and photographers. In 1900 the Point Alones fishing village was the largest and oldest Chinese community in the Monterey Bay Region. How had it managed to survive for so long?

First, the village was located in a jurisdictional blind spot, on the border between Pacific Grove and Monterey, far from the center of municipal development and scrutiny. The other major Chinatowns in the Monterey Bay Region (Salinas, Watsonville, Santa Cruz) had all been located close to business districts and had been pressured because of it. Second, the Point Alones village had developed Monterey's only major industry in 1900; with the exception of tourism, sporadic efforts at mining coal and sand, and the military encampments, fishing was the only industry on the Monterey Peninsula, and the Chinese brought dollars into the local economy. Third, the Chinese had a very powerful landlord. The Pacific Improvement Company, the land-development arm of the Southern Pacific Railroad, tacitly

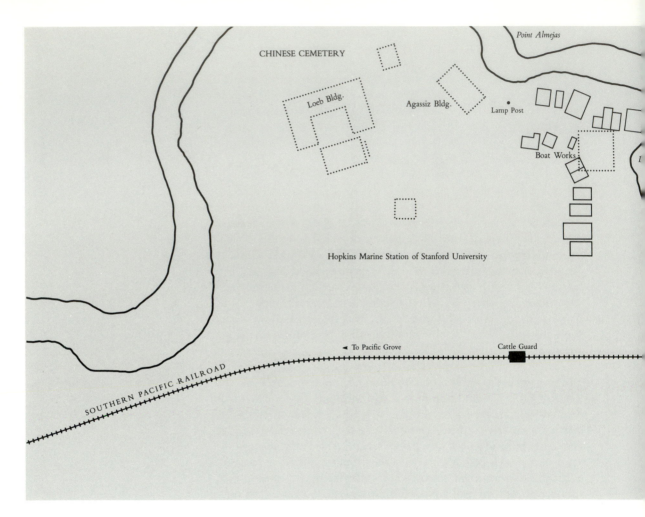

Map 11–1

POINT ALONES FISHING VILLAGE, c. 1900

This composite map is derived from a Pacific Improvement Company map made
following the 1906 fire and historic photographs taken before the fire. Map also

352

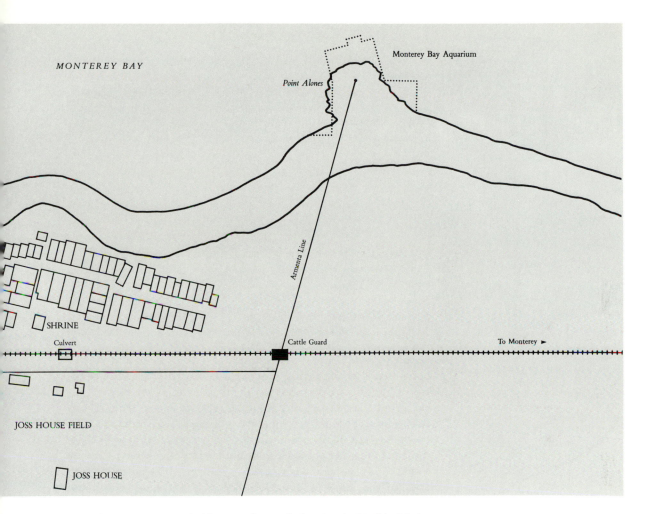

MONTEREY BAY

Point Alones

Monterey Bay Aquarium

Armenta Line

SHRINE

Culvert

Cattle Guard

To Monterey ▶

JOSS HOUSE FIELD

JOSS HOUSE

shows location of existing buildings on the Stanford University Hopkins Marine Station. Original maps provided by the Pebble Beach Company, Pat Hathaway, and Bob Ayres.

Point Alones Village, c. 1900. After a half-century the village began to look rickety. One of the few photographs taken before 1906 fire. Buildings in distance on right were the family section of the village. ROY CHRISTIAN

354

supported the Chinese community by renting its land to the villagers; the Chinese village had been woven into the fabric of the tourist business promoted by the Pacific Improvement Company and Southern Pacific Railroad. Fourth, most of the objections raised about other Chinatowns concerned gambling, opium smoking, and prostitution; these were not concentrated in Point Alones but in the small Chinatown in downtown Monterey on Franklin and Washington streets. The main reason the village still thrived in 1900, however, was that Monterey was about thirty years behind in its development. Between 1850 and 1880 Monterey had gone into a state of suspended animation, and even after the arrival of the Pacific Improvement Company on the peninsula in 1880, development had been slow because most of the peninsula's property was controlled by the company.

Point Alones Village main street, c. 1900. Photograph taken looking west.　　　BANCROFT LIBRARY

*Below*: Point Alones Village, c. 1900. Looking east. Building beyond the trees in the distance is part of the cannery expansion which put pressure on the village at the turn of the century.

PAT HATHAWAY

## THE TOWN PRESSURES THE VILLAGE
## TO MOVE

The Chinese fishing village could not continue to exist indefinitely—the property was too valuable, and the Chinese toehold too tenuous, to permit it. The Spanish-American War in 1898 broke the depression of the 1890s, and the town's development began to pick up speed. Residential development of ocean-front property spread along the coast toward the village; houses such as the Tevis house, about a half-mile east of the Point Alones village, equipped with indoor plumbing, electricity, and modern fixtures, demonstrated how archaic the Chinese fishing village had become. To the west the Pacific Improvement Company continued to subdivide sections of Pacific Grove until, by 1905, the only large ocean-front parcel remaining to be subdivided was the fishing village itself. To the south the United States Government began to restore the presidio it had abandoned years earlier in order to accommodate troops returning from the war in the Philippines. In 1902 the Army began constructing a military post on the hill south of the Chinese village, and the first troops stationed there were a squadron of Ninth U.S. Cavalry returning from two years of duty in the Philippines.

To the east the arrival of fish canneries brought the greatest pressure on the Chinese village. The first fish cannery to locate between Monterey and Point Alones was the Sacramento River Packers Association in 1896. After negotiating agreements with Italian, Portuguese, and Japanese fishermen, the canning business began to flourish. In 1901 a second cannery was built by M. R. Robbins and by early 1902 two more canneries were under construction. The canneries made the Chinese system of fish drying obsolete. Complaints about the odor of drying squid coming from the village became more insistent as the village became less important to the economy. As Monterey matured, so did its anti-Chinese feeling.

In May 1902 Mayor Johnson of Monterey presented a number of citizen complaints about the odor to the Pacific Improvement Company. Mr. B. A. Eardley, the superintendent of the company's properties in Pacific Grove, sympathetically responded with a promise that the drying of squid at Point Alones would stop. When Eardley was asked what would happen to the Chinese if they could no longer dry the squid, he observed that Chinatown would probably "cease to exist." As the editor of the *Monterey New Era* observed, ". . . any decrease in the town's business which may result [from the Chinese leaving] will be more than made up by the increased number of visitors and residents who must surely have been kept away by the smell of the squid drying in the fields and stored at the wharf . . ." He concluded his editorial by pointing out that Chinatown's abolition "would not only make building sites on the water front at the western end . . . immensely more valuable, but Chinatown itself would in time form as beautiful and desirable villa sites as can be found in America." To ensure that the Pacific Improvement Company understood the gravity of the town's interests, Mayor Johnson visited the company's headquarters in San Francisco and extracted assurances from the company's president, Horace Platt, that in addition to prohibiting squid drying, the company would not renew its leases with the Chinese once they expired.

For the next two years, the Chinese dried their squid elsewhere on the peninsula. Convinced that the issue of the odor had died down, the Chinese resumed drying squid at Point Alones in May 1904; the odor "hung like a dark brown cloud over Monterey from the city limits to the custom house." Several Chinese squid dryers were arrested for maintaining a nuisance, but this did not deter the Chinese, and the drying continued.

In early 1905 the Pacific Improvement Company gave notice to the Chinese that their leases would not be renewed, and later that year the Company stopped collecting rent from the Chinese to remove any legal right the Chinese might have to occupy the property. The Chinese asked for several extensions of time so they might continue to search for a new site for the village, but the Pacific Improvement Company ordered them to remove their buildings and fish-drying racks and vacate the premises not later than February 1906. (The fact that the Chinese were not paying rent to the Pacific Improvement Company at the time of the fire led several historians to conclude that the Chinese at Point Alones were squatters on the property. Neither David Jacks nor the Pacific Improvement Company ever let one day go by rent-free for the Chinese at Point Alones until the beginning of 1906.)

In 1905 the Chinese began negotiations for a location along the beach near Seaside, but in early 1906 the deal fell through. Faced with the February deadline and no alternative site, the Chinese went back to the Pacific Improvement Company and asked for another extension which the company granted: "The Pacific Improvement Company does not wish to be harsh with their Chinese tenants . . ."

The Chinese were stalling. It is not clear whether they actually wanted to find an alternative site or whether they believed that if they dragged their feet long enough the Pacific Improvement Company would give up trying to evict them. During these negotiations the village was led by a group of America-born Chinese including Tuck Lee and Yen Tai, and they skillfully played the various spokesmen of the Pacific Improvement Company against each other. The village had survived municipal bluster and threats before, and the Chinese were confident that time would again resolve the problem. After all, they had been at the site as long as they or anyone else could remember, fishing, drying, paying their rents and taxes on time. The squid drying operation had been there *first*—people who chose to live in the neighborhood of the village had no right to complain about the odor.

The 1906 earthquake cancelled Chinese hopes of stalling off their opponents. San Francisco lay in ruins after the April 18 earthquake and fire, while Pacific Grove suffered a "trifling" amount of damage, mainly fallen chimneys. Like Santa Cruz, its resort counterpart across the Bay, Pacific Grove quickly mobilized to make its tents and summer homes available to refugees from San Francisco, taking up collections of clothing and blankets to help the victims of the disaster.

Chinese refugees from the San Francisco fire found temporary housing in Chinatowns throughout the San Francisco Bay Area; an estimated 150 Chinese refugees came to the Point Alones village. Some, like the remarkable woman who walked with her children from San Francisco to Castroville before boarding a train to ride the last few miles to Pacific Grove, were Point Alones villagers who had been temporarily residing in San Francisco. Another refugee, young Ben Hoang, had been asleep in a fishing boat near San Francisco when the earthquake struck. He returned with his uncle to his mother's home village of Point Alones in late April to wait until the fate of San Francisco's Chinatown was resolved.

Two weeks after the fire and earthquake, the Pacific Improvement Company once again resumed its eviction efforts at Point Alones village, possibly concerned that the San Francisco Chinese population dispersed by the earthquake to Point Alones would settle permanently, making eviction that much more difficult. In early May 1906, A. D. Shepard, General Manager of the Pacific Improvement Company, suggested that "the removal could be accomplished quietly and effectively if the Company would put up some shacks, somewhere near the light house, and charge a nominal rent." J. P. Pryor, General Agent of the Company in Pacific Grove, responded with a lengthy analysis of the situation based on the assumption that nothing "can get the Chinamen out of there except process of law, or unless the Company should undertake to use force to eject them and risk the

consequences." Pryor was convinced that "another location is
not in their thoughts at all, and they have no intention of moving." Instead, Pryor recommended that eviction suits be instituted against several of the village leaders; once they had been
evicted, the others would follow. Pryor concluded his recom-
mendation to Shepard by saying that "Moral suasion or tem-
porizing with them any further is, in my opinion, out of the
question. . . . Something must be done to show the Chinese that
we mean business." Shepard suggested that Pryor make one last
effort to convince the Chinese to move to an alternative site out
near the lighthouse and Pryor agreed, though he was pessimistic
about getting the Chinese leadership even to walk the land with
him.

Eight days later the Point Alones village burned to the ground.

## THE 1906 FIRE

To painters and poets the village was picturesque and quaint,
but to public health officials and fire inspectors, the village was
an anachronism—a hodgepodge of wooden buildings scattered
among the rocks, lacking a sewage system or sufficient water
pressure to put out a major fire, while elsewhere the twentieth
century had brought plumbing and electricity. Fire had acted as
an instrument for municipal redevelopment in the nineteenth
century; Chinatowns in Santa Cruz and Salinas had been destroyed by fires and then modernized. The Point Alones village
had been visited by major fires three times before the final one in
1906 but had changed very little along the way.

The first major fire occurred on November 9, 1889. While the
village was cleaning up in preparation for the funeral of a prominent merchant, a rubbish pile caught fire and 75% of the village
burned to the ground. Since the Chinese owned the buildings

they bore the entire burden of the loss. Undaunted by the fire, they quickly rebuilt the village almost exactly as it had been before. When the rebuilding was complete, the Pacific Improvement Company distributed fire barrels throughout the town, and the Chinese promised to buy some fire hose and establish a fire company, but there is no evidence they did so.

The second fire came in October 1898 when a kerosene lamp exploded, starting a fire which might have destroyed the entire village. The only available water to fight the fire came from a single garden hose, so the Chinese residents created a fire break by tearing down a row of buildings in the path of the flames. In addition to the houses destroyed to make a fire break, four houses burned along with fishing nets, trawl lines, and assorted household goods, for a total loss of an estimated $1,200.

The third fire came in 1902, and once again, a row of buildings had to be torn down to create a fire break in order to stop the fire. This time the Chinese had help from the all-black Ninth Cavalry unit which was encamped on the hill behind the village. The fires brought few improvements to the village; buildings were rebuilt in the same cheek-by-jowl manner, fire hydrants were not installed, nor were fire companies formed, and the village creaked into the twentieth century.

The 1906 fire broke out in a barn at the west end of the fishing village at 8 P.M. on May 16. The Chinese tried to contain the fire with a bucket brigade, but the westerly wind spread the flames to nearby buildings, so a call went out for the Pacific Grove volunteer fire fighters. As in all the previous fires, the water supply was insufficient to fight the fire. Fire breaks were created at several points by tearing down buildings, but this time the wind was too strong, and the flames jumped each fire break. Realizing that the fire would continue to spread, Chinese residents rescued personal belongings, fowls, and fishing gear, while the volunteer firemen made one last futile effort to halt the flames. Within an

Point Alones Village, May 17, 1906.
Remains of the village after the fire.
Smoke is still rising from embers.
          J. K. AND MYRON A. OLIVER
COLLECTION, COLTON HALL, MONTEREY

hour the firemen gave up and joined hundreds of spectators to watch the fire from the railroad tracks. By 10 P.M. the fire had done its work, and all but sixteen of the over one hundred buildings in the fishing village were destroyed. The fire spared only a few buildings (including the temple) on the south side of the railroad tracks and a small cluster of barns and buildings on the extreme west end of the village. Damage was estimated at $25,000, and since the Chinese owned everything in the village except the land, they bore the entire loss. As in the previous three major fires in the village, no lives were lost; the only injury was sustained by a spectator who fell backwards off the small railroad overcrossing and into the underpass.

But the Chinese lost more than their homes to the fire. The hundreds of spectators lining the railroad tracks cheered the fire as it roared through Chinatown, and many of the white spectators joined in looting. Vandals broke into stores and dwellings not touched by the fire and carted their contents away. When

363

Point Alones Village, May 17, 1906. Souvenir hunters picking through the ashes. Whites looted the Chinese houses and buildings during the fire and picked through the ashes creating what, to some observers, was a "deplorable and disgusting spectacle."

J. K. AND MYRON A. OLIVER COLLECTION, COLTON HALL, MONTEREY

Point Alones Village, May 17, 1906. Chinese residents of the village gathered around the safes which survived the fire.

J. K. AND MYRON A. OLIVER COLLECTION, COLTON HALL, MONTEREY

Chinese piled their belongings beyond the range of the fire, spectators stole them as soon as the Chinese ran back into the village to save more of their possessions. Several officers took up stations on the roads leading away from the village and apprehended some of the thieves, relieving them of their booty. As one observer noted, "Had it not been for a few of the officers present the Chinese would have lost everything they possessed." The next morning dozens of townspeople poked about in the warm ashes looking for valuables.

Numerous letters protesting the actions of the thieves were written to local newspapers. As Edward Berwick put it in a letter to the *Pacific Grove Review*, "Conscience, honor, delicacy, decency, seemed thrown to the winds." Dr. Kupelwieser, a visiting German biologist who had witnessed the fire, declared,

> I hope I may never in my life feel so ashamed of my white skin or white civilization as I then felt . . . I wondered why they were taking things away from the poor unfortunates instead of bringing them some token of Christian sympathy . . . it was a deplorable and disgusting spectacle.

Editorials and letters lamented the behavior of the looters and wondered aloud about the morality of such actions in a community dedicated to Christian principles.

There were also many acts of kindness toward the hundreds of Chinese refugees standing homeless before the smoldering ruins of the village. Many residents offered shelter to the Chinese and their families, and Pacific Grove Mayor Will Jacks took a family of six with a newborn baby to his family cottage in Pacific Grove. Many of the Chinese crowded into the unburned buildings on the west side of the village for the night, while others were put up in the old Pacific House Hotel in Monterey. A relief fund was organized the day following the fire, beginning with a donation from Dr. Kupelwieser. Despite the acts of contrition, the people of Pacific Grove made it clear that they wanted

Point Alones Village, May 17, 1906. Chinese resident searches the ashes while whites socialize on the right.

J. K. AND MYRON A. OLIVER COLLECTION, COLTON HALL, MONTEREY

Point Alones Village, May 17, 1906. Souvenir hunters pick through the rubble. The souvenir hunting and looting occasioned a lengthy debate in the local newspapers.

J. K. AND MYRON A. OLIVER COLLECTION, COLTON HALL, MONTEREY

Point Alones Village, May 17, 1906. Well-dressed Pacific Grove women sightseeing in the ashes of the village.
J. K. AND MYRON A. OLIVER COLLECTION, COLTON HALL, MONTEREY

the Chinese out of the Grove—not west to the alternative site originally offered by the Pacific Improvement Company, but out: "We wish them to be removed so far that they will never be any more trouble . . ." Perhaps the size of the relief fund gave an even clearer measure of the feelings of the community toward the Chinese—the fund reached a grand total of twenty-nine dollars (mainly from Berwick and Kupelwieser). No arrests for looting were ever made.

Many articles have been written about the May 16 Point Alones fire, and some of them speculate that the Pacific Improvement Company deliberately burned the village, but the evidence used to implicate the Company is circumstantial. The exact origin of the fire will probably never be known, but if the Company believed they could resolve the issue by burning most of the village, they clearly underestimated the resolve of the Chinese villagers. Two days following the fire, the *Pacific Grove Review* stated: "The question of the removal of Chinatown is now settled." They could not have been more wrong.

Point Alones Village, May 17, 1906. Chinese residents scramble to collect their belongings.    J. K. AND MYRON A. OLIVER COLLECTION, COLTON HALL, MONTEREY

Point Alones Village, May 17, 1906. Monkey face rock remains as a lasting reminder of the village. Today the rock is on the grounds of Stanford University's
Hopkins Marine Station.

J. K. AND MYRON A. OLIVER COLLECTION, COLTON HALL, MONTEREY

## THE BATTLE—MAY 1906 TO MAY 1907

After the fire at Point Alones, the Chinese waged a fierce battle to retain their village, once again contradicting the stereotype of meek, submissive people fleeing before mobs. Far from being the end of the struggle between the Pacific Improvement Company and the Chinese, the fire was really the beginning. In scenes comparable to the civil rights sit-ins of the 1960s, the Chinese at the Point Alones village made a heroic effort to remain there.

The morning after the fire, A. D. Shepard received two telegrams from Monterey. The first, from George Snell, manager of the Del Monte Hotel, simply said, "About two thirds of Chinatown destroyed by fire last night." J. P. Pryor, the ranking Company official in Pacific Grove, also sent a telegram about the fire, but he added, "Shall I appoint watchman to prevent any attempt at rebuilding." Shepard telegraphed his answer to Pryor the same day: "Do anything necessary to prevent rebuilding." The next day the Pacific Improvement Company built a fence around the burned village site and posted several guards at the entrance. Meanwhile, an estimated one hundred Chinese crowded into the unburned buildings outside the fence and made it clear that they intended to remain and to rebuild the village on the burned site as well. The Chinese began a small guerilla war to gain re-entry into the burned section. They distracted the guards, tore down the fence, and entered the burned section of the village to build temporary shacks out of squid-drying racks which had survived the fire. The guards, armed with shotguns, forcibly evicted the group, and when one Chinese woman sat down and refused to leave, the guards dragged her kicking and screaming out the gate.

The internal correspondence of the Pacific Improvement

Telegram sent by J. P. Pryor, Superintendent of the Pacific Improvement Company's properties on the Monterey Peninsula, to A. D. Shepard, General Manager of the Company.
SPECIAL COLLECTIONS,
STANFORD UNIVERSITY

Form No. 168.

**THE WESTERN UNION TELEGRAPH COMPANY.**
INCORPORATED
**23,000 OFFICES IN AMERICA.    CABLE SERVICE TO ALL THE WORLD.**

This Company TRANSMITS and DELIVERS messages only on conditions limiting its liability, which have been assented to by the sender of the following message.
Errors can be guarded against only by repeating a message back to the sending station for comparison, and the Company will not hold itself liable for errors or delays in transmission or delivery of Unrepeated Messages, beyond the amount of tolls paid thereon, nor in any case where the claim is not presented in writing within sixty days after the message is filed with the Company for transmission.
This is an UNREPEATED MESSAGE, and is delivered by request of the sender, under the conditions named above.
ROBERT C. CLOWRY, President and General Manager.

**RECEIVED** at
204 xn y ot. 14-paid

PacificGrove,Calif.,May 17th-06

A.D.Shepard,

No.1006 Broadway

Oakland,Calif.

Greater portion Chinatown burned Shall I appoint watchman to prevent

any attempt at rebuilding.

J.P.Pryor.

337-p

A. D. Shepard's response. The Pacific Improvement Company wanted to take the opportunity of the fire to move the Chinese village to another site. Whether or not the company actually set the fire is still a matter of some debate among Monterey historians.
SPECIAL COLLECTIONS,
STANFORD UNIVERSITY

Form No. 2.

**THE WESTERN UNION TELEGRAPH COMPANY.**
INCORPORATED
**23,000 OFFICES IN AMERICA.    CABLE SERVICE TO ALL THE WORLD.**
ROBERT C. CLOWRY, President and General Manager.

| Receiver's No. | Time Filed | Charge P I Co | Check |

**SEND** the following message subject to the terms on back hereof, which are hereby agreed to.    Oakland May 17th ,1906,    190

To    J.P.Pryor,

Pacific Grove,Cal.

Do anything necessary to prevent rebuilding. .

AD. SHEPARD.

☞ READ THE NOTICE AND AGREEMENT ON BACK. ☜

Company provides a fascinating perspective on the conflict between the company and the Chinese. Far from being the omniscient and powerful corporation, the company was perplexed by the actions of the Chinese protestors at Point Alones. The Pacific Improvement Company was on the defensive from the beginning of the struggle, concerned about public opinion and afraid of the consequences should someone be injured or killed in the conflict. A week after the fire, Chinese occupied buildings west and south of the burned section, while guards patrolled the fence surrounding the remainder of the village site. Minor skirmishes between guards and Chinese punctuated the uneasy peace. The company erected some new cottages on the south side of the railroad tracks so the Chinese would move out of the buildings on the west end. But after three of the cottages had been begun, Pryor learned that the Chinese refused to move into them: "I therefore prefer to spend . . . money on the guards, rather than waste it on cottages which the Chinese refuse to occupy." As

Point Alones Village, late May 1906. Pacific Improvement Company guards stand behind the fence erected to prevent the Chinese from rebuilding on the burned site. Approximately seventy Chinese protestors occupied the unburned buildings in the distance on the right, and it took a year of legal struggle before the last Chinese resident of the village moved to the McAbee Beach site. In the distance on the left are the cottage frames which the Pacific Improvement Company began building to lure the Chinese off the site. The Chinese refused to move into the cottages and they were never completed. CALIFORNIA STATE LIBRARY

371

Point Alones Village, late May 1906. The outdoor altar in the right foreground was not completely destroyed, and on the left, beyond the railroad tracks, is the Chee Kong Tong temple which was eventually moved to McAbee Beach.     PAT HATHAWAY

time passed Pryor became increasingly concerned for the safety of his guards: "I am reliably informed that the Chinese have purchased every firearm to be had in Monterey. I know that they have threatened to shoot and kill my men." The Chinese had begun to build new buildings on the south side of the railroad tracks near the temple, and when the guards tore the buildings down, the Chinese threatened to shoot, but they did not. Instead they filed charges of assault and destruction of private property against the company's guards; the local Justice Court judge dismissed the charges.

In late June 1906 the Chinese again took the offensive in the courts. On June 25 attorneys Sandholdt and Shaw filed a suit titled "Demand for Surrender of Real Property" on behalf of thirty-five named Chinese. The suit asked that the burned district be returned to the Chinese. While this suit and various counter-suits by the Pacific Improvement Company began their laborious journey through the courts, the guards patrolled the fence and the Chinese occupied the buildings to the west and south.

Beyond the principle of resisting an unfair eviction, most Chinese fishermen fought because the loss of the site and the drying yards meant they would be without a livelihood. There were few places in California that Chinese fishermen could work, as anti-Chinese fishing restrictions had driven most of the Chinese out of the Sacramento River Delta and San Francisco Bay. Monterey was the last stronghold of extensive fishing in Northern California. Most leaders of the Chinese resistance, such as Tom Yuen, Tom Wong, and Tuck Lee, were California-born fishermen who had grown up at a time when educational opportunities in Monterey (except for the Mission school) were nonexistent. Tuck Lee, in particular, was a persistent foe of the Company's efforts to move the village. Arrested several times and named in most of the suits filed by the Company, Tuck Lee was a direct descendant of one of the original Monterey Chinese fishing families of the 1850s.

Why did the Pacific Improvement Company, a historic champion (and employer) of the Chinese in California, work so hard to oust the Chinese from Point Alones? All available evidence suggests that the company was responding to public opinion against the Chinese in Pacific Grove and neighboring Monterey. The towns wanted the Chinese evicted. While the Company was embroiled in the first week of the struggle, Shepard learned that one of the local newspapers was taking the side of the Chinese and angrily instructed Pryor to go to the offices of the newspaper and tell the editor that should his editorial policy continue, "we are disposed to immediately tear down the fence and permit the Chinamen to re-occupy the old premises, and will never again attempt anything toward their removal, leaving the Chinese and their squid-drying affairs wholly in the hands of others. This is no threat, but straight business." The company's willingness to give the Chinese an alternative (and cheaper) location on company property attests to the fact that the Pacific Improvement Company had no desire to hound them. The company took a hesitant and gingerly approach to evicting the Chinese after the fire; sensing this hesitation to use outright force, the Chinese tied up the property while Shephard, Platt, and Pryor hemmed and hawed about what to do. In a letter to Reverend R. H. Willey in June 1906, Shepard gave a candid assessment of his plans:

> *I would like to drop everything in the way of legal proceedings* [against the Chinese] *. . . leaving the fence in place and the Chinamen out of the burned district. I am satisfied everything will quiet down, and our only controversy will be with the people remaining outside of the fence. This, I think, can be settled later . . . I think we have proceeded far enough for one season.*

Just as Gandhi was lucky to have a civilized adversary in the British, so were the Chinese at Point Lobos fortunate to have a civilized adversary in the Pacific Improvement Company.

During the summer and early fall of 1906, the Chinese negotiated with J. B. McAbee for a lease on his beach, a quarter-mile east of Point Alones, within the city limits of Monterey. Officially named Arena Gorda (Thick Sand) Beach, the beach and adjacent property were the only ocean-front property not subdivided when New Monterey was laid out in 1889. During the 1890s J. B. McAbee built a small cluster of cottages and attracted sea bathers to the beach with a small fleet of pleasure boats. McAbee's beach was closer to Monterey and the wharves than the alternative site offered the Chinese by the Pacific Improvement Company. In the fall of 1906, while the Chinese were crowded together in the remaining buildings at Point Alones, representatives from the Chinese village as well as Chinese from San Francisco approached McAbee about leasing the beach for a fishing village site. In October 1906 McAbee agreed to a long-term lease of the property.

The news of the tentative arrangement reached the Monterey public and the Pacific Improvement Company at about the same time. The company was delighted; the people of Monterey, though they sympathized with the plight of the Chinese when they were outside city limits, were furious. Residents of New Monterey, led by W. N. Furlong, the Prebles, and the Murrays (who had purchased the nearby Tevis mansion), quickly formed a committee and offered to purchase the land from McAbee to prevent the Chinese from signing a lease and moving there. McAbee gave the committee a week to raise a first payment of five thousand dollars, but before the week had elapsed, McAbee signed the lease with the Chinese. The citizens continued to meet for the next six months, trying unsuccessfully to purchase or condemn the land.

When A. D. Shepard learned of the move, he pledged the Pacific Improvement Company's support:

> This Company is favorable to location of Chinatown on McAbee Beach, and will do all [it] can to assist, i.e., . . . place necessary water mains and fire hydrants, without charge, within the new section. Will also not object to the Chinamen removing any of the buildings from our lands; instead [we] will assist them.

When J. P. Pryor expressed doubts as to the benefit of the move, Shepard reiterated his pleasure at the prospect:

> Personally, I am inclined to rejoice, that we have escaped an incubus on our premises and the transfer means a heavy increase in value of the P.I. Co.

*properties. I do not believe that Chinatown will be detrimental to New Monterey. In any event, it is not a trouble of our making, and the people who have been antagonistic to us, because of the Chinese colony we have been thought to encourage, can now turn their attention elsewhere."*

The Chinese were slow to leave the Point Alones site, and they trickled out of the few remaining buildings through the winter of 1906–07. Eviction proceedings continued against them, keeping the pressure on until the last of the Chinese left the site in April 1907. Some of the shacks were moved to the new Chinatown at McAbee while the more flimsy ones were torn down. Exactly 365 days after the 1906 fire, Tuck Lee, the last to depart, left Point Alones and the Chinese surrendered the village site. Only the temple south of the railroad tracks remained, and it was later moved to McAbee Beach.

Public opinion had favored the underdog Chinese in their year-long struggle with the powerful Pacific Improvement Company, and the Company abandoned its plans to subdivide the village site into ocean-front home sites. Instead, in November 1906, Shepard instructed Pryor to announce "that the Board of Directors of the Pacific Improvement Company have donated Chinatown Point to the University of California for park and laboratory purposes." The company's new plan called for the construction of a subdivision (named University Park) in which faculty at the laboratory could purchase homes, thus extracting some profit from the gift. In December Benjamin Ide Wheeler, President of the University, conveyed the Board of Regents' thanks for the gift. The transfer of the point to the University of California was an ingenious solution to a sticky public relations problem for the Pacific Improvement Company.

The Pacific Improvement Company squeezed another advantage out of the move of the Chinese to McAbee Beach. McAbee had long been a favorite beach for local sea bathers as it was one of the warmest locations on the north side of the Monterey Peninsula, so when the Chinese leased the beach, effectively closing it to sea bathing, the Pacific Improvement Company decided not to open the beach at Point Alones for public bathing, forcing local sea bathers to board the street railway and travel to the Del Monte Hotel's beach and baths. "We have a bath house and beach at Del Monte which is not paying expenses, and the closing of McAbee beach [to bathers] should bring additional revenue," said A. D. Shepard. "It would be quite as convenient for the people of Pacific Grove to continue the street car ride to Del Monte Bath House . . ."

## McABEE BEACH

In negotiating the McAbee Beach site, the Chinese won a bittersweet victory. The location of McAbee Beach was excellent, but the price of victory was a great loss of population. In 1900, 155 Chinese lived at Point Alones, and 61 of those were fishermen. In 1910 the Chinese population at McAbee Beach was 86, with only 18 fishermen.

The Chinese village erected at McAbee faced Ocean View Avenue (now Cannery Row) between Prescott and Hoffman Avenues. In addition to the buildings that had been moved from the Point Alones site, the Chinese lived in refurbished cottages that the McAbees had formerly rented to summer visitors. Ben Hoang, whose family lived at the McAbee Chinatown for many years, remembered that at first some of the buildings were constructed partially of striped canvas, reminders of McAbee Beach's resort years. The lots which faced Ocean View Avenue were narrow (fifteen to eighteen feet wide) and deep (sixty feet), a configuration typical of all Chinatowns in the Monterey Bay Region; most of the buildings were two stories tall. Most of the

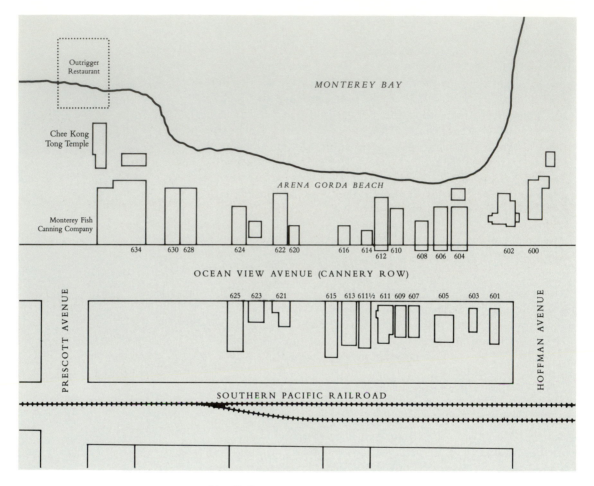

Map 11–2

McABEE BEACH CHINATOWN, MONTEREY, 1912

Map shows Chinese-occupied buildings and businesses between the beach and railroad track. Monterey Fish Canning Company building is on the left. Present-day Outrigger Restaurant is now on the point at far left. Map derived from Sanborn Map Company maps, Map Library, UCSC.

378

Chinese living in the McAbee Chinatown had long-term leases with the McAbees. The typical lease ran for twenty years at a monthly rental of five dollars. The Chinese were free to build on the lots or alter buildings already there, but each of the leases concluded with the condition that the lessee would "not sell liquor without a permit, nor shall he sell any opium to any white person, nor as a house of prostitution, or any unlawful business." This morality clause probably helped maintain the family nature of the Point Alones fishing village; women still comprised nearly 40% of the population in 1910, and eleven children under ten years of age lived there.

McAbee Beach Chinatown, Monterey, c. 1911. White building on extreme right is the Chee Kong Tong temple which was moved from the Point Alones village site following the fire. Large building with smokestack in the center is the Monterey Fish Canning Company which specialized in turning fish entrails and heads into oil and fertilizer. Note fish hanging on the drying racks in center of picture.

PAT HATHAWAY

The Chinese christened their new village by hosting the Ring Game in March 1907. As always, representatives from Watsonville and Salinas came in on a special train, and colorful costumes, the noise of firecrackers, and the scramble for the ring marked the festival. Several Chinese made speeches predicting that the McAbee Beach Chinatown would soon rival San Francisco, but the fire and struggle had dispersed many of the Chinese fishing families, and McAbee Beach never became the cultural center that the old Point Alones village had been. Its population never exceeded one hundred.

By moving inside the Monterey City limits, the Chinese had lost the protective isolation of their little corner at Point Alones. The secrecy with which the Chinese had negotiated their lease with McAbee, along with McAbee's disdain for public opinion, guaranteed that the Monterey City government would do everything it could to make life uncomfortable for the Chinese, particularly for the squid fishermen, who continued to dry their catch on vacant lots in McAbee. By 1908 complaints about the odor of drying squid from neighboring residents reached such a point that the trustees passed an ordinance prohibiting the drying of squid inside the Monterey City Limits.

Following the ordinance of 1908, the squid-drying industry continued fitfully, but neither the quantity nor quality of squid indicated a good prognosis for the industry. Each year the squid were dried on the outskirts of Monterey, beyond the reach of the Monterey City Trustees. An enterprising Chinese merchant brought several innovations which gave the industry a last and very profitable decade. Won Yee came to California from his native Toishan in 1913, and after several years operating a business in San Francisco, he came to Monterey and opened a small store west of the McAbee Chinatown on Ocean View Avenue. Like most Chinese businessmen, he gave the store a grand name—

Won Yee and his squid-packing machine, Monterey, c. 1920. Won Yee's machine cleaned and baled the dried squid, revolutionizing the dried-squid industry on the Monterey Peninsula.
JACK YEE

Wing Chong—"glorious, successful." Wing Chong was a general store geared to serving the cannery workers living and working nearby; Won Yee stocked not only food but also the equipment the cannery workers needed—gloves, rubber boots, and fishing tackle.

Won Yee saw that there was still a strong market for dried squid in China, so in 1924 he set up a squid-drying operation adapted to the changes which had come to Monterey. First, with the number of Chinese fishermen down to a handful by the 1920s, Won Yee began buying fresh squid from the Sicilian fishermen. Yee paid the Italians eight dollars per ton for the squid at the wharf. Won Yee leased some acreage outside the city limits on the Monterey-Salinas highway across from the Monterey air field (now Monterey Airport); owned by T. A. Worth and sometimes called "Tarpey Flats," the area soon became known as "Squid Mountain." Trucks hauled the fresh squid to the drying

Won Yee in the squid-drying fields at Tarpey Flats (c. 1920), located beyond the Monterey City limits to avoid the anti squid-drying ordinances. The squid were spread on the ground to dry. Workers in the distance (left) are raking the squid, and piles of dried squid line the edge of the field in the distance. The drying field was adjacent to Monterey's airport, hence the airplane above Won Yee's head.

JACK YEE

fields where they were soaked in brine and spread on the ground to dry. With so few Chinese laborers available to work in the drying yard, Won Yee hired anyone willing and able to stand the strong odor and work for twenty-five cents per hour. Depending on the weather, the drying took from twelve to fifteen days.

Won Yee invented a machine which cleaned the accumulated straw and dirt from the dried squid and then compressed them into tight, heavy bales, a significant improvement over old methods. This reduced shipping charges from San Francisco to Hong Kong, which were calculated on volume rather than weight. The dense squid cubes were sold to brokers who resold them in Hong Kong and China. The use of trucks to move the squid to the drying fields and the wonderful machines which cleaned and packed them gave the squid-drying industry new life on the Monterey Peninsula.

The best years of the squid business were between 1928 and

Won Yee standing before a truckload of baled and dried squid, c. 1920. The squid were shipped to China. Won Yee developed a baler which packed the squid into tight, heavy bales because the shipping companies charged by volume, not weight.    JACK YEE

1932; in 1932 Won Yee signed a contract to ship 10,000 tons of dried squid to Hong Kong, a deal estimated to be worth between $50,000 and $80,000. The worldwide economic depression began to cut into the business, however, while Japan began to replace China as the primary market for dried squid. When Won Yee died in 1934, the Chinese dried squid era ended on the Monterey Peninsula. From the 1880s to 1934, the strange little mollusk had carried the Chinese through thick and thin; after 1934 the Chinese community had grown too small to support a healthy industry. Won Yee's son Jack continued to operate the Wing Chong store which is now a landmark on Cannery Row.

After 1900 two new immigrant groups competed with the Chinese for the fishing catch. The twenty-eight Japanese who arrived in 1900 grew to one hundred by 1910, and most of them owned their own boats. The Japanese fishermen supplied sardines and salmon to the canneries and also revived the abalone

Packing Label from Wing Chong Company, Won Yee's squid company. Row of characters on the left say, "Dried Squid," while those on the right spell out "Wing Chong Company."                                    JACK YEE

*Opposite*: The fishermen who came to the Monterey Peninsula in the early 1850s and their descendants pioneered commercial fishing in the Monterey Bay Region. They were highly-skilled boat builders, navigators, and fishermen, and their faces are a study of pride and determination.

PAT HATHAWAY

industry. Sicilian immigrants swelled the ranks of the local fishing community beginning in the late 1890s. The lampara net introduced by Pietro Ferrante in 1905 was much better suited for catching large numbers of squid than the traditional Chinese dip net, and the Sicilian fishermen dominated the night waters off Monterey by 1910, catching both sardines and squid.

The few remaining Chinese fishermen reversed roles with the Sicilians. In the 1880s the Chinese had gone to sea at night to avoid competing directly with the Genovese who caught fresh fish during the day; after 1905 the few remaining Chinese fishermen went to sea during the day. The sight of any Chinese fishermen on the water became rare; in 1920 six Chinese fished commercially in the Monterey Bay Region, and that number dropped to one by 1930. Only those older Monterey Chinese fishermen unable to accumulate enough money to return to China continued to fish around the Bay after World War I, fishing off piers or sculling out in old sampans to catch enough fish to live on. Most of them lived and died alone in small fishing shacks near the water. Man Sing had come to Monterey in 1874 and had headed one of the early Chinese fishing companies. After the Point Alones fire in 1906, Man Sing moved to a small shack at McAbee Beach, and several days each week he would scull his sampan out and catch a hundred pounds or so of rock fish:

> For fifty years he has been fishing from his skiff and he doesn't propose to change his habits now. And why should he? Old as he is he can go out to China point, where he knows every rock on the bottom, and catch a boat load of the finest fish in Monterey Bay. Man Sing's catch included codfish, blue fish, yellow-tail, gopher-fish, devil-fish and sea trout . . . which he pulled up the wharf of the San Francisco International Fishing company at 10 o'clock this morning. This catch was valued at $9.68, which wasn't such a poor morning's work for one old man.

By the 1920s the canneries had pushed down the street and engulfed the McAbee village, and several serious cannery fires

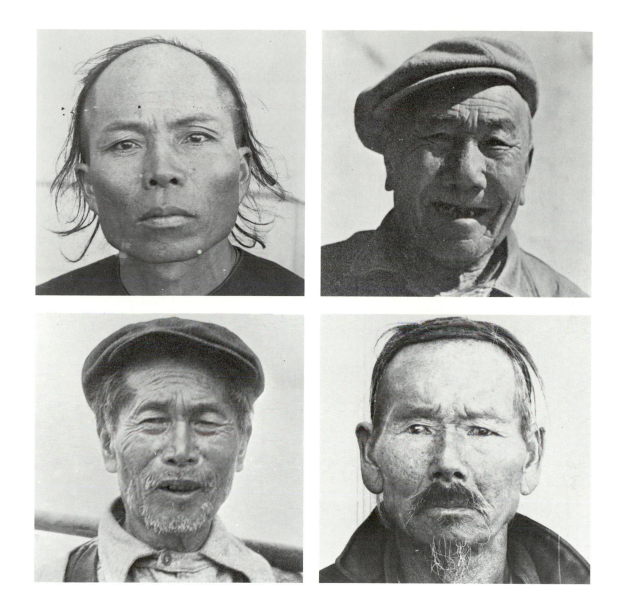

destroyed many of the old Chinese buildings. Some buildings were moved up to Foam Street to make way for the canneries. The few remaining Chinese fishing families found other professions as well as new homes.

The elements which led to the decline of the Chinese fishing industry at Monterey were repeated in each Chinese community in the region. The combined effects of immigration restrictions, the return of Chinese pioneers to China, death, municipal restrictions, and fire forced the Chinese out of industries they had dominated. Many moved to San Francisco or Oakland where the new Chinatowns offered more opportunities, while others stayed and attempted to adjust to the changing economic and political climate. Where the Chinese dominated a place or industry in the 1890s, only a few remained by World War II. The Chinese fishing industry at Monterey dramatically exemplifies that phenomenon; in the 1870s four major Chinese fishing villages thrived in the region, but in 1935 no commercial Chinese fishermen were left in the region. Before the 1906 Point Alones fire, the story of the Chinese fishermen was one of large groups of Chinese families and companies; after 1907 it was a story of a few individuals struggling to survive.

## CANNERIES

During the gold-mining era in the California Sierra Nevada, a number of Chinese companies gained substantial profits by following crews of white miners and re-mining the mountains of gravel they left behind—mining the tailings. After 1900, when canneries in Monterey made the fish-drying methods of the Chinese virtually obsolete, the Chinese again found a niche on the periphery of the industry. Charley Chin Yep, Jeung Yurn Tai, and Lee Chong recognized the potential profit in the fish heads and guts that the canneries were throwing into the bay. In 1910 they founded the Monterey Fish Canning Company.

The fish offal had become a nuisance at Monterey because the prevailing ocean current carried most of the refuse to the Del Monte Hotel's beach and deposited it there; by 1907 A. D. Shepard asked the canneries not to dump their refuse into the bay. In 1910 the Monterey Fish Canning Company opened a small factory on the point of rocks at the west end of McAbee Beach (location of the present-day Outrigger Restaurant) and processed fish waste products into fish oil and fertilizer. During the first year of operation, the large canneries were only too willing to give the heads and guts to the Chinese, but when the potential profit became apparent to the larger canners, they began processing the refuse themselves, and the Monterey Fish Canning Company went bankrupt. The Chinese founded an industry (called fish reduction) which came to dominate the Monterey sardine industry.

The Chinese also attempted to take part in the canning industry directly. The Bayside Canning Company, founded in 1917, combined some Oakland and Monterey Chinese capital. The Bayside cannery did well during World War I (as did all the canneries in Monterey), but when the post-war slump hit the fish-canning industry, the Bayside did not have enough resources to weather hard times; the company went bankrupt in 1920.

## THE FRANKLIN/WASHINGTON STREET CHINATOWN

As early as the 1870s several Chinese laundries were located near downtown Monterey. The first reference to these laundries was in 1875 in the *Monterey Weekly Herald*, and in 1888 the *Monterey Argus* referred to a Chinese laundry on California Street

Nea Lee, head gardener, Del Monte Hotel, Monterey, 1880s, standing on the hotel grounds with a handful of narcissus. Nea Lee lived on the hotel grounds and raised ten children, many of whom moved to Monterey's Franklin/Washington Chinatown as they grew older.

CALIFORNIA STATE LIBRARY

(now Munras) "just beyond the bridge." Chinese laundries eventually formed the nucleus of a small Chinatown at the intersection of Franklin and Washington Streets, specializing in gambling, opium selling, and prostitution. This small Chinatown served the male Chinese hotel staff after the Del Monte Hotel was constructed in 1880. Employees without families lived on the hotel grounds, but if they married, they often moved into the small downtown Chinatown. The 1907 Directory of Monterey lists three Chinese stores and one Chinese laundry in the little Chinatown, but these businesses were outnumbered by six Chinese lotteries and four *fan tan* parlors.

The resurrection of the military base at the presidio above New Monterey brought hundreds of United States Army troops to the Monterey Peninsula. The recreational activities in the little Chinatown expanded dramatically after the presidio's dedication in 1902, and a number of the houses of prostitution and gambling halls patronized by the troops were Chinese-owned and -operated. The district was centered on a block-long section of Franklin Street between Tyler and Washington with the Washington/Franklin intersection the hub. The area became nicknamed "The Badlands." Opium, gambling, and prostitution represent perfect examples of the Chinese "working the edges," providing services or products which the majority community either overlooked or disdained to provide for itself. The Chinese took the risks and were arrested when a show of "law and order" was required. In the nineteenth century the Chinese gambling halls catered primarily to Chinese patrons, but in the twentieth century, particularly the 1920s and 1930s, most of the gamblers were non-Chinese.

The Sanborn Map Company map of 1912 combined with the manuscript census of 1910 gives an excellent idea of the extent of the Monterey downtown Chinatown. The manuscript census lists seventy-two Chinese including two professional gamblers

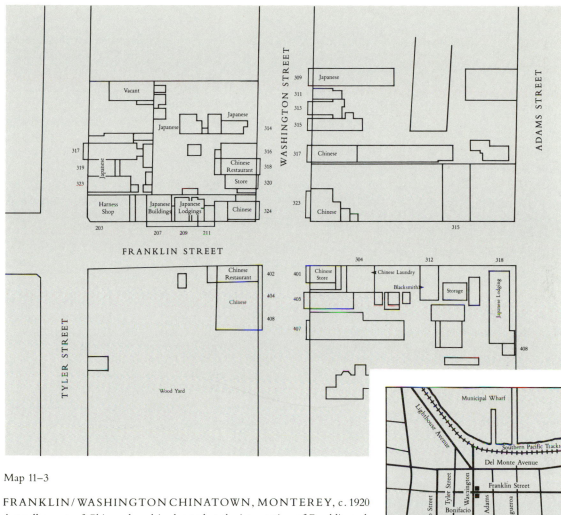

Map 11–3

FRANKLIN / WASHINGTON CHINATOWN, MONTEREY, c. 1920

A small group of Chinese laundries located at the intersection of Franklin and Washington streets was joined by a number of Chinese residents and businesses after the May 1906 Point Alones fire. Note the Japanese-occupied buildings in the vicinity.

(Ah Sit, Lee Mu Yet), seven laundrymen, nineteen merchants, and thirteen cooks. A remarkable mix of Chinese businesses, gambling halls, and families (there were eleven children under the age of eighteen) lived together in Chinatown. Several Chinese who grew up in the Franklin/Washington Chinatown remembered the camaraderie and friendships which developed among the children living there.

After the Point Alones fire of 1906, a number of the Chinese fishing families moved to the Franklin/Washington Chinatown. One week after the fire, Quong On Tai signed a five-year lease with Louis Little for a lot on Washington Street at an annual rent of sixty dollars. Quong On Tai agreed not to establish a "China wash house or laundry on the land." Other families moved to McAbee Beach but worked in the Franklin/Washington Chinatown. Though Ben Hoang's father was a professional gambler, the Hoang family lived at the McAbee Beach Chinatown and Ben's father walked along the railroad tracks to work in a gambling hall downtown.

Charley Ming, nicknamed "Little Pete," was a merchant in the Chinatown who became extremely interested in early movie technology. In 1907 he purchased one of the first moving picture projectors in Monterey, and he began showing movies in his Chinatown store to Chinese and white patrons. Sensing the business potential of movies, particularly in China where the magic of movies was virtually unknown, Charley Ming left for China in early 1908, taking his movie projectors and a plan to travel about China showing movies.

Monterey's downtown Chinatown thrived during the 1920s and 1930s but civic pressures and the opening of Fort Ord (farther from town than the presidio) finally drove under the Franklin/Washington Chinatown, and today, parking garages mark the site of the little Chinatown.

# POSTSCRIPT: THE VIETNAMESE FISHERMEN

In 1979 a new group of immigrant fishermen from Asia appeared in the Monterey Bay Region, and their experiences since their arrival have been strikingly similar to those of the Chinese fishing pioneers in the nineteenth century. This time, the immigrants were Vietnamese refugees who had fled Vietnam after the end of the Vietnam War in 1975. Out of an estimated six hundred commercial fishing boats operating in the Monterey Bay Region, thirty were Vietnamese.

Limited by a federal law making it illegal for a resident alien to own a vessel of more than five-ton displacement (twenty-eight to thirty feet in length), the Vietnamese fishermen pooled their resources and adapted older pleasure boats (Chris-Craft, for example) for commercial fishing use. Using the most inexpensive equipment, including monofilament gill nets, the Vietnamese concentrated on fishing for species which the other fishermen were ignoring—rock fish, king fish, halibut—and selling them to fresh fish wholesalers and dealers. Like their Chinese predecessors before them, the Vietnamese found a niche in an industry and concentrated their energies there. What they lacked in equipment, they made up for by working long hours, and by the end of 1979 a vigorous Vietnamese fresh fish industry had grown at Moss Landing and Monterey.

In the early 1980s an economic recession coupled with a warming of the ocean currents and a drop in the commercial catch in the region brought extreme pressures on commercial salmon and squid fishermen at Monterey, fostering tension between the commercial fishermen and their Vietnamese counterparts. Espousing the same arguments against the Vietnamese fishermen that had been used against the Chinese throughout the region in the nineteenth century, commercial fishermen and conservation organizations began to pressure the state of California to pass laws which would restrict the fishing techniques used by the Vietnamese. Ultimately their efforts focused on restricting the depth at which gill nets could be used in the Monterey Bay. Several hearings were held, and while the commercial fishermen testified that the Vietnamese were killing sea birds and depleting the fish, the Vietnamese quietly explained that they had come to the Monterey area in hope of a better life. One fisherman said he understood the concern for the sea birds, but hoped that the state officials were "concerned about us [the Vietnamese] too." Later in 1982 a bill was passed banning gill nets from being used in waters less than sixty feet deep.

Limited by the federal law which forbids their owning boats longer than thirty feet, the Vietnamese fishermen have great difficulty using their gill nets in waters more than sixty feet deep. The gill net law is similar to the cubic air or pole ordinances passed against the Chinese in the nineteenth century. These ordinances claimed a public health or conservation purpose, but in practice singled out and harassed the Chinese.

Many of the non-Vietnamese fishermen also voiced fears that the Vietnamese were depleting the natural supply of fish in the bay. One fisherman put it very directly: "They're raping the bay, that's what they are doing." More cool-headed observers, on the other hand, dismissed the detrimental impact of the Vietnamese on the resources as exaggerated. Bill Wimmer, retired Moss Landing Harbor Master, said, "Of course [the Vietnamese] haven't fished out the bay . . . a purse seiner pulls more out of the bay in one load than the Vietnamese can catch in a month of Sundays."

Beneath the emotional arguments, the economic realities, and the actual impact of the Vietnamese fishermen on the marine resources of the Monterey Bay lies the issue of race. Easily identified by their appearance, their language, and their cultural practices, the Vietnamese have become the scapegoat for all the economic ills facing commercial fishermen in the region. The guilt and anger many Americans feel over the Vietnam War may well have been attached to these refugees.

The anti-Vietnamese tension has brought violence to the fishing industry. A Vietnamese fishing boat was burned at Moss Landing in July 1983, causing $38,000 worth of damage, and the Vietnamese responded by holding a demonstration. One of the signs carried by a Vietnamese fisherman read, "There's Room on the Sea for You and Me." Some of the Vietnamese have left the fishing industry because of the harassment, taking temporary jobs in high technology industries in Santa Cruz and San Jose. Others have hired out as deckhands on other fishing boats, saving their money for the time they can reenter the fishing business.

The conflict involving the Vietnamese fishermen echoes the conflicts experienced by the Chinese fishermen a century earlier. But where the Chinese fishermen had a few alternatives available to them (including returning to China), today's highly regulated fishing industry (and a closed homeland) affords the Vietnamese even fewer. Despite the difficulties, most of the Vietnamese continue to hope the situation will improve: "I truly believe, you know, that the fishermen and other groups will understand us."

An entire generation of us America-born Chinese learned about hard work by working in those Watsonville apple dryers.

Charlie Leong, 1982.

# 12

# Watsonville

THE CHINESE IN AMERICA passed through their darkest years between 1900 and 1930. Strangled by immigration restrictions and decimated by the emigration or death of many of the pioneer immigrants, the Chinese population in America dropped to its lowest point in 1920. The Chinese population in the Monterey Bay Region was no exception; elderly Chinese men died in Chinatown back rooms or gathered their meager resources together and returned to China. With the decline of the fishing industry and the advent of hundreds of young Japanese farm laborers, economic uncertainty drove Chinese from the Monterey Bay Region. San Francisco's Chinatown was an ever-present magnet, particularly to the China-born, offering economic opportunity and a healthy community to refugees from smaller, shrinking Chinatowns in central California. San Francisco tugged so relentlessly on the Chinese in the region that, had it not been for the apple-drying industry which evolved in the Pajaro Valley just after the turn of the century, the Chinese population in the region might have dropped completely out of sight. The China Dryers (the name given to the Chinese-owned and -operated apple driers) carried many Chinese families through those difficult years, providing a capital base wide enough to launch a second generation into other businesses or the professions.

When Claus Spreckels pulled up stakes and left the Pajaro Valley in 1898, it was a sure bet that the Chinese businesses which supported the sugar beet contractors and their laborers would follow Spreckels to Salinas, and Brooklyn would wither and die. Instead, the Chinese demonstrated their ability to shift with the wind and adapt. As owners and managers of apple-drying businesses, the Chinese gained a stability impossible for farm laborers or labor contractors. When they reached this second step of the economic ladder, they married and raised families, demonstrating dramatically that, when given the opportunity, they metamorphosed naturally from Chinese immigrants to Chinese-Americans.

The last example of that Chinese alchemical equation which combined a marginal commodity with intense labor to produce Chinese Gold, the apple-drying industry kept Brooklyn alive for several more decades. While the Chinese population declined drastically from 1900 to 1910, that of the Pajaro Valley dipped only slightly, making Brooklyn the unofficial capital of the region's Chinese community.

## FROM SUGAR CITY TO APPLE CITY

When the sugar beet dethroned King Wheat in the Pajaro Valley in the late 1880s, farmers began to expand their horizons well beyond sugar beets, planting strawberries, raspberries, apricots, and apples. When Spreckels pulled the economic rug out from under the Pajaro Valley in 1898, Watsonville landed on its feet, rebounding quickly from what could have been a devastating blow. In the amount of time it took an apple orchard to mature, Watsonville permanently retired the nickname Sugar City which it had worn so proudly (even arrogantly) in the 1890s and donned a new one—Apple City. By 1910 Watsonville had several businesses named Appleton, had staged an October Apple festival, and had changed the name of the town's semi-professional baseball team from the Sugar Beets to the Pippins.

Credit for the early development of the apple industry in the Pajaro Valley must go to Slavic immigrants who came into the area after the 1870s and organized efficient systems of growing, packing, and marketing apples. Known in the Pajaro Valley as "Slavonians," the Slavs came primarily from Dalmatia, on the east coast of the Adriatic. By 1890 they dominated the Pajaro Valley apple industry. The Slavs introduced an innovative contract system in which apple packers bought apples at a set price while they were still immature, hoping to lock up the apple crop at a price lower than that which would be prevalent in the fall. The pre-season contracts were extremely risky: if successful at predicting the fall prices and sure of dependable markets, the apple packers could make a lot of money, but if they guessed wrong, they stood to lose their shirts. Slav apple packers and fruit brokers set up an extensive interlocking network throughout the United States for selling and shipping Pajaro Valley apples.

It was unusual for Chinese businessmen to compete directly with non-Chinese during the nineteenth and early twentieth century in California. Chinese in the Monterey Bay Region concentrated on peripheral or side industries (squid fishing, fish drying) to avoid direct competition, a legacy of the anti-Chinese hysteria of the 1870s and its resurgence in the 1880s and 1890s. Chinese enterprises were also limited because few Chinese immigrants could accumulate enough capital to effectively finance competitive businesses.

Therefore, the entry of a Chinese into the risky and somewhat closed apple-packing business in 1899 was a singular event in the history of the Pajaro Valley. Chong Wo, a successful merchant, owned several stores in Brooklyn and a number of vegetable fields around the Pajaro Valley; he was often described by the local newspaper as one of the Chinese community's "best known merchants." In May of 1899, in "the first appearance of a Chinaman in the business of buying apples in the Pajaro Valley," Chong Wo bought the rights to ten railroad cars of apples which he planned to ship to ports around the Pacific Ocean. Because Slav apple packers dominated the larger orchards in the valley, Chong Wo concentrated on buying apples from smaller orchards near Corralitos and Pajaro. In 1900 the Chinese packer began shipping some of his apples to points in the United States as well as across the Pacific. Chong Wo's success in the apple-packing business exemplifies the transition of a Chinese immigrant from sojourner to merchant to successful permanent resident. Had more Chinese been able to overcome the obstacles placed before them in the 1880s and 1890s, more Chong Wo's would have gone into other businesses in California. Few Chinese joined Chong Wo to start similar apple-packing businesses in the Pajaro Valley, partly because of the evolution of a spin-off branch in the apple industry which the Chinese came to dominate.

During those early years the bulk of the apple crop was sold fresh, a characteristic which put the apple growers at the mercy of the law of supply and demand. As the number of acres of apples in the Pajaro Valley grew, the profit margin narrowed; during a bad year (the depression year of 1893, for example) the price dropped so low that it did not pay to harvest the fruit. Increasing pressures to set standards of quality for apples sold and shipped in California further tightened the profit margin. Some years, when the crop was particularly hard-hit by insects, blight, or bad weather, a large part of the crop failed to meet the minimum marketing standards and was either pressed into cider and vinegar or destroyed. Eventually the apple industry became so finely tuned that finding a market for the culls represented the margin between profit and loss for a season.

Although dried apples and apple cider or vinegar were the two most obvious secondary products for the culls, only a few farmers had experimented with sun drying apples in the Pajaro Valley during the 1880s and 1890s. But the fog which characterized the valley's summers made outdoor drying difficult, and some fruit growers took their culls to drying yards in Gilroy to take advantage of the hot, fog-free climate in the southern Santa Clara Valley.

The first recorded mechanical fruit dehydrator in the Pajaro Valley was built by Thomas Beck in 1885. Beck's machine was based on a design used to dry prunes in the Santa Clara Valley; the apples were placed in a large drum which resembled a Ferris wheel (it was called the Ferris-wheel dryer) and were dried as they tumbled inside a furnace. Beck's dryer operated fitfully during the remainder of the 1880s and early 1890s, but never achieved enough success to catch on. Two similar Ferris-wheel dryers were built during the 1893 depression to handle the surplus of fruit caused by the failure of many of the fruit canners in the Santa Clara Valley, but none of these dryers were able to operate at a profit.

The Spanish-American War brought an increased demand for dried apples, and the United States government offered a number of contracts to ship dried apples to the troops in the Philippines; in 1900 a group of Slav apple growers/packers, Luke Scurich, S. Scurich, F. P. Marinovich, and N. Banaz, built another revolving-drum dryer, but once the government contract was filled, the dryer began to lose money just as its predecessors had. J. F. Unglish made the necessary technological breakthrough when, in Pajaro in 1901, he built a dryer in which the apples were sliced, sulphured, spread on trays, and dried in large kilns. The Unglish method produced better quality dried apples than the revolving-drum dehydrators, but the process demanded constant attention and a tremendous amount of hand labor.

Given the unpredictability of the dried fruit business, the owner and operator of an apple dryer, even an efficient one, took an extreme risk. By 1904 the Slav apple growers devised the solution to the dilemma—build Unglish-style dryers and lease them to someone having a source of skilled but inexpensive labor. The Slav apple growers assured themselves of steady income from the lease and a market for their culled apples, while someone else had the headache of operating the dryer, finding the necessary skilled labor, and taking the financial risk.

In 1904 F. P. Marinovich, Luke Scurich, and C. W. Adamson built a tray-loaded, kiln-type dryer on Walker Street in Watsonville and leased it to a Chinese named King Kee. Operating under the company name Quong Sang Lung, King Kee hired fellow Chinese to work in the dryer and by the end of the 1904 season the success of the Chinese-operated apple dryer made it the prototype of the Pajaro Valley apple-drying industry for the next twenty years. The Chinese so dominated Pajaro Valley apple drying that the Unglish-style apple dryer became known as the "China Dryer."

## THE CHINA DRYERS

As with mustard, slough lands, and squid, Chinese muscle and ingenuity transformed a discarded commodity into a valuable product. As one historian of the industry put it, successful apple drying began with King Kee's operating the Unglish-style dryer in 1904 because "the Chinese were able to overcome the great difficulty which the Americans and Slavonians had encountered, the obtaining of an adequate supply of comparatively cheap and efficient labor."

A few of the China Dryers were owned outright by the Chinese operators, usually China-born merchants, but more often the dryers were leased from non-Chinese owners. Under a typical lease recorded in Monterey County between Marion T. Rowe and Charley Fang, Rowe agreed to build a two-kiln fruit dryer and "one bunk-house 18 feet by 36 feet, a lean-to and toilet," and Charley Fang agreed to pay $850 yearly rent for the use of the dryer and surrounding buildings.

Each dryer had a bunkhouse which housed the seasonal Chinese workers who came from throughout California to work during the apple-drying season. The Pajaro Valley apple dryers became part of the seasonal migratory labor loop which extended from the fields of California to the canneries in Alaska, and the older men who came to work in the dryers were veterans of many harvests and campaigns throughout the West. The apple-drying season began with the early apple harvest in September and usually ended in December, dovetailing perfectly with the squid-drying season, so that many fishermen came to Watsonville after the squid-drying season ended in summer. When legal restrictions forced the squid-drying operations into a decline, some Monterey Chinese moved to Watsonville.

But the period 1904–1924 overlapped the period of the lowest Chinese population in the United States. Although the Chinese dryer operators followed the traditional practice of contracting Chinese laborers in San Francisco, that pool of labor had been so decimated by death, age, or return to China that it could no longer be depended upon as the sole source of labor for the dryers. The Chinese dryers also drew on a new supply of labor—the America-born Chinese children of relatives and neighbors. Many of the Chinese who grew up in the Pajaro Valley in the 1920s and 1930s worked in the apple dryers during their youth, making boxes, peeling apples, or stacking trays; they remembered with fondness the odor of apples drying in the kilns. Charles Leong, a

*Overleaf:* Charley Fang and family, Watsonville, 1914. One of the successful China Dryer operators in the Pajaro Valley, Charley Fang poses proudly with his young family for a portrait.

PAJARO VALLEY HISTORICAL
ASSOCIATION

successful San Francisco journalist who grew up in Watsonville, recalled the long hours and hard work and theorized that China Dryers provided an important training ground for the first generation of America-born Chinese in Watsonville.

The first step in the apple-drying process was coring and peeling; each apple was placed onto a spindle and the peeler operator turned a crank which caused a series of knives to skim the surface of the apple, removing the peel. The core was removed when the apple was taken off the spindle (peels and cores were saved for making vinegar). Then the apples were sliced, washed, and spread in a single layer on large wooden trays. In stacks of

Hoy Lew inside the Pacific Evaporating Company Dryer, Watsonville, c. 1918. Rare interior view of a China Dryer showing the racks of apples (left) in the kiln. Hot air rose through the trays, so the apples needed to be rotated from top to bottom to insure they dried evenly. Hoy Lew came to Watsonville from China in 1916 to work in his father's dryer.   HOY LEW

403

China Dryer, Watsonville, 1911. A
classic two-chimney dryer stands isolated by the 1911 flood.
PAJARO VALLEY HISTORICAL
ASSOCIATION

ten the trays were placed for an hour or so in a room filled with
the smoke from burning sulphur before they were ready to be
placed in the kilns.

The heart of the drying operation, brick kilns (from one to six
per China Dryer) operated vertically, with the apple-laden trays
placed above the furnace, and the heat finally leaving the dryer
through a chimney. The dryers were ranked by the number of
chimneys—Pacific Evaporation (the Lew dryer) was a six chimney as were Hop Lee, Quong Sang Lung, and the Appleton
dryer; Charlie Chin Goon had a five chimney on Grove Street in
Watsonville, and the Lam-Mattison dryer in Aptos was a two
chimney. The Aptos and Watsonville dryers burned oil which
came by rail in tank cars. Some of the earlier experiments in
apple drying had used coal and wood, and Sam Eng's Corralitos
dryer continued to use wood for fuel because cordwood was
close at hand and inexpensive.

Charlie Chin Goon's China Dryer on Grove Street, Watsonville. Dryer is building in distance with the four chimneys; apple boxes are stacked to the left. South Watsonville also flooded just as Brooklyn did across the river.
EARL GOON

The trays fit into the walls of the brick kilns much like the racks fit into the sides of a household oven, with the dryer operator sliding twenty trays (two stacks of ten) into the kiln. The apples usually dried in six to eight hours, with the dryer operator monitoring them and rearranging the trays from time to time to ensure that all the apples dried at the same rate. (This unevenness was one of the drawbacks of using wooden trays stacked one over the other, and most contemporary apple dryers now spread the apples on one large, permanent rack so that all the apples are at the same distance from the furnace. Only one of the present-day dryers still uses wooden trays, the Hiura drier in Watsonville.) When the apples dried, they were removed and allowed to cool, then packed in wooden boxes, each of which held fifty pounds of dried apples. In 1918 it took approximately eight pounds of fresh apples to produce a pound of dried apples, a ratio which has not changed appreciably to this day.

Lam Pon's family, c. 1915. Lam Pon, the successful Aptos apple dryer operator, poses with (left to right) his wife, his daughter Anna, and Lam Sing, a cousin.          BARSON FAMILY

Every effort was made to supply a steady flow of apples to the dryer so that a twelve-hour day was sufficient to keep up with deliveries. However, when more apples were delivered, the dryer was operated twenty-four hours a day. During the peak of the harvest, sweat-shiny Chinese, often shirtless, worked in the glow of the extremely hot kilns.

The combination of wooden frames and furnace made fire an ever-present hazard in the China Dryers, and before the era ended in the mid-1920s most of the dryers had been destroyed by fire at least once, a fact which explains why the Sanborn Map Company went to such pains to locate each of the apple dryers on its maps.

The Lam family had the longest connection to apple drying in the Monterey Bay Region. Lam Pon came to America sometime before the turn of the century and began as a laundryman and cook. By 1910 he had been joined in Santa Cruz by other relatives, including Lam How and Lam Sing. In 1905 Lam Pon entered a lease arrangement with Ralph J. Mattison of Aptos and built a two-chimney dryer on the field behind the Bay View Hotel. Each fall Lam Pon moved to a small house near the dryer in Aptos while several dozen Chinese moved into the bunkhouse adjacent to the dryer. At season's end Lam Pon moved back into Santa Cruz to work as a cook. By 1910 Lam Pon was secure enough in his business to consider marriage to a young California-born Chinese woman from Pleasanton, California.

Around 1918 Lam Pon was joined by another relative, Otto Lam, who became a partner with him in the Aptos apple dryer, which had become a landmark. Lam Pon branched out into the restaurant business, and in the 1920s he also set up a small credit institution for his fellow Chinese. Having become a successful merchant did not exempt Lam Pon from the prejudice accorded his fellow Chinese, and he became increasingly frustrated as the old patterns did not change. Lam Pon had traveled to China on several occasions during the 1920s, and finally, to achieve the respect to which he felt entitled, Lam Pon returned to China in the early 1930s.

The Aptos dryer and the partnership between the Mattisons and the Lams lasted well beyond the heyday of the China Dryers in the Pajaro Valley, possibly because their dryer was the only one operating in Aptos and the competition was limited. When the China Dryers declined in the early 1920s, many of the partnerships which had been formed to pool resources or to circumvent the Alien Land Law of 1913 (and its successor in 1920) dissolved, often into bitter feuds between ex-partners. Some of the Chinese dryer operators went deeply into debt gambling that the dried-apple business would turn around in the early 1920s, but the price stayed low, and a number of dryers were deliberately set on fire for the insurance.

Otto Lam and Ralph Mattison dissolved their partnership amicably in 1940, and three years later Ralph Mattison sold the dryer to the LaValley and Cecil Company. Otto Lam continued in the apple-drying business, operating a dryer in the Branciforte

The Lam-Mattison Apple Dryer, Aptos, c. 1920. The two-chimney dryer can just be seen in the distance on the left. The Bayview Hotel is on the right peeking through the trees.
CAROLYN SWIFT

Creek area during World War II and building his last apple dryer, the Santa Cruz Fruit Company, on Mattison Lane in Soquel in 1945. In 1982 Otto Lam sold the Santa Cruz Fruit Company, ending a Lam family tradition of apple drying that began with Lam Pon in 1905 in Aptos.

Santa Cruz County is still one of the nation's apple drying centers as three of the seven apple dryers still operating in the United States are there—the Valentine Dryer, the Hiura Dryer (owned and operated by a Japanese-American), and the Santa Cruz Fruit Company (up to 1982, the only China Dryer in the United States). Machinery was added to the process over the years, but the apples are still spread, turned, and tested by hand.

## THE ALIEN LAND LAW OF 1913

Just when the China Dryers were proving to be successful, the Chinese of the Pajaro Valley were caught up in a net cast for someone else—the Alien Land Law of 1913. From 1913 to 1948 China-born Chinese were prohibited from owning real property in California. Other than small isolated lots (the lots owned by Sam Kee and Jim Lee in Castroville, for example), few Chinese had bought land in the Monterey Bay Region in the nineteenth century, even though it was legal in California until 1913. Chinese "enjoyed the same rights of purchase, ownership, and lease of real property as those enjoyed by citizens."

The Japanese immigrants who came into California beginning in the 1890s evolved to the second economic plateau much more quickly than did the Chinese, and during the first decade of the twentieth century, a number of Japanese began to lease and ultimately purchase farm land in the state. Like the Chinese, they were not eligible to become naturalized citizens and were plagued by the same racist sentiment that had haunted the Chinese. When the federal government appeared to be stalled in its efforts to restrict or prohibit Japanese immigration into the United States, the California legislature took matters into its own hands and struck a blow which was designed to discourage further Japanese immigration into California. California Attorney General Ulysses S. Webb stated that the Japanese "would not come in large numbers and long abide with us if they may not acquire land . . ." As one of the leading historians of the relationship between Asian immigrants and American law put it, the Alien Land Law was "a measure directed to exclude the Japanese from California."

The law did not succeed in its primary objective. The many restrictions placed on Japanese immigrants did *not* bar women from immigrating, so that they were able to found families. Land ownership could be registered in the name of America-born children who were citizens. This option was not widely available to the Chinese; immigration restrictions placed on the Chinese beginning in 1882 had effectively barred Chinese women from entering the United States in large numbers. The Japanese also resorted to other tactics, such as owning land in partnership with white citizens, and continued to acquire real estate in California despite the Alien Land Law.

Though the number of America-born Chinese was growing despite the obstacles, the number was not nearly large enough to provide a legal refuge for all the Chinese wishing to put the land in their names. The Chinese also seemed to have greater difficulty setting up successful partnerships. The reasons for this are not completely clear, but it may have been caused, at least in part, by the cultural differences between the older China-born men and their younger America-born partners. Many stories within the Chinese community tell of China-born partners losing most or all of their investments in jointly owned businesses; such ventures were viewed with mistrust.

Hoy Lew, the patriarch of today's Watsonville Chinese community, is still bitter about the Alien Land Law and its effects on his family during the 1920s. Born in China in 1896, Hoy joined his merchant father in Watsonville in 1912. One of Hoy's responsibilities was to pick up fresh produce, eggs, and chickens and deliver them to his father's store. While driving about the Pajaro Valley, he became very familiar with the region; he also became familiar with the location of the good farm land, particularly if it was for sale. Whenever he came upon a good buy, however, he was stopped cold by the Alien Land Law.

In 1919 Hoy married Margaret Eng, an America-born girl from San Jose. Believing that he would be able to put land in Margaret's name, Hoy Lew began to pursue the purchase of a small piece of prime Pajaro Valley farm land. It was then that Hoy Lew discovered that by marrying him, an alien ineligible for citizenship, Margaret had *lost* her American citizenship. State law blocked him from owning land, and federal law stripped his wife of her citizenship, so that neither Hoy Lew nor his wife could purchase property in the Pajaro Valley: "I was offered many good farms and pieces of property during those early years, but I could not buy the property because of the law. 'Buy my ranch,' said some of the farmers, but I could not."

For many Chinese in the Pajaro Valley, the combination of Alien Land Law and citizenship restrictions kept them from purchasing property and relegated them to the status of tenants for another generation. By the time the citizenship-loss law was repealed and Chinese became eligible for naturalization (1943), the Watsonville Chinese community had been dispersed. The 1913 Alien Land Law and subsequent restrictions to land ownership passed in 1920 closed to Chinese the possibility of investing in real estate, and many made their investments in their children's education instead.

## BROOKLYN IN THE 1900s

The China Dryers in and around the Pajaro Valley acted as a counterbalance to the forces which were whittling away at other regional Chinese communities. Discounting the number of seasonal Chinese farm laborers (probably not permanent residents) from both the 1900 and 1910 census, the resident Chinese population in the Pajaro Valley was 171 in 1900 and 140 in 1910. More important than the total numbers, however, was the increase in the percentage of children and women in this permanent Chinese community. Where there were 24 children under the age of 18 (14%) in the Pajaro Valley in 1900, there were 36 (26%) in 1910, and the number of women increased from 22 (13%) to 34 (25%). The percentage of America-born Chinese also increased in the permanent community, from 17% (30 of 171) in 1900 to 38% (54 of 140) in 1910.

Because of the apple dryers, many Chinese were able to establish an economic base from which to launch families. The experience of Eng Chung (known as Sam Eng) typified that of many immigrants. Born in China in 1843, Sam Eng came to California

Sam Eng, Watsonville, c. 1920. Sam Eng owned several apple dryers including the wood-burning dryer in Corralitos. As did many of his China-born generation, Sam Eng married late in life.          ANNIE DE LA PENA

as a teenager, working on various railroad projects before arriving in the Pajaro Valley in the 1870s. Sam worked for various farmers in the valley clearing land, planting orchards, and grafting fruit trees. At various times between 1906 and 1924, Sam Eng ran apple dryers in Watsonville, Freedom, and in Corralitos. Sam Eng's wood-burning apple dryer on Corralitos Creek was his most famous, and older residents of Corralitos still remember the smell of woodsmoke mixed with apple which characterized each apple harvest.

Once he had achieved economic security, Sam Eng married and raised a family of four children. Sam's marriage was less typical of Chinese in the region as he married Semona Salzaze, a California native of Mexican ancestry. Two years after Semona died suddenly (the children were grown by then), Sam traveled to China and returned with a second wife who bore him three more children. The local newspaper wrote of him:

> Sam's activities in the Pajaro valley have been largely agricultural and his efforts have been uniformly successful, due to his industry and thrift and pleasing personality which has enabled him to make and keep friends.

Like most of the China-born men, Sam was middle-aged (forty-four years old) before he started a family. It took decades of scrimping and hard work before these Chinese immigrants had enough security to raise a family, marry California-born women in their twenties, and surround themselves with families of up to a dozen children. Dong Teng Seng, also forty-four years old when he married, fathered eleven children; Charlie Chin Goon waited until he was in his early forties before marrying a younger California-born Chinese woman who bore him nine children.

The children of these and other marriages like them in the Monterey Bay Region grew up between two cultures. The hardworking, China-born father was often a distant authority figure linked with the land of his birth. With one eye on their dryers and the other on the changing political and economic events in China, these men represented traditional Chinese culture to their children. The younger mothers were often more Americanized (several were Christians) and more intent on seeing that their children received training which would assist them in America. The Chinese children could have been faced with the dilemma of an either/or choice, but most parents in these transitional families wisely decided to train their children in *both* cultures.

Although several of the new Chinese families listed in the 1910 census lived in south Watsonville, drawn out of Brooklyn to the neighborhoods of the China Dryers, and the vacancy rate of Brooklyn had increased from none in 1900 to six in 1910, Brooklyn in the early part of the century continued to be a cultural and economic center. The children of the newly established families vividly recalled a healthy Chinatown.

Collin Dong's father, Dong Teng Seng (T. S. Dong), established a successful restaurant in Brooklyn in the 1890s, and Collin was the second son born to the Dong Teng Seng family in 1901. In a speech to the Pajaro Valley Historical Society in 1971, Collin shared his memories of growing up in Brooklyn in the early part of the twentieth century. The temple and the seasonal Chinese religious festivals made a lasting impression on him:

Charlie Chin Goon, Watsonville, c. 1920. Charlie Chin Goon owned several China Dryers during his successful career, and he also married late in life. He is shown here with one of his young children.   EARL GOON

> [The temple] was graphed with some Chinese ornamentation, with carved pillar decorations, and topped with the traditional curved Chinese roof. . . . Next to [it] was a small voluntary fire department.

Collin also described the Ch'ing Ming and the lunar New Year festivals. Chinese from throughout the region came to Brooklyn during the New Year celebration "to renew old acquaintances and friendships, to visit relatives, and to participate in burning fireworks for good luck."

> [The Chinese] came to contribute money for the poor by giving to the collectors during the lion and dragon ceremonial dances. They

enjoyed listening to the Chinese orchestras with the cymbals and drums playing the Chinese songs, which brought back fond memories of their younger days in China. The colorful banners and lanterns along the streets and the seasonal delicacies of the banquets were a great treat for the hard-working Chinese immigrants.

His boy's-eye-view of Chinese New Year gives a special feeling to this happiest day of the year:

> Mother would dress us in colorful costumes, and along with Father, who was dressed in his best Chinese silken gown, we went from door to door to pay respects to the store owners and to every household in the Chinese communities. The adults of the whole community had prepared little red packages containing 25 cent pieces, called *li shee*, to give to the children. It is an old legend that the giver of *li shee* on New Year's Day will have a lucky year. After a day's collection of these red packages, our pockets were usually quite full. In our early teens I remember my older brother, Gene, and I would open a few of these packages and race across the bridge to Trevethan's tamale parlor. There we would gorge ourselves with two or three beef tamales.

Collin remembered the Chinese community traveling to the Chinese cemetery north of Watsonville on Ch'ing Ming to pay respects to the departed members of the community:

> Horses and buggies, bicycles, and other modes of transportation carried most of the community to Whiskey Hill, where the Chinese cemetery was situated. The purpose of the trip was to pay respects to the dead by renewing the markers on the graves, planting greens and flowers, and making the area clean and beautiful. The ceremony at the gravesite included lighting red candles, burning incense, burning idol paper money, and shooting firecrackers to eliminate the demons and specters that may be around. A small amount of red wine was poured in front of the gravesite and a feast for the dead and the guardian of the cemetery was spread out on the ground. When the dead had partaken, the living, who were waiting near, consumed the good food.

From 1912 to 1919, when he moved into Watsonville, Hoy Lew lived at his father's store, Bow Ching Chong, located at the south end of Brooklyn Street, #34. Hoy's father sold produce and Chinese staples to the community, but he was famed for his whole roast pigs. The Lews raised up to one hundred pigs at a time on a plot of land behind the store, and Hoy remembers that they fed the pigs a "special diet" of vegetables. As a young man, Hoy Lew purchased a Model T Ford:

> I had a blacksmith modify the back of the car so that I could use it as a pick-up truck. They put wooden sides and a wooden top on the back of the car so I could carry up to six pigs in it. The top kept the pigs from climbing out.

For Ch'ing Ming the Chinese Association would purchase a whole roast pig from Hoy's father and take it to the graveyard for the ceremonies commemorating the dead. The pig was usually returned to Brooklyn and divided up among the Association members who had donated money toward its purchase. Hoy learned the secrets of raising and preparing the pigs from his father by watching the process, and he also watched him buy crates of flounder, salt the fish, and hang them by their tails to dry. His father's dried fish were also famous throughout the region.

According to Hoy Lew, once each year the Porter family would have Brooklyn Street plowed up along its entire length; the Chinese residents of Brooklyn would lay planks across the plowed earth so they could walk from one side of the street to the other until the earth was packed down again. Hoy believes that the Porters plowed the street so they could convince the Monterey County tax assessor that Brooklyn Street was actually a field and should be taxed lower than a town street. Whatever the reason for the plowing and the planks, Hoy Lew leaves an unforgettable image of his Model T thumping along Brooklyn Street, the pigs swaying back and forth as he inched over the planks laid across the street.

## THE KUOMINTANG PARTY AND THE
## CHINESE SCHOOL

While the China Dryers were infusing the Pajaro Chinese with hope for the future, events occurred in China which
promised to bring the Middle Kingdom out from under the
cloud which had hung over it since the mid-nineteenth century.
The Chinese immigrants in America had had little to be proud of
as China was saddled with a series of humiliating, unequal treaties and defeated by Japan in the Sino-Japanese War of 1894–95.
As a rule, the Chinese in the region rarely discussed Chinese
politics outside their communities. But when the hated Manchu
government began to totter, the Chinese began to speak openly
of their concern for China. They watched the Boxer Uprising
with great interest and discussed the complicated events with
anyone who would listen.

Dr. Sun Yat-sen, one of the most outspoken forces for revolu-
tionary change in China, sent his fund raisers through the Pajaro
Valley Chinese community several times during the first decade
of the twentieth century, and the Brooklyn Chinese contributed
"several thousand dollars" to help him overthrow the Manchu
dynasty. When the news of the successful October 10, 1911, Revolution reached Brooklyn, a rush of optimism and excitement
swept through the community. On October 26, 1911, the Kuomintang's flag rose on a pole at the south end of Brooklyn Street,
and many of the Chinese men participated in a public queue-
cutting ceremony in front of the temple. The 1911 revolution
promised that China would be a democracy and would take her
rightful position as a respected nation.

After October 1911 the Chinese in Brooklyn made their support for Sun Yat-sen and his Kuomintang (Nationalist Party)
well known. By 1913 the Kuomintang had rented #35 for a local

The Kuomintang Hall, Brooklyn, c. 1915. The KMT rented #35 Brooklyn Street, and this photo shows what probably is a fund-raising gathering as the crowd is made up of both Chinese and whites.

HENRY AND ALICE LEONG

headquarters and opened a reading room which made Chinese newspapers and Sun Yat-sen's writings available to the Chinese community. As complicated events in China unfolded during and after World War I, the Watsonville Kuomintang often took out newspaper ads to inform the Pajaro Valley public of Chinese events and how they might assist the KMT. In 1921 the Watsonville KMT took out a bold-type ad in the Watsonville newspaper requesting the United States government to stop lending money to the Peking government: "Please lend no money to kill our people." The following year, the KMT sent a public telegram to the delegation representing China at the Washington disarmament conference urging them not to permit Japan's increasing influence over Chinese affairs, declaring, "If you do, we know the Chinese people here and in China will never forgive you . . ." This increasing interest in Chinese politics, plus a desire to have their children learn something of Chinese history and language, sparked the opening of the first Chinese School in Brooklyn in 1916, funded by the KMT and operated in their building at #35 Brooklyn Street.

It was difficult for Chinese children to find educational opportunities in any language in the 1890s in the Pajaro Valley; by 1920 they could not avoid it. After the opening of the Chinese School in 1916, Chinese children had a dual-track school system available to them. All attended the public school in Pajaro and then Watsonville High School. (Dr. Emma Dong believes that all the children from the 1900–1920 generation graduated from Watsonville High School.) When public school ended in mid-afternoon, most of the Chinese children walked home, had a quick meal, and then walked down to #35 Brooklyn Street for Chinese school, which began at 4:30 and ended at 8:30. Chinese school met six days each week, with a half-day session on Saturday. Many of the children also spent part of their Sunday at Sunday school, receiving Christian instruction.

This emphasis on education reflected not only the traditional Chinese feeling about the value of education, but also the conclusion of parents in these transitional families that education was a better investment than land. Land was subject to the caprice and vagaries of political and economic changes in both China and America (the Alien Land Law of 1913 was just another example of that), but education was not.

The classroom of the Chinese school was dominated by a large map of China and the KMT flag, and high on the wall at the front of the room hung the ever-present portrait of Sun Yat-sen. Most of the funding for the school came from the KMT, but local parents were expected to make small monthly contributions to help defray the salary of the teacher. Hired by the KMT, usually from San Francisco, the young male teacher taught his classes of Chinese language, history, and culture through rote memorization. Students were required to demonstrate their skills

民國十二年 九月十二日 影撮念紀立成會治自生學 學校立公 華僑 委埠慎 美洲

in periodic public recitations; many remembered the trauma of standing before their classmates to recite. Emma Dong recalls a curriculum that included Chinese calligraphy, history, geography, and lessons on the use of the abacus. Students memorized entire Chinese readers and recited lengthy passages, in Chinese, from memory. That Emma went on to graduate at the top of her public high school class and at the top of both her University of California undergraduate class and her University of California Medical School class bore out the value of the Chinese school. The discipline imposed by the strict Chinese teachers taught the young Chinese-Americans perhaps their most valuable lesson.

The Chinese School operated on a regular basis in Brooklyn from its opening in 1916 through the spring of 1943, though it had two different locations during that period. The first school, located at #35 in the KMT building, was destroyed in the fire of 1924, but within a year a second Chinese school was built on the opposite side of Brooklyn at #18 where it continued to operate

Chinese School, Brooklyn, September 22, 1923. Brooklyn's first Chinese School was founded around 1916 and was led by members of the KMT. Caption reads, "Watsonville USA, founding of Chinese American Public School students self-government club." Those identified in the photograph include, first on left, back row, Edward Dong; third from left, back row, Charlie Leong; fifth from left, back row, Hubert Dong; second from left, middle row, Emma Dong; ninth from left, middle row, Leong Mon Way; first from left, seated, Edward Way; second from left, seated, Elmer Shew; fifth from left, seated, Lena Way; sixth from left, seated, Emma Shew; seventh from left, seated, Anna Bell Wong; eighth from left, seated, Annie Goon; second from right, seated, Tommy Chan. HENRY AND ALICE LEONG

Second Chinese School, Brooklyn, September 18, 1932. After the 1924 fire destroyed the KMT building, funds were collected and a second school building erected at #18 Brooklyn Street. The building still stands at #18 Brooklyn Street. Those identified in the photograph include, back row, standing, first from left, Mr. Wong; back row, fourth from left, Dong Doo Yee; back row, fifth from left, T. S. Dong; back row, sixth from left, Mr. Wong; back row, second from right, Tai Yee Chin; young men standing in middle row, left to right, Edward Wong, Billy Lee, Johnson Chin, Henry Lew; seated, front row, left to right, Annabel Wong, Elizabeth Lee, Mary Lee, Mabel Wong, Marian Dong, Dorothy Wong, May Wong, Betty Wong, Hazel Wong, Bette Eng, Jenny Lee, Evelyn Lew, Dorothy Lee, Mary Goon.

HENRY AND ALICE LEONG

until World War II. The school closed due to the dispersal of the Chinese community and the declining numbers of Chinese-American children in Watsonville. The Chinese community also became nervous about their "cultural school" after the Japanese School was used as one of the excuses to round up and relocate the Japanese community after Pearl Harbor. After World War II some Chinese planned to revive the Chinese school, but they could not generate enough community support, and the school building was eventually sold.

## FIRE—MARCH 1, 1924

Following World War I, the balance of risk began to tip against the Chinese dryer operators as the pre-season contract price for apples on the trees remained high, but the price of dried apples

Brooklyn and South Watsonville, c. 1920. A rare aerial photo of Brooklyn taken before the 1924 fire. Bridge which connected Brooklyn and Monterey County with Watsonville is in the center with San Juan Road angling down to the right and Brooklyn Street angling down to the left. The Chee Kong Tong temple is on the extreme lower left toward the end of Brooklyn Street. Charley Fang's apple dryer is the light-colored building next to the river in the center of the picture, while two dryers (the single chimney in the center and the four chimney on the right) can be seen on the Watsonville side of the river.

PAJARO VALLEY HISTORICAL
ASSOCIATION

(without the sizable government contracts) plummeted. Quong Sang Lung, the six chimney on Walker Street, was put up for sale in 1921; in 1922 Charley Fang went into bankruptcy with assets totalling $485 and obligations totalling $26,362; and Hoy Lew's father lost his interest in two dryers during the early 1920s. Mrs. John T. Porter's ledger book shows increasing vacancies in Brooklyn in 1922 and 1923—in 1924 fourteen of the forty-two buildings along Brooklyn Street were listed as vacant. As Henry Valentine, veteran Watsonville apple dryer (and one of the last three apple dryers in Santa Cruz County) remembered, most

Chinese honored their commitment despite the enormous losses which resulted: "They delivered their contract, but they lost their property doing it."

The Chinese were leaving Brooklyn for the San Francisco Bay Area or making the symbolic move from China to America by moving across the river into Watsonville. As early as 1916 the Watsonville newspaper had noted that the Chinese in Brooklyn were becoming "Americanized." The ornate parades which heralded the beginning of the Ring Game or the birthday of Kuan Kung were abandoned, and the Chinese community concentrated on entering floats in Watsonville's annual Fourth of July parade. In 1919 the newspaper noted that if the Chinese float entered in the parade that year was any measure, the Brooklyn Chinese were making the transition from Chinese to Americans very successfully.

The fire that started in Brooklyn at 5:30 A.M. on Saturday, March 1, 1924, consumed a Chinatown already decimated by assimilation. Starting behind the buildings facing San Juan Road on the east side of Brooklyn, the fire spread south down the east (odd-numbered) side of the street and then jumped across the street to the temple, coming to a stop at the alley between #18 and #16. All the buildings facing Brooklyn Street were destroyed save eight, #2 through #16 on the west side of the street. The fire also burned the buildings facing San Juan Road and most of the out-buildings behind the main row of buildings facing Brooklyn Street.

On the scene soon after the fire began, the Watsonville fire department used the single hydrant on San Juan Road and also ran a hose across the bridge from Watsonville, but in spite of these efforts, the fire swept unchecked down the street. Most of the efforts of the firemen focused on rescuing sick and invalid elderly Chinese men from the buildings. Four elderly men were reported missing later in the day, and firemen searched the ruins

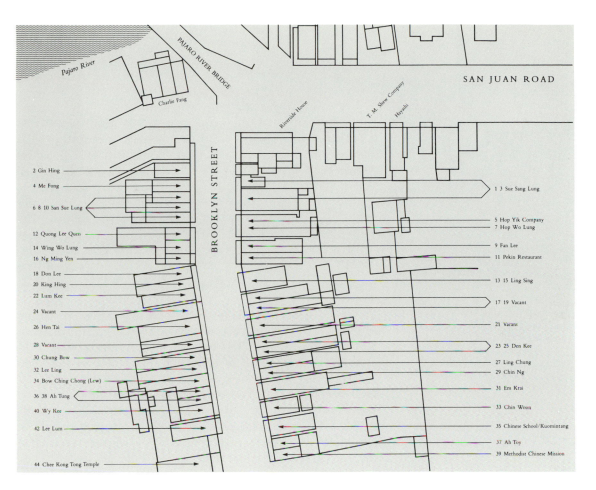

Map 12-1

THE 1924 FIRE, BROOKLYN

Map shows the extent of fire of March 1, 1924. Names on the buildings were those listed in Mrs. Porter's ledgers the month before the fire. Remaining buildings were destroyed in a second fire in 1933. Map derived from Sanborn Map Company maps, Map Library, UCSC.

423

for several days before deciding that only one of the forms found
in the ashes could be positively identified as human; the body
was later identified as Chin Joe Kim, aged seventy-five years.

Hoy Lew's father was away in Oakland on business that weekend, and Hoy, then living on Front Street in Watsonville, was
awakened by the alarm. He dashed across the bridge and down
Brooklyn Street to #34 to rescue as much as possible from the
flames before the fire reached the store. He first rescued two
small safes which contained the company's ledgers; he picked up
the first safe, took it out into the middle of the pig sty behind the
store, and then returned to get the second safe which he placed
safely alongside the first. His father had lost one of his earlier
stores in the 1906 fire in Chinatown, San Francisco, and he had
drummed it into Hoy that the company's ledgers had top priority in the event of a fire. When the business was again re-
established after the fire, his father announced that the books had
been destroyed; those owing and owed money by Bow Ching

Chong were asked to help reconstruct the records, with the ledgers providing the Chinese businessman with a measure of the honesty of his business associates.

With the flames but a short distance away, Hoy had one more opportunity to rush into the store and retrieve some valuables. When confronted with a final choice between saving a pistol or a gold watch in the company desk, Hoy selected the pistol. As the flames consumed the store, Hoy Lew realized the folly of his final choice and in a rage threw the pistol into the mud of the pig sty.

A frightened, ten-year-old Elmer Shew was roused from his bed and ran down the stairs from the living quarters over his father's store at #4 San Juan Road and out into the street. Elmer remembers that the fire burned his father's house and store before stopping at the alley which separated the store from the blacksmith shop next door.

All of the important buildings in the Chinese community were destroyed, including the temple, the KMT/Chinese School building, and the Methodist Chinese Mission. The loss in personal property sustained by the Chinese tenants was estimated in excess of $60,000, while the destroyed buildings (all owned by the Porter family and all uninsured) were estimated to be worth $25,000. A dozen safes of various sizes and descriptions survived the fire with their contents intact.

In contrast to the less than enthusiastic help given to the Chinese at Point Alones in 1906, the non-Chinese responded generously to the stricken Chinese. The Watsonville Chamber of Commerce sent several hundred blankets, food, quilts, bedding, and clothing to the Chinese, while the Japanese Association gave one hundred dollars cash and forty blankets. The Red Cross and local charitable organizations also assisted the Chinese community, and later in the week, several loads of rice and clothing arrived from the Chinese Six Companies in San Francisco. Many

Memorial for Sun Yat-sen, April 1925, Brooklyn. The Brooklyn KMT staged this commemoration for Dr. Sun Yat-sen when they received news that he had died in China. Because the KMT building had been destroyed in 1924 and not rebuilt, the organization rented the Justice Court building of Northern Monterey County to hold their celebration. Some of the people identified in the photograph include, fourth from left, standing, Emma Dong; back row, standing on extreme right, Charlie Leong; front row, standing, second from right, Steven Way; front row, standing, fourth from right, Elmer Shew; second row, standing, third from right (with V-neck sweater), Parker Chan; front row, standing, fifth from right, Tommy Chan.

HENRY AND ALICE LEONG

of the homeless Chinese found temporary housing in the bunkhouses of the China Dryers; Charlie Fang temporarily took in dozens of Chinese at his large apple dryer at the head of Brooklyn Street. The Chinese community took up a collection of $175 which was presented to the fire department "for their generous efforts to put out the fire in Chinatown, Pajaro."

As with other Chinatown fires, the 1924 Brooklyn fire acted as an agent of redevelopment, razing buildings which had become dilapidated and unsafe since their initial construction in 1888. One of Mrs. Porter's grandchildren, Edward Pfingst, acted as the family's agent in the aftermath of the fire and, after meeting with some of the residents, decided to rebuild some of the destroyed buildings. The Shew grocery at #4 San Juan Road was the first building reconstructed, in part because Elmer Shew's father, Tom Shew, had carried insurance on the store. In contrast to the previous arrangement in which the Porters owned the

buildings, the new buildings were owned by the Chinese occupants and rent was charged for the land. The second building reconstructed in July 1924 was a dryer for the Wah Lung Company. In Mrs. Porter's ledger book for 1925–27, only a handful of tenants were listed in Chinatown: Charley Fang, Kay Dan, Gin Hing, Me Fong, San Sue Lung, Quon Lee Quen, Wing Wo Lung, Ng Ming Yen, J. M. Shew, J. P. Shew Co., Wah Lung, Chin Deck Lung, and Len Chung.

The Chinese school was rebuilt later in 1924 with contributions solicited from Chinese communities all over Northern California. The temple was not rebuilt. Dr. Edwar Lee, working in the Chinese Mission in Brooklyn at the time of the fire, went to see the Porter family about rebuilding the Methodist Mission. Mrs. Porter told Edwar Lee that the Methodists could rebuild their mission and have the land rent-free, but the Pfingsts responded with a "we'll see" attitude; without a firm commitment

Drum and Bugle Corps, Brooklyn, July 2, 1931. "Watsonville Chinese American School band playing drums in front of school to celebrate recess." Photograph was taken on Brooklyn Street facing southwest showing the area that was not rebuilt after the 1924 fire. FLORABELLE WONG

427

to rebuild the mission, the Methodists decided not to rebuild in
Brooklyn. The mission used various rented locations in Watsonville during the 1930s and 1940s.

Within a year the Watsonville newspaper published a "Reminiscence of Old Chinatown" which described the pre-fire Brooklyn as a town of "winding streets" and buildings with signs of
"squirming letters of black," while the smaller post-fire Chinatown still existed with "much of its old lure and Oriental witch-
ery." But the era of the China Dryers was ending, and with the
solid center of the Watsonville Chinese economy fast disappear-
ing, Brooklyn Chinese began to leave the region as Chinese in
other communities had already done.

## BROOKLYN BURNS DOWN

Apple City and the Pajaro Valley underwent yet another agricultural transformation as lettuce—"green gold"—became an
important crop in the valley. As Chong Wo had pioneered in apple packing in the 1890s, Sing Wo Kee, a Chinese company, pioneered in the Pajaro Valley lettuce industry in the 1920s.
Founded by five America-born brothers of a Monterey fishing
family, the Kwoks (G. J. Sing, Tom K. Quock, William J. Duck,
G. J. Leen, and Joe Gok—all variants on Kwok representing the
usual distortion of Chinese name-order by whites), Sing Wo Kee
established its headquarters and packing shed next to the railroad
line in Pajaro on the Brooklyn side of the Pajaro River. Connected with a San Francisco wholesale produce firm, Sing Wo
Kee was the lone representative of the Chinese in the lettuce
farming, packing, and wholesale business in the Pajaro Valley.
The driving force behind the company was G. J. Sing (Jong Sing
Gok), who developed some of the early techniques for shipping
lettuce in refrigerated railroad cars.

Though Sing Wo Kee was not nearly large enough to fill the gap left by the failing apple dryers in the Watsonville Chinese economy, the lettuce-packing firm helped forestall the complete demise of the Chinese community in Watsonville and provided summer employment for a generation of Chinese-American college students. Edwar Lee remembers working in the Sing Wo Kee lettuce fields while an intern at the Chinese Methodist Mission in 1923–24, and Charlie Leong also spent some time working for Sing Wo Kee during his college summers.

The death of Mrs. John T. Porter in 1930 marked the end of an era for the dwindling Chinatown. As a testimony to their affection for Mrs. Porter's kindness over the years, the Chinese took up a collection and purchased two bronze vases which were donated to the Watsonville Episcopal Church in Mrs. Porter's memory.

The final, fatal blow to the old Chinatown came with yet another early morning fire—March 22, 1933. This time the Fire

Sing Wo Kee packing company, Watsonville, 1931. Sing Wo Kee was the pioneer Chinese-owned lettuce-packing firm which provided employment for many Chinese-American college students during the late 1920s and early 1930s. G. J. Sing, partner and driving force behind the company, is standing on the loading dock behind the group. The group standing in front of the automobile on the right includes (left to right) Tom Kwok, Philip Kwok, Loy Kwok, two sons of G. Wing Kwok, Hazel Kwok, George Kwok, and William Jung. The large group on the left includes Chinese college students and Filipino laborers hired by the company.

MUNSON KWOK

429

Sing Wo Kee packing company, Watsonville, 1931. G. J. Sing is standing to the right wearing the hat, while college students and Filipino employees can be seen packing lettuce.

HENRY AND ALICE LEONG

God finished the work he had begun in 1924 by destroying the small row of buildings which had escaped the flames in 1924; before the Watsonville Fire Department was able to control it, the fire burned buildings #2 through #16 on the west side of Brooklyn Street. This fire was anti-climactic as the plans to subdivide the Porter property and sell the lots were already in the works when the fire broke out. Miraculously, no one was injured in the fire, though the K. H. Chinn family, living above the Kong Sam restaurant at #2, escaped with nothing but the clothing they were able to grab on the way out of the burning building.

When seventy-eight-year-old T. S. Dong, living on Front Street in Watsonville, heard the fire alarm that morning, he rushed across the river to bring assistance to the homeless. His son Collin recalled:

In spite of a severe cold, Father rushed down to help his old friends. He brought blankets, food, and clothing and made coffee for the

430

homeless. He continued without sleep long into the night to arrange for the comfort of his helpless and bewildered friends. He exhausted himself seeking shelter for them. The next day he was stricken with pneumonia. And nine days later, on March 31, 1933, at the age of 78, a wonderful man passed away.

T. S. Dong and the Brooklyn Chinatown died together. Soon after the fire the Porter estate realigned Brooklyn Street and subdivided the old Chinatown into lots. The Chinese Association purchased the lot on which the Chinese school was built (several of the directors of the Association were America-born), but other than the Chinese school and a couple of the other long, narrow buildings which survived the 1933 fire, Watsonville no longer had its Chinatown across the river. For forty-five years Watsonville's Chinatown had been the social and cultural lodestone for the Chinese in the Pajaro Valley.

The Chinese New Year is being celebrated the quietest of any time in the history of the city, and by the smallest number of Chinese, as the population has continually dwindled.

*Santa Cruz Sentinel*, January, 1928.

# 13

# Santa Cruz and Salinas

## SANTA CRUZ CHINATOWN

AFTER THE APRIL 1894 fire which destroyed the Front Street Chinatown, the Santa Cruz Chinese split into two camps. Neither had difficulty in finding a location on which to rebuild. (The desire of landlords to have Chinatowns located on their properties testifies not only to the regularity with which the Chinese paid their rents, but also to the Chinese reluctance to complain about the conditions of the property. Having Chinese tenants meant a steady flow of rent money with few requests for repairs.) A small number of non-Christians led by Wong Kee moved to Mrs. Blackburn's property on the southwest side of Santa Cruz. A larger, predominantly Christian group moved to the Fagen-Birkenseer island known as the Midway (it had often been used as a circus midway). The Chinatowns took on the names of the property owners, Blackburn's and Birkenseer's Chinatowns.

On April 23, 1894, six separate leases were signed between Birkenseer and Pon Fang, Yu Kee, Sam Sing Lung, Quong Chung-Ling Kee, Quong Chung-Yuen Kee, and Sing Kee. The leases ran for twenty years, and each property rented for $10.50 per month. The property leased by Pon Fang was rented at $12

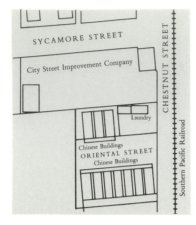

Map 13-1

BLACKBURN'S CHINATOWN,
SANTA CRUZ, c. 1900

Blackburn's Chinatown lasted from
1894–1905 and was located in the
southwest corner of Santa Cruz. The
site is now near the Union Ice Company. Map derived from Sanborn Map
Company maps, Map Library, UCSC.

per month and was to be used for the Chinese Congregational
Mission church. The Chee Kong Tong headquarters and temple
(all of which had been destroyed in the 1894 fire) were rebuilt on
Mrs. Blackburn's property and re-dedicated in 1895.

The 1900 manuscript census shows that the Birkenseer Chinatown was far and away the larger of the two. Birkenseer's Chinatown had fifty-nine residents in 1900, including one identifiable
family (Chin Tai Kim) with four children under sixteen. Other
than the Chin family, which had five females, there were only
four other women, all living at #18, listing their occupations
as servants or boardinghouse keepers. The Birkenseer Chinese
community, composed of cooks, servants, laundrymen, and laborers, primarily served the white Santa Cruz community. The
Blackburn Chinatown, on the other hand, listed but five households, and a total of nineteen men, with no families and no
women or children. A number of Chinese market gardeners still
lived on the west side of Santa Cruz in 1900, but like all Chinese
in the region, they were getting older.

Despite the dwindling Chinese population, gambling halls
continued to thrive in Birkenseer's Chinatown until after World
War II. Japanese and Filipinos joined the Chinese gamblers to play
*fan tan* or buy lottery tickets, but it was the steady patronage of
Santa Cruz whites that kept the gambling halls operating. The
police would raid the halls periodically to keep up appearances
(the Santa Cruz jail was less than a block away from Chinatown),
but after a few nights passed, the lotteries and tables were back in
business. The Sanborn Map Company even labeled several of the
1930s buildings in Chinatown as "Gambling Halls." Gambling
was still extensive enough in the Santa Cruz Chinatown during
World War II that the United States Army made it off-limits for
soldiers on leave from duty at nearby Fort Ord.

Birkenseer's Chinatown, Santa Cruz, c. 1900. China Lane angles off to the river on the right, while the buildings in the left foreground (Bowman's Carriage works) face Front Street. Part of the Garibaldi Hotel can be seen on the far left. San Lorenzo River can be seen beyond the Chinatown, and there is snow visible on the Santa Cruz Mountains in the distance. Most of the residents of Birkenseer's Chinatown were domestics, cooks, and laundrymen.

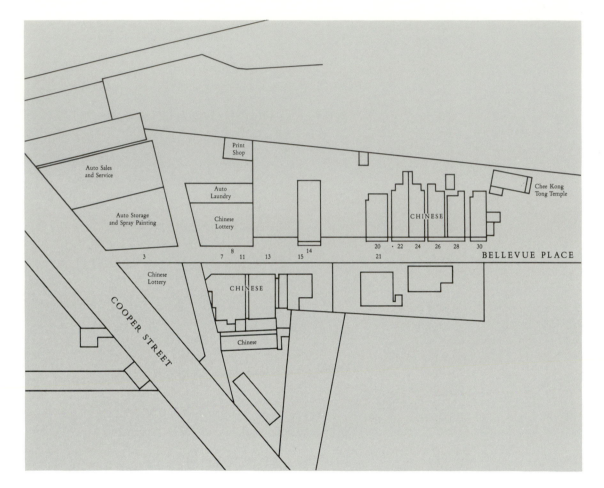

Map 13–2

BIRKENSEER'S CHINATOWN, SANTA CRUZ, c. 1930

Santa Cruz's last Chinatown. Bellevue Place ended to the right in the San Lorenzo
River. The last temple is labeled in the upper right. The S. S. Lee and Ow families lived in numbers 26, 28, and 30 on the north side of the street. Map derived
from Sanborn Map Company maps, Map Library, UCSC.

436

The Chinese Mission, Birkenseer's Chinatown, c. 1900. Chinese congregation standing in front of mission building on China Lane. Bearded man on left is Reverend William H. Pond. In the distance the street dropped off into the San Lorenzo River.

SPECIAL COLLECTIONS, UCSC

In September 1905 the Southern Pacific Railroad announced that it planned to buy twenty acres west of Chestnut Avenue, including the Blackburn Chinatown, to erect a railroad yard. Though several local real estate developers offered to buy the Chinatown buildings from Mrs. Blackburn or the Southern Pacific, the railroad company chose to purchase the buildings and demolish them. The only building to survive the sale and removal was the Chee Kong Tong headquarters and temple which was disassembled and reconstructed at the extreme east end of the Birkenseer Chinatown, facing the river.

In November 1905 the new temple was dedicated in a huge celebration. Over fifty members of the Chee Kong Tong participated in the festivities, which included a Chinese band, and the temple was adorned with new decorations. Each member then entered the new building:

Each brought his offering of punks and Chinese candles and then kow towed before the joss with burning punk in hand, offered his libation of wine, pouring it on the floor, while bowing, and then burned his lucky paper representing cash, while outside firecrackers were discharged.

Two roast pigs were laid on the altar, and the air was filled with incense smoke. A large banquet followed at which members were served "roast pork, chicken, dried oyster, bird's nest soup, sharks' fins, and delicacies so palatable to the Chinese." The place of honor on the altar was occupied by an image of Kuan Kung, and he was surrounded by "red banners, and tablets of green." At the conclusion of the celebration, ten new members were initiated, and then each participant departed with some roast pork and betel nuts.

The Chee Kong Tong, very strong in nineteenth-century Santa Cruz, continued to exert influence into the twentieth century. Ernest Otto estimated that only three of the fifty male Chinese residents of Santa Cruz were not members of the Chee Kong Tong in early 1911.

In anticipation of the coming overthrow of the Manchu dynasty, Santa Cruz's Chinese community went through a frenzy of queue cutting beginning in December 1910:

> A number chose Christmas day for the innovation, stating they wished a day that they could always remember it, and since then it has become epidemic in Chinatown, especially the past few days, as the New Year season approaches. It has struck all classes, old and young, the progressive and conservative.

The community anxiously followed events in China, and when news of the overthrow of the Manchus in October 1911 finally reached Santa Cruz, the new nationalist flag ("red with a blue corner on which is a sixteen pointed star") was raised over the temple. By February 1912 only five of the older Chinese men living in Santa Cruz still wore their queues.

The 1910 manuscript census confirms the declining Chinese

population in Santa Cruz. With no secure foothold in the community's economy (such as the China Dryers in Watsonville or the canneries and squid fishing at Monterey), the Chinese drifted away. Birkenseer's Chinatown had a population of fifty-nine Chinese in 1910, with but two children under eighteen; most of the residents were older men, many of whom would die or move back to China before 1920.

Public observances of Chinese holidays and festivals in Santa Cruz declined as the Chinese population dwindled, until even the Chinese New Year celebrations were "mere reminders of past days." The feasts held in the Congregational Chinese Mission were ended when the building was torn down in 1920, and by 1922 only three open houses were still being held by Chinese businessmen: Wo Gap and Lam Pon held feasts at their stores in Chinatown, and Sun Fat (the only Chinese merchant still maintaining an active shrine) had a big open house and dinner at his laundry on Front Street.

The last elaborate old-fashioned Chinese wedding ceremony and feast was held in August 1910 when the China Dryer owner and merchant, Lam Pon, married a California-born woman from Pleasanton:

> The bride went home to China when about twelve, and returned on the last steamer and for the first time saw the man whom she was to marry, as was also the case with the groom. This is according to Chinese custom, as the parents arrange the marriages for their children.

The marriage was performed at Lam Pon's home in Chinatown. Bride and groom wore traditional finery:

> The bride had an elegant brocaded silk gown. Her blouse was of a dainty pink shade with lower garment of lavender. A wonderful jeweled headdress adorned her coiffure, while high-heeled Chinese green silk slippers were worn. The groom wore a long dark blue brocaded silk blouse, reaching to the ankles. Over this was a shorter

wine-colored blouse. A double sash of dark pink brocaded silk was across each shoulder and crossed over the chest. His headgear was a silk turbaned effect with golden trimming and peacock feathers. The walls of the front room of the house were completely hidden from view by red scrolls sent by friends as gifts.

The feast that followed was considered to be "the biggest and greatest event ever held in Chinatown," and over a hundred sat down to the wedding dinner; Lam Pon's friends at the wedding filled six houses in the Chinatown.

One of the earliest success stories of a Santa Cruz Chinese was that of Dong Toy. A member of the Chinese mission at the Congregational Church who sometimes played the organ at the annual recitals, Dong Toy had been a cook for many years in Santa Cruz, and in 1895 he moved to San Francisco where he opened a small store in Chinatown selling American clothing. By 1910 he had built his single store into a small merchandising empire which stretched from Dupont Street (later Grant Avenue) in San Francisco's Chinatown to Hong Kong; his net worth in 1910 was estimated to exceed $100,000. By the early 1920s Dong Toy had organized a bank in Hong Kong and built a hotel in San Francisco. Two members of the Congregational mission achieved success in China: Soo Hoo Dong, an assistant in the mission, eventually received a medical degree and opened a practice in Tientsin, and Fong Sec, a visiting lecturer for the Congregational mission, graduated from the University of California and received a Chinese government position in Shanghai. The early successes of these members of the Congregational mission can partially be attributed to the Santa Cruz missionary effort which began very early and was extremely successful in recruiting students for the English language classes essential to success in education and the professions.

But as the Chinese population shrank, many successful merchants left Santa Cruz. Wo Gap, the unofficial mayor of the

Members of the Chinese Mission, Santa Cruz, c. 1900. Wearing their traditional queues, seven members of the church posed for photographers. Many of the members of the mission went on to successful careers in business and education.

SPECIAL COLLECTIONS, UCSC

Santa Cruz Chinatown after 1905 and a successful merchant, bought a cattle ranch in the Sacramento Valley and moved there in 1918: "The Chinese population has gradually dwindled until it is less than 50 in Santa Cruz, so [Wo Gap] decided to enter another line of business." (Wo Gap's wife died during the 1919 flu epidemic, and he eventually returned to Santa Cruz.) During the 1920s Jue Chong, Ah Hing, Lue He Li, and Lam Pon left Santa Cruz for China so that by the end of the decade, the Santa Cruz Chinese community consisted of five younger families and a group of older men. In 1930, except for the gambling enterprises that came and went, only two active Chinese businesses remained in Birkenseer's Chinatown. The New Year celebration in 1930 was a muted affair:

> The Chee Kong Tong joss house is practically deserted. Several of the old timers visit to worship, but none of the younger men are seen there . . . The [private] dinners are as elaborate as ever, but with none of the old time music of drum, cymbal and gong. The Santa

Cruz orchestra was always a three piece affair. The instruments are in the joss house, but untouched. No stores have the elaborate shrines in the front room with silk hangings, large banners and the many Chinese lillies . . .

The departure of many prosperous merchants not only reduced the Chinese population to a handful, it also relegated the next generation to starting anew without a property or capital base to build on. Lam Pon left Santa Cruz a financially successful man, but his China-born son arrived in Santa Cruz in 1937 with a total of sixteen dollars in his pocket. For the next generation the struggle of the first pioneers, who never became an integral part of Santa Cruz's economy, left no foundation on which to build. As the temple fell into disrepair, a handful of Chinese families—Wo Gap, Chin Jung, Lam Sing, Lam Pon, and S. S. Lee—began the process of pioneering all over again.

Chinese who grew up in Chinatown during its waning years describe a quiet multicultural community. The single street was a cul-de-sac that ended at the river, so pedestrians rarely came into Chinatown; the dirt street and the river were the playground for the dozen or so Chinese children who spent their leisure time climbing fruit trees or searching for creatures in the marshy river bottom. Some residents remember at least one black family living near the end of the street along with Filipinos and Italians in the surrounding area. The Lee and Ow children walked across Santa Cruz each morning to Laurel School where they spoke only English, and returned to Chinatown where their parents and grandparents spoke Chinese. The school principal complained to Emily Ow that her children were speaking a "double-talk" combination of Chinese and English and asked her to minimize the amount of Chinese spoken at home so their level of English might improve. The Chinese children sometimes were teased at school for their accents and appearance, and Chinatown was a warm, safe refuge for them—just it had been for the cooks and domestics a century before.

Santa Cruz Chinatown in the 1940s. Photo taken looking north toward Santa Cruz.    GEORGE LEE

Birkenseer's Chinatown, Santa Cruz, 1930s. Looking south toward the San Lorenzo River, photograph shows the wooden buildings that remained as the Chinese community in Santa Cruz dwindled to a handful of families.
SPECIAL COLLECTIONS, UCSC

Flood replaced fire as the bane of Santa Cruz's last Chinatown. Soon after the dedication of the new temple in 1905, the San Lorenzo River overflowed into the Chinatown until the water covered the wooden sidewalk which connected the buildings. The residents of Chinatown usually responded to floods by moving their belongings upstairs to the second story. In 1940 three elderly residents were rescued from the balcony of the temple, and the last residents of Chinatown, Jun Lee and his mother, Gue Shee Lee, left during the devastating December 1955 flood. The remaining buildings of Santa Cruz's last Chinatown were razed during the redevelopment of the area following the flood.

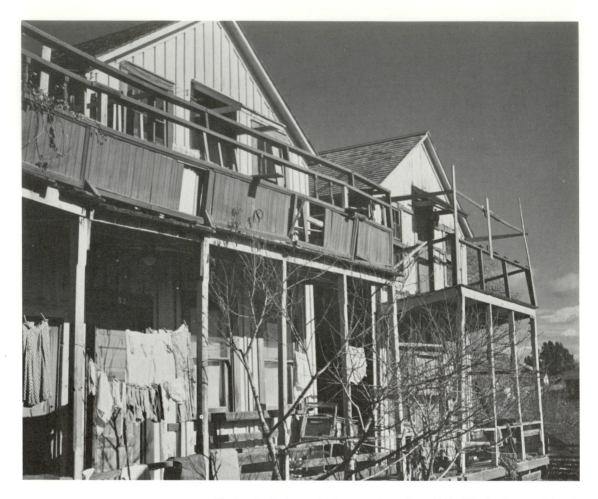

The Lee family home, Chinatown, Santa Cruz, 1940s. The San Lorenzo River is behind the building. The Lee family grew up here, and they were the last residents to leave Chinatown after the flood of 1955. Note the flounder drying beside the door upstairs on the building to the right.
GEORGE LEE

444

Santa Cruz's Chinatown coming down, c. 1950. Long-neglected buildings in
Chinatown were torn down in the 1940s and 1950s. This building had been a
gambling hall and association hall before the Chinese community in Santa Cruz
grew too small to support such activities.                    GEORGE LEE

446

Chee Kong Tong Temple being dismantled, 1950, Santa Cruz. After years of disuse, the once-busy Chee Kong Tong temple was dismantled. Old incense can be seen in the holder on the altar and in the container on the left. The Chinese characters are couplets meaning good luck, good fortune, etc.

## SALINAS CHINATOWN

The Salinas Chinatown began as a small service community for the seasonal Chinese farm laborers in the Salinas Valley in the 1870s, and that role continued to be its primary focus well into the twentieth century. Like a magnet, Spreckels' sugar factory pulled most of the aging Chinese farm laborers into the Salinas Valley in 1898, virtually emptying the Castroville Chinatown, and many of them ended their careers in Salinas. The Chinese did not make the transition into a new industry in the Salinas Valley as they had at Monterey with the squid drying or in the Pajaro Valley with the China Dryers. A few of the farm laborers and market gardeners made the transition to full-fledged farmers in the Salinas Valley, but most of the Chinese in Salinas after 1910 were merchants in the Salinas Chinatown on Soledad Street. Chinese families did not appear in Salinas until after 1910, and then only in merchant families; seasonal laborers did not have the security to follow their example.

Two years after the opening of the Spreckels sugar factory, the 1900 census listed forty-three residents in the Soledad Street Chinatown, all male and all but one China-born. Wong Yee, the one California-born Chinese in the community, was also the only one under the age of eighteen. Two barbers, four cooks, four farmers, two laundrymen (the Chinese laundries were still operating at Main and Central in downtown Salinas), one restaurant owner, and eighteen merchants worked in the Chinatown. Because the census taker conscientiously wrote down the house numbers of the Chinatown residents, the census list and a Sanborn map made the same year provide a precise picture of Chinatown in 1900. Approximately six months prior to the census, the Monterey County Assessor listed Chinatown by *business name* rather than personal name, so this second map shows the common business name used by the Chinese residents; only a

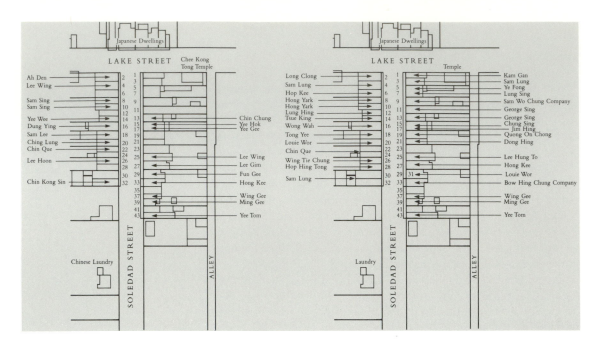

Map 13-3

SOLEDAD STREET CHINATOWN, SALINAS, CENSUS, 1900

Names on buildings are those listed by the federal census taken in 1900. Note the buildings occupied by the growing Japanese population (at the top of the map). Map derived from Sanborn Map Company maps, and manuscript census, Monterey County.

Map 13-4

SOLEDAD STREET CHINATOWN, SALINAS, ASSESSOR, 1900

Names on buildings are those listed by the Monterey County assessor in 1900. Chinese residents were known to the assessor by business names, while they told the census takers their personal names (map 13–3). The differences between the two lists of names points up the difficulty in finding specific Chinese individuals in the records. Map derived from Sanborn Map Company maps and Monterey County assessor's rolls, 1900.

few of the names match those from the census, dramatizing the difficulty of tracking individual Chinese through the historical records.

Rebuilt after the fire in 1893, the temple burned again in August 1901, and was again rebuilt on lot #1 in November of that year. From 1901 to 1937 the temple stood on that corner. The queue cutting in Salinas took place at the time of the lunar New Year in 1910, and Lee Dong, the unofficial mayor of the Soledad Street Chinatown, explained his feelings about the braids:

> The Chinese government no longer insists on its subjects wearing them, and many Chinese, especially the young men, are discarding them. They are very troublesome at the best, and are good for nothing. Therefore, I had mine removed. I like the change and will hereafter wear my hair like the American people. As soon as I took the lead, six other Chinese followed suit. I expect a Chinese with a queue will be a curiosity before long.

From 1900 to 1910 the Chinese population of Salinas increased to a total of eighty-one, seventy of whom lived on Soledad Street. The all-male nature of the Chinatown had not changed very much; only two Chinese women lived on Soledad Street. The number of merchants had doubled to twenty-seven, and their average age had increased to forty-four. All of the merchants listed in the 1910 census were China-born.

Perhaps the most significant development in the 1900–1910 decade was the arrival of a sizable group of Japanese farm laborers. A small Japantown formed on the north side of Lake Street, and the new Japanese residents attracted Chinese merchants and gambling hall operators to Soledad Street. The Japantown that grew up at the end of Soledad Street brought new economic life to Chinatown. Brooklyn Chinatown in Watsonville was separated from the Japanese community by the Pajaro River, and Japanese merchants moved more quickly into businesses to

Bing Kong Tong, Soledad Street, Salinas. Located at #10 Soledad Street, the Bing Kong Tong was one of two tongs which were powerful in Salinas' Chinese community. Bing Kong rebuilt their headquarters after a fire and their headquarters still stand on Soledad Street. Characters above the door are the name, Bing Kong Tong.

MONTEREY COUNTY LIBRARY

serve the Japanese community on south Main Street in Watsonville, whereas in Salinas Japantown snuggled right up against Chinatown, and the Chinese were able to secure more of the business of the Japanese farm laborers. Where Brooklyn's Chinese community began to disperse in the 1900s, Salinas' Chinatown and Japantown remained insulated, on the "other side of the tracks," making it easier for gambling and prostitution to flourish.

Tong influence came to Salinas with the gambling and prostitution, and the struggles between the various highbinder tongs in San Francisco sometimes spilled over into the Salinas Valley. The tong wars were usually disagreements over gambling territory or prostitutes; in 1912 "Shorty" Lee (Lee Yin) was almost killed in a gunfight in Salinas. Several more Chinese were killed in Salinas in 1912 during a tong disagreement. The San Francisco Chinese community set up a Peace Association in 1913 to mediate the conflicts and stop the violence, but the wars simmered into the 1920s with occasional assassinations and raids erupting throughout California. The decline in population and immigration as well as the growing influence of America-born Chinese weakened the influence of the tongs, and by World War II they lost both their influence and their control over illegal activities. Today the tongs perform primarily social functions within the Chinese community.

The Bing Kong Tong and the Suey Sing Tong had the greatest and most long-lived influence in Salinas. Both operated gambling halls, beginning in the early twentieth century, but any rivalry between the two organizations has mellowed over the years. The two tong halls face each other across Soledad Street, and each tong holds one or two social events each year.

Outliving the Chinese laborers it had been created to serve, the Soledad Street Chinatown became the recreational center for the farm laborers who replaced the Chinese—first the Japanese, and then the Filipinos, and even later the braceros and Mexicans. As the China-born merchants passed away or moved on, their places were taken by America-born merchants, many of whom were able to start families. The America-born Wong Yee (Harry Yee Wong), a clerk in the 1900s, became an established merchant, married a young Chinese woman from Monterey, and raised a family of seven children. Wong Yee later opened several Chinese restaurants in Salinas in addition to the original family store at 10½ Soledad Street.

The Lee family, headed by "Shorty" Lee (Lee Yin), was the second merchandising family to take root on Soledad Street and begin the process of developing a financial base that could support a large family. Lee Yin was born in China in 1887 and came to California in 1897. He came to Salinas in 1908, establishing a general merchandising store (Hop Hing Lung) at 12½ Soledad Street. Lee Yin was associated with the Bing Kong Tong (whose headquarters were next door), and he ran a small gambling room in the back of his store. Lee Yin's grandson, Wellington Lee, remembers going next door to the Bing Kong Tong:

> As a little boy, I often shivered at the sight of the ferocious-looking Chinese men painted on a scroll behind the altar in the clubhouse and marvelled at the fine teakwood tables and chairs that lined two sides of the room.

"Shorty" Lee became the "mayor" of Salinas' Chinatown in the 1920s, and he acted as official greeter and spokesman for the community during the lunar New Year and Salinas Rodeo (known as "Big Week," the busiest week in the year for gambling halls in Chinatown). Lee's store closed shortly after his death in 1944, but the Lee family continued to live in the building until redevelopment came to Soledad Street in 1961.

Children from families such as the Lees and Wongs went to Chinese school downstairs in the Chee Kong Tong temple. When

Lee Yin ("Shorty" Lee) and his wife, Salinas, 1920s. Shorty Lee was the unofficial mayor of the Soledad Street Chinatown during the 1920s and 1930s.
MONTEREY COUNTY HISTORICAL SOCIETY

Shorty Lee in front of his store, Sole-
dad Street Chinatown, Salinas.
MONTEREY COUNTY HISTORICAL
SOCIETY

the temple was torn down in 1937, the school was transferred to a new building on California Street a block to the east. With the name "Salinas Confucius Church" emblazoned on its eaves, the new Chinese building served as Chinese community center, meeting room, and Chinese school.

## CHINESE FARMERS IN THE SALINAS VALLEY

Hundreds of Chinese farm laborers worked in the Salinas Valley during the 1880s and 1890s; dozens of Chinese sugar beet contractors worked the fields, and dozens more Chinese farmers worked the land under reclamation leases. By 1920 no more than a dozen Chinese farmers worked in the Salinas Valley. Immigration restrictions and California's Alien Land Laws prevented Chinese farm laborers from making the transition to farm owners. The Chinese Exclusion Act of 1882 and its off-shoots specifically forbade the immigration of Chinese *laborers* while permitting Chinese students, scholars, and merchants to enter the United States. While Chinese merchants had some freedom to travel back and forth, to marry in China, and to maintain their businesses in the Monterey Bay Region, the farm laborer was severely restricted. When Chinese farm laborers in the Pajaro and Salinas Valleys got older, averaging over fifty years of age by 1900 and almost sixty in 1910, no new Chinese immigrants took their place.

In 1900 a half-dozen Chinese farmers working leaseholds and reclamation projects had achieved some financial independence: Jim Bow, Tom Kee, Quong Fee, Fung Gee, Lee Hoon, and Lee Wing. Many more returned to China or died in Salinas. When the Alien Land Law of 1913 specifically prohibited Chinese farm

Salinas Confucius Church, California Street, Salinas. Home of the Salinas Chinese community, this building also houses community meetings and the Salinas Chinese School. PHOTO TAKEN BY AUTHOR

453

laborers from evolving to leaseholder or landowner, it completed the destructive work of immigration restrictions. The loophole in the Alien Land Law allowing aliens to put their farms in the name of the America-born (and thus United States citizens) children gave some relief to the Japanese, but very little to the Chinese. Where Japanese women were coming to California in increasing numbers following the Gentleman's Agreement between Japan and the United States in 1908, most Chinese men had to journey to China to find a wife; the Quota Act of 1924 effectively stopped that practice by prohibiting even the wives of America-born Chinese from coming into the United States. The end result of these restrictions was that most Chinese farmers had to let leases expire or sell their land and return to China. The very men who had the experience and initiative to recognize and develop the rich swamp lands in the Salinas Valley were not around to partake of the bonanza which came in the valley in the 1920s and 1930s with the lettuce boom. Once again, the Chinese had to work the edges of the Green Gold Rush, providing services to the Japanese and Filipino farm laborers in Chinatown. If things had evolved naturally, the Chinese would have owned many of those lettuce fields by the 1920s.

There is one further cruel twist to the story. Many of the Chinese who returned to China invested in land in their home villages and settled down to reap the rewards of a lifetime of hard work on the Golden Mountain. Their legacies provided a land base for their family's next generation, and slowly and steadily the sweat-money that had been earned in the swamps and sloughs of the Salinas Valley grew in China. When land reform came to the People's Republic of China in the early 1950s, many Chinese lost those properties during the process of land reform. Land proved to be a difficult if not poor investment for many Chinese in the Salinas Valley, causing, at least in part, the tremendous emphasis on investing in education rather than property for the next generation of Chinese.

Instead of participating directly in the Green Gold Rush of the 1920s and 1930s, the Chinese worked in the gambling halls and stores on Soledad Street, mining the pockets of the farm workers. Today, out of the hundreds of Chinese market gardeners and farmers, only one Chinese family still farms in the Monterey Bay Region.

# PART FOUR

# THE GENERATIONS AFTER

Politics can change and maybe someday they can take away your money or property, but they can't take away what you have in your head. They can't take away your education.

Hoy Lew,
Watsonville, 1983.

# 14

# The Chinese Markets and the America-born Pioneers

Somewhere back in the history of almost every Chinese family in the Monterey Bay Region is a market or restaurant. Small retail businesses carried most of the families through the 1920s and 1930s. The evolution from the small market in Chinatown which sold Chinese products to Chinese customers to the all-purpose, Chinese-owned supermarket of the 1980s further illustrates the theme of adaptation and tenacity which characterized Chinese immigrants from the squid fishermen to the China Dryers. The Chinese market is a study of the Chinese in microcosm.

Conditions in the United States almost required that the Chinese be merchants, particularly after the passage of the Chinese Exclusion Act in 1882. Subsequent immigration laws refused entry to "Chinese employed in mining, fishing, huckstering, peddling, laundrymen, or those engaged in taking drying or otherwise preserving shell or other fish for home consumption," but permitted Chinese merchants to continue to enter the United States:

> A merchant is a person engaged in buying and selling merchandise, at a fixed place of business, which business is conducted in his name,

and who during the time he claims to be engaged as a merchant, does not engage in the performance of any labor, except as is necessary in the conduct of his business as such merchant.

Merchants had the freedom to move back and forth between China and the United States (though they had to undergo habeas corpus proceedings when they re-entered), and to bring their wives and families to the Golden Mountain (until 1924) when they felt financially secure. The merchants sustained the Chinese presence in the Monterey Bay Region between the imposition of Exclusion in 1882 and its relaxation in 1943.

Chinese cultural attitudes also motivated many immigrants to go into business for themselves. Maurice Freedman, a thoughtful observer of the Chinese, believed this was due to their proverbial capacity "for regular and sustained work" combined with a sophisticated understanding about money. Though most of the Chinese immigrants were peasants, they had been exposed to Chinese loan associations (*hui*) where they learned about "credit, interest and cooperation." The "respectability of the pursuit of riches" also helped to nudge the Chinese immigrants into business. Finally, the Chinese immigrant desired to be independent, to work for himself rather than for someone else. George Ow, Sr., a successful supermarket owner in Santa Cruz County, explained that for the Chinese, whether in China or America, going into business was the only way to succeed; he quoted a Chinese saying: "Work [alone] will never get you ahead."

Although the days of the grand labor-demanding projects where a Jim Jack or Jim Toy could order a large group of Chinese laborers to come down from San Francisco and work on a project were over, the principle of interdependence within the Chinese community prevailed. The Chinese market depended on the interdependence between family or village members. Capital was limited, so partnerships between family members were common, and community or family members often loaned start-up money on a handshake. Once the business was in operation, the new owners could depend on having help from family members or other Chinese in the community when it was needed, and conversely, a Chinese needing work could pretty well count on employment in a Chinese business. Years of harassment developed the community's resources and created an extensive, supportive infrastructure.

Though organized anti-Chinese sentiment died away by the 1930s, second-generation Chinese met discrimination in both housing and employment. Going into business for oneself was one avenue open to young Chinese who found themselves thwarted in their search for access to the professions. Educational opportunities for Chinese-Americans ran a generation ahead of the jobs available to them, and a number of the region's second generation returned to the family business when they found that their college education was not enough. "We were suppressed," says Salinas market owner Henry Chin, "there were many jobs that were not open to Orientals." The Depression did not help matters either, as the number of jobs available to anyone shrank each year. Small businesses carried the Chinese in the Monterey Bay Region through those transitional years from the 1920s to the 1950s.

The Chinese markets, like the early Chinese fishing companies, had little or no competition in the Chinatowns when they began, and when the Chinese merchandise stores evolved to general-purpose small markets, they usually had no competition except each other. The chain supermarkets (Safeway, Purity, Lucky) entered the Monterey Bay Region in the 1940s, and faced with that kind of competition, the Chinese market operators had to adapt just as the early pioneer fishermen did. The chain stores took over the center of the market business, and the Chinese market owners had to work the edges to stay alive. Showing the same tenacity and ingenuity that the earlier Chinese did, the Chinese mined locations, customers, and hours that the chain supermarkets did not—staying open late at night and on weekends and holidays and providing personal services which supermarkets could not (many knew their customers by name).

## FROM CHINESE STORE TO
## ALL-PURPOSE MARKET

The early Chinese stores in the region's Chinatowns sold a little bit of everything to the surrounding Chinese community. Ah Moon, Quong Chong, and Wong Kee, three Santa Cruz merchants, dealt primarily in Chinese goods:

> These merchants handled Chinese goods, mainly groceries from China, canned or dried, such as dried oysters, abalones, etc—choice victuals. Especially about the New Year season would arrive a large supply of birds' nest soup, sharks' fins, etc. There were the usual Chinese sausages, roast duck, roast pork, brown to a turn, from San Francisco. There were vegetables such as their lettuce, bean sprouts, okra, yams, water lily bulbs, etc. In cans were bamboo sprouts; lichee nuts, etc. in jars, preserved ginger, and the always piled high rattan-covered bundles of rice. They also sold the Chinese shoes, slipper-like, most of them made from black horse hair but some were very pretty ones of velvet.

As long as a sizable Chinese community existed in and around Santa Cruz or the region's other communities, the merchants were very successful. But when the Chinese population declined after the turn of the century, many of the Chinese store owners returned to China. If the Chinese store was to survive into the twentieth century, it would have to adapt to the changing demographics and begin to broaden its appeal to include the white population as well as the Chinese.

Hoy Lew's career in the Watsonville market business provides an excellent opportunity for us to study the evolution from Chinese store to all–purpose market. Hoy Lew worked in his father's Chinese store, Bow Ching Chong, at #35 Brooklyn Street, and as a young man he learned all facets of the business, from buying chickens, eggs, and produce to stocking the shelves and preparing the special roast pork for which Bow Ching Chong was famous throughout the region. The Brooklyn fire of 1924 destroyed the store and forced Hoy Lew and his father to decide whether or not to rebuild the store on Brooklyn Street. Hoy Lew and his father, who was getting along in years, decided not to rebuild the store. With the apple dryers no longer economically viable, Hoy Lew knew that he needed to re-learn the market business if he were to be able to continue in it. Later in 1924 he was offered a job working for Charlie Chin Goon at his market at 169 South Main Street. Charlie Chin Goon wanted Hoy Lew's skill and knowledge of Chinese products, and Hoy Lew wanted to learn about how to order and stock shelves for a market geared to whites. After working for Charlie Chin Goon for ten years, Hoy Lew opened his own market in 1935 on the corner of Bridge and Main Street and called it the California Market.

Hoy Lew, Watsonville, 1984. Hoy Lew is the patriarch of Watsonville's Chinese community.     GEORGE LEE

The California Market was stocked to cater to all elements of south Watsonville's multi-cultural population—Japanese, Filipino, Chinese, and white. "That's what I want, I want a market that appeals to all kinds of people, not just one kind. If your market appeals to only one kind, you take a big chance." The memory of Bow Ching Chong's dependency on Chinese customers and the devastating effect the 1924 fire and exodus had on the Chinese stores remained strong for Hoy.

From 1935 to 1950 Hoy Lew attempted to serve the broadest spectrum of people, but over the years several other markets had entered the field in south Watsonville, notably one owned by O. S. Chinn and the Daily Market owned by the Wongs. So

Hoy Lew shifted gears again, and from 1950 to 1964 he ran his store as a variety store until his retirement in 1964. During the last years Hoy's son Wally, a graduate in accounting, returned to help his father run the business.

During his years working at Bow Ching Chong in Brooklyn, Hoy had learned what he considers to be the most important lesson for running a business: "My father had a reputation for honesty, and I saw how important honesty was in running a business." "I never got rich in the market business," says Hoy Lew, but the market carried his family through the Depression and provided enough income and capital to support college educations for the next generation. The story is echoed, with slight variations, throughout the Monterey Bay Region.

Not all the Chinese markets in Brooklyn moved across the river after the 1924 fire; Shew's Market stayed on the same spot until 1970. Tong Mo Shew (known as Tom or T. M.) was born in San Jose in 1883, and soon after the turn of the century came to the Brooklyn Chinatown where he opened a store in partnership with his brother, T. P. Shew. The store was located at #4 San Juan Road, a through street that brought traffic passing through Watsonville, in contrast to a store such as Bow Ching Chong on Brooklyn Street, which was not a through street. Elmer Shew was born in 1914 and grew up above the store. The store burned in the 1924 fire, but the Shew brothers quickly made arrangements with the Porter family to rebuild it, and in 1933, when the Porters subdivided the old Chinatown, the Shews purchased the land and the building. Elmer worked in the store as a youngster and remembers that the patrons were primarily Japanese farmers; he remembers selling huge bags of rice, barrels of *shoyu* (soy sauce), and large packages of dried shrimp and other fish. T. M. Shew delivered the groceries in a horse-drawn wagon, and for the Japanese farm laborers who found it difficult to get to town, such a service was essential.

When Elmer Shew graduated from high school and was preparing to go to college, his father, T. M., became very ill, and Elmer stayed on to work in the store. Elmer continued working in the store for the next thirty-eight years, and as the clientele shifted, so did his stock, from goods for Japanese farm laborers to staples for the Mexican farm laborers who came into the area after World War II. When Elmer retired and sold the store in 1970, Shew's market had been operating over half a century in the same spot.

Daylite Market is an institution on Watsonville's South Main Street and represents the transition from small Chinese store to larger modern supermarket. Fred Wong owned a number of small markets in the San Joaquin Valley during the 1920s, learning to be both a merchandiser and butcher in the process. In 1939 Fred moved his family to Watsonville and opened the Daily Market at 227 South Main Street. The family lived above the market, and the Wong children worked in the store; the oldest son, Ernie, learned the butcher's trade from his father. After serving in the Air Force during World War II, Ernie had plans to go to college on the GI Bill, but his father was having health and financial difficulties, so Ernie returned to Watsonville to assist the family. "I was the number one son," says Ernie, "and it was my responsibility to look out for the family." When the Daily Market failed, Ernie began to search for a way to get another market started: "I wanted to be in business for myself, rather than work for someone else." In 1953 Ernie's mother took him to the San Joaquin Valley and introduced him to some Chinese businessmen there who loaned Ernie enough money to buy a one-twelfth partnership in a new supermarket in Watsonville. "I was astonished that they loaned me all that money, but when I asked my mother why they would do so on just a handshake, she just said, 'They believe in you.'" Ernie had received his starting capital from a form of *wui*, or money pool. The money pool oper-

The Fred Wong family of Watsonville, March, 1943. Back row, left to right, Wally Wong, Ernie Wong, Harry Wong; front row, left to right, Francis Wong, Ida Wong (mother), Fred Wong (father), and Johnny Wong. Ernie was one of the founders of Daylite Market in Watsonville in the 1950s, and was the first Watsonville City Councilman of Chinese ancestry.    IDA WONG

ated on oral agreement and was a common feature of early twentieth-century Chinese businesses.

Ernie Wong was one of twelve Chinese partners who opened Daylite Market in the fall of 1953, two doors south of the site where his father, Fred, had opened the Daily Market in 1939. During the first years Ernie worked one hundred hours a week, earning $150 a month for his efforts. Ernie helped manage the store and worked as a butcher, but his first love was working the check-out stand where he could meet the customers. Daylite Market served a multi-cultural clientele, and most of the Chinese working in the market spoke Chinese, English, and Spanish. Now semi-retired, Ernie Wong still works four days a week at Daylite Market, spending most of his time at the check-out stand: "I love meeting the people, talking to them, talking about our grandchildren and things that changed in our lives."

Ernie Wong's contacts with the public made him well known

Chin Brothers Market, Salinas, 1954.
HENRY CHIN

in Watsonville, and in 1969 he was asked if he would be willing to be considered for an appointment to the Watsonville City Council when an unexpected vacancy occurred. "They told me that there would be a list of five people from which the Council would select the replacement, so I figured there was not much of a chance of being selected. I jokingly said, 'Go ahead, put me on the list, I don't have a Chinaman's chance.'" His remark about a "Chinaman's chance" was picked up by the local press and eventually appeared in Herb Caen's column in the *San Francisco Chronicle*. Ernie Wong was selected as a City Councilman and became the first and only Chinese councilman Watsonville ever had. After serving the term's remaining year and a half, Ernie decided not to stand for election. "There was just too much homework in that job, and I wanted to work on my golf game." Today, when not working the check-out stand or caring for grandchildren, Ernie continues to work on his golf game.

467

The Chin Brothers Market is a landmark on Salinas' North Main Street. It is less than a half-mile from the center of the Soledad Street Chinatown, where California-born Chin Bow operated a store in the 1920s and 1930s. Located at 7½ Soledad Street, the store specialized in Chinese herbs. Chin Bow had nine children, and three of them comprise the Chin Brothers Market. Henry Chin, sixth in line, was born in Salinas in 1924, and he and his brothers, Parker and David, first entered the market business when they bought the Sausal Market in Salinas in 1949; half the six thousand dollars capital was borrowed from their father and the other half from the bank. "The market business was one of the few businesses we could enter without a college education," says Henry, "and there were a lot of occupations that we Chinese were not welcome in during those days."

In 1954 the three brothers built their present store, the Chin Brothers Market, just north of the railroad tracks on North Main Street. The three brothers have worked in the market since the store opened, and now that they own the property and building free and clear, their operating expenses are low enough to allow them to stay in business despite the heavy competition from the chain markets. "We can't compete with Safeway's prices," declares Henry, "no matter how low our overhead is. We provide friendly, individual service to our customers. And we have a good location." (Much of Salinas' recent growth has been in the neighborhood of the Chin Brother's Market.)

None of the brothers' children are following their fathers in the market business. Henry's three children have become a court reporter, a park ranger, and a cinematographer. "There is much less discrimination [against Chinese] these days," concludes Henry, "and our children have had much wider opportunities."

When the apple dryer Lam Pon returned to China in the late 1920s, he sold valuable holdings including a restaurant and a store. With this wealth he built a three-story brick home in Can-

The Lam Pon Family, c. 1924. Taken before Lam Pon's return to China, this photograph shows daughter Anna on left and Mrs. Lam Pon. Lam Pon's son George Ow came to the United States in 1937.          HENRY AND ALICE LEONG

ton (which still stands) and was able to afford several servants in his home. A son George was born to the family in Canton to join an older sister, Anna, who had been born in Santa Cruz. When the Japanese began to attack northern China in the mid-1930s, Lam Pon became fearful for his family, moving them temporarily to Hong Kong. The threat of a Japanese invasion in southern China and Hong Kong finally convinced Lam Pon that he should send George to America, and in 1937 George boarded the *U.S.S. President Hoover*. The ship was struck by a Japanese bomb (causing minor damage) as it embarked.

Lam Pon had taken much of his wealth back to China, but his network of friends and relatives in and around Santa Cruz was still in place. George Ow (he had come into the United States on his mother's family name) rode the train from San Francisco to Santa Cruz and found a home with his uncle, Lam Sing. Lam Sing, a product of the Congregational Church's Chinese Mission, owned the Canton Market on Pacific Avenue. George enrolled in Santa Cruz High School while working in the market

George Ow, Sr. and the New Monterey Market, December 1956. In a sea of canned and bottled goods, George Ow poses in the New Monterey Market. Active in the Exchange Club, George Ow, Sr. was elected National President of the Exchange Clubs of America in 1984, the first person of Chinese ancestry to lead the 150,000 member organization.                                GEORGE OW, SR.

in the evenings. Though his command of English was still unsteady, George Ow graduated from Santa Cruz High School in 1940.

George married a Santa Cruz Chinese girl, Emily Lee (daughter of S. S. Lee), just before being drafted into the United States Army during World War II for a three-year hitch in the South Pacific. After the war George went back to the market business, borrowing $3,500 from his uncle Lam Sing to buy a small market in New Monterey—the New Monterey Market.

The New Monterey Market was what George calls a typical "Mom and Pop" grocery store—small enough to be staffed by George and Emily. The Monterey economy was quite healthy in the late 1940s, with soldiers being mustered out at Fort Ord and the sardine canneries enjoying what would turn out to be their last hurrah. The market was only a couple of blocks above the canneries and old McAbee Beach at the corner of Lighthouse and Prescott. Within a year the Ows paid back the loan, and by 1957 they bought a lot on Lighthouse Avenue and built a new, medium-sized grocery store called the Avenue Market.

The Ows succeeded in their market because they worked the edges. They had to compete with Safeway and Purity in New Monterey, but with their low overhead and flexibility, they worked around the chains, staying open later (usually to 11 P.M.) and on Sundays and holidays. Though they planned to work only a half-day on Christmas and Thanksgiving, it sometimes took most of the day to serve the customers who showed up at the store. The Ow children helped in the store after school, and the Ows would sometimes employ other Chinese in the community when they needed help. George and Emily Ow worked as a team, with George concentrating on the meat section (like many other market owners, he was a skilled butcher) while Emily set up the produce department, each alternating on the cash register as required.

In 1962 the Ng family (from the San Joaquin Valley) opened a modern, 20,000-square-foot supermarket (Monte Mart) just down the street from the Avenue Market. George Ow saw the writing on the wall: "I'm a very proud man, and I did not want to sit back and not be able to compete with them." So the Ows looked around for a new site to build a more modern market. They traveled all over the Monterey Bay Region and eventually settled on a site just west of Capitola on 41st Avenue. "I did a lot of reading, and I always remembered that the most valuable intersection was the first four-way intersection off a freeway interchange." Though it was only a cow pasture, the intersection of Capitola Road and 41st Avenue was just such an intersection, and the Ows purchased the southwest corner and built their own 30,000-square-foot modern supermarket.

They named it King's, for the most pragmatic of reasons:

> Actually, I had driven around the San Francisco Bay Area and had noticed a store named King's; it had a nice, regal sound to it, and, it was a short name—a large neon sign for King's would cost half what a sign that said something like Albertson's would cost.

Though observers had predicted that the huge supermarket way out in the middle of nowhere would fold within six months, George Ow's vision paid off; the proceeds from the store more than met the family's expectations at the end of the first year, and the Ows purchased adjacent acreage and began building a shopping center. Meanwhile, Sears, Albertson's, and Long's had bracketed the intersection, confirming that they too knew about the "first four-way intersection off a freeway interchange."

King's market may have looked like a super-slick and modern supermarket from the outside, but inside it was a traditional Chinese-American market. The Ows lived above the store in large living quarters, and they provided living facilities for other Chinese who might be employed in the store. George Ow had a

Intersection of Capitola Road and Forty-first Avenue, Santa Cruz County, c. 1965. Selected by George Ow, Sr. because it was the first four-way intersection off the freeway, the corner became the hub for major development in the 1960s and 1970s. The building on the lower left hand corner is the Ow's King's Market. Today the King's Market building houses Orchard Supply. CAROLYN SWIFT

restaurant-sized Chinese kitchen built above the store (with a wok big enough to swim in), and one of the Chinese employees usually volunteered to cook for the Ow family and crew, taking off for lunch an hour early to prepare the meal for everyone. The store may have been modern, the kitchen facilities all shiny and new, but the system was the same as that used by Chinese in the Monterey Bay Region a century before.

King's Market was successful enough that, in 1966, George Ow began looking for yet another site for a grocery store, this time a cow pasture in Scotts Valley, also on a major four-way intersection off the freeway. Here the Ows built a second supermarket and shopping center.

George Ow, Sr. had strong feelings about the value of an education: "In this modern world, you need a college education even if you have a good financial base to work from." All seven of the

Ow children attended college, and most of them (though George Ow, Sr. did not push them into it) studied business administration. Today the children have taken over operation of the Ow's property and shopping centers, and George and Emily Ow have retired.

"Some people envy our being able to retire, but we don't feel guilty about it; Emily and I just remind them that we put in two lifetimes of forty-hour weeks working in the markets in the evenings and on weekends." In his retirement George Ow finally returned to Canton and saw that three-story brick house that his father had built so many years before; he has become an expert on Chinese ceramics and has surrounded himself with a veritable museum of cloisonné, porcelain, and art.

The two shopping centers buzz with activity, testimony to George Ow, Sr.'s vision—Capitola has grown out to engulf the first shopping center, and Scotts Valley is undergoing a boom in the electronics industry which has brought a staggering increase of patronage to the Scotts Valley center. The centers testify to the hard work, tenacity, and vision of George Ow. George also gives some credit to the timing of his arrival in the region. During the 1940s there was an old man living in Chinatown Santa Cruz whom everyone called Uncle Mun Lai. "He always used to say, 'I was born in the wrong time,'" says George, "and when I asked him what he meant, he just said, 'when we came into America young, there was hardly any work or real opportunity. Now there is, but I am too old.'" "I was lucky to be here at the right time," says George Ow, Sr., "and I am grateful for the opportunities."

## THE NATIONAL DOLLAR STORES

Not all of the merchandising done by the Chinese in California was on a small scale. In 1928 Joe Shoong founded the National Dollar Store chain which had its beginnings in a small

Vallejo, California, store in 1903. Based in Oakland, the National Dollar Stores eventually expanded to cover the entire western United States. The National Dollar Stores concentrated on selling dry goods (clothing was 80% of the stock) to working-class people. A cut below J. C. Penney's in price, National Dollar Stores were usually built in working-class neighborhoods. Eventually National Dollar Stores were built in every major community in the Monterey Bay Region, and during the 1930s the stores helped some of the Chinese in the region to get through the Depression. Almost every family had someone working in the "Dollar Store." The National Dollar Stores did on a large scale what local Chinese businesses did—provided secure employment for Chinese, especially during hard times, at a lower wage.

The National Dollar Store branch in Watsonville brought a young man with Monterey Bay roots back into the region. Henry Leong's mother, Leong Low Shee, was a member of a Monterey fishing family, the Kwocks, and had been born at the Point Alones fishing village in September 1874. At the age of twenty, she married a successful China-born merchant from Bakersfield, Leong Bow, and the couple eventually moved to San Francisco. They had one son before Leong Bow died in 1911; the son, Leong Guy (Henry), was three years old. Leong Low Shee, a hairdresser, knew she would have to travel a great deal to make a living, so she placed Henry with a "god-family."

Much is often made about how the responsibilities of the traditional Chinese family stopped at the door of the family home and how Chinese were reluctant to assist anyone not a member of the family or clan. That may have been true in traditional China, but it was not true in the Monterey Bay Region. Stories of temporary "adoptions" and children being cared for by other families are legion. Henry Leong was raised in his god-family just as if he was a member of that family; his mother sent financial support and visited him often.

Leong Low Shee, Monterey, 1894. Born in Monterey, Low Shee is pictured here as she filed a writ of habeas corpus to re-enter the United States after a visit to China.
NATIONAL ARCHIVES

Henry Leong and his mother, Leong Low Shee. Henry Leong was raised by a "god-family" and eventually went to work for the National Dollar Store chain, managing stores in Watsonville and Santa Cruz during his forty-year career with the company.

HENRY AND ALICE LEONG

Henry grew up in San Francisco, and as a young man in the early 1930s, he got a job as a chauffeur for Joe Shoong (founder of the National Dollar Stores) in Oakland. In August 1934 Henry went to work in the Oakland branch of the chain and learned the business from the ground up. Two years later Henry moved to Watsonville to manage the National Dollar Store branch there. The National Dollar Store was on South Main Street very near Charlie Chin Goon's Independent Market and Hoy Lew's California Market. Patronized by working-class Japanese, Chinese, Filipinos, Mexicans, and whites, the store undercut prices at Ford's Department Store and J. C. Penney's at the other end of Main Street.

Henry married Alice Chin, a girl with roots in the China Dryer era; her family was related to Charlie Chin Goon's, and she had grown up next to the Grove Street dryer and attended Watsonville High School. Alice's father had worked at Charlie Chin Goon's Independent Market just as Hoy Lew had. Henry Leong managed the Watsonville National Dollar Store for twenty-three years and remembers how important the store was for the Chinese community during the Depression: "The Dollar Stores were one of the few places that Chinese could find employment during those hard times." In 1959 Henry transferred to Santa Cruz where he managed the Santa Cruz National Dollar Store on Pacific Avenue; after brief service in branches in Hawaii and San Francisco, he returned to Santa Cruz in 1967, retiring from the company in 1974 after serving for forty years. Henry and Alice Leong now live in San Jose to be closer to their only son and his family.

## TRAILBLAZERS

Using the economic base provided by hard-working parents in restaurants, markets, and China Dryers, a group of America-born Chinese broke new ground and moved into fields and professions that had been closed to the first generation of Chinese pioneers. As Uncle Mun Tai said, timing had a lot to do with success on the Golden Mountain. Most of the America-born children in the Point Alones village met tremendous resistance because they were making demands a generation too early; young Tim Wong was one of the first casualties. A decade later Len Puk was able to leave the Point Alones village and eventually help found the Chinese American Citizen's Alliance, fighting for the rights of his community on a statewide and national level.

During the first half of the twentieth century, a series of young Chinese men and women born and raised in the Monterey Bay Region broke into the professions, making it easier for the generations of America-born Chinese that followed. Behind each of these young pioneers were parents, brothers, and sisters working long hours to support his or her education. The following biographies best exemplify what the Chinese family stood for in the Monterey Bay Region—pride, interdependence, love, and discipline.

The accomplishments of the children of T. S. Dong (Dong Teng Seng—Dong Heavenly Star) of Watsonville are legendary in California's Chinese community. In the 1890s, after operating a small market in Gonzales, China-born T. S. Dong established what is believed to be the first Chinese restaurant in Brooklyn, upstairs at #3 Brooklyn Street; Dong also operated a small mercantile store on the street level. In November 1899, secure and modestly successful, T. S. Dong married America-born Yook Gee (Jennie) from Marysville. In 1901 the first of eleven children was born. Emma Dong, one of the eleven, explains the large family quite simply: "Fertility, I guess—there was no family planning in those days; you accepted whoever came." Collin Dong, the second-born son, remembers the ever-present diapers drying on the back porch of the family home.

T. S. Dong built up his business until he was able to buy the

International Cafe, a restaurant at 101 Main Street in Watsonville (he put the property in the name of a son to evade the Alien Land Law), and the family moved from Brooklyn to Elm Street in Watsonville. All the children helped in the restaurant, but the first priority was their education; all graduated from Watsonville High School and most went on to college or university immediately following school graduation. The children of the Watsonville restaurateur broke new trails wherever they went.

In the traditional Chinese family, the education of daughters was put aside in deference to any sons in the family; if all the sons got an education, then, maybe, the daughters might be able to go on to college. But T. S. Dong wanted all of his children to receive an education, and when it came time for Emma to go to school, she was supported both by her parents and her older brothers. Valedictorian of her high school graduating class, Emma was elected to Phi Beta Kappa her junior year at the University of California, Berkeley, and graduated at the top of her class at the University of California Medical School. In medical school during the Depression, Emma lived with older brothers and sisters in the San Francisco Bay Area, and she feels she could not have made it through school without their assistance; her brothers often paid her tuition.

Three years following her graduation from medical school, Emma married Dr. Harry Chong. She studied for years to become an ophthalmologist and taught at the University of California Medical School for one year, until she and Harry began to look for a place to start a practice. Eventually they chose Salinas:

> When we first came to town we were wondering, are they going to accept a woman, a Chinese woman? We had a little reservation, but I had something no one else had and that was being a specialist in ophthalmology. My husband was an ear, nose, and throat specialist. Within six months we knew there was no problem. We were accepted as physicians with skills that were needed in the medical community . . . I think that there were areas earlier that we could not have lived in, but that was later broken down.

Emma and Harry were following the tradition set by the Point Alones fishermen—find an underutilized area and develop it. After thirty years of practice in Salinas, Emma and Harry have retired, leaving in their place a son, Byron, also a physician, to carry on the family practice.

Emma explains the ambition of the Dong children simply: "You do the best you are able to do. We had a tremendous respect for Dad and Mother who worked as hard as they could to put us kids through school." Several times, when her older brothers threatened to quit school and go to work to help support the family, T. S. Dong would discuss the situation with the children and then quote his guiding philosophy: "Heaven brought us here, and Heaven will take care of us." Whenever the Dong children would become discouraged in their educational careers, Collin would erect a simple sign: "Remember Dad and Mother."

As a rule, the China-born men who stayed in the region married late, often in their forties, to women sometimes twenty years younger. Again, the anti-Chinese legislation and hostility in California can be held responsible; it delayed the acquisition of the financial security necessary to raise a family. The children in such a family were sometimes fifty years younger than their father. As a result, many children were just reaching college age when their father entered old age, and almost every family relates a story in which an elder son interrupted his career or education to return and care for the family business, younger sisters and brothers, or their mother. Wally Lew, Elmer Shew, and Ernie Wong all came back to help the family when their families needed them. Walter Wong's father, Harry Yee Wong, died when Walter was in the eighth grade, and Walter began working part-time to help support his family.

California-born Harry Yee Wong was a restaurateur in Salinas, owning several different restaurants in Salinas over the years as well as a store on Soledad Street; the family (which eventually had seven children) lived at 10½ Soledad Street. The middle child in the family, Walter Wong, worked his way through high school (where he was active in student government), two years at Hartnell College, and pre-med studies at the University of California, Berkeley. His responsibilities to his mother and younger brothers and sisters were too great to permit going on to medical school, so Walter Wong went into the field of public health. He began his professional career as a sanitarian for Stanislaus County, California, but when his mother died in 1955, he had to return to Salinas to care for his younger brothers and sisters, eventually putting them all through college. Fortunately, Monterey County had an opening for a sanitarian, and in September 1955 Walter Wong began his career with the Monterey County Health Department. One of his duties over the years was to inspect Monterey County restaurants: "I think it is ironic that my father owned restaurants, I worked in them while going to school, and now I am inspecting them."

Walter rose steadily through the ranks of the Health Department until in 1971 he became the Director of the Environmental Health Department of Monterey County—he was the first person of Chinese ancestry to hold such a position in California. He has been President of the California Association of Environmental Health Administrators (also the first Chinese to hold that post) and President of the California Conference of Directors of Environmental Health. At this writing, Walter Wong is the most highly placed government employee of Chinese ancestry in the Monterey Bay Region.

Walter encountered discrimination and prejudice during his education and professional career, but it just made him more determined: "If you have to work hard or harder because you are Chinese, then you accept it and you do it." Occasionally being called "Charlie Chan" by disgruntled Monterey County citizens has not deterred Walter Wong, and in 1982 the Salinas Area Chamber of Commerce named him Member of the Year. Walter feels a strong commitment to public service and to the Salinas community: "I believe in giving something back to the community, but my first loyalty is to my family."

Jun Lee grew up in Santa Cruz's tiny Chinatown, listening to the "Cavalcade of America" on the radio and believing that he could someday be President of the United States. When Jun was twelve, his father (S. S. Lee) died, and with his older brothers and sisters, he helped support the family. While attending Mission Hill Junior High School and Santa Cruz High School, Jun Lee worked in the fields around Santa Cruz on weekends and delivered newspapers during the week. "My mother and the kids picked strawberries and blueberries, and older brother George helped with money he made working at the photography store." The family bought the least expensive chicken parts (wings and necks) from a nearby Italian poultry shop, grew their own vegetables, and each child got one new pair of Levis and a new shirt at the beginning of the school year. But they did not think of themselves as being poor: "Growing up in Santa Cruz as a minority and living in the ghetto seemed natural to us—nobody told us it was a ghetto."

Jun went to Lassen Junior College and graduated from San Jose State College with a degree in industrial design. A job in the Fremont City planning department eventually led him back to Santa Cruz County. Two years after Scotts Valley incorporated as Santa Cruz County's fourth city, Jun Lee was hired as Assistant to the City Administrator in 1968. One of only five city employees, Jun was not only the city's planner but also wore a number of different hats in the city government. Scotts Valley began to grow in the early 1970s and growth brought increasing interest in city politics; in the spring of 1975 a newly elected city council

Mrs. S. S. Lee (Gue Shee Lee) in Chinatown, Santa Cruz, c. 1940. Mrs. Lee is holding daughter Emily (Mrs. George Ow, Sr.), while son George stands beside her. The Lee family home is on the left of the photograph.
SPECIAL COLLECTIONS, UCSC

Jun Lee's campaign card, 1978. Re-elected to the Scotts Valley City Council, Jun Lee was eventually selected Mayor of Scotts Valley in 1980, the first Chinese-American mayor in the Monterey Bay Region.    JUN LEE

**RE-ELECT**
**Councilman**
**☒ JUN LEE**

The man who listens to you
and votes with the people
★★★
2 years on the City Council
Assistant City Administrator
& Planning Director for 8 years

decided to fire Jun Lee because of his identification with past planning decisions in the city. Jun refused to go quietly: "I reject the offer that I submit a voluntary resignation and disappear from local affairs." Jun sued the city council for what he believed to be a wrongful dismissal (the suit was later settled out of court). When one of the council members was recalled, Jun Lee ran for and was elected to the Scotts Valley City Council in March 1976.

"I went into politics to prove a point," says Jun Lee. Re-elected to a full term in 1978, Jun Lee served six and a half years on the Scotts Valley City Council. In 1980 Jun Lee was selected by his fellow council members to be Mayor of Scotts Valley, the first Mayor of Chinese ancestry in the Monterey Bay Region. "I did not think of myself as being Chinese," says Lee, "they were voting for me as a person; I could have been purple and they would have elected me." In 1982 Jun Lee decided not to seek re-election, and he retired from Scotts Valley politics. Jun Lee now does consulting work as a designer and planner in the Scotts Valley area, and he looks back with pride on his political career: "I am proud of what we accomplished both while I worked for the city of Scotts Valley and while I was on the city council." Those years when he worked in the fields and delivered newspapers to help support his family have stayed with him: "You know, I still feel guilty about taking a vacation."

Charlie Leong grew up in a Watsonville China Dryer family, and though he spent most of his fifty-year career as a professional journalist outside the Pajaro Valley, he never forgot his boyhood in Watsonville and never lost his love for the smell of drying apples. Charlie worked in the apple dryer after school and on weekends during the fall, and when he graduated from Watsonville High School in 1930, he was headed for a career as a pharmacist. He was something of a poet and writer, however, and while a student at San Jose State College ("the school for us poorer Chinese kids"), he became a journalism major, eventually becoming the first Chinese-American editor of a college newspaper in America—the *Spartan Daily*. He received his Master's degree in Journalism from Stanford University: "There were still barriers against Chinese in those days, so I figured I'd better fortify myself with something extra." His illustrious half-century career in journalism including writing for Chinese community newspapers, *The Stars and Stripes* while serving with the Flying Tigers during World War II, and all the major San Francisco newspapers. Charlie was the first Asian-American to join the San Francisco Press Club.

Throughout his career Charlie wrote about growing up in Watsonville, and in his weekly column in *Asian Week*, a San Francisco-based weekly newspaper, he often described his childhood years and the China Dryers:

> I am up and about shortly after six in the morning and I say 'Hello Ray' to the Filipino foreman of our apple drying plant. After the Chinese meal with the rest of the 50-person working crew it is the

484

Charlie Leong and James Lam, Santa Cruz, 1983. Charlie Leong, a pioneer Chinese-American journalist, returned to Santa Cruz in 1983 to visit the last China Dryer still in operation. James Lam, manager of the dryer, discusses the drying operation with Charlie. PHOTO TAKEN BY AUTHOR

morning duty to feed the chickens and greedy pigs. Then clean up and walk to the grammar school a mile away from our plant. This was a hard working routine, but that is the way life was for people in the early 1900s . . .

In November 1983 the San Francisco Press Club honored Charlie Leong for his pioneering efforts as a Chinese-American journalist and his half-century contribution to the profession of journalism. Charlie died in early 1984.

Sure, things were tough on the early Chinese immigrants, like my father, Lam Pon, but you must remember that compared with life in China, America was the land of opportunity, the Golden Mountain. America is still the land of opportunity.

George Ow, Sr.,
Scotts Valley, 1982.

# Conclusion

ONE OF THE OBJECTIVES of this book is to dispel the stereotypes that have followed the Chinese since their arrival in the region in the 1850s. The image of Chinese immigrants as contract laborers, saving their earnings and returning to China without leaving a trace, does not apply to the Chinese who came to the Monterey Bay Region. The first Chinese came directly from China by sea, founding Monterey's fishing industry; agricultural workers were not mere laborers but skilled and inventive farmers. The Point Alones village, with its families and children, testifies to the desire of many Chinese to remain in this country. It also suggests that many others would have brought their families had conditions allowed it; merchants, once they became financially secure, married and established families with alacrity.

The Chinese were often depicted as submissive, passive people who did not resist the legal and physical harassment they suffered at the hands of the white community, an even more damaging stereotype. The fierce determination of the Chinese to pursue their legal rights is amply proven by events in the region: the refusal of the railroad workers to enter the Summit Tunnel after devastating explosions; the fishermen's court battle with the Portuguese whalers who were cutting their nets; the efforts of an enraged Santa Cruz Chinese community to investigate the murder of Lou Sing in 1884; the negotiations by the Watsonville Chinese in 1888; and the occupation of Point Alones village after the 1906 fire.

The stereotype of Chinese immigrants in California as illiterate peasants has also been contradicted by the history of the Chinese in the Monterey Bay Region. From the sophisticated boat builders and fishermen at Monterey to the scholarly Chung Sun, the composition of the Chinese immigrant group more clearly represented a cross-section of Chinese culture and society. An equally untrue stereotype emphasized the mystic, exotic Oriental—honeycombs of tunnels beneath every Chinatown, mass graves, and secret rituals. Those who attributed esoteric philosophies to the "spiritual, philosophical" Chinese were contradicted by the facts. The philosophies which the Chinese brought with them to the Monterey Bay Region had much more to do with getting along in the everyday world, adapting and using every means possible to make a living.

We should also discard once and for all the sojourner stereotype when describing Chinese immigrants in California. Either that or attach the term to all other immigrant groups and speak of the sojourner Italians, the sojourner Greeks, the sojourner Irishmen, the sojourner Slavs, and so on. Had the Chinese met a less hostile reception in California, they would have metamorphosed naturally into permanent residents and citizens. The term *sojourner* implicitly defines Chinese immigrants as less loyal than other immigrants, less willing to make a commitment to the United States. It should never be forgotten that between 1790 and 1943, the Chinese were prohibited from becoming naturalized citizens of the United States. As a letter writer to the *Monterey Gazette* asked in 1867, "Would any of us make a permanent home here, if we should meet with as many discouragements as the poor Chinaman does?" The Chinese traditionally placed a high value on duty and commitment and demonstrated loyalty to their new country even in the face of crippling discrimination; the flag-waving Chinese parades of the 1890s exemplify this spirit.

## CHINATOWN AND VILLAGE SITES TODAY

Today little evidence remains of the region's once bustling Chinatowns and villages. In many cases, this is no mere accident but the result of cultural blinders; the Chinese, a race and culture distinct and isolated from the majority community, have been overlooked. At Point Lobos State Reserve, on the cove where the first Chinese village was located in the early 1850s, there is a single gray weatherworn house described as "Whaler's Cabin" on park maps. The cabin sits exactly where the Chinese village was located in the 1870s, and there is a good chance that before it

Santa Cruz market gardeners, 1940s. Many of the Chinese immigrants of the nineteenth century were not able to move into business or return to China, and their lives eventually ended in Chee Kong Tong buildings or county hospitals. They were the unfortunate victims of a seventy-year series of immigration and naturalization restrictions.

SPECIAL COLLECTIONS, UCSC

489

was occupied by Portuguese whalers, it was occupied by Chinese fishing families.

Across Carmel Bay from Point Lobos, the waters of Stillwater Cove still shimmer like crystal. Where Jung San Choy's house and garden once looked down on the beach, the tinted windows of the Pebble Beach Company's Beach and Tennis Club now overlook the cove. The only objects remaining from the days of the Pescadero Chinese fishing village are the grand cypress trees originally planted by the Chinese fishermen a century ago; the trees now shade the parking lot behind the Beach Club. Curiously, the point on which Jung San Choy's house was located has no official name. Most often referred to as the Seventeenth Green Point because of the famous golf green nestled there, the point is unnamed on the nautical charts, Monterey County Maps, the United States Geological Survey Maps, and the Pebble Beach Company maps. Perhaps now is the time to see to it that the pioneer Chinese fishermen on Carmel Bay receive some official recognition. Rather than name the point after the Chinese in the usual collective manner ("China Point" or "Chinese Point"), we should name it after the family whose presence was most associated with the point—Jung Point, to honor Jung San Choy.

At Point Alones the land upon which most of the largest Chinese fishing village rested is still vacant, a monument to the victory of the Chinese in their struggle with the Pacific Improvement Company in 1906–07. Stanford University's Hopkins Marine Station is located just to the west on Point Almejas (sometimes called China Point by local residents). A mushroom-shaped rock, often called "Monkey-Face" rock because it has the profile of a monkey's head, juts above the beach. The Point Alones village surrounded that rock, and many of the early photographs show buildings actually built around it. Burn marks can still be seen on parts of the rock, perhaps from that fateful May 1906 fire. In the only other reminder of the village, citizens of Pacific

Grove unwittingly pay homage to the Chinese squid fishermen in their annual Spring Lantern Festival.

The name "China Beach" is no longer in common usage to describe the cove where the Chinese fishermen lived just around the corner from Capitola in Santa Cruz County, and only one photograph has been found of the village. Today the site is near beach-front restrooms of New Brighton Beach State Park. At the south end of the parking lot a plaque commemorating the Chinese fishermen was erected by the Monterey Viejo Chapter of

Ah Fook, old fisherman, Santa Cruz, c. 1945. Ah Fook was a figure on the Santa Cruz Municipal Wharf for years. He lived alone in the Chee Kong Tong building in Chinatown, and to make spending money, he rewove the bottoms of cane chairs. GEORGE LEE

E Clampus Vitus in October 1984; this was the first plaque in the Monterey Bay Region dedicated to the memory of the Chinese pioneers. If you walk east down the beach from the restrooms in the summer or fall, you will notice clusters of pale yellow evening primroses on the bluff. Those are the primroses that framed the Chinese village.

With the exception of Chinatown Salinas in which two tong buildings and several of the older Chinatown buildings still stand, the sites of the region's Chinatowns are anonymous. Watsonville's Maple/Union Chinatown sports a hot dog stand and parking lot, Santa Cruz's Birkenseer Chinatown is now a shopping complex, and Monterey's Franklin/Washington Chinatown is now a parking garage. Castroville's Chinatown site is now a small subdivision.

Brooklyn (now known as Pajaro), once the home for hundreds of Chinese, has no residents of Chinese ancestry. John T. Porter's mansion still looms at the end of Brooklyn Street, but only three of the Chinese-occupied buildings survived the fire and subsequent subdivision in 1933. One of those buildings, though its characteristic balcony has been removed, still stands on Brooklyn Street. Originally the two-story school house built after the 1924 fire, #18 Brooklyn was sold by the Chinese in the 1940s. The Chinese Association reinvested the proceeds in another potential school site, a lot on the north side of Riverside Drive in Watsonville, but a third building was never constructed. Instead, in 1968 the Chinese Association built a public park on the Riverside Drive property.

## CONTRIBUTIONS

Like the sites of the Chinatowns, the monuments to the Chinese presence in the region are obscured, difficult to recognize, unknown to most of the residents. The Chinese comprised less than 7% of the population of the region in the nineteenth century and approximately 1% in the twentieth century. Even at their peak, Brooklyn and the Point Alones village never exceeded two hundred permanent residents. Yet this small group of people accomplished feats disproportionate to their numbers despite exclusion and discrimination.

Many of the Chinese who came to the United States in the nineteenth century were discouraged by the wall of racism and prejudice that met them when they landed; even thoughtful, patient Chung Sun returned to China rather than face the continual harassment. For those who stayed, the toll was extremely high; suicide, insanity, and "eccentricity" bear witness to the effects of restrictions and discrimination. For each Emma Dong, Lam Pon, or Walter Wong, many older men lived out their lonely lives in the Chee Kong Tong temples, died in county hospitals, and were buried in pauper's graves.

Despite all the obstacles, the list of industries the Chinese founded or to which they made major contributions is a long one—fishing, agriculture, reclamation, tourism, transportation, merchandising, the professions. The Chinese were an integral part of the region's development; in almost every case, it was necessary to develop the history of an industry (sugar beets, fishing, agriculture) in order to tell of the contributions of the Chinese. Like many other immigrants, the Chinese have been denied credit for contributions central to the development of the region. No official monuments have been erected to Chinese who pioneered the fishing industry, reclaimed "worthless" land and inspired diversification of crops, built the railroads which brought tourists and enabled local industry to flourish, or provided the labor essential to the sugar beet industry. The evidence of Chinese achievements can only be pieced together from scattered and often obscure clues.

Of all the nineteenth-century Chinese groups in the Monterey Bay Region, the railroad workers are the most difficult to document. Living in tent villages along the railroad tracks, they made little contact with local communities and moved on when the railroad was completed. Few jumped their crews to remain in the region. As a result, very little remains to remind us of these workers. When the rails of the Southern Pacific Railroad were removed from the upper Aptos Canyon, nature began to erase the railroading and logging scars, leaving virtually no traces. The name the loggers gave the ridge which separates Aptos Creek from Bridge Creek is all that remains—China Ridge, for the China Men who cut a railroad into a canyon which most considered impassable.

The railroad rails which still remain and the Wright's tunnel portal remind us of the enormous sacrifice made by the Chinese railroad workers. Buried in the hills, the bodies of those killed also give evidence of the dependable, loyal, and hard-working Chinese, long forgotten. At the Laurel Tunnel Portal, the tunnel face has been boarded up, and if you put your ear to the wood, you can hear the water dripping inside, echoing deep beneath the ridge. There is a monument here, but it is to Frederick Hihn, the man who developed the redwood lumber in the region, and the man who spearheaded the construction of many miles of railroad in Santa Cruz County. No official monument, no brass plaque commemorates the efforts of the thousands of Chinese who built the railroads. But the rails and tunnels themselves commemorate the Chinese. I like to imagine an aerial view from which the pattern of all those railroad rails can be read as a single Chinese character, written large across the Monterey Bay Region—China Man.

Forest Lake, in the middle of the Del Monte Forest, is now owned by the California-American Water Company, and is part of the water system serving the residents of Pebble Beach and

Pacific Grove. The reservoir has undergone little alteration over the years, and as Red Reynolds, engineer for the Pebble Beach Company, explained it, the weight of the horse and mule teams which drew the scrapers in 1888 compacted the earth as well or better than any modern equipment could today. Surrounded by a cyclone fence topped with barbed wire, the lake is off the beaten track, and except for a few people living in houses built above it, most residents and visitors to the Del Monte Forest do not even know the lake is there. Even fewer know of the Chinese laborers who made this project and many others a reality.

The Chinese also deserve their share of credit for the five-story sugar factory which Claus Spreckels built at Spreckels in 1898. From the first experiments by Benjamin Flint in 1870 to the early twentieth century, the Chinese beet contractors and laborers were the ball-bearings upon which the sugar beet industry rolled. In 1899, as the new sugar mill was being readied for its first season, a crew of middle-aged Chinese beet workers cultivated five hundred acres of beet land adjacent to the factory. There, in the shadow of the world's largest and most advanced sugar beet mill, the Chinese turned the earth with an old-fashioned wooden plow. Beaten by immigration laws and restrictions, the Chinese passed the burden of working in the beets to younger Japanese farm laborers. In 1982, after eighty-three years of uninterrupted operation, the Spreckels plant suspended operations. Now quiet, the building stands as a monument not only to the vision and energy of Claus Spreckels, but to the sweat and blood of thousands of Chinese beet workers who made Spreckels' dreams a reality.

In a region once populated by China Dryers, only the Santa Cruz Fruit Company dryer—begun by Otto Lam early in this century and run by his family until 1983—remains. Adjacent to Highway 1 between Santa Cruz and Soquel, the beige building has two ventilators with huge propellors, the modern indication that it is a two-kiln or two-chimney dryer. The Santa Cruz Fruit Company is the last evidence of the resourceful Chinese apple dryers.

## THE LAST OF THE OLD TRADITIONS

Today two descendants of early Chinese pioneers have carried on the traditional work of their forebears, living reminders of a proud heritage. Mrs. Margaret Lam, the last practitioner of Chinese-style fish drying in the Monterey Bay Region, stopped drying fish in 1976. Margaret was born and raised in the Franklin/Washington Street Chinatown of Monterey. One of eleven children in the Haw family (the name eventually evolved to Hall), Margaret learned the art of fish drying from her mother. The two secrets which her mother imparted were the ability to feel the fish and tell when they were dry, and a recipe for soaking the fish to keep the flies from landing on them while they were drying. In the small town of Seaside, just east of Monterey, Margaret established a fish-drying business in the 1950s.

Margaret concentrated on drying Petrale sole which she bought from Sicilian fishermen in Monterey. Margaret cleaned the fish and soaked them in her secret solution before hanging them on hooks to dry in the sun. Margaret Lam's dried fish became famous in Chinese communities all over the United States; she often air-freighted crates of her popular fish to Hawaii and New York. Seaside was an unincorporated town when Margaret began drying her fish in the 1950s, but the town grew steadily and houses were built all around her home. Following incorporation, the City of Seaside's Health Department put increasing pressure on Margaret to close down; health inspectors were frequent visitors to her fish-drying operation. Finally, rather than make the adjustment that Won Yee had made a half-century earlier and take her fish-drying racks out of town, Margaret chose to retire, and the Chinese fish-drying tradition in the Monterey Bay Region came to an end.

When you realize how many Chinese farmers have been winnowed out over the years, Sam Chinn's physical presence does not surprise—he is a strong man. You first notice the twinkle of humor in his eyes, then the direct, forceful voice, and then, beneath the workshirt, the shoulders and arms toned by decades of hard work. Sam Chinn and his son Ronald are the last Chinese farmers in the Salinas Valley, and the history of Chinn Farms demonstrates those Chinese traits which appeared so often in the historical record—tenacity and ingenuity.

Sam Chinn was born in Castroville in the early 1920s. His father had come to the United States in 1905, surviving in the ship's hold for almost a month on a box of crackers. He came on someone else's papers and went by the name of Jim Toy. Jim Toy came to the Salinas Valley because his grandfather before him had worked in Salinas as a gambler before returning to China. In 1916 Jim Toy sent for his wife (she also came in on false papers), leaving behind a young daughter to be raised by the family in China. Jim Toy was a farmer, and he entered into reclamation leases with landowners who still did not know the value of the "willow land" they had. Eventually Jim Toy had moderate success growing potatoes, sugar beets, and beans. As a young man Sam Chinn drove a six-horse team which hauled sugar beets to the railroad dump near Castroville for shipment to Spreckels' sugar beet factory south of Salinas. Sam was the only child born to Jim Toy in America, and he did not meet his sister until a trip to China several years ago. "It was uncanny," Sam said. "I picked her out of the crowd at the airport in Hong Kong easily—she looks just like my mother."

When Sam Chinn was fourteen, he lost his left hand in an auto accident, and a high school counselor convinced him to forget about farming as a career and concentrate on commercial/

business training. Sam took a job in a bank after graduation. In the middle of the Depression, Sam Chinn quit his job at the bank: "The job had no challenge—anyone can push a pencil with one hand." In spite of the counsel he received from all sides ("how can a man with one hand be a farmer?"), he got a job digging ditches, clearing land for a landowner just as his father and all those Chinese pioneers before him had done. While a ditch digger he studied farming and impressed those he worked for with his drive and tenacity. As a United States citizen, Sam Chinn did not face all the legal obstacles that his father, uncles, and their forebears had, and he evolved from ditch digger to sharecropper to farmer.

In 1941 Sam Chinn bought sixty acres of that worthless willow land and began to farm on his own. He learned quickly that he could not compete with the larger lettuce growers, so he developed peripheral specialty crops in which the large farmers had no interest. He pushed back the willows and reclaimed the rich, black peat soil which is so much like a sponge it retains an even moisture content, providing excellent conditions for his crops, particularly carrots and cardone. Today he grows parsley, table beets, broccoli, anise, cardone, and carrots. Sam Chinn found Chinese Gold in his carrots—he has grown carrots for Gerber's Baby Food for almost forty years, and his carrots have the highest quality and highest sugar content of any carrots that Gerber's buys.

An Italian from Castroville first urged Sam to grow cardone (an Italian spice), and he planted five acres of it, "though I didn't know what the hell it was." His cardone sold so well that he expanded the acreage and began shipping it all over the United States; a bus-load of Italian tourists from New Jersey made a special trip to Salinas to see Sam Chinn's farm and the source of all that wonderful cardone. "Cardone is Italian soul food," says Sam with a smile. It is also a winter crop, providing income at a time when most farmers are forced to let their land lie fallow.

Sam Chinn on his carrot machine, Salinas, 1983. Sam Chinn has been reclaiming farm land since his boyhood in Castroville. Retired from active farming, Sam Chinn is Secretary-Treasurer of the National Association of Conservation Districts and an advisor to the United States Secretary of Agriculture. SHMUEL THALER

Sam knows and appreciates the contributions of the Chinese pioneers who came into the Salinas Valley and drained the swamps to farm the rich, black soil beneath. But he is somewhat bitter about the meager resources with which the second- and third-generation of Chinese in the valley had to work. With no capital or land base to work from, each farmer worked from scratch. Sam wishes that his uncles and their peers had not given up and returned to China, but he understands the pressures that drove them back. Sam also speaks with fondness about the nineteenth-century Chinese pioneers who used paddle wheels and flumes to irrigate land in the Salinas Valley. Over the years Sam has become a missionary, preaching the value of reclamation and soil conservation.

Today Sam Chinn is Secretary-Treasurer of the National Association of Conservation Districts and has been an advisor to the Secretary of Agriculture under many different administrations. He makes frequent trips to Washington to testify before Congressional panels writing legislation affecting American farmers. ("They don't know very much about real farming in Washington.") Sam also arranges tours for visiting dignitaries so that they might better understand the realities of Salinas Valley agriculture.

Sam is a living reminder of the Chinese contribution to the Monterey Bay Region, particularly in terms of hard work and ingenuity. Faced with a strike by his carrot pickers in the early 1950s, Sam went into his barn and began building a machine that would pull, clean, and pack his carrots, and over the years, by trial and error, Sam has built just such a machine. "I have the Chinese trait of pondering," he says, "I just pondered about the problem a lot and eventually solved it." The machine works extremely well but has been difficult to duplicate—agricultural engineers from all over the world have come to Salinas to measure and photograph the machine, but have been unable to make a replica of it that will work. Something spiritual? "Nah," says Sam, "it's just that most of the engineers don't know very much about real farming." Sam Chinn's carrot machine stacks up with Won Yee's dried-squid cleaner and baler as monuments to the fine art of Chinese pondering. Like his predecessors, Sam has worked the edges. He hands me a carrot with lumps of thick, black soil still stuck to it: "Break it open," he says proudly. When I do, I can see no discernible core, only pure golden carrot. Chinese gold.

## CHINESE IN THE REGION TODAY

In 1980, after a long slow climb from the low of 759 in 1910, the Chinese population in the Monterey Bay Region finally equalled its nineteenth-century high of 2,400. (see Appendix pp. 505) However, the total population of the region has increased over tenfold, from 37,907 in 1890 to 478,585 in 1980. The percentage of Chinese in the region's population has declined from a high of 6.5% in 1890 to .5% in 1980. The San Francisco Bay Area continues to act as a magnet for people of Chinese ancestry, and whether they are second- and third-generation America-born Chinese or recent immigrants from Hong Kong, Taiwan, or the People's Republic of China, the number of opportunities in and around San Francisco is greater. China-born cooks working in Santa Cruz often insist on a weekly trip to San Francisco as a condition of their employment, so they may touch base with their fellow Chinese in Chinatown, San Francisco.

One of the primary purposes of this study was to determine if there was ever a regional Chinese community in the region, and whether or not it continues to exist. During the 1890s the Ring Games held at the Point Alones village were the focus of a regional Chinese community, but once immigration laws, fires, and changing economic patterns dispersed the region's Chinatowns, the Chinese no longer had any institutions to connect the region's communities. As the community dispersed, tenuous contacts were maintained through marriages between families from each of the Chinese communities. Marriages, birthday celebrations, and family reunions kept the few Chinese families

Chin Lai and his nephew, George Ow, Jr., January 1947. Chin Lai had been a logging camp cook for many years in the San Lorenzo Valley, and was eighty-one when this photograph was taken. He later died in poverty. George Ow, Jr., son of the King's Market developer, went on to college and a degree in business, returning to help manage his father's many businesses. Photo was taken to commemorate the lunar New Year.

SPECIAL COLLECTIONS, UCSC

living in the region in contact with each other. Among the older Chinese who grew up in the region, there is still a village tied together by telephone and family celebrations. Chinese publications from San Francisco also disseminate news from one part of the area to the entire region; Chinese in Salinas can read of their Monterey neighbors in the columns of newspapers such as *Asian Week* and *East/West*.

Today Salinas has the most organized Chinese community, with an active chapter of the Chinese American Citizen's Alliance (C.A.C.A.) and a Chinese school operating in the Confucius Church on Pajaro Street. Membership in the C.A.C.A. has remained stable, and it appears that the organization will continue to provide a focus for the Chinese in Salinas.

After the Chinese Exclusion Law was repealed in 1943, new Chinese immigrants began entering the region. It is now possible to define two groups within the total Chinese population—those whose forebears immigrated before World War II and those who came since Exclusion was repealed; the earlier group seems to be much more cohesive than the latter. This tendency to separate "newcomers" and "old-timers" was best demonstrated when the Watsonville Chinese community organized a reunion in May 1982; invitations were sent primarily to those whose families had lived in Watsonville or Brooklyn before 1940.

## CHINESE GOLD

The Chinese called America the Golden Mountain, and images of gold fueled their desire to emigrate to the United States. There was very little actual gold to mine in the Monterey Bay Region, but that did not deter the Chinese, for they could see value where others could not. Today we would call the process appropriate technology or recycling, and we would label them as ecologists; in the nineteenth century they were dismissed as "heathen Chinee." Perhaps the greatest contribution the Chinese made to the Monterey Bay Region was the gift of vision—the ability to see the potential value in the most mundane creatures, crops, and discarded items. The Chinese worked the edges, taking fish heads, mustard, sea urchins, culled apples, and willow swamps and elevating them from the status of waste products to healthy peripheral industries. More often than not, bemused white observers usually followed suit and copied what the Chinese did, whether in squid drying, the mustard harvest, or sardine reduction. Through their particular form of alchemy (insight plus ingenuity plus energy), the Chinese turned what they found into gold, to the lasting benefit of the Monterey Bay Region.

# Appendix

## CHINESE IN THE MONTEREY BAY REGION BY COUNTY

| Year | Monterey County Total Pop. | Chinese | San Benito County Total Pop. | Chinese | Santa Cruz County Total Pop. | Chinese |
|---|---|---|---|---|---|---|
| 1850 | 1,872 | 0 | (San Benito County | | 643 | 1 |
| 1860 | 4,739 | 23 | formed in 1874) | | 4,944 | 6 |
| 1870 | 9,876 | 230 | | | 8,743 | 156 |
| 1880 | 11,302 | 372 | 5,584 | 242 | 12,802 | 523 |
| 1890 | 18,637 | 1,667 | 6,412 | 85 | 19,270 | 785 |
| 1900 | 19,380 | 857 | 6,633 | 69 | 21,512 | 614 |
| 1910 | 24,146 | 575 | 8,041 | 66 | 26,140 | 184 |
| 1920 | 27,980 | 748 | 8,995 | 104 | 26,269 | 215 |
| 1930 | 42,646 | 613 | 11,311 | 9 | 37,433 | 238 |
| 1940 | 73,032 | 589 | 11,392 | 9 | 45,057 | 363 |
| 1950 | 130,498 | 713 | 14,370 | 33 | 66,534 | 384 |
| 1960 | 198,351 | 1,080 | 15,396 | 71 | 84,219 | 402 |
| 1970 | 250,071 | 1,345 | 18,226 | 34 | 123,790 | 607 |
| 1980 | 290,444 | 1,590 | 25,005 | 33 | 188,141 | 830 |

Source: US Bureau of the Census, annual reports and manuscript census.

# Notes

Notes are listed by first words of a direct quotation or by subject. References in each note are abbreviations of sources. To find complete sources, check alphabetical list of references which follows these notes.

## INTRODUCTION pp. 1–9

"Original Spanish subjects": *Watsonville Register-Pajaronian*, August 10, 1982.

Subscription histories: *Santa Cruz County*; Elliott and Moore, *Monterey County*.

E. S. Harrison: Harrison, *Santa Cruz County*; Harrison, *History of Santa Cruz County*. See also Francis, *Santa Cruz County*.

A new generation of local and regional histories: Fisher, *Salinas*; Fink, *Monterey*; Koch, *Santa Cruz County*; Lewis, *Watsonville*.

Academic papers and limited-edition books: Breschini and Hampson, "Reconnaissance of Hopkins Marine Station"; Catbagan, "Chinatown"; Elstob, *Old Cannery Row*; Elliott, "Chinatown"; Roop, "Hopkins Marine Laboratory"; Woolfenden, "Chinese Village."

All but 7 of the 5,000 voters: Supervisors' Minutes, Santa Cruz County, Vol. 4, 52; *Index*, September 11, 1879.

## CHAPTER 1. THE FIRST IMMIGRANTS pp. 13–16

The Kuroshiro, or Black Tide: Needham, *Science*, Vol. 4, Part 3, 548–51.

"A mountain of evidence": Needham, *Science*, Vol. 4, Part 3, 545.

"There is said to be an authentic record": Chapman, *California*, 23.

"He saw a strange wreck": Ibid.

Alex Early began giving guided tours: Card, "Point Lobos," 6–7. Naturalists now believe the Monterey Cypress to be indigenous.

Fusang: Steiner, *Fusang*; also, for a more impassioned argument, see Mertz, *Pale Ink*.

## SPANISH RULE IN THE PACIFIC pp. 16–20

The Manila galleon: Schurz, *The Manila Galleon*.

"We found ourselves to be in the best port": Bolton, *Spanish Explorations*, 91–92.

Antonio Rodriquez: Steiner, *Fusang*, 80.

First documented Chinese resident: Chinn, Lai, and Choy, *Syllabus*, 41; Otto, "Old Santa Cruz," June 8, 1949 (hereafter referred to as Otto); Woolfenden, "Chinese Village."

"Arroyo del Chino": Leonard, letter.

Sanquie: Manuscript census, 1850, Santa Cruz and Monterey Counties.

CHAPTER 2. FISHING pp. 29–31

In a 1967 interview: Chen, *Chinese*, 22.

"She was born at Point Lobos": Hoang, interview.

Munson Kwok, another Monterey descendant: Kwok, letter.

The boat people: Gray, *China*, Vol. 2, 282–83; Osgood, *The Chinese*, Vol. 3, 973; Ward, "Hong Kong Fishing Village," 195–214.

"Boat people": Otto, March 27, 1955.

*THE ABALONE RUSH* pp. 31–35

"It is safer to live on the seashore": M. Lam, interview.

Periodically harvest abalone for their shells: Gordon, *Monterey Bay Area*, 23–29; 53–55.

*Aulon: Pacific Sentinel*, Nov. 15, 1856.

"Corruption of the Spanish '*orejones*'": Fish Commission, 1883, 425.

Otter hunters set the stage: Webster, interview.

"Five or six hundred": *Daily Alta California*, May 20, 1853.

Working in the rocks near Point Sur: J. B. R. Cooper to T. O. Larkin, June 22, 1856, *Larkin Papers*, Vol. 10, 283.

"Cleaned nearly all": *Pacific Sentinel*, Nov. 15, 1856.

Abalone supply was exhausted: *Sentinel*, Feb. 10, 1866.

"In a decade or two more": *Index*, Nov. 6, 1890.

Complaints were exaggerated: Armentrout-Ma, "Chinese in Fishing," 142–46.

Abalone hunters took some risks: *New Era*, Oct. 3, 1900.

"With singular improvidence": *Sentinel*, Aug. 23, 1859.

Mother-of-pearl cabinet inlays: *Pajaro Times*, Jan. 28, 1865.

Price rose to $50 per ton: *Weekly Herald*, Aug. 11, 1874; Nov. 17, 1874.

Continued to ship shells to France: *Weekly Herald*, May 22, 1875; Nov. 27, 1875.

$100 per ton in 1888: Fish Commission, 1888, 23.

Japanese shipped one and a half tons: Edwards, "Abalone Industry," 11.

*DIVERSIFICATION* pp. 36–40

"Everything from a shark to a shiner": *Gazette*, Jan. 15, 1864.

Shipped three hundred tons of dried fish by steamer: *Gazette*, Aug. 17, 1866; March 2, 1867.

"Platforms covered with the fish": *Democrat* (Monterey), July 20, 1872.

"A visit to Chinatown": *Weekly Herald*, Aug. 15, 1874.

Genitals of sea lions: Choy, interview.

Dead whale washed ashore: *Weekly Herald*, Oct. 31, 1874.

"They ship the sinew to China": *Democrat* (Monterey), April 6, 1872.

Dried kelp: Spangenberg, "Long Road," 38; Chinn, Lai, and Choy, *Syllabus*, 41; H. Lew, interview; Jung, interview; Yee and Yee, interview.

Sea urchins were eaten raw: M. Lam, interview.

*CHINESE BOATS AND FISHING PRACTICES* pp. 41–45

Chinese boats not built to standard specifications: Needham, *Science*, Vol. 4, Part 5, 396–406.

"The redwood board": Armentrout-Ma, *Sampans*, 7.

Total of thirty boats between them: *Weekly Herald*, May 22, 1875.

Visions of a hold full of opium: *Cypress*, April 6, 1889.

"Broad, flat and clumsy": Jordan, *Fisheries*, 603.

"Odd-shaped and lumbersome-looking": *Weekly Herald*, July 3, 1875.

Set lines, trawl lines and gill nets: Jordan, *Fisheries*, 604.

"The gill-nets are placed": Goode and Collins, "Fishermen," 40.

## COMPETITION FOR THE FISHING GROUNDS pp. 45–48

Small company of Italian fishermen arrived in Monterey: *Weekly Herald*, Oct. 17, 1874.

The fall of 1875, a second Italian company: *Weekly Herald*, Oct. 2, 1875; Oct. 16, 1875.

"The Italian Fishing Companies": *Index*, Nov. 23, 1876.

"As a rule the Latin fishermen": Jordan, "Fisheries," 477–78.

An informal census published in 1875: *Weekly Herald*, May 22, 1875.

"Almost entirely outside the bay": *Weekly Herald*, Nov. 6, 1875.

The arrangement was set: *Weekly Index*, Nov. 23, 1876.

## FISHING ON THE NORTH SIDE OF MONTEREY BAY pp. 48–53

Fishing for mackerel off Soquel: *Sentinel*, Sept. 6, 1862.

177,000 pounds of Chinese-caught fresh fish: Jordan, "Fisheries," 606.

They rigged davits to the wharf: Goode and Collins, "Fishermen," 30.

The 1880 manuscript census: Manuscript census, 1880, Santa Cruz County.

"The houses were about six feet above ground": Otto, March 27, 1955.

"The catches included smelt": Otto, Jan. 21, 1953.

In 1877 nine Chinese were arrested: *Weekly Courier*, March 16, 1877.

Blocked no more than one-third: *Sentinel*, Jan. 4, 1879.

Fresh shad ten inches long: *Sentinel*, June 28, 1879.

Santa Cruz County sheriff arrested three Chinese:

*Sentinel*, May 22, 1880; *Pajaronian*, May 17, 1880; June 17, 1880.

Camp San Jose opened: *Sentinel*, May 25, 1878.

Last fishing camp at Camp Goodall: *Pajaronian*, July 21, 1887.

No Chinese fishermen remained in Santa Cruz County: Collins, "Fisheries," 63–66.

## SQUID FISHING pp. 54–59

Portuguese whalers cut the nets of Chinese fishermen: *Monterey Californian*, March 27, 1880; *Sentinel*, April 3, 1880.

Squid would eventually swim to the surface: Gray, *China*, Vol. 2, 292–94.

Organized into three boat teams: Collins, "Fisheries," 60.

"Hovering just beneath the surface": *Argus*, May 1, 1886.

In the 1888 squid season, shipped 230,000 pounds: Collins, "Fisheries," 63.

Chinese actually purchasing salt: Hoang, interview; H. Lew, interview; Yee and Yee, interview; M. Lam, interview.

"Abominable stench": *New Era*, May 26, 1892.

"The lights of eleven Chinese boats": *Salinas Democrat*, May 28, 1892.

The first Lantern Festival: *Review*, July 21, 1905.

"Resembles a bit our Chinatown": *Review*, July 28, 1905.

## CHAPTER 3. AGRICULTURE pp. 61–63

In 1832 the missions San Antonio, Soledad, etc: Johnson, *Missions*, 316.

"Ranching is the principal interest": Manuscript census, 1850, Monterey and Santa Cruz Counties.

In 1881 King Wheat reigned: Hittell, *Commerce*, 279.

## THE FIRST CHINESE FARM LABORERS IN THE REGION—SUMMER, 1866 pp. 63–65

Beleaguered farmers in the Monterey Bay Region: *Pajaro Times*, July 28, 1866; *Gazette*, Aug. 24, 1866.

"They [Chinese] make excellent hands": *Pajaronian*, July 15, 1869.

They were willing to extend credit to the farmers: *Pajaronian*, July 15, 1869.

Census counted 120 Chinese farm laborers: Manuscript census, 1870, Monterey and Santa Cruz Counties.

"Crops are excellent, freights low": *Pajaronian*, Oct. 9, 1873.

## TOBACCO AND HOPS pp. 65–67

A small cigar and chewing tobacco factory: *Sentinel*, Feb. 13, 1864.

Culp built a huge three-story cigar factory: *Pajaronian*, Jan. 30, 1873; July 15, 1875.

Huge cigar factory on San Felipe Road: Manuscript census, 1880, San Benito County.

Virulent lobbying against Chinese-made cigars: Bauer, "Crops that Failed," 48; Chinn, Lai, and Choy, *Syllabus*, 49.

Attempts were made to grow hops near Natividad: *Democrat* (Salinas), Sept. 10, 1879.

"Four of whom are busily engaged": *Sentinel*, May 28, 1870.

Smith's small hop yard: *Pajaronian*, Oct. 5, 1871.

Owen Tuttle employed Chinese: *Pajaronian*, Sept. 27, 1877.

James Tynan's widow Margaret entered into a typical lease: Lease Book, Santa Cruz County, Vol. 3, March 30, 1895, 368.

Hop acreage steadily declined: *Pajaronian*, May 30, 1933.

## MUSTARD—CHINESE GOLD pp. 67–70

"The most sublime scene": Shumate, *Boyhood Days*, 65–66.

"Poison Jim": Treleaven, "Poison Jim," 40–45.

Dodge and Millard employed twenty Chinese: *Sentinel*, Oct. 21, 1865.

Upwards of 400,000 pounds of mustard seed: *Index*, Sept. 28, 1876; Sept. 16, 1880.

"The yellow mustard fields": *Chronicle*, Dec. 25, 1882.

"Yellow mustard on David Jacks' ranch": *Index*, Aug. 11, 1887.

Monterey County Assessor often listed mustard: Assessor's Rolls, Monterey County, 1890, 255; 1894, Book #3, 315; 1895, Book #2, 181.

"A prosperous San Juan Mongolian": *Pajaronian*, Jan. 4, 1900.

## THE BEET SUGAR INDUSTRY pp. 70–75

The California Beet Sugar Company: McGinnis, *Beet-Sugar*, 7–8.

Flint distributed sugar beet seed: *Democrat* (Monterey), Aug. 12, 1871.

The soil around Alvarado unsuitable for beets: *Sentinel*, Nov. 28, 1874.

Factory moved from Alvarado to Soquel: *Sentinel*, March 12, 1874; April 11, 1874; June 11, 1874.

"Here we are in the field": *Sentinel*, Nov. 28, 1874.

"One can scarcely help but be surprised": *Index*, Nov. 15, 1877.

Contract between Ah Dong and John T. Porter: Porter manuscripts, May, 1879.

"Quite a source of revenue": *Index*, Nov. 15, 1877.

This three-level system: *Sentinel*, May 6, 1875; Sept. 16, 1876; Oct. 14, 1876; *Pajaronian*, May 6, 1875; June 1, 1876; *Index*, Sept. 27, 1877.

"Persist in employing a good many heathen": *Sentinel*, Oct. 14, 1876.

"Was of such a nature that only Chinamen could be obtained": *Pajaronian*, June 20, 1878.

The company was unable to pay: Porter manuscripts, Box 2, Feb. 7, 1880; F. A. Hihn to J. T. Porter, Feb. 16, 1880.

Factory buildings and equipment were sold: Porter manuscripts, agreement, 1879; *Sentinel*, Dec. 4, 1880.

### STRAWBERRIES pp. 75–77

The first sizable and successful: Wilhelm and Sagen, *Strawberry*, 175–76.

300 Chinese were working in strawberry: *Pajaronian*, April 22, 1886.

A number of Pajaro Valley farmers enter into leases: *Pajaronian*, April 8, 1886.

"The method of conducting this farm": Harrison, *History of Santa Cruz County*, 30.

In the Struve and Hansen sloughs: *Pajaronian*, May 7, 1891.

"Wherever Chinamen have cleared land": *Pajaronian*, March 24, 1892.

"Acreage in orchards is increasing every year": *Index*, Aug. 7, 1890.

### CHAPTER 4. RAILROADS pp. 79–82

The Central Pacific released an estimated five thousand: Chiu, *Chinese Labor*, 49.

A railroad south from San Francisco to San Jose: Ibid., 42.

The M&SRR: *Gazette*, June 30, 1869; *Democrat* (Monterey), Sept. 2, 1869.

The first line went south from Gilroy: Hamman, *Central Coast Railways*, 25.

A sketchy picture of over five hundred Chinese: *Pajaronian*, May 13, 1871; *Democrat* (Monterey), Sept. 2, 1871.

### THE MONTEREY AND SALINAS VALLEY RAILROAD pp. 82–87

Encouraged by Salinas Valley farmers: *Index*, Sept. 15, 1898; see also Jacks Collection.

Surveyors moved across the Salinas Valley: *Index*, April 2, 1874; April 23, 1874.

Leland Stanford came to Salinas: *Index*, April 30, 1874.

The first Chinese railroad workers: *Index*, May 7, 1874.

Few white workers came forward: *Weekly Herald*, June 13, 1874.

Farmers took back their horses: *Weekly Herald*, June 6, 1874; June 27, 1874; July 4, 1874.

The Salinas River was the second obstacle: *Weekly Herald*, July 25, 1874; Aug. 1, 1874; Aug. 8, 1874; Aug. 22, 1874; Sept. 12, 1874.

The M&SVRR completed: *Weekly Herald*, Oct. 10, 1874.

"Monterey County has solved the problem": *Weekly Herald*, Dec. 5, 1874.

Forced Southern Pacific to drop its rates: *Index*, Nov. 23, 1876.

*H. L. Richardson* came alongside: *Weekly Herald*, Oct. 10, 1874.

Railroad was unable to make the payments: *Index*, Oct. 31, 1878; *Monterey Californian*, Dec. 24, 1878.

Southern Pacific Railroad paid final respects: *Monterey Californian*, Sept. 30, 1879; *Index*, Sept. 4, 1879; Nov. 13, 1879; P. I. Co. Files, JL 1, Box #1, ledger entry, Aug. 23, 1879.

### THE SANTA CRUZ AND FELTON RAILROAD pp. 87–90

The Santa Cruz and Felton Railroad was incorporated: MacGregor and Truesdale, *Centennial*, 248–49; Hamman, *Central Coast Railways*, 83–85.

"Not a single Mongolian": *Weekly Courier*, Oct. 6, 1876.

*THE SANTA CRUZ RAILROAD* pp. 90–92

"The village is empty during the day": *Sentinel*, July 3, 1875.
Lotteries sent salesmen: *Sentinel*, Nov. 13, 1875.
Brakes failed on the construction train: *Sentinel*, April 15, 1876.
Railroad cut fell: *Sentinel*, May 6, 1876.
Most melancholy accident: *Sentinel*, Jan. 15, 1876; Jan. 22, 1876; Jan. 29, 1876.

*THE SOUTH PACIFIC COAST RAILROAD* pp. 92–101

James Fair not awed by the challenges: MacGregor and Truesdale, *Centennial*, 7–13.
SPCRR employed 700 men: *Sentinel*, Nov. 10, 1877.
Approximately one thousand Chinese: *Sentinel*, Jan. 25, 1879.
Paid the crews' wages directly to the Ning Yeung Company: *Sentinel*, Aug. 31, 1878.
Chinese tunnel workers were lured back: *Sentinel*, Dec. 20, 1879.
"Possessed of retentive memories": *Sentinel*, Jan. 10, 1880.
"With Chinamen to the right of him": *Sentinel*, July 13, 1878.
Wrights tunnel was begun in December: *Sentinel*, Dec. 8, 1877.
"Besides the tunnel's portal": "County Scrapbook," 7.
"O. B. Castle carried one [Chinese]": *Sentinel*, Feb. 15, 1879.
A San Jose doctor got to the tunnel: *Sentinel*, Feb. 15, 1879; Feb. 22, 1879; March 1, 1879.
The company installed pipes: *Sentinel*, March 1, 1879.
Chinese fired for "being lazy": *Sentinel*, March 1, 1879.
"Utterly failed": *Sentinel*, March 8, 1879; April 26, 1879; May 24, 1879.
"A shower of picks and drills": *Sentinel*, June 7, 1879.

The night of November 17, 1879: *Sentinel*, Nov. 22, 1879.
"The stench of burning flesh": Ibid.
Bodies buried on a flat: *Santa Cruz News*, Oct. 31, 1936.
Wounded were taken to Chinatown: *Sentinel*, Nov. 22, 1879; Nov. 29, 1879.
"The devils they asserted were in the tunnel": *Sentinel*, Jan. 17, 1880.
The Chinese won easily: *Sentinel*, Feb. 7, 1880; March 20, 1880.
An excursion train derailed: *Sentinel*, May 29, 1880; MacGregor and Truesdale, *Centennial*, 286.
Buried a camp of Chinese: *Sentinel*, Feb. 5, 1881; Feb. 19, 1881; March 5, 1881.

*THE SOUTHERN PACIFIC TAKES OVER* pp. 101–8

Southern Pacific bought M&SVRR: Jacks Collection, Box #3, C. Crocker to D. Jacks, Sept. 16, 1879.
Crews tore up the narrow-gauge tracks: *Index*, Jan. 8, 1880.
"Not a vestige of this bridge": *Monterey Californian*, April 24, 1880.
"Poorest [Stanford] ever made": *Sentinel*, March 20, 1880.
San Lorenzo River trestle knocked down: Hamman, *Central Coast Railways*, 30.
Chinese broad-gauge the line: *Sentinel*, Oct. 6, 1883; Oct. 20, 1883.
Branch into Aptos Canyon: Sentinel, June 16, 1883.
Paymaster "made himself scarce": *Sentinel*, Aug. 4, 1883.
Railroad extended up the canyon: Hamman, *Central Coast Railways*, 39–57.
SPCRR fell to the Southern Pacific: MacGregor and Truesdale, *Centennial*, 307–8; Hamman, *Central Coast Railways*, 100–102.

"Six miles out of Soledad": *Index*, May 20, 1886.

Carmel Valley coal mine: *Monterey Californian*, March 28, 1878; Nov. 28, 1878; Jan. 2, 1879; Feb. 11, 1879.

Line would be extended to Carmel Valley: *Index*, Feb. 26, 1888.

"Mongolians busy as bees": *Cypress*, May 18, 1889.

Moved the cemetery: *Cypress*, May 11, 1889.

Sand brought $2.50 per cubic yard: *Index*, July 25, 1889.

### THE PAJARO VALLEY CONSOLIDATED RAILROAD pp. 108–11

Line extended to Moss Landing: *Index*, Aug. 28, 1890.

Extended to Salinas: *Pajaronian*, Sept. 24, 1891.

It turned a profit: *Pajaronian*, Oct. 3, 1895.

### CHAPTER 5. THE ANTI-CHINESE MOVEMENT pp. 115–17

"If the grants were just cut up": *Pacific Sentinel*, Nov. 29, 1856.

Clash between Protestant and Catholic values: For the best discussion of this conflict, see Pitt, *Decline*.

### ANTI-CHINESE LEGISLATION pp. 117–19

A cocoon of legal restrictions: Coolidge, *Chinese Immigration*, 69–82; R. Heizer and A. Almquist, *Other*, 154–77.

The watershed event: Chan, "Chronology," 13–14; Konvitz, *Alien*, 1–5.

The Scott Act: Chan, "Chronology," 15.

The Geary Act: Chan, Ibid., 16.

"An Act to Prevent Kidnapping": Heizer and Almquist, *Other*, 164–65.

An unusual California referendum: Coolidge, *Chinese Immigration*, 123; Sandmeyer, *Anti-Chinese*, 62–63.

The results were even more astonishing: Supervisors' Minutes, Santa Cruz County, Vol. 4, 52; *Index*, Sept. 11, 1879.

### THE ANTI-CHINESE MOVEMENT IN THE MONTEREY BAY REGION pp. 119–29

The Order of Caucasians: *Sentinel*, Dec. 18, 1875.

The Santa Cruz Chapter of Caucasians: *Sentinel*, Dec. 22, 1877; Lydon, "Anti-Chinese," 227; Saxton, *Indispensable*, 18, 196.

The Workingmen's Party eclipsed: Saxton, *Indispensable*, 116–27.

"The dignity of labor must be sustained": Ibid., 118.

The Santa Cruz Workingmen's Party: For an analysis of the party, see Lydon, "Anti-Chinese," 219–42.

"No Nationality!": *Sentinel*, April 13, 1878.

"The Chinamen are an unmitigated curse": *Sentinel*, Jan. 5, 1878.

"A calamity to this State": *Sentinel*, April 8, 1882.

McPherson flogged the issue: Lydon, "Anti-Chinese," 234–235.

"To drive [the Chinese] from town to town": *Pajaronian*, March 18, 1886.

"Depreciation of property value": *Pajaronian*, April 8, 1886.

"The Strawberry Rebellion": Wat, "Strawberry."

"Most pronounced pro-Chinese sentiment": *Pajaronian*, May 7, 1886.

Salinas quickly acquired a reputation: *Index*, Nov. 23, 1876.

The March 1878 election: *Monterey Californian*, March 5, 1878.

A Workingmen's Party in Monterey: *Monterey Californian*, Aug. 12, 1879.

Only issue was David Jacks: *Monterey Californian*, March 11, 1879.

Ratification of a new state Constitution: Sandmeyer, *Anti-Chinese*, 66–74.

"Captain Jacks, the Chief": *Monterey Californian*, March 11, 1879.

"A general feeling of disappointment": *Index*, March 13, 1879.

"Profanity, vulgarity, and obscenity": Ibid.

Reasonable minds were at work: *Index*, Jan. 24, 1878; Jan. 31, 1878.

Watsonville's reaction to Kearney: *Sentinel*, March 15, 1879.

Kearney's last stop was Santa Cruz: *Sentinel*, March 15, 1879.

Chinese were "needlessly" frightened: *Sentinel*, Feb. 28, 1886.

Watsonville Workingmen's Party folded: Lydon, "Anti-Chinese," 228.

"The Chinese must go forth—to bind": *Pajaronian*, July 3, 1879.

Salinas held no public demonstrations: *Index*, April–May, 1882.

Salinas Non-Partisan Anti-Chinese: *Index*, Feb. 18, 1886; July 8, 1886.

Scott Act signed into law: *Index*, Oct. 4, 1888.

"One day when Dan Ragan": McDougall, "Looking Back," 22–23.


## *IMPACT ON THE CHINESE* pp. 129–33

The Six Companies came into the region: See chapters on Monterey and Santa Cruz for development of these events.

Burial brick "for identification later": Otto, Nov. 22, 1943.

"Travel over the State": *San Francisco Evening Bulletin*, June 29, 1861.

"They [the bone pickers]": Ibid.

Bone pickers came to Watsonville: *Pajaronian*, June 19, 1913.

"An Act to Protect Public Health": Heizer and Almquist, *Other*, 168–69.


## *A CHINESE VIEW* pp. 133–35

Chung Sun's first letter: *Pajaronian*, Nov. 9, 1871.

Chung Sun's second letter: *Pajaronian*, Nov. 16, 1871.


## CHAPTER 6. MONTEREY pp. 137–38

Map shows "China Camp" at Salmon Creek: U.S. Coast and Geodetic Survey manuscript map #1829, "San Carpoforo Creek to White Rock No. 2," 1887.


## *THE VILLAGES OF CARMEL BAY* pp. 138–49

"The little bay . . . is dotted": *Gazette*, Aug. 5, 1864.

Six Chinese fishermen lived at Point Lobos: Manuscript census, 1860, Monterey County.

Joined by a company of Portuguese whalers: *Weekly Herald*, Aug. 1, 1874.

Point Lobos "still as a millpond": *Weekly Herald*, Aug. 29, 1874.

Traveler to Carmel Bay in 1875: *Weekly Herald*, Sept. 28, 1875.

United States Coast Survey in 1876: U.S. Coast Survey manuscript map #1458b, "Coast Between Monterey Bay and Point Sur South of Carmel Bay," 1876.

*Halcyon* smuggling: *New Era*, Sept. 8, 1892.

Jacks acquired Pescadero and built a wharf: Jacks Collection, Journal and Ledger, 1863.

The cove had a "good wharf": *Gazette*, Aug. 5, 1864.

China Man Hop Company and David Jacks lease: Jacks Collection, Lease, Dec. 8, 1868.

Chinese fishermen burning brush: Jacks Collection, Ledger, 1868–79.

Professor Jordan counted forty Chinese: Jordan, *Fisheries*, 603.

Moored their boats to a heavy chain: Morse, manuscript history.

Jacks leased it back from Pacific Improvement Company: Jacks Collection, Lease Box 14, Pacific Improvement Co., lease to David Jacks, Dec. 1, 1880.

"Occupied by Chinese for dwellings": Ibid.

"At Pescadero, on Carmel Bay": Collins, "Fisheries," 57.

Herd of buffalo: *Index*, Dec. 4, 1890.

The village dropped to twelve in 1900: Manuscript census, 1900, Monterey County.

"San Choy, Ge Wah, Tai Wo": P. I. Co. Files, Map of Pescadero Chinatown, dated May 1, 1906.

Had three shell stands: "Carmel-by-the-Sea," 33.

Pacific Improvement Company renewed lease: P. I. Co. Files, Lease, San Choy and the Pacific Improvement Company, July 3, 1906.

Jung San Choy visited China in 1907: *Cypress*, Nov. 5, 1907.

Company began to subdivide Pescadero Ranch: *Monterey Peninsula Herald*, Oct. 20, 1974; Manuscript census, 1910, Monterey County.

### POINT JOE pp. 149–52

Wreck of the steamer, *St. Paul*: *Review*, Dec. 19, 1896.

"The proverbial thrift": Ibid.

"Chinaman Joe": O'Donnell, "Peninsula Diary," *Peninsula Herald*, April 13, 1951.

### THE POINT ALONES VILLAGE pp. 152–63

Chinese living on the cove in 1857: Jacks Collection, Rancho Box 19, map sketch of Point Pinos Ranch; *Weekly Herald*, Dec. 11, 1875.

"Fifteen or twenty" Chinese at the cove: *Sentinel*, Oct. 24, 1861.

Jacks charged an annual rent of $200: Jacks Collection, Journals, 1869–79.

"The Chinatown of Monterey is located down the shore": *Democrat* (Monterey), July 23, 1870.

Fourteen distinct Chinese family units: Manuscript census, 1870, Monterey County.

"Some of the women here go fishing": Goode and Collins, "Fishermen," 38, 40.

Village organized into "companies": *Weekly Herald*, May 22, 1875.

Wong Wah Foo, also called Tim Wong: Manuscript census, 1870, Monterey County; *Monterey Republican*, Aug. 14, 1870.

Tim collected the rents: Jacks Collection, Ledger Book A, 1875, 35, 246.

Tim quickly asserted his rights: *Weekly Herald*, Sept. 4, 1875; *Sentinel*, Sept. 11, 1875; *Index*, Nov. 16, 1876.

"An American citizen claiming the equal rights": *Sentinel*, Jan. 15, 1876.

### THE LEGEND OF CHINA'S WAR WITH MONTEREY—1875 pp. 164–65

According to a Monterey legend: Eastwood, "Strange Tale;" Schurmacher, *Lost Treasures*, 114–24.

Only reference to a Chinese fleet: *Gazette*, Feb. 19, 1864.

### SOUTHERN PACIFIC COMES TO MONTEREY pp. 165–76

Monterey was "essentially and wholly Mexican": Stevenson, *Scotland*, 160.

Southern Pacific brought Chinese to Monterey: *Monterey Californian*, Aug. 21, 1880.

By 1886, 1,500 lots sold: *Index*, May 6, 1886.

Methodist Episcopal Church establishes Chinese Mission in 1883: *Review*, Sept. 5, 1896.

Lease expired in 1890: Jacks Collection, Box 14, 1890.

Mission into "inocuous quietude": *Review*, Sept. 5, 1896.

"They present themselves clean": *Index*, July 19, 1894.

Leong Qui Pak (Len Puk): *Review*, Sept. 26, 1896.

"Few, upon casually meeting this handsome": Ibid.

"A natty young man is [Robert] Leon Park": *San Francisco Examiner*, Sept. 20, 1896.

Inspector for Immigration and Naturalization Service: Logan, letter; Leon, personal communication.

Chinese built a pipeline down Carmel Valley: *Index*, Aug. 10, 1882; March 22, 1883.

Hotel's Chinese running ashes through sluice: *Index*, April 21, 1887.

One hundred Chinese at the reservoir site: *Argus*, Aug. 25, 1888; Oct. 6, 1888.

"Long rows of white tents": *Index*, Oct. 4, 1888.

"It wouldn't be healthy policy": *Argus*, Oct. 6, 1888.

The 140-million-gallon reservoir: *Cypress*, Jan. 5, 1889.

Chinese sent to terminus of railroad line: *Index*, Nov. 8, 1888.

### THE MURDER OF TIM WONG pp. 176–79

The first hint of difficulty: *Weekly Herald*, Feb. 12, 1876.

His body was found hanging from a tree: *Index*, July 16, 1885.

His murderer "could be strung up": Ibid.

"The above reward ($600) will be paid": *Index*, Aug. 13, 1885.

Tim's widow and four children: Manuscript census, 1900, 1910, Monterey County.

### CHAPTER 7. WATSONVILLE pp. 181–84

Ordish opened a new street: *Pajaro Times*, March 11, 1865.

By 1869 at least one Chinese laundry: *Pajaronian*, May 17, 1869.

Owned by John T. Porter: Porter Manuscripts, Box 2, File 1880, Tax receipts for 1880.

Five businesses: Manuscript census, 1870, Santa Cruz County.

"It is a well-known fact": *Pajaronian*, Oct. 12, 1871.

Chinatown had grown to ten buildings: Porter Collection, Sanborn Map Company Map, Watsonville, 1874.

A total of seventy-nine residents: Manuscript census, 1870, Santa Cruz County.

### THE MOVE—1888 pp. 184–91

"This delectable sink hole of barbarism": *Pajaronian*, Sept. 3, 1874.

"When the green, and black, and oily smoke": *Pajaronian*, Oct. 1, 1874.

The announcement that Spreckels would locate in Watsonville: *Pajaronian*, Feb. 2, 1888.

A meeting of interested property owners: *Pajaronian*, Feb. 23, 1888.

The committee presented its proposal: *Pajaronian*, March 3, 1888.

Vice-Consul F. A. Bee asked to contribute: *Pajaronian*, Feb. 23, 1888; March 1, 1888.

"The Chinese are cunning and crafty": *Pajaronian*, March 8, 1888.

Vice-Consul Bee's trip to Watsonville: *Pajaronian*, April 5, 1888; April 12, 1888.

Porter quickly set to work: *Pajaronian*, June 20, 1888; July 12, 1888; July 26, 1888; Aug. 9, 1888.

"The old Chinese quarters look desolate": *Pajaronian*, Sept. 20, 1888.

"The first time in the history of the Pacific slope": *Pajaronian*, April 26, 1888.

Precedent for the move set in 1885: *Pajaronian*, Sept. 1885.

Warren R. Porter a "Chinaman-lover": Porter, interview.

"I am sorry to be compelled to go to war": Porter Manuscripts, F. A. Bee to J. T. Porter, April 16, 1891.

Watsonville farmers found themselves apologizing: *Pajaro Times*, July 18, 1866.

Santa Cruz sneered: *Sentinel*, July 13, 1878.

"The Pajaro Valley does not want the Chinese": *Pajaronian*, May 27, 1886.

"Watsonville will be the first town in the country": *Pajaronian*, July 19, 1888.

"An undesirable lot of being": Francis, *Santa Cruz County*, 167.

Watsonville "passed an ordinance": Coates, "Old Custom House."

## BROOKLYN'S EARLY YEARS pp. 191–97

Origin of the name Brooklyn: Francis, *Santa Cruz County*, 167; *Pajaronian*, Aug. 16, 1888.

Mrs. Porter's ledger book: Porter Collection, Brooklyn Ledger Book.

Brooklyn's first flood: *Sentinel*, Jan. 28, 1890; *Pajaronian*, Jan. 30, 1890.

Porter purchased an old fire cart: *Pajaronian*, Oct. 10, 1889; Jan. 23, 1890.

He called off the fire drill: *Pajaronian*, Feb. 13, 1890.

"John T. Porter made a good investment": *Pajaronian*, June 16, 1892.

Porter also provided security: Manuscript census, 1900, Monterey County.

Rileys developed an early reputation: *Pajaronian*, March 14, 1889.

## ORGANIZATION OF WATSONVILLE'S CHINATOWN pp. 198–201

Basic three-tiered organization: See Chinn, Lai, and Choy, *Syllabus*, 66–67; Lai and Choy, *Outlines*, 114–30.

Origins of the Chee Kong Tong: Lyman, *Asian in the West*, 39–41.

Six Companies felt Geary Act unconstitutional: *Pajaronian*, March 30, 1893; Lai and Choy, *Outlines*, 91.

"Not rushing to the registration office": *Pajaronian*, March 30, 1893.

April 10 mass meeting in Brooklyn: *Pajaronian*, May 13, 1893.

The wishes of the Six Companies prevailed: Ibid.

"Great big hunks of gloom": Ibid.

Charles E. Peckham registered an estimated 1,100 Chinese: *Pajaronian*, Jan. 4, 1894; Jan. 11, 1894; Feb. 22, 1894.

## THE TONGS IN BROOKLYN pp. 201–4

The Chee Kong Tong: Lyman, *Asians in the West*, 34–38.

Chee Kong Tong builds a temple: *Pajaronian*, Jan. 10, 1894.

Mrs. Porter did not charge rent: Porter Collection, Brooklyn Ledger, 13.

Hop Yick returned from China: *Pajaronian*, Sept. 26, 1895; Oct. 10, 1895.

Kuan Kung: Chinn, Lai, and Choy, *Syllabus*, 74.

Temple was tended: H. Lew, interview; Chai, interview.

Highbinder tongs: Lai and Choy, *Outlines*, 123–124.

Suey Sing and Bing Kong Tong: H. Lew, interview; F. Wong, interview.

"Little Pete" visit: *Pajaronian*, July 31, 1890.

Five San Francisco highbinders: *Pajaronian*, Nov. 22, 1891.

## GAMBLING, PROSTITUTION, AND OPIUM SMOKING pp. 204–8

Traditional Chinese view of the universe: Bloodworth, *Looking Glass*, 223–25.

"The mass of the people": Culin, *Gambling*, 14–15.

"The expressionless Oriental": *Pajaronian*, March 21, 1925.

*Fan tan* and *pok kop pew*: Ibid.; Culin, *Gambling*; Culin, "Fan Tan," 153–55.

"The lottery, perhaps, was the most colorful": *Pajaronian*, March 21, 1925.

"In those [early] days gambling games were conducted in little rear rooms": Ibid.

"Brooklyn is deserted except on Sundays": *Pajaronian*, June 21, 1894.

Interest rates charged by the moneylenders: *Pajaronian*, Feb. 12, 1891.

"The Chinese lottery games across the river": *Pajaronian*, Nov. 2, 1893.

Chinese merchants complained: *Pajaronian*, April 13, 1896.

Prostitution was common: Chen, *Chinese*, 182–83.

"A number of white women": *Pajaronian*, Aug. 19, 1897.

Chinese remember the houses of prostitution: F. Wong, interview.

Riley brothers made a concerted effort: *Pajaronian*, March 14, 1889.

## BROOKLYN IN THE MID-1890s—FROM LABOR CAMP TO COMMUNITY pp. 208–15

Reconstructing Brooklyn: Monterey County Assessor's Rolls, 1894, Book 4, Pajaro Chinatown, 430; Assessor's Rolls, 1895, Book 4, 432; Porter Ledger Book.

Ng Yee Yick's habeas corpus case: Habeas corpus case #10988, Ng Yee Yick, June 6, 1894.

"A small army of Chinese children": *Pajaronian*, Aug. 13, 1896; Jan. 17, 1897.

## SUGAR CITY pp. 215–21

Spreckels chose Watsonville: *Pajaronian*, Nov. 5, 1887—Dec. 15, 1887.

Western Beet Sugar Co. factory became economic flagship: *Pajaronian*, May 10, 1888.

"33 two-horse teams": *Index*, Dec. 31, 1896.

"There is no record": *Pajaronian*, Oct. 13, 1894.

"Pandora's horn": Francis, *Beautiful Santa Cruz*, 108.

"Men, women and children": *Pajaronian*, Jan. 3, 1889.

The appearance of white faces: *Pajaronian*, March 12, 1896.

Sugar beet crews along ethnic lines: *Index*, June 27, 1895.

"There is a shortage of berry pickers": *Pajaronian*, May 25, 1893.

The trend to leases: *Pajaronian*, April 8, 1886.

First mention of Japanese contracts: *Pajaronian*, Feb. 28, 1895; May 9, 1895.

"Chinese labor is rapidly becoming scarcer": *Pajaronian*, Sept. 20, 1900.

The 1900 census caught the transition: Manuscript census, 1900, Monterey County.

Acreage of sugar beets began to creep south: *Pajaronian*, Oct. 3, 1895.

"The heart which pumps the life blood": Francis, *Beautiful Santa Cruz*, 108.

## CHAPTER 8. SANTA CRUZ pp. 223–27

California Powder Works: See Reedy and Reedy, *Paradise Park Site*.

"If they get blown up in the powder mills": *Sentinel*, Sept. 17, 1864.

Masked and armed vigilantes stormed the powder factory: *Sentinel*, Oct. 29, 1864.

"The dexterity with which the ingenious Chinamen": *Sentinel*, Dec. 8, 1866.

"The Chinese cook their own food": *Sentinel*, March 14, 1874.

New Year at the Powder Works: Otto, July 30, 1944; Jan. 21, 1952; March 27, 1955.

June 1875 celebration at Powder Works: *Sentinel*, June 26, 1875.

Powder Works fired all Chinese: *Sentinel*, July 6, 1878.

## THE FIRST CHINATOWN—1862–1877
pp. 227–30

The Willow Street Chinatown: Otto, March 27, 1955.

Ung Yah's cigar factory: Internal Revenue Assessment Rolls, Santa Cruz County, July, 1866.

Santa Cruz families who had Chinese servants: Manuscript census, 1870, Santa Cruz County.

Willow Street renamed Pacific Avenue: Survey, 1866.

The last Chinese move from Willow Street: *Sentinel*, April 14, 1877.

## THE FRONT STREET CHINATOWN
pp. 231–35

Less than half of the ninety-eight lived in Chinatown: Manuscript census, 1880, Santa Cruz County.

"They [the Chinese] were the most loyal": Otto, Aug. 6, 1944.

White domestics earned fifteen dollars per month: Labor Statistics, 126–28.

A good Chinese cook earned forty dollars per month: Chen, *Chinese*, 59.

John Dong: Dong, interview; J. Dong, "Cowell Ranch," 10–11.

Mock Get hanged himself: *Pajaronian*, March 30, 1905.

## THE MARKET GARDENS pp. 236–38

Market gardens common in California: Chiu, *Chinese Labor*, 73–77.

George Treat leased five acres to Ah Hop and Ah Foo: Lease Books, Santa Cruz County, Vol. 2, May 19, 1876, 50.

Six acres in Santa Cruz leased from Judge Rice: *Sentinel*, June 18, 1881.

Santa Cruz encircled by market gardens: Otto, Aug. 6, 1944.

Strawberries for seventy-five cents per quart: *Sentinel*, March 31, 1877.

Fresh strawberries shipped to San Francisco: Wilhelm and Sagen, *Strawberry*, 173–75.

"Last Monday Chinamen were selling green peas": *Sentinel*, March 18, 1876.

A day's fresh produce for five cents: *Sentinel*, Nov. 5, 1881.

"He had one large protruding sharp tooth.": Otto, May 25, 1947.

Passed to Italian gardeners: Manuscript census, 1900, 1910, Santa Cruz County.

## LAUNDRIES pp. 238–45

Wah Lee first laundry in San Francisco: Chen, *Chinese*, 58.

More Chinese laundrymen lived in Santa Cruz: Manuscript census, 1880, Santa Cruz and Monterey Counties.

Laundry ratios: Ibid.; statistics derived by author.

David Jacks sold to Charley Hop Kee: Jacks Collection, Letter Box #3, W. H. Davies to D. Jacks, March 25, 1879; R. McElroy to D. Jacks, May 27, 1880.

Laundries organized into guilds: Chinn, Lai, and Choy, *Syllabus*, 63.

"At the side of each [Chinese] engaged in ironing": Otto, March 20, 1955.

"Ulcerated tonsils and throats": *Sentinel*, April 29, 1882.

"Seldom cost more than a dollar": Otto, March 20, 1955.

Average Chinese laundryman made a profit of sixteen dollars: Labor statistics, 128.

"There were no stiffer shirt bosoms": Otto, March 20, 1955.

Jim Jim's laundry at New Year: *Review*, Feb. 5, 1896; *Salinas Democrat*, Aug. 22, 1891.

"The event of the week *par excellence*": *New Era*, Dec. 19, 1900.

Pacific Grove prohibited laundries: *Review*, April 13, 1906.

"Stagnant pools and sink spots": *Sentinel*, Aug. 2, 1884.

"A skilled workman, instead of a low grade drudge": *Sentinel*, Jan. 10, 1886.

Japanese began to replace Chinese: Manuscript census, 1900, 1910, Santa Cruz County.

## CHINESE MERCHANTS pp. 245–55

". . . dried oysters always attached": Otto, Aug. 6, 1944.

"Ill-smelling" Chinese tobacco: Otto, Sept. 5, 1943.

"Herbs, sea horses, horned toads": Otto, Dec. 28, 1952.

Wing Sing practiced traditional customs: Otto, May 25, 1947.

Quong Chong wore a "brocaded silk blouse": Ibid.

"He would proudly sit": Otto, Dec. 19, 1954.

"Flags were flying": *Sentinel*, Oct. 7, 1886.

Ah Moon on River Street: *Sentinel*, May 4, 1878.

Wong Kee on Front Street: Otto, May 25, 1947.

Ham Tung's habeas corpus case: Habeas corpus case #10932, Ham Tung, April 1894.

## CHINESE CULTURE pp. 255–61

Chinese calendar and festivals: See Eberhard, *Festivals*.

"Windows never washed during the year": Otto, Jan. 23, 1947.

"If [the lilies] were in full bloom": Otto, Feb. 19, 1950.

"From house to house with sacks of silver": Ibid.

"At three o'clock a skirmish attack": *Sentinel*, Jan. 22, 1890.

"Grapefruit, piles of oranges": *Sentinel*, Jan. 19, 1890.

". . . in the center of the altar was an alcove": Otto, July 30, 1944.

Wong Kee expected to lose $2,000: *Sentinel*, Feb. 4, 1886.

Two Chinese men did not wear queue: Otto, Dec. 19, 1954.

"The customer sat on a small, hard, wooden bench": Otto, Dec. 28, 1952.

"On the tray were the lamp and opium pipes": Otto, Sept. 5, 1943.

## CHINESE FUNERALS pp. 261–66

"The hearse would be preceded by numbers in line": Otto, Nov. 22, 1943.

"He [the nephew] followed . . . the hearse": *Surf*, April 13, 1906.

"Roast pork, chickens, food": *Surf*, March 3, 1915.

Chinese buried in simple coffin: Otto, Nov. 22, 1943.

Ch'ing Ming: Eberhard, *Festivals*, 116.

"An express wagon left Chinatown": *Surf*, April 6, 1907.

Spirits' Festival: Chinn, Lai, and Choy, *Syllabus*, 77.

Set fire to the dry grass: *Index*, Aug. 28, 1881.

Ching Sing died destitute: *Surf*, March 3, 1915.

## THE CHEE KONG TONG IN SANTA CRUZ pp. 266–71

Chee Kong Tong: Lyman, *Asians in the West*, 34–41.

"Wong Kee would display his pin proudly": Otto, Dec. 19, 1954.

"Here and there lay several Chinamen smoking": *Sentinel*, Sept. 15, 1883.

Wong Kee estimated five hundred members in Monterey Bay Region: *Sentinel*, Sept. 2, 1884.

"There was also a circular steel rim and sword":
    Otto, April 12, 1942.
Lou Sing found dead: *Sentinel*, Sept. 11, 1884.
"We would like to ask, how could Lou Sing": *Sentinel*, Sept. 12, 1884.
Hired Dr. Charles Stivers: *Sentinel*, Sept. 14, 1884.
"The coffin was placed on a pedestal": *Sentinel*, Sept. 13, 1884.

### THE CHRISTIAN MISSION IN THE MONTEREY BAY REGION pp. 271–79

William Speer opened the first Chinese mission: Sung, *Chinese*, 220, 230–31.
"The [Chinese] believe in praying": Ibid., 218.
Missionaries concentrated on teaching Christian ethics: E. Lee, interview.
"Some could read the [English] alphabet": *Sentinel*, April 24, 1869.
Santa Cruz Congregational Church's Chinese Mission: Congregational History, 39–40.
"Closed with devotionals and Bible study": Otto, April 28, 1946.
"Forty baptized members": Ibid.
"His tightly-wound queue . . . [reflecting] back the rays": *Sentinel*, April 26, 1884.
"The exhibition on the whole": Ibid.
"Mr. Pond is one of the most unacceptable preachers": *Sentinel*, May 3, 1884.
"The men . . . who are intent": *Sentinel*, May 3, 1884.
Wong Ock transferred to Stockton: *Sentinel*, Sept. 6, 1884.
"Long table filled with Chinese confectionary": *Sentinel*, Jan. 25, 1887.
Pon Fang official interpreter: Warrant Book, Santa Cruz County, Book 5, Jan. 5, 1891.
Pon Fang "taught, sang, preached": Otto, Dec. 12, 1954.

Pon Fang returned to Santa Cruz in 1894: Manuscript census, 1900, Santa Cruz County.
Pon Fang leased new mission site: Lease Book, Santa Cruz County, Vol. 3, 277.

### FRONT STREET CHINATOWN DESTROYED pp. 279–81

"The Chinese mourn the loss of their Joss": *Sentinel*, April 18, 1894.
Chinese offered alternative sites: Otto, Jan. 23, 1953.
"There was some disagreement among themselves": Ibid.

### CHAPTER 9. SALINAS AND CASTROVILLE pp. 283–86

Establishment of Salinas: See Johnston, *Beginnings*.
Luco signed agreement with Ah Yuk: Lease Book, Monterey County, Book A, March 1866, 216.
Ah Yuk agreed to send 550 Chinese: *Gazette*, April 6, 1866.
Surplus of Chinese miners: Chiu, *Chinese Labor*, 9.
". . . develop, perhaps, something": *Gazette*, April 6, 1866.
"They won't be able to bring much water": *Gazette*, May 4, 1866.
"Cadaverous looking" miners: *Gazette*, May 25, 1866.
"We have no business, no commerce": *Gazette*, April 13, 1866.
"Don't come [to Monterey]": *Gazette*, May 4, 1866.
Carr, Vanderhurst, and Sanborn owned five hundred acres: *Index*, April 12, 1877.
"With huge knife-like spades": Ibid.
"White men refused to work up to their knees": *Index*, Aug. 9, 1877.

## *EARLY SALINAS VALLEY AGRICULTURE* pp. 286–90

"It is sincerely to be hoped that at an early day": *Sentinel*, Dec. 18, 1858.

Irrigation company formed during drought of 1876–77: *Index*, June 21, 1877.

Jacks lease with Sam Kee in 1877: Jacks Collection, Box 14, Jan. 1877.

"Lessees will use all effectual efforts": Jacks Collection, Box 14, Lease between Jacks and O. Jim, A. Len, and Cong Sue Kee, Jan. 1885.

Bardin signed lease with Jim Sing: Lease Book, Monterey County, Book C, March 23, 1888, 167.

Rafael Estrada lease with Jim Kee: Lease Book, Monterey County, Book B, July 3, 1882, 572.

Reclaiming process: S. Chinn, interview.

In 1881, 140,000 acres in wheat: *Index*, July 27, 1882.

## *EARLY SALINAS CHINATOWN* pp. 290–99

First reference to Chinese in Salinas: *Pajaronian*, July 1, 1869.

A special census in 1872: *Democrat* (Salinas), July 19, 1872.

First reference to Chinatown in Salinas: *Index*, April 2, 1874.

Attempt to burn house of prostitution in "the Chinese quarters": *Index*, May 21, 1874.

Occupation Chart, 1880: Manuscript census, 1880, Monterey County.

Salinas Town Trustees prohibit washing clothes: *Index*, July 1, 1886; July 8, 1886; July 15, 1886.

Ordinance repealed in 1897: *Index*, March 11, 1897.

Chama Zamora and Chin Yik lease: Lease Book, Monterey County, Book B, May 23, 1878, 454.

Fire of 1888: *Index*, Feb. 2, 1888.

"Want of gratitude is not one of the shortcomings": Ibid.

First Chee Kong Tong temple: *Index*, Nov. 2, 1882.

"From early dawn on Sunday": *Index*, Dec. 14, 1882.

"Harvest hands are exceedingly scarce in Monterey County": *Sentinel*, July 24, 1880.

Chinese laborers did "not get drunk": *Index*, June 23, 1881.

An evening in Chinatown, 1891: *Salinas Democrat*, Feb. 14, 1891.

Most of Salinas Chinese from Toishan: Lai and Choy, *Outlines*, 116.

"Here Confucius sits enthroned": *Salinas Democrat*, Feb. 14, 1891.

The haunted house: *Index*, July 26, 1877; Aug. 2, 1877.

Staging the bar bet: *Index*, Jan. 20, 1898.

## *THE 1893 FIRE* pp. 300–301

Big Salinas Chinatown fire, 1893: *Salinas Democrat*, June 17, 1893.

"In most civilized countries": Ibid.

"Chinatown of Salinas will never again mar": Ibid.

## *THE SOLEDAD STREET CHINATOWN* pp. 301–3

Sherwood agreements with Lee Saw, *et al*: Lease Book, Monterey County, Book C, 471–72.

Twelve new buildings: *Journal*, July 14, 1893.

Assessor's personal property records: Assessor's Rolls, Monterey County, 1894, 1895, Book #3, 157, 319.

Charley Mack developed potato: S. Chinn, interview.

## *THE CHINESE ECCENTRICS* pp. 303–5

"Joe" at Point Joe: Hoang, interview.

"Charley Lee" of Watsonville: *Pajaronian*, April 19, 1921; April 3, 1922; *Sentinel*, April 13, 1922.

"Finnegan": *Salinas Democrat*, May 12, 1894; *Index*, May 3, 1894; *Pajaronian*, Oct. 22, 1891.

Sam Sing dies at mental hospital: *Index*, Dec. 23, 1897.

"The insanity and death of Sam Sing": *Pajaronian*, Jan. 6, 1898.

### SPRECKELS FACTORY TO SALINAS—1898 pp. 305–9

Last campaign in which Pajaro Valley made up bulk: *Index*, Jan. 26, 1893.

Two hundred carloads of beets shipped daily: *Index*, Aug. 30, 1894.

Spreckels planned move of factory: *Index*, Feb. 20, 1896; March 19, 1896; March 26, 1896.

"If you farmers guarantee to grow the beets": *Index*, Aug. 6, 1896.

"The difficulty lies in changing the grain farmers": *Index*, June 12, 1890.

"To banish hard times": *Index*, Aug. 6, 1896.

Spreckels announced Salinas location: *Index*, Aug. 13, 1896; Aug. 20, 1896; Sept. 10, 1896.

"From the edge of the Salinas River": *Index*, Dec. 3, 1896.

Sugar mill rocketed Salinas out of the doldrums: *Index*, April 1, 1897.

Streetcar line built: *Index*, Oct. 8, 1896.

Spreckels tore down Aptos hotel: *Index*, Nov. 25, 1897.

Several communal experiments: *Index*, see year of 1897.

Wing Tai Chung lease: Lease Book, Monterey County, Book D, Dec. 1899, 398.

### CHINATOWN, CASTROVILLE pp. 309–15

"Over 1,000 acres of solid beet field": *Pajaronian*, Aug. 27, 1891.

Fifteen Chinese companies farming beets: Assessor's Rolls, Monterey County, Castroville Book, 1892, 423.

Token Chinese laundry in Castroville: *Pajaronian*, Sept. 30, 1869.

### CHAPTER 10. THE RING GAME pp. 319–22

"The Point Alones [village] as seen in the afternoon": *Index*, Nov. 6, 1890.

### THE RING GAME pp. 322–27

T'u Ti and the Festival: Gray, *China*, Vol. 1, 257–58.

First ring game in the region: *Cypress*, March 10, 1894.

"As soon as the ring would descend": Ibid.

Bomb exploded prematurely: *New Era*, March 15, 1899.

Chinese participant died: *New Era*, Feb. 18, 1900.

The expense was $5,000: *New Era*, March 15, 1899.

### PARADES pp. 327–44

"This process was one of the most unique": *New Era*, Feb. 23, 1898.

The Watsonville Chinese rented costumes: *Pajaronian*, Feb. 24, 1898.

An order for over $3,000 worth: *Pajaronian*, March 3, 1898.

"Expected to surpass anything that the Chinese societies": *Pajaronian*, June 9, 1898.

Chinese staged a grand celebration in July: *Pajaronian*, July 7, 1898.

"The variety and richness of costumes": Ibid.

". . . in full regalia, with their banner": Ibid.

Ring Game parade in Monterey, March 1899: *New Era*, March 15, 1899; *Cypress*, March 18, 1899.

"Long silken folds of our glorious Stars and Stripes": *Review*, March 18, 1899.

"Chinese vision with beautiful silken banners": *New Era*, July 9, 1902.

## THE WELCOME WEARS THIN pp. 345–49

"You will come upon a space of open down": Stevenson, *Scotland*, 154–55.

"Some [who] went to satisfy curiosity": *Monterey Republican*, Feb. 3, 1870.

"Could be seen winding through the narrow streets": *Cypress*, Feb. 2, 1889.

Lists of sights to see: *Cypress*, April 10, 1897, special tourist issue.

"Among the many attractions": *Review*, March 16, 1895.

"Well-dressed" young men climbed up on a drying frame: *Review*, March 13, 1897.

"Peering into open doorways": Ibid.

"Was of no consequence": Ibid.

"A deplorable reflection upon the manners": *Review*, Feb. 26, 1898.

"Imagine a band of lawless Chinese": Ibid.

"Just think; on the 22nd of February, 1898": *Review*, March 5, 1898.

Dropped a firecracker in Quong Wah's lamp: *Salinas Democrat*, Feb. 14, 1892.

Native Sons of the Golden State: Chinn, Lai, and Choy, *Syllabus*, 79.

## CHAPTER 11. MONTEREY

## THE TOWN PRESSURES THE VILLAGE TO MOVE pp. 356–60

First fish cannery: *New Era*, June 17, 1896.

Second cannery built by M. R. Robbins: *New Era*, Sept. 25, 1901; Oct. 30, 1901.

Chinatown would probably "cease to exist": *New Era*, May 14, 1902.

". . . any decrease in the town's business": Ibid.

Mayor Johnson visited the company's headquarters: *New Era*, June 18, 1902.

"Hung like a dark brown cloud": *New Era*, May 25, 1904.

Several Chinese squid dryers were arrested: *New Era*, June 15, 1904.

The Pacific Improvement Company gave notice: *Review*, Nov. 24, 1905; *Pajaronian*, Nov. 30, 1905.

Led several historians to conclude: Woolfenden, "Chinese Village;" Catbagan, "Chinatown," 8.

"The Pacific Improvement Company does not wish to be harsh": *Review*, Feb. 16, 1906.

"Pacific Grove suffered a 'trifling'": *Review*, April 20, 1906; April 27, 1906.

The remarkable woman who walked with her children: *Review*, April 27, 1906.

Another refugee, young Ben Hoang: Hoang, interview.

"The removal could be accomplished quietly": P. I. Co. File JL1, Box 53. A. D. Shepard to J. P. Pryor, May 3, 1906.

Nothing "can get the Chinamen out of there": P. I. Co. File JL1, Box 53, Pryor to Shepard, May 5, 1906.

Shepard suggested Pryor make one last effort: P. I. Co. File JL1, Box 53, Shepard to Pryor, May 7, 1906.

Pryor was pessimistic about Chinese leadership: P. I. Co. File JL1, Box 53, Pryor to Shepard, May 8, 1906.

## THE 1906 FIRE pp. 360–68

First major fire: *Index*, Nov. 14, 1889; *Democrat* (Monterey), Nov. 16, 1889.

Company distributed fire barrels throughout town: *Salinas Journal*, Jan. 14, 1890.

The second fire: *New Era*, Oct. 16, 1898; *Review*, Oct. 29, 1898.

The third fire: *New Era*, May 16, 1902.

The 1906 fire: *Review*, May 18, 1906.

"Had it not been for a few officers present": *Pajaronian*, May 22, 1906.

Dozens of townspeople poked about in the ashes: *Review*, May 18, 1906.

"Conscience, honor, delicacy": *Review*, May 25, 1906.

"I hope I may never in my life feel so ashamed": Ibid.

Many acts of kindness: *Pajaronian*, May 22, 1906.

"We wish them to be removed so far": *Review*, May 25, 1906.

Some speculate that the Pacific Improvement Company deliberately burned: See Catbagan, "Chinatown;" Woolfenden, "Chinese Village."

"The question of the removal of Chinatown is now settled": *Review*, May 18, 1906.

### THE BATTLE—MAY 1906 TO MAY 1907
pp. 369–77

Two telegrams: P. I. Co. File JL1, Box 53, R. Snell to Shepard, May 17, 1906; Pryor to Shepard, May 17, 1906.

"Do anything necessary": P. I. Co. File JL1, Box 53, Shepard to Pryor, telegram sent from Oakland, May 17, 1906.

Pacific Improvement Company built a fence: *Review*, May 25, 1906.

Chinese began a small guerilla war: Ibid.

"I therefore prefer to spend": P. I. Co. File JL1, Box 53, Pryor to Shepard, May 26, 1906.

"I am reliably informed": Ibid.

Chinese had begun to build new buildings: P. I. Co. File JL1, Box 53, Pryor to Shepard, June 15, 1906.

Chinese filed charges: P. I. Co. File JL1, Box 53, Pryor to Shepard, June 16, 1906.

"Demand for Surrender of Real Property": P. I. Co. File JL1, Box 53, copy of suit addressed to J. P. Pryor, June 25, 1906.

Tuck Lee: Hoang, interview.

"We are disposed to immediately tear down the fence": P. I. Co. File JL1, Box 53, Shepard to Pryor, May 26, 1906.

"I would like to drop everything in the way of legal proceedings": P. I. Co. File JL1, Box 53, Shepard to R. H. Willey, June 19, 1906.

Arena Gorda Beach not subdivided in 1889: *Cypress*, Jan. 7, 1889.

J. B. McAbee built a small cluster of cottages: *Review*, Jan. 8, 1897.

Residents quickly formed a committee: *Review*, Nov. 2, 1906; P. I. Co. File JL1, Box 53, Pryor to Shepard, Nov. 6, 1906.

"This Company is favorable to location of Chinatown": P. I. Co. File JL1, Box 53, Shepard to Pryor, Nov. 5, 1906.

"Personally, I am inclined to rejoice": P. I. Co. File JL1, Box 53, Shepard to Pryor, Nov. 7, 1906.

Last Chinese left the site: *Cypress*, May 17, 1906.

"That the Board of Directors have donated Chinatown Point": P. I. Co. File JL1, Box 53, Shepard to Pryor, Nov. 14, 1906.

Benjamin Ide Wheeler conveyed his thanks: P. I. Co. File JL1, Box 53, Wheeler to Shepard, Dec. 13, 1906.

"We have a bath house and beach at Del Monte": P. I. Co. File JL1, Box 53, Shepard to Pryor, Nov. 7, 1906.

### McABEE BEACH pp. 377–86

Great loss of population: Manuscript census, 1900, 1910, Monterey County.

Some of the buildings were of striped canvas: Hoang, interview.

"Not sell without a permit": Lease Books, Monterey County, Book G, 341; Lease between C. L. Smith and Quong Yick signed March 11, 1909.

Women still comprised nearly 40%: Manuscript census, 1910, Monterey County.

Ring Game in March 1907: *Cypress*, March 15, 1907.

Monterey City trustees passed an ordinance prohibiting squid drying: *Cypress*, May 19, 1908; June 10, 1908.

Won Yee's life: Yee and Yee, interview.

Best years of the squid business: *Monterey Peninsula Herald*, April 20, 1932.

The sight of any Chinese fishermen became rare: Rosenberg, "Fishing and Canning," 40.

"For fifty years he has been fishing": *Pajaronian*, April 30, 1924.

No commercial Chinese fishermen were left: Rosenberg, "Fishing and Canning," 40.

### CANNERIES: pp. 386–87

Monterey Fish Canning Company: Lease Books, Monterey County, Book H, lease between C. L. Smith and Tsue Yuen Ling Co., June 8, 1910, 127.

Monterey Fish Canning Company went bankrupt: Hoang, interview.

Bayside Canning Company: Hoang, interview.

### THE FRANKLIN/WASHINGTON STREET CHINATOWN pp. 387–90

First reference to laundries: *Herald*, Oct. 2, 1875.

*Monterey Argus* refers to "just beyond the bridge": *Argus*, July 28, 1888.

The 1907 Directory of Monterey: Perry, *Directory*, 44.

Outnumbered by six Chinese lotteries: *Cypress*, March 28, 1907.

"The Badlands": *New Era*, March 23, 1904.

Quong On Tai's lease with Louis Little: Lease Books, Monterey County, Book F, May 23, 1906, 182.

Charley Ming: *Cypress*, Sept. 28, 1907; Dec. 12, 1907.

### POSTSCRIPT: THE VIETNAMESE FISHERMEN pp. 391–93

Out of an estimated six hundred commercial fishing boats: *San Francisco Chronicle*, Nov. 27, 1980; *Monterey Peninsula Herald*, July 9, 1980.

Limited by a federal law: Law was enacted in 1792. See *Monterey Peninsula Herald*, Aug. 20, 1982.

Hearings were held: *Monterey Peninsula Herald*, Nov. 27, 1981; March 5, 1982.

"Concerned about us": *Monterey Peninsula Herald*, March 5, 1982.

"They're raping the bay": *San Francisco Chronicle*, Nov. 17, 1980.

"Of course the Vietnamese haven't fished out the bay": Ibid.

A Vietnamese fishing boat was burned: *Watsonville Register-Pajaronian*, July 26, 1983; *Monterey Peninsula Herald*, April 15, 1983.

"I truly believe": *Monterey Herald*, March 5, 1982.

## CHAPTER 12. WATSONVILLE

### FROM SUGAR CITY TO APPLE CITY pp. 396–400

Early development of the apple industry: Meler, *Slavonic Pioneers* 52–54; see also *Watsonville Evening Pajaronian*, Jan. 10, 1910.

Chong Wo "best known merchant": *Pajaronian*, May 12, 1898.

"The first appearance of a Chinaman in the business": *Pajaronian*, May 11, 1899.

Chong Wo began shipping apples: *Pajaronian*, Aug. 31, 1899; March 15, 1900; Aug. 6, 1900.

The first recorded mechanical fruit dehydrator: Tate, "Apple Drying;" see also, Fong, "Apple Drying."

In 1904 F. P. Marinovich built a tray-loaded dryer: Tate, "Apple Drying."

*THE CHINA DRYERS* pp. 400–408

"Because the Chinese were able to overcome": Tate, "Apple Drying."

Marion T. Rowe and Charley Fang: Lease Books, Monterey County, Book 1, June 13, 1911, 25.

Each dryer had a bunkhouse: C. Leong, interview; J. Lam, interview.

Dovetailing perfectly with squid season: Hoang, interview.

The first step in the apple-drying process: H. Lew, interview; C. Leong, interview; J. Lam, interview.

Sam Eng's Corralitos dryer: de la Pena, interview.

In 1918 it took eight pounds of fresh apples: Tate, "Apple Drying;" J. Lam, interview.

Lam Pon came to America: G. Ow, Jr., "Grandpa," G. Ow, Sr., interview; Manuscript census, 1910, Santa Cruz County.

Lam Pon entered a lease arrangement with Ralph Mattison: O. Lam, personal communication; Cartier, "Aptos Village Project," 13.

Lam Pon traveled to China on several occasions: G. Ow, Sr., interview.

Some of the Chinese dryer operators went deeply into debt: H. Lew, interview.

Otto Lam and Ralph Mattison dissolved their partnership: Cartier, "Aptos Village Project," 22–23.

*THE ALIEN LAND LAW OF 1913* pp. 408–11

Chinese "enjoyed the same rights of purchase": Konvitz, *Alien*, 160.

The Japanese immigrants who came into California: Wilson and Hosokawa, *East to America*, 62–63.

Japanese "would not come in large numbers": Konvitz, *Alien*, 159.

"A measure directed to exclude": Ibid.

Hoy Lew is still bitter: H. Lew, interview.

Federal law stripped his wife of her citizenship:

Chinn, Lai, and Choy, *Syllabus*, 27. The law was in effect until 1943.

"I was offered many good farms": H. Lew, interview.

*BROOKLYN IN THE 1900s* pp. 411–15

Sam Eng: de la Pena, interview.

"Sam's activities": Undated newspaper article from collection of Annie de la Pena.

Charlie Chin Goon: Goon and Goon, interview; Manuscript census, 1910, Santa Cruz County.

Vacancy rate of Brooklyn had increased: Porter Collection, Brooklyn Ledger Book.

"[The temple] was graphed": C. Dong, "Dong Family," 4.

"[The Chinese] came to contribute money": Ibid., 14.

"Mother would dress": Ibid.

"Horses and buggies": Ibid., 15.

Hoy Lew and Bow Ching Chong: H. Lew, interview.

"I had a blacksmith": Ibid.

Porter family would have Brooklyn Street plowed: Ibid.

*THE KUOMINTANG PARTY AND THE CHINESE SCHOOL* pp. 416–20

They watched the Boxer uprising: *Pajaronian*, July 26, 1900.

Brooklyn Chinese contributed "several thousand dollars": *Pajaronian*, Oct. 26, 1911.

The Kuomintang's flag rose: Ibid.

Kuomintang rented #35: Porter Collection, Brooklyn Ledger Book; H. Lew, interview.

"Please lend no money to kill our people": *Pajaronian*, Jan. 31, 1921.

"If you do, we know the Chinese people": *Pajaronian*, Jan. 11, 1922.

First Chinese School in Brooklyn: H. Lew, interview.

Dr. Emma Dong believes all graduated from high school: McPherson, "Emma Dong," 99.

The classroom of the Chinese school: Shew, interview; F. Wong, interview; E. Dong, interview.

School was rebuilt at #18 after the fire: E. Dong, interview; F. Wong, interview.

## FIRE—MARCH 1, 1924 pp. 420–28

Price of dried apples plummeted: H. Lew, interview; *Pajaronian*, June 30, 1921; April 4, 1922.

"They delivered their contract": Fong, "Apple Drying," 102–3.

Chinese in Brooklyn becoming "Americanized": *Pajaronian*, Feb. 3, 1916.

1919 Chinese float in the parade: *Pajaronian*, July 5, 1919.

Fire of March 1, 1924: *Pajaronian*, March 1, 1924; March 3, 1924.

Hoy was awakened by the alarm: H. Lew, interview.

Ten-year-old Elmer Shew: Shew, interview.

All important buildings were destroyed: *Pajaronian*, March 3, 1924.

Non-Chinese responded with help: *Pajaronian*, March 20, 1924.

Shews were first to rebuild: Shew, interview; *Pajaronian*, July 11, 1924.

Chinese school was rebuilt: E. Dong, interview.

Methodists decided not to rebuild: E. Lee, interview.

The mission used various rented locations: F. Wong, interview.

"Reminiscence of Old Chinatown": *Pajaronian*, March 21, 1925.

## BROOKLYN BURNS DOWN pp. 428–31

Sing Wo Kee: Kwok, letter to author.

Employed Chinese-American college students: E. Lee, interview; C. Leong, interview.

Fire of 1933: *Pajaronian*, March 22, 1933.

"In spite of a severe cold": C. Dong, "Dong Family," 18.

## CHAPTER 13. SANTA CRUZ AND SALINAS

## SANTA CRUZ CHINATOWN pp. 434–46

Six separate leases: Lease Books, Santa Cruz County. Vol. 3, 277–99.

Chee Kong Tong temple rebuilt on Mrs. Blackburn's: *Sentinel*, Aug. 21, 1895.

Fifty-nine residents in 1900: Manuscript census, 1900, Santa Cruz County.

Gambling halls continued to thrive: Lee and Lee, interview; G. Ow, Sr., interview.

Southern Pacific Railroad planned to buy twenty acres: *Surf*, Nov. 9, 1905.

Chee Kong Tong temple reconstructed in Birkenseer's: *Surf*, Oct. 10, 1905.

The new temple dedicated: *Surf*, Nov. 13, 1905.

"Each brought his offerings": Ibid.

"Roast pork, chicken": Ibid.

Three of the fifty male Chinese residents were not members: *Surf*, Jan. 28, 1911.

"A number chose Christmas day for the innovation": *Surf*, Jan. 26, 1911.

The new nationalist flag: *Surf*, Dec. 1, 1911.

Only five of the older men still wore queues: *Surf*, Feb. 5, 1912.

"Mere reminders of past days": *Sentinel*, Sept. 17, 1920.

By 1922 only three open houses: *Sentinel*, Jan. 28, 1922.

The last elaborate old-fashioned Chinese wedding: *Surf*, Aug. 20, 1910.

"The bride went home to China": Ibid.

"The bride had an elegant brocaded silk gown": Ibid.

"The biggest and greatest event ever held": *Surf*, Aug. 22, 1910.

Dong Toy: *Surf,* July 6, 1910.

Dong Toy organized a bank in Hong Kong: *Sentinel,* July 5, 1922.

Soo Hoo Dong opened a practice in Tientsin: *Surf,* Jan. 24, 1918.

Fong Sec graduated from University of California: *Surf,* Feb. 25, 1918.

Wo Gap moved to Sacramento Valley: *Surf,* Oct. 26, 1918.

"The Chee Kong Tong joss house is practically deserted": *Sentinel,* Jan. 30, 1930.

The school principal complained to Emily Ow: E. Ow, interview.

Flood after 1905 dedication: *Surf,* Jan. 19, 1906.

The last residents left in 1955: J. Lee, interview; Lee and Lee, interview.

## SALINAS CHINATOWN pp. 447–52

Forty-three residents: Manuscript census, 1900, Monterey County. Sanborn map: Sanborn Map Company Maps.

Temple rebuilt on lot #1: *New Era,* Nov. 6, 1901; Dec. 11, 1901.

"The Chinese government no longer insists": *Surf,* Feb. 9, 1910.

Chinese population of Salinas increased to eighty-one: Manuscript census, 1910, Monterey County.

"Shorty" Lee almost killed in 1912: Leyde, "Rich and Notorious," 17.

Chinese killed in 1912: *Pajaronian,* Aug. 21, 1912.

San Francisco Chinese community set up Peace Association: Lai and Choy, *Outlines,* 124–25; Chinn, Lai, and Choy, *Syllabus,* 67–68.

Wong Yee (Harry Yee Wong) raised a family: W. Wong, interview.

Lee Yin was born in China in 1887: Leyde, "Rich and Notorious," 17.

"As a little boy, I often shivered": Lee, "Chinatown Vanished."

Lee's store closed after his death in 1944: W. Lee, interview.

School transferred to new building: Ibid.

## CHINESE FARMERS IN THE SALINAS VALLEY pp. 452–55

A half-dozen Chinese farmers working lease-holds: Manuscript census, 1900, Monterey County: S. Chinn, interview.

## CHAPTER 14. THE CHINESE MARKETS AND THE AMERICA-BORN PIONEERS pp. 459–62

"A merchant is a person engaged in buying and selling": Chan, "Chronology," 16.

Maurice Freedman: Freedman, *Chinese Society,* 22–26.

"Work [alone] will never get you ahead.": G. Ow, Sr., interview.

"We were suppressed": Chin, interview.

## FROM CHINESE STORE TO ALL-PURPOSE MARKET pp. 462–74

"These merchants handled Chinese goods": Otto, May 25, 1947.

Hoy Lew's career: H. Lew, interview; W. Lew, interview.

Shew's Market: Shew, interview.

Daylite Market: E. Wong, interview; I. Wong, interview.

Chin Brothers Market: Chin, interview.

King's Market and the Ow family: G. Ow, Sr., interview; E. Ow, interview; G. Ow, Jr., interview.

## THE NATIONAL DOLLAR STORES pp. 474–76

Henry Leong and the Dollar Stores: Leong and Leong, interview.

*TRAILBLAZERS* pp. 476–85

The Dong Family: *Pajaronian*, November 23, 1899; E. Dong, interview; C. Dong, "Dong Family;" McPherson, "Emma Dong."

"When we first came to town": McPherson, "Emma Dong," 102.

Many children were just reaching college age: Lai and Choy, *Outlines*, 97.

Walter Wong: W. Wong, interview.

Jun Lee: J. Lee, interview.

Jun Lee elected to Scotts Valley City Council: *Scotts Valley News*, March 3, 1976; *Sentinel*, May 18, 1975.

Charlie Leong: C. Leong, interview.

"I am up and about shortly": *Asian Week*, Nov. 11, 1983.

CHAPTER 15. CONCLUSION pp. 487–88

"Would any of us make a permanent home": *Gazette*, June 20, 1867.

*CONTRIBUTIONS* pp. 492–96

Chinese turned the earth with an old-fashioned wooden plow: *Index*, Feb. 2, 1899.

*THE LAST OF THE OLD TRADITIONS* pp. 496–501

Margaret Lam: M. Lam, interview.

Sam Chinn: S. Chinn, interview.

# References

Only the works cited in the book are listed here. The most useful sources in piecing together the various Chinatowns were the Sanborn Fire Insurance Maps housed in Map Library, University of California, Santa Cruz (UCSC), the Assessor's Supplemental Tax Rolls, the Manuscript Census for each county, and the local newspapers. There are no indices for the newspapers, so a thorough search requires the reading of all extant issues. Most of the newspapers are available on microfilm, and the locations of the more obscure newspaper files are noted in the reference list. Collections and repositories are abbreviated below: Archaeological Research Center, Cabrillo College (ARC); Bancroft Library, University of California, Berkeley (Banc); California State Library, Sacramento (CSL); Federal Archives and Records Center, San Bruno (FARC); Monterey Public Library, Monterey (MPL); University of California, Santa Cruz (UCSC). Primary and secondary sources are alphabetized together for easier use with the chapter notes.

[*Argus*]. *Monterey Argus*. Newspaper published in Monterey, Ca. Banc.

Armentrout-Ma, Eve. "Chinese in California's Fishing Industry, 1850–1941." *California History* 60, No. 2 (Summer 1981): 142–57.

———. *Sampans, Junks and Chinese Fishermen in the Golden State*. San Francisco: National Maritime Museum, 1979. (pamphlet)

*Asian Week*. Newspaper published weekly in San Francisco.

[Assessor's Rolls]. Monterey County. Assessor's Rolls, unsecured taxes. County Clerk's Office, Salinas, California. Microfilm.

Bauer, John E. "California Crops that Failed." *California Historical Quarterly* 45 (March, 1964): 41–68.

Bloodworth, Dennis. *The Chinese Looking Glass*. New York: Dell, 1966.

Bolton, Herbert. *Spanish Explorations in the Southwest, 1542–1706*. New York: Scribner's, 1916.

Breschini, Gary S., and R. Paul Hampson. "Preliminary Archaeological Reconnaissance of the Hopkins Marine Station, Pacific Grove, Monterey, California." Prepared for Hopkins Marine Station, Pacific Grove, March 22, 1984. ARC.

Card, Carol. "Point Lobos Folk Lore and Fancies." *Game and Gossip* 5, No. 4 (May 10, 1951): 6–7.

*Carmel-by-the-Sea*, photocopy of booklet published in 1967. Pebble Beach Company collection.

Cartier, Robert. "Archival Background to the Aptos Village Project." Prepared for Archaeological

Consulting, November, 1979. ARC.

Catbagan, Mariano, Jr. "Pacific Grove's Chinatown." Unpublished manuscript. June, 1980. Author's collection.

Chai, Jimmy. Interview with author. Kohala, Hawaii, 1981.

Chan, Charles. "Chronology of Treaties and Major Federal Laws Affecting Chinese Immigration to the United States." In *Chinese Studies in Federal Records*, 12–15. San Bruno: Federal Archives and Records Center, 1975.

Chapman, Charles E. *A History of California: The Spanish Period*. New York: Macmillan, 1921.

Chen, Jack. *The Chinese of America*. San Francisco: Harper and Row, 1980.

Chin, Henry. Interview with author. Salinas, California, 1984.

Chinn, Sam. Interview with author. Salinas, California, 1983.

Chinn, Thomas, Him Mark Lai, and Philip Choy, eds. *A History of the Chinese in California: A Syllabus*. San Francisco: Chinese Historical Society of America, 1969.

Chiu, Ping. *Chinese Labor in California, 1850–1880: An Economic Study*. Madison, Wisconsin: State Historical Society of Wisconsin, 1967.

Choy, Philip. Interview with author. Monterey, California, 1983.

[*Chronicle*]. *San Francisco Chronicle*. Newspaper.

Coates, J. S. "Official Occupants of the Old Custom House." *Game and Gossip* 13 (1946), No. 1: 4–7.

Collins, Joseph W. "Report on the Fisheries of the Pacific Coast of the United States." *Report of the Commissioner*, Part 16: 3–141. United States Commission of Fish and Fisheries. Washington, D.C.: Government Printing Office, 1892. Some reports of the United States Fish Commission are listed by author. All Fish Commission reports from 1860 through 1900 were surveyed.

[Congregational History]. First Congregational Church. *A Century of Christian Witness: History of First Congregational Church, Santa Cruz, California, 1857–1963*. Santa Cruz: First Congregational Church, 1963.

Coolidge, Mary. *Chinese Immigration*. New York: Henry Holt, 1909.

"County Scrapbook." Immigration Association of California, 25. California Room, CSL.

Culin, Stewart. *Gambling Games of the Chinese in America*. Pennsylvania: University of Pennsylvania Press, 1891.

———. "The Origin of Fan Tan." *Overland Monthly* 28, 2nd series (August, 1896): 153–55.

[*Cypress*]. *Monterey Cypress*. Newspaper. Title varies: *Monterey Weekly Cypress* (CSL), *Monterey Daily Cypress* (MPL).

*Daily Alta California* San Francisco, newspaper. CSL.

de la Pena, Annie. Interview with author. Corralitos, California, 1981.

[*Democrat*]. *The Democrat*. Newspaper. Originally published in Monterey, then moved to Salinas. Name of city follows reference. Banc.

Dong, Collin H. "The Saga of the Dong Family." Transcript of speech, Pajaro Valley Historical Association, Watsonville, July 4, 1971.

Dong, Emma. Interview with author. Salinas, California, 1982.

Dong, John. "John Dong: The Cowell Ranch Cookhouse." Unpublished interview. Special Collections, UCSC, 1967.

Eastwood, Ron. "Strange Tale of Chinese 'Attack' on Monterey." *Monterey Peninsula Herald*, June 14, 1981.

Eberhard, Wolfram. *Chinese Festivals*. New York: Henry Schuman, 1952.

Edwards, Charles Lincoln. *The Abalone Industry in California*. Fish Bulletin No. 1. Sacramento: State of California Fish and Game Commission, 1913.

Elliott and Moore. *History of Monterey County, California, with Illustrations.* San Francisco, 1881. Reprinted. Fresno: Valley Publishers, 1979.

Elliott, Ronna Zinn. "Monterey's Chinatown." *Coasting* (May 19, 1982): 30–31.

Elstob, Winston. *Chinatown: A Legend of Old Cannery Row.* San Francisco: Condor's Sky Press, 1965.

Fink, Augusta. *Monterey: The Presence of the Past.* San Francisco: Chronicle Books, 1972.

[Fish Commission]. U.S. Congress. Senate. *Report of the Commissioner.* Prepared for the United States Commission of Fish and Fisheries. Miscellaneous Documents of the U.S. Senate. Washington, D.C.; Government printing office. Those reports cited include date of publication. Reports which bear the name of an author (David Starr Jordan, for example) are listed here by author.

Fisher, Anne B. *The Salinas: Upside-down River.* New York: Farrar & Rinehart, 1945.

Fong, Richard. "Apple Drying and the Chinese in Watsonville, California." In *The Other Side of Main Street: A Collection of Oral Histories of Ethnic Peoples: Watsonville, California,* 97–106. Santa Cruz: University of California, 1979.

Francis, Phil. *Beautiful Santa Cruz County.* San Francisco: H. S. Crocker, 1896.

Freedman, Maurice. *The Study of Chinese Society.* Stanford: Stanford University Press, 1979.

[*Gazette*]. *Monterey Gazette.* Newspaper. Published in Monterey. Banc.

Goode, George Brown and Joseph W. Collins. "The Fishermen of the United States." In *Fisheries and Fishery Industries of the United States,* Vol. 8, 29–42. Prepared for the United States Commission of Fish and Fisheries. Miscellaneous Documents, 1st session, 47th Congress. Washington, D.C.: Government Printing Office, 1889.

[Goon and Goon]. Goon, Earl and Evelyn. Interview with author. Watsonville, California, 1983.

Gordon, Burton. *Monterey Bay Area: Natural History and Cultural Imprints.* Pacific Grove: Boxwood Press, 1974.

Gray, John Henry. *China: A History of the Laws, Manners, and Customs of the People.* 2 vols. London: MacMillan, 1878.

[Habeas corpus case]. U.S. District Court of Northern California, in Admiralty Case Files, 1851–1934. Filed by Case Number. Federal Archives and Records Center, San Bruno.

Hamman, Rick. *California Central Coast Railways.* Boulder, Colorado: Pruett Publishing, 1980.

Harrison, E. S. *History of Santa Cruz County California.* San Francisco: Pacific Press, 1892.

———. *Santa Cruz County.* Published for the Santa Cruz County Board of Supervisors, 1890.

Heizer, Robert F. and Alan F. Almquist. *The Other Californians.* Berkeley: University of California Press, 1971.

Hittell, John S. *Commerce and Industries of the Pacific Coast.* San Francisco: A. L. Bancroft, 1882.

Hoang, Ben. Interview with author. Monterey, California, 1982; 1983.

[*Index*]. *Salinas Weekly Index.* Newspaper. Title varies: *Salinas Daily Index*; *Salinas City Index.* Steinbeck Library, Salinas.

[Internal Revenue Assessment Rolls]. U.S. Internal Revenue, Assessment Lists, 1862–1866. FARC. Microfilm.

[Jacks Collection]. David Jacks Collection, uncatalogued. The Huntington, San Marino, California.

Johnson, Paul C., ed. *The California Missions.* Menlo Park: Lane Publishing, 1979.

Johnston, Robert B. *The Beginnings of Salinas: A Brief History to 1874.* 2nd edition. Salinas: Salinas Chamber of Commerce, 1974.

Jordan, David Starr. "The Fisheries of California." *The Overland Monthly* 10 (July–December 1892): 477–78.

————. *The Fisheries of the Pacific Coast*, Vol 7: 599–618. U.S. Congress. Senate. Miscellaneous Documents, 1st session, 47th Congress. Washington, D.C.: Government Printing Office, 1888.

[*Journal*]. *Salinas Daily Journal*. Newspaper published in Salinas, California. CSL.

Jung, Alfred and Rose May. Interview with author. Pacific Grove, California, 1983.

Koch, Margaret. *Santa Cruz County: Parade of the Past*. Fresno: Valley Publishers, 1973.

Konvitz, Milton R. *The Alien and the Asiatic in American Law*. Ithaca: Cornell University Press, 1946. Press, 1946.

Kwok, Munson. Letter to author, March 13, 1983.

[Labor Statistics]. California. Bureau of Labor Statistics. *First Biennial Report*, for the years 1883–1884. Sacramento, 1884.

Lai, H. Mark and Philip P. Choy. *Outlines: History of the Chinese in America*. San Francisco: Chinese-American Studies Planning Group, 1973.

Lam, James. Interview with author. Santa Cruz, California, 1982; 1983.

Lam, Margaret. Interview with author. Seaside, California, 1983.

Lam, Otto. Telephone conversation with author, 1982.

[Larkin Papers]. Hammond, George P., ed. *The Larkin Papers*. 10 vols. Berkeley: University of California Press, 1964.

[Lease Books]. Monterey County. Lease Books. County Clerk's Office, Salinas, California.

[Lease Books]. Santa Cruz County. Lease Books. County Clerk's Office, Santa Cruz, California.

Lee, Edwar. Interview with author. Berkeley, California, 1982.

[Lee and Lee]. Lee, George and Priscilla. Interview with author. Santa Cruz, California, 1982.

Lee, Jun. Interview with author. Scotts Valley, California, 1984.

Lee, Wally. "Salinas Chinatown Vanished." *East/West*, September 4, 1968.

Lee, Wellington. Interview with author. San Francisco, California, 1982.

Leon, Louella. Telephone conversation with author, 1983.

Leonard, Vincent. Letter to author, July 17, 1973.

Leong, Charles. Interview with author. San Francisco, California, 1982; Santa Cruz, 1983.

[Leong and Leong]. Leong, Henry and Alice. Interview with author, San Jose, California, 1983.

Lew, Hoy. Interview with author. Watsonville, California, 1981; 1982; 1983.

Lew, Wally. Interview with author. Watsonville, California, 1983.

Lewis, Betty. *Watsonville, Memories that Linger*. Fresno: Valley Publishers, 1976.

Leyde, Tom. "Local Chinese History Rich and Notorious." Living Section of *Salinas Californian*, June 5, 1982, 17.

Logan, Lorna. Letter to author, September 22, 1983.

Lydon, Edward C. [Sandy]. "The Anti-Chinese Movement in Santa Cruz County, California: 1859–1900." In *The Life, Influence and the Role of the Chinese in the United States, 1776–1960*, edited by Thomas W. Chinn, 219–242. San Francisco: Chinese Historical Society of America, 1976.

Lyman, Stanford. *The Asian in the West*. Reno: University of Nevada, 1970.

McDougall, J. "Looking Back Down an Age Old Trail." Originally published in *Salinas Journal Index*, June 13, 1930–February 21, 1931. Typescript copy, Steinbeck Library, Salinas.

McGinnis, R. A. *Beet-Sugar Technology*. New York: Reinhold Publishing, 1951.

MacGregor, Bruce A. and Richard Truesdale. *A Centennial: South Pacific Coast*. Boulder, Colorado: Pruett Publishing, 1982.

McPherson, Chris. "Emma Dong." Interview in

*Watsonville: I Would Have Told It If I Had A Chance*, edited by Lynn Burkett, Robán San Miguel, Estella García and Dana Frank, 96–104. Santa Cruz: University of California Press, 1978.

[Manuscript census]. U.S. Bureau of the Census. Manuscript census rolls for 1850, 1860, and 1870; Santa Cruz and Monterey counties. 1880, 1900, and 1910 for San Benito, Santa Cruz, and Monterey counties. Microfilm.

Meler, Vjekoslav. *The Slavonic Pioneers in California*. San Francisco: Slavonic Pioneers of California, 1932.

Mertz, Henriette. *Pale Ink: Two Ancient Records of Chinese Exploration in America*. 2nd edition. Chicago: Swallow Press, 1972.

*Monterey Californian*. Newspaper published in Monterey, California. MPL. Microfilm.

*Monterey Peninsula Herald*. Newspaper.

*Monterey Republican*. Newspaper published in Monterey, California. Banc. Microfilm.

Morse, Samuel F. B. Manuscript history of Del Monte Forest, n.d. Pebble Beach Company collection.

Needham, Joseph. *Science and Civilization in China*. 8 vols. London: Cambridge University Press, 1971.

[*New Era*]. *Monterey New Era*. Newspaper published in Monterey, California. MPL. Microfilm.

O'Donnell, Mayo Hayes. "Peninsula Diary," a regular column in the *Monterey Peninsula Herald*. Cited by date.

Osgood, Cornelius. *The Chinese: A Study of a Hong Kong Community*. 3 vols. Tucson: University of Arizona Press, 1975.

Otto, Ernest. "Old Santa Cruz," a regular column in the *Santa Cruz Sentinel-News* and *Santa Cruz Sentinel*. Cited by date.

Ow, Emily. Interview with author. Scotts Valley, California, 1982.

Ow, George, Jr. "Grandpa and the Golden Mountain." Unpublished manuscript.

Ow, George, Jr. Interview with author. Scotts Valley, California, 1982; 1983.

Ow, George, Sr. Interview with author. Scotts Valley, California, 1982; 1983.

[P. I. Co. Files]. Pacific Improvement Company Files, Manuscript Division, Special Collections, Stanford University Library, Stanford, California. Cited by File number and Box number.

*Pacific Sentinel*. Newspaper published from 1854–1856 in Monterey, California.

[*Pajaronian*]. *Watsonville Pajaronian*. Newspaper. Published in Watsonville, California. Title varies. *Watsonville Evening Pajaronian*, etc. UCSC. Microfilm.

*Pajaro Times*. Newspaper published in Watsonville and later, Santa Cruz, California. CSL.

Perry, T. F. *Directory of Monterey, Pacific Grove, Seaside, Del Monte Grove and Vista Del Rey, 1907*. MPL.

Pitt, Leonard. *The Decline of the Californios*. Berkeley: University of California Press, 1968.

[Porter Collection]. Porter family collection in possession of Mrs. Bernice Porter, Watsonville, California.

[Porter Manuscripts]. John T. Porter manuscript collection. California Historical Society, San Francisco, California.

Porter, Mrs. Bernice. Interview with author. Watsonville, California, 1981; 1984.

[Reedy and Reedy]. Reedy, Thomas L. and Alice M. *A History of the Paradise Park Site*. Santa Cruz: The Paradise Park Masonic Club, 1967.

[*Review*]. *Pacific Grove Review*. Newspaper published in Pacific Grove, California. CSL. Microfilm.

Roop, William, Edna Kimbro, and Pat Hathaway. "Archaeological Test Excavations at 4-Mnt-104 on the property of Hopkins Marine Laboratory, Pacific Grove, Monterey County." Prepared for

Stanford University, July, 1977. ARC.

Rosenberg, Earl. "A History of the Fishing and Canning Industries in Monterey, California." Master's thesis, University of Nevada, Reno; July, 1961.

*Salinas Democrat*. Newspaper. Published in Salinas, California. Banc.

Sanborn Fire Insurance Maps. Map Library, UCSC.

Sandmeyer, Elmer Clarence. *The Anti-Chinese Movement in California*. Urbana, Illinois: University of Illinois Press, 1939.

*San Francisco Evening Bulletin*. Newspaper. Published in San Francisco, California. Banc. Microfilm.

*San Francisco Examiner*. Newspaper. Published in San Francisco, California.

*Santa Cruz County, California*. San Francisco: Wallace W. Elliott & Co., 1879.

*Santa Cruz News*. Newspaper. Published in Santa Cruz, California.

Saxton, Alexander. *The Indispensable Enemy*. Berkeley: University of California Press, 1972.

Schurmacher, Emile C. *Lost Treasures and How to Find Them*. New York, 1968, photocopy, Steinbeck Library, Salinas.

Schurz, William Lytle. *The Manila Galleon*. New York: Dutton, 1939.

*Scotts Valley News*. Newspaper. Published in Scotts Valley, California.

[*Sentinel*]. *Santa Cruz Sentinel*. Newspaper. Published in Santa Cruz, California after 1856. Title varies: *Santa Cruz Daily Sentinel*; *Santa Cruz Sentinel-News*. UCSC. Microfilm.

Shew, Elmer. Interview with author. Watsonville, California, 1982.

Shumate, Albert. *Boyhood Days: Ygnacio Villegas' Reminiscences of California in the 1850s*. San Francisco: California Historical Society, 1983.

Spangenberg, Helen. "The Long Road Began in China." *Game and Gossip* 17, No. 12 (September 15, 1972): 10–11.

Steiner, Stan. *Fusang: The Chinese Who Built America*. New York: Harper & Row, 1979.

Stevenson, Robert Louis. *From Scotland to Silverado*. Cambridge: Harvard University Press, 1966.

Sung, Betty. *The Story of the Chinese in America*. New York: Collier Books, 1967.

[*Supervisors Minutes*]. Santa Cruz County. Board of Supervisors Minute Books. County Governmental Center, Santa Cruz, California.

[*Surf*]. *Santa Cruz Surf*. Newspaper. Published in Santa Cruz, California. UCSC. Microfilm.

[*Survey*, 1868]. Santa Cruz. City Planning Department. Survey Maps, A and B, 1868.

Tate, A. W. "Development of the Apple Drying Industry in the Pajaro Valley." *Watsonville Pajaronian*, September 5, 1918.

Treleaven, Owen Clarke. "Poison Jim Chinaman." *Overland Monthly* 74, No. 1 (July, 1919): 40–45.

U.S. Coast Survey. After 1885, referred to as U.S. Coast and Geodetic Survey. Manuscript Maps. Map Library, UCSC.

Ward, Barbara E. "A Hong Kong Fishing Village." *Journal of Oriental Studies* 1 (1954): 195–214.

[*Warrant Book*]. Santa Cruz County. Special Collections, UCSC.

Wat, Raymond. "The Strawberry Rebellion." Unpublished manuscript in possession of author.

Watkins, Rolin C., and M. F. Hoyle. *History of Monterey, Santa Cruz and San Benito Counties, California*. 2 vols. Chicago: S. J. Clarke Publishing, 1925.

Webster, Steven. Interview with author. Monterey, California, 1983.

[*Weekly Courier*]. *Santa Cruz Weekly Courier*. Newspaper. Published in Santa Cruz, California. UCSC. Microfilm.

[*Weekly Herald*]. *Monterey Weekly Herald*. Newspaper. Published in Monterey, California. Banc and MPL. Microfilm.

Wilhelm, Stephen, and James E. Sagen. *A History of the Strawberry*. Berkeley: University of California Press, 1974.

Wilson, Robert A., and Bill Hosokawa. *East to America: A History of the Japanese in the United States*. New York: Morrow, 1980.

Wong, Ernie. Interview with author. Watsonville, California, 1984.

Wong, Florabelle. Interview with author. Watsonville, California, 1982.

Wong, Ida. Interview with author. Watsonville, California, 1982.

Wong, Walter. Interview with author. Salinas, California, 1983.

Woolfenden, John. "Chinese Village Flourished Along Monterey Bay." *Monterey Peninsula Herald*, October 21, 1972.

[Yee and Yee]. Yee, Jack and Frances. Interview with author, Pacific Grove, California, 1983.

# Index

Designer:     Mark Ong, Berkeley, California
Compositor:   G&S Typesetter, Austin, Texas
Text:         10/12 Bembo
Display:      Bembo
Printer:      Malloy Lithographing, Ann Arbor, Michigan
Binder:       Malloy Lithographing, Ann Arbor, Michigan